# Framing the Race in South Africa
*The Political Origins of Racial-Census Elections*

Post-apartheid South African elections have borne an unmistakable racial imprint: Africans vote for one set of parties, whites support a different set of parties, and, with few exceptions, there is no crossover voting between groups. These voting tendencies have solidified the dominance of the ruling African National Congress (ANC) over South African politics and turned South African elections into "racial censuses." This book explores the political sources of these outcomes. It argues that although the beginnings of racialized election outcomes lie in South Africa's past, in the effects apartheid had on voters' beliefs about race and destiny and the reputations parties forged during this period, their endurance reflects the ruling party's ability to use the powers of office to prevent the opposition from evolving away from its apartheid-era party label. By keeping key opposition parties "white," the ANC has rendered them powerless, solidifying its hold on power in spite of an increasingly restive and dissatisfied electorate. The ruling party's ability to frame the opposition's image in the electorate thus lies at the heart of both its continued dominance and the persistence of racial-census elections in South Africa.

Karen E. Ferree is an associate professor of political science at the University of California, San Diego. She has traveled extensively in Africa, particularly South Africa. Her research focuses on elections in Africa's new and consolidating democracies, and she has published research articles in a variety of journals, including *American Political Science Review*, *British Journal of Political Science*, *Journal of Politics*, and *Political Analysis*.

*Cambridge Studies in Comparative Politics*

*General Editor*
Margaret Levi *University of Washington, Seattle*

*Assistant General Editors*
Kathleen Thelen *Massachusetts Institute of Technology*
Erik Wibbels *Duke University*

*Associate Editors*
Robert H. Bates *Harvard University*
Stephen Hanson *University of Washington, Seattle*
Torben Iversen *Harvard University*
Stathis Kalyvas *Yale University*
Peter Lange *Duke University*
Helen Milner *Princeton University*
Frances Rosenbluth *Yale University*
Susan Stokes *Yale University*

*Other Books in the Series*
David Austen-Smith, Jeffry A. Frieden, Miriam A. Golden, Karl Ove Moene, and Adam Przeworski, eds., *Selected Works of Michael Wallerstein: The Political Economy of Inequality, Unions, and Social Democracy*
Andy Baker, *The Market and the Masses in Latin America: Policy Reform and Consumption in Liberalizing Economies*
Lisa Baldez, *Why Women Protest: Women's Movements in Chile*
Stefano Bartolini, *The Political Mobilization of the European Left, 1860–1980: The Class Cleavage*
Robert Bates, *When Things Fell Apart: State Failure in Late-Century Africa*
Mark Beissinger, *Nationalist Mobilization and the Collapse of the Soviet State*
Nancy Bermeo, ed., *Unemployment in the New Europe*
Carles Boix, *Democracy and Redistribution*
Carles Boix, *Political Parties, Growth, and Equality: Conservative and Social Democratic Economic Strategies in the World Economy*
Catherine Boone, *Merchant Capital and the Roots of State Power in Senegal, 1930–1985*
Catherine Boone, *Political Topographies of the African State: Territorial Authority and Institutional Change*

*Continued after the Index*

# Framing the Race in South Africa

*The Political Origins of*
*Racial-Census Elections*

**KAREN E. FERREE**
*University of California, San Diego*

CAMBRIDGE UNIVERSITY PRESS
Cambridge, New York, Melbourne, Madrid, Cape Town, Singapore,
São Paulo, Delhi, Dubai, Tokyo, Mexico City

Cambridge University Press
32 Avenue of the Americas, New York, NY 10013-2473, USA

www.cambridge.org
Information on this title: www.cambridge.org/9780521765091

© Karen E. Ferree 2011

This publication is in copyright. Subject to statutory exception
and to the provisions of relevant collective licensing agreements,
no reproduction of any part may take place without the written
permission of Cambridge University Press.

First published 2011

Printed in the United States of America

*A catalog record for this publication is available from the British Library.*

*Library of Congress Cataloging in Publication data*
Ferree, Karen E.
  Framing the race in South Africa : the political origins of racial-census
  elections / Karen E. Ferree.
    p. cm. – (Cambridge studies in comparative politics)
  Includes bibliographical references and index.
  ISBN 978-0-521-76509-1 (hardback)
  1. Elections – South Africa.   2. Voting – South Africa.   3. Political campaigns – South
  Africa.   4. Political parties – South Africa.   5. South Africa – Race relations – Political
  aspects.   I. Title.   II. Series.
  JQ1992.F47 2010
  324.968'06–dc22          2010012049

ISBN 978-0-521-76509-1 Hardback

Cambridge University Press has no responsibility for the persistence or
accuracy of URLs for external or third-party Internet Web sites referred to in
this publication and does not guarantee that any content on such Web sites is,
or will remain, accurate or appropriate.

*For my mother, Betty, and for Bari,
with love and gratitude*

# Contents

| | | |
|---|---|---|
| *List of Tables* | | *page* x |
| *Acknowledgments* | | xiii |
| 1 | Introduction | 1 |
| 2 | Voters | 32 |
| 3 | The 1994 Campaigns | 65 |
| 4 | The 1999 Campaigns | 82 |
| 5 | The 2004 Campaigns | 107 |
| 6 | Can a Leopard Change Its Spots? Candidate Demographics and Party Label Change | 141 |
| 7 | Why So Slow? The Political Challenges of Candidate Transformation for Opposition Parties | 163 |
| 8 | Negative Framing Strategies and African Opposition Parties | 193 |
| 9 | Conclusion: South Africa in Comparative Perspective | 222 |
| *References* | | 243 |
| *Index* | | 263 |

# Tables

| | | |
|---|---|---|
| 1.1 | 1994 Reported Vote by Race (percent) | *page* 6 |
| 1.2 | 1999 Reported Vote by Race (percent) | 6 |
| 1.3 | 2004 Reported Vote by Race (percent) | 6 |
| 1.4 | African Impressions of the NP's Image (percent) | 19 |
| 1.5 | African Impressions of the DP's Image (percent) | 19 |
| 2.1 | Prevalence of Racial Identities in South Africa (percent) | 42 |
| 2.2 | African Partisanship over Time (percent) | 43 |
| 2.3 | Best Way to Create Jobs: Private Enterprise versus Government (percent) | 44 |
| 2.4 | Who Should Take Responsibility for Reducing Crime? (percent) | 45 |
| 2.5 | Performance Evaluations (percent) | 46 |
| 2.6 | Views of Exclusivity of Different Parties for 1994, 1999, and 2004 (percent) | 52 |
| 2.7 | Logit Models of African Vote Choice (1998–1999 *Opinion99* Survey). Standard Errors in Parentheses | 55 |
| 2.8 | Fitted Values and 95 Percent Confidence Intervals for Models 1, 2, and 3 (African Probability of Supporting the ANC, of Being Uncertain, and of Supporting the NNP) | 57 |
| 2.9 | Ordered Probit Model of African Performance Evaluations (1998–1999 *Opinion99* Survey). Standard Errors in Parentheses | 59 |
| 2.10 | Ordered Probit Models of Africans' Views of the Trust and Credibility of the Opposition (1998–1999 *Opinion99* Survey) | 60 |
| 2.11 | Logit Models of African Vote Choice (1994 Idasa Survey). Standard Errors in Parentheses | 62 |

| | | |
|---|---|---|
| 2.12 | Logit Models of African Vote Choice (2000 *Afrobarometer* Survey). Standard Errors in Parentheses | 63 |
| 2.13 | Logit Models of African Vote Choice (1998–1999 *Opinion99* Survey). Standard Errors in Parentheses. Split Sample: Partisans versus Independents | 64 |
| 5.1 | Campaign Events (All) | 115 |
| 5.2 | Rhetorical Sparring Partners | 116 |
| 5.3 | Type of Rhetoric by Different Parties | 119 |
| 5.4 | Issues Emphasized by Different Parties | 120 |
| 5.5 | Policies Named by Different Parties | 122 |
| 5.6 | The ANC/NNP and Racial Rhetoric | 132 |
| 5.7 | Type of Rhetoric about Different Parties | 133 |
| 5.8 | The DA and Racial Rhetoric | 133 |
| 5.9 | Most Frequent Topics in Party Discourse in the 2004 Election | 134 |
| 5.10 | Media Coverage of Parties | 137 |
| 6.1 | The Racial Breakdown of the ANC's Candidates, 1994–2004 | 152 |
| 6.2 | The Racial Breakdown of the NP's Candidates, 1994–2004 | 153 |
| 6.3 | The Racial Breakdown of the DP's Candidates, 1994–2004 | 154 |
| 6.4 | The Racial Breakdown of the New Candidates, 1999 and 2004 | 155 |
| 6.5 | African Impressions of the NP and Party Demographics | 156 |
| 6.6 | African Impressions of the DP and Party Demographics | 156 |
| 6.7 | White/Coloured Impressions of the ANC and Party Demographics | 158 |
| 6.8 | Indian Impressions of the ANC and Party Demographics | 159 |
| 6.9 | Indian Impressions of the DP and Party Demographics | 159 |
| 6.10 | Indian Impressions of the NP and Party Demographics | 159 |
| 7.1 | Control over Seats by the ANC, DA, and NNP | 172 |
| 7.2 | Explaining Candidate Rankings, 1999 | 173 |
| 7.3 | Explaining Candidate Rankings, 2004 | 174 |
| 7.4 | Retention Rates for 1994–1999 and 1999–2004 Periods | 176 |
| 7.5 | Logit Analysis of Returning versus Leaving Candidates | 177 |
| 7.6 | Probability a Candidate on the 1994 List Returned in 1999 (95 Percent Confidence Intervals) | 179 |
| 7.7 | Probability a Candidate on the 1999 List Returned in 2004 (95 Percent Confidence Intervals) | 179 |
| 7.8 | Probability a Candidate on the 1994 List Returned in 1999 (95 Percent Confidence Intervals) | 180 |

| | | |
|---|---|---|
| 7.9 | Probability a Candidate on the 1999 List Returned in 2004 (95 Percent Confidence Intervals) | 180 |
| 7.10 | New, Returning, and Poached Candidates in 1999 and 2004 (Percentages Sum by Column) | 181 |

# Acknowledgments

Over the course of writing this book, I have benefited from the intellectual, logistical, emotional, and financial support of many individuals, communities, and institutions. My gratitude for these gifts is immeasurable, as I hope the following remarks will express.

I began this book as a dissertation in the Government Department of Harvard University. When I started at Harvard, I intended to study international monetary institutions. By the end of my first year, I had jumped into the deep end of African politics, a decision that reflects, in part, the unique group of scholars and students collected at Harvard at that time. I thank Jennifer Widner for kindling my interest in Africa and Robert Putnam for encouraging my intellectual curiosity. Jim Alt, Ken Shepsle, and Gary King asked difficult questions and gave me the tools and freedom to answer them. Robert Rotberg and the late Leroy Vail introduced me to the history and politics of South Africa and provided useful practical advice regarding my first trip to the country in 1997. Robert Bates, to whom I owe so much, was a generous patron and a patient mentor. When I told him of my interest in ethnic politics, he told me to read *The Reasoning Voter*. When I talked to him about South African elections, he pushed me to think about Mexico. Thus began the journey that ended in this book. I also benefited from a truly extraordinary community of graduate students: Kanchan Chandra, Eric Dickson, Anna Grzymala-Busse, Shigeo Hirano, Macartan Humphries, Orit Kedar, Dan Posner, Ken Scheve, Naunihal Singh, Smita Singh, Jeremy Weinstein, and Steven Wilkinson (to name just a few). I had to run hard to keep up with them – and still do! A special thanks to Smita, for being a lively and fascinating friend, and to Ken, for his early enthusiasm for this project.

In South Africa, the web of people to thank is enormous and impossible to enumerate fully. In 1997, Tom Lodge and the Political Studies Department at the University of Witwatersrand gave me a home away from home. Lodge, whose work on South African campaigns has been an inspiration, was patient with my questions and generous with his knowledge. While at Wits, I was fortunate to meet two historians, Peter Delius and Stefan Schirmer, who facilitated my early attempts to understand the history of identity formation in South Africa. In 1999, the Politics Department at the University of Pretoria opened its doors to me. Bill Johnson at the Helen Suzman Foundation was more than kind in sharing his knowledge of South Africa. Bob Mattes has been unfailingly generous with his data and insights into South African politics, providing invaluable feedback at various critical junctures in this project. I have been strongly influenced by his pioneering work on South African voting behavior. I also wish to thank Cherrel Africa, for research assistance and many interesting conversations, and Jonathan Faull, for collecting newspaper clippings in 2004 and for general advice and insights on South African parties and elections. Outside of academia, I met many South Africans of all origins and circumstances who shared with me, often in a language so vivid it brought tears to my eyes, the excitement and tribulations of their experiences in the new South Africa. I began this book believing it would be about mobilization, how racial polarization in South Africa had closed off opportunities for persuasion, inducing parties to focus exclusively on getting core supporters to the polls. While I saw plenty of evidence of mobilization during my field experiences in South Africa, South Africans themselves revealed to me the fluidity of their politics. African voters repeatedly told me of their frustrations with the ruling party and their desire for alternatives, yet balked when I asked them about the opposition parties, opening the puzzle that inspired this book. Listening to their stories, I began to realize that the interesting questions in South African politics were not about mobilization, but about persuasion, and the political factors that impeded it. For their candor, I thank the ordinary citizens of South Africa.

Most of this book came together well after graduate school, and I have been very fortunate in the community of scholars I have found at the University of California at San Diego (UCSD). Gary Cox, Zoli Hajnal, Sam Popkin, Matt Shugart, and Tracy Strong all provided insightful comments to earlier drafts of this book. Special thanks to Zoli, for useful discussions on American racial politics, for reading the book manuscript in its entirety, and for many helpful comments. Special thanks also to Sam Popkin, who read the full manuscript, coached me on ways to improve its framing, and helped me draw out the political story. More broadly, I thank my colleagues in the Political Science Department for simultaneously supporting and challenging me. I am especially indebted to David Lake, Gary Cox, and Clark Gibson for their mentorship. Further thanks to Clark for helping to name the book and for making UCSD a great place to study African politics. I also thank the many excellent graduate students I have worked with at UCSD, especially Jeremy Horowitz and James Long, for many long discussions about ethnicity and African elections, and Sarah Knoesen for help in coding South African surnames.

I have had the great good fortune to participate in two research groups: the Laboratory in Comparative Ethnic Processes (LiCEP) and the Working Group on African Political Economy (WGAPE). These groups have spanned universities, disciplines, and substantive focus, but share a commitment to theoretically

## Acknowledgments

grounded, empirically rigorous research, and I have benefited tremendously from my participation in them. My fellow members have taught through example and have been patient and constructive with their advice. I would especially like to acknowledge Kanchan Chandra and Dan Posner for founding these groups, for their generosity of spirit and intellect, and for the many ways in which they have supported me throughout this project. If there is any merit in this book, it is in no small part due to their influence and advice over the years. Thanks also to David Laitin, for his acute insights, intellectual enthusiasm, and mentorship, and to Ted Miguel for co-creating and sponsoring WGAPE. Thanks also to the universities and organizations that provided financial support for LiCEP and WGAPE, especially the National Science Foundation (NSF), UCLA, Berkeley, and Stanford.

In addition to LiCEP and WGAPE, I have benefited from the support and advice of a wider group of scholars that work on African politics, ethnicity, and/or elections in new democracies. I would especially like to thank Michael Bratton, who provided excellent feedback on various portions of this manuscript and published an early version of one of my chapters in the *Afrobarometer* working papers series. With his work on the *Afrobarometer*, Michael has given all scholars of African politics a truly amazing public good, and for this I thank him. Many thanks also to Shaheen Mozaffar, James Scarritt, and Jessica Piombo for comments on early drafts of chapters in this book. I would also like to acknowledge Libby Wood, David Holiday, Christine Wade, and Carrie Manning for advice on my section on El Salvador, and David Forman-Barzilai for advice on Israel.

In the later stages of preparing this manuscript, I benefited greatly from the editorial advice of Margaret Levi and Lewis Bateman and Cambridge University Press. Two anonymous reviewers provided excellent constructive advice. Deborah Patton cheerfully and professionally indexed the manuscript and Elise M. Oranges painstakingly weeded the manuscript for omissions and errors. I am grateful to all for their assistance.

Conducting research on a country half a world away is logistically difficult and expensive, and without the support of numerous organizations and individuals, this book would have been impossible. The International Predissertation Fellowship Program of the Social Science Research Council funded my first trip to South Africa in 1997, during which I had the luxury to study South African history and languages and "soak and poke" my way into an understanding of South African politics. An NSF Dissertation Improvement Grant allowed me to return to South Africa to gather data, conduct interviews, and witness the campaigns for the 1999 election. Robert Bates personally funded a final invaluable year at Harvard, during which I completed the writing of my dissertation. While at UCSD, I benefited from several Committee on Research (COR) grants from the Academic Senate, as well as a generous grant from the Chris and Warren Hellman Fellowship Program that allowed me to hire South African research assistants to complete various data collection projects that were crucial to this book.

Writing a book is a long and frequently solitary journey, and I am most thankful to my friends and family for diversions, support, and entertainment along the way. Thanks to Maureen and Bill for good wine and pizza, to Alexia for yoga and conversation, and to Carmela and David for beautiful days in Laguna. Thanks to Gia for more than two decades of friendship. Thanks to Ray and Eileen and the other Weicks for their warm web of family. Thanks to my brother Andrew, who always has a shoulder I can lean on. Thanks to my father, Bill, for his perpetual optimism, and for investing in my education and teaching me to swing for the fences. Thanks to my wonderful Samuel, Leila, and Marcus, for being such very good children and making me laugh, regardless of how the book was going. And most fundamentally, thanks to my husband, Bari, and my mother, Betty. Bari followed me to Boston, then to Africa, and finally to California, and made a home with me in all of these places. Together we have drunk from the fire-hose of parenthood, and I will forever be grateful to him for his companionship, stamina, and loving support. My mother, Betty, has been endlessly generous to me and my family, indulging us in a thousand kindnesses. For the hours, days, months, and years that she took care of my children, I am truly and most profoundly thankful. I could not have completed this book without her.

# 1

# Introduction

From an aerial viewpoint, post-apartheid South African elections bear an unmistakable racial imprint: Africans vote for one set of parties, whites support a different set of parties, and, with few exceptions, there is no crossover voting between these groups, which together make up more than 90 percent of the South African population. Such sharp racial contours of voting have earned South African elections the dubious distinction of being "racial censuses:" Voters line up with their racial groups, seemingly without thought to issues, performance, or any of the other politics-as-usual factors that drive elections in other countries. Indeed, elections look so deeply racial that one wonders if politics has anything to do with it at all. What role can persuasion play if voters simply register their social identity when they enter the polling booth?

However, behind the racial imprint lies a puzzle, for racial identities in South Africa are neither pervasive enough nor unique enough to account for South African voting outcomes. African voters – who comprise around three-quarters of the electorate and drive the census – are a highly diverse group; some place primary importance on race, but many more emphasize nonracial identities. Moreover, liberation jubilation aside, Africans have not been uniformly committed to the ruling African National Congress (ANC). Even in 1994, during the very first post-apartheid election campaigns, African voters expressed uncertainty about the ANC. Surveys consistently show a large group of independent Africans, up to 50 percent at some points in the recent past. And many Africans express frustration and weariness with their continued impoverishment in the new South Africa: Political transformation is clearly not enough. They cannot eat liberation. As one South African recently put it: "Freedom turned out to be just a word."[1] South Africans want economic change, yet they remain unsure about the ANC's ability to generate it. At the same time, the ANC has not yet developed a patronage machine to buy the

---

[1] Vincent Ntswayi, resident of Mvezo in the Eastern Cape. Quoted in Perry, Alex. "South Africa Looks for a Leader." *Time*, April 27, 2009: 41.

votes of disgruntled Africans; clientelism, while it might still develop in South Africa, has not been a significant factor to date.

So if Africans are not blinded by identity, liberation euphoria, or partisanship, and if their votes are not purchased, what keeps them loyal to the ruling party? The answer is simple. The barriers to persuasion rest not in the racial identity of voters but in the successful realization of a political strategy employed by the ruling party to discredit and delegitimize the opposition. Africans stick with the ANC because they do not see the strongest of the current opposition parties – the (New) National Party until 1999 and now the Democratic Alliance – as credible alternatives. Moreover, the opposition's lack of credibility with Africans, and its negligible role in South African elections, are not socially given facts – as is often suggested by South African political observers – but a product of politics past and present. Because of their participation in apartheid-era governments, most African voters (quite reasonably) view the opposition parties as "white," out to protect and further the interests of white voters. In order to attract African votes, opposition parties must transform themselves from "white" to something more inclusive. They have attempted to accomplish such a transformation through electoral campaigns and the racial diversification of their candidate pools. However, the ANC has been able to neutralize such efforts by running skillful campaigns, playing on opposition missteps and weaknesses, and controlling the supply of high-quality African politicians. As hard and as loudly as the opposition claims to have transformed, the ANC claims the opposite. With more resources and more attractive representatives, the ANC has fought and won the battle to define the opposition's image in the electorate. By blocking the opposition from changing its image – by keeping the opposition "white" – the ANC has destroyed its opponents' credibility and preserved its own hold on African voters, even those who do not claim strong partisan attachments or favorable views of the ruling party's performance. Race and identity are therefore red herrings: An exclusive focus on them ignores the hard political work underlying the racial-census outcome in South African elections. What seems organic, a natural expression of a pervasively held social identity, is in fact *politically engineered*, the end result of a negative framing strategy employed by the ruling party to neutralize its competition.

If the origins of the census are political, then political change – not identity change – is the key to its erosion. Divisions within the ruling party that produce a schizophrenic and disorganized political campaign, or – more damaging – elite defections to other parties, could provide the ANC's competitors with the window they need to change their images. They might also pursue image change by winning elections at the local level and developing a reputation for even-handed delivery of services or through alliances with legitimately multiracial parties – all options that the arrival of the new party, Cope (Congress of the People), makes more plausible. And although the current opposition parties seem insignificant, relatively small changes in support could lead to major changes in South African politics. A shift in voting of even 15 to 20 percent of the African vote could push the ANC close to the 50 percent mark, possibly forcing it into a coalition government.² Moreover, and perhaps more importantly, it would end the ruling party's aura of invincibility.³ This process of change – inherently political and quite possibly violent – is very different from the one implied by a social identity perspective of South African politics. Because the pathways implied by different theories of origin diverge significantly, understanding the political roots of South Africa's racial census is critical to understanding the country's future.

Viewed from a political light, South Africa has a surprising amount in common with nonracially or ethnically divided countries like Japan and Mexico, where a large party has used its size and position to weaken the opposition and cement its dominance. Like Japan's Liberal Democratic Party (LDP) or Mexico's Institutional Revolutionary Party (PRI), the ANC protects its position through the flow of resources, controlling who gets what, where, and when in a country where a new road or clean water has a huge impact on the quality of voters' lives. Less obviously – and the focus of this book – the ANC also protects its position through the control of information and reputation, the ability to frame election campaigns through a deeper campaign chest and bigger media presence, and a monopoly of African political talent. Using these powerful tools, the ANC has prevented the opposition from evolving, from changing its party label in a way that would make it more credible to the African electorate. The ANC is not the first party to use negative framing strategies to cement its dominance, and it does not use these strategies only on the white opposition: Dominant parties in Israel and El Salvador have used similar techniques, and the ANC has employed them to discredit other competitors, including the Inkatha Freedom Party (IFP) and, more recently, the Congress of the People (Cope). So long as the ruling party remains successful in framing elections and defining the opposition's image, it will maintain its dominance and the racial census will persist. In the remainder of this chapter, I discuss the racial census in greater detail, outline traditional explanations for it, and then provide an overview of my argument, which forms the rest of the book.

THE RACIAL CENSUS

South Africa has held four sets of post-apartheid national elections (1994, 1999, 2004, and 2009). The African National Congress (ANC) walked away

---

² Assuming Africans are about three-quarters of the electorate and the Democratic Party wins 20% of the vote based on non-African votes (for example, the NP's performance in the 1994 elections), then winning 20% of the African vote would put it at around 35% of the total vote. If other small parties continue to attract small chips of the electorate, this shift in African support could drag the ANC down to close to 50%.

³ Magaloni (2006) argues that dominant parties cultivate an image of invincibility to deter would-be challengers by winning strong majorities of the vote. Shifts in support away from dominant parties that damage this image can be significant even if they do not result in turnover.

from all with a dominating majority: In 1994, it won 63 percent of the vote; in 1999, 66 percent; in 2004, 70 percent; and in 2009, 66 percent. In South Africa's parliamentary system, these commanding majorities have allowed the party to form governments without partners.[4] The fates of the primary opposition parties have varied. In 1994, the largest opposition party was the National Party (NP), which won around 20 percent of the vote. In 1999, the Democratic Party (DP) superseded the NP – by then called the New National Party or NNP – with about 10 percent of the vote to the NNP's.[5] In 2004, the DP – by then the Democratic Alliance or DA – grew to 12 percent of the national vote, while the NP had slipped down to 2 percent.[6] In 2005, the NNP folded its cards altogether. In 2009, the DA won almost 17 percent of the vote, while newcomer Cope took 7 percent. The Inkatha Freedom Party (IFP) has also challenged the ANC, winning between 11 (in 1994) and 7 (in 2004) percent of the vote, almost all in KwaZulu-Natal. In 2009, the IFP's support collapsed to less than 5 percent of the national vote. A panoply of smaller parties compete and win enough votes to capture a seat or two in the 400-person legislature. Of these, the African Christian Democratic Party (ACDP), the United Democratic Movement (UDM), the Pan African Congress (PAC), the Freedom Front (FF), and, most recently, the Independent Democrats (ID) are the most significant. Because only two of the opposition parties – the NP/NNP and the DP/DA – have maintained a national presence in repeated elections, they are parties I speak of when I refer to "the opposition."[7] This is obviously a simplification, but one I hope readers will tolerate until Chapter 8, when I address the experiences of other opposition parties – notably the IFP, the UDM, and Cope – and show that the ruling party has used negative framing strategies against these parties as well.

The ANC and its opposition attract different racial constituencies. Horowitz (1985) coined the term "ethnic census" to describe elections in which ethnicity so strongly predicts voting behavior that the election is simply a "head count"

---

[4] Clause 88 of the Interim Constitution (1994–1997) stipulated that parties winning twenty or more seats were eligible for a government portfolio. The National Party and the IFP both took advantage of this, and the Government of National Unity (GNU) was formed. The National Party left the GNU in 1997. The current constitution of South Africa does not have the consociational Clause 88. The ANC has sometimes included junior partners in government, but out of choice, not necessity.

[5] The National Party changed its name to the New National Party in 1997 in an explicit effort to divorce itself from its past.

[6] The Democratic Alliance was born in 2000, a coalition of the Democratic Party, the New National Party, and the Federal Alliance formed to contest the 2000 local elections. It survived until 2001, when the New National Party pulled out. The Democratic Party continued under the name Democratic Alliance, or DA.

[7] Until recently (with the birth of Cope), the Inkatha Freedom Party (IFP) was the only "African" party to challenge the ANC on a significant scale. However, it is by and large a regional party, winning all but a handful of its votes in KwaZulu-Natal. It has failed to develop any kind of national presence or organizational infrastructure. And even in KwaZulu-Natal, its strength is ebbing.

or "census" of the size of each group. Multiple parties may represent each group (there may be within-group competition for votes), but there is little to no crossover voting, that is, voters stick to own-group parties. As demonstrated by Tables 1.1–1.3, South Africa provides a nearly perfect example of this kind of election.[8] Along with the IFP, the ANC attracted the vast majority of African votes, while the NP, DP, and a handful of more conservative parties dominated the white electorate. Coloured and Indian voters split their votes across the racial divide, but these voters together only comprise about 10 percent of the electorate and therefore do not detract much from the overall impression of racial polarization.[9] Racialized voting patterns have appeared in every election to date and emerge consistently in mass surveys.[10] There is, therefore, little controversy that "racial census" accurately describes South African elections.[11]

According to standard thinking on ethnicity and democracy, this outcome bodes ill for the long-term health of the country. Lijphart (1977, 1999) argues that democracy is unstable in the face of fixed majorities, as one group is permanently locked out of power, disaffected, and more likely to pursue violent means of influencing the political system. Moreover, parties that feel

---

[8] The figures in Tables 1.1 and 1.2 are based on the estimates in Reynolds (1994, 1999). While ecological inference problems usually make it hazardous to estimate group-specific behaviors from aggregate data, the homogeneity of behavior in South Africa significantly reduces this problem. The figures in Table 1.3 are based on the September 2004 Comparative National Elections Project (CNEP) of 1,200 individuals (837 Africans, 113 coloureds, 67 Indians, and 183 whites). The CNEP survey followed the election by five months and is based on respondent recall.

[9] Horowitz establishes no specific cut-points for how much crossover voting can occur before an election is no longer a census. We might therefore envision voting as a continuum, with a pure census on one end. In the pure census, there is zero crossover voting. On the other end of the continuum, voters behave without regard to group membership. In between are mixed cases. The closer to the pure census end of the continuum, the more clearly the case falls in the "census" camp. As close to 90% of the South African electorate sticks within racial boundaries when voting, we can think of it as a fairly strong census example.

[10] Survey evidence leaves little doubt about the persistence of racialized voting in the 2009 election. In a Markinor poll of 3,531 likely voters in February and March of 2009 (six weeks prior to the election), 79% of African voters supported the ANC, whereas the DA drew almost all of its support from whites, coloureds, and Indians. See Mataboge, Mmanaledi, Mandy Rossouw, and Matuma Letsoalo, "What the ANC's Victory Means." *Mail and Guardian*, April 17 2009.

[11] A word on racial terminology and groups in South Africa: Per common usage, "Africans" in South Africa are those people who speak one of the Bantu languages (isiNdebele, isiXhosa, isiZulu, Sepedi, Sesotho, Setswana, SiSwati, Tshivenda, Xitsonga); "white" South Africans are those of European descent; "coloured" South Africans are a people of mixed African, European, and Asian descent; and "Indian" (also sometimes called "Asian") people are those of primarily South Asian ancestry. Coloured people live mostly in the Western and Northern Capes, where they are the majority group. Africans form the majority group in all other provinces and tend to be geographically concentrated by ethnolinguistic group (Xhosa in the Eastern Cape, Zulu in KwaZulu-Natal, Tswana in the North West province, and so on). Whites are dispersed throughout the country. Indians live primarily in KwaZulu-Natal.

TABLE 1.1. *1994 Reported Vote by Race (percent)*

|  | Africans | Whites | Coloureds | Indians |
|---|---|---|---|---|
| *"White" Parties* | 4 | 90 | 67 | 50 |
| Democratic Party | 0 | 10 | 0 | 0 |
| National Party | 4 | 66 | 67 | 50 |
| Other White | 0 | 14 | 0 | 0 |
| *"African" Parties* | 91 | 9 | 28 | 42 |
| African National Congress | 81 | 2 | 28 | 25 |
| Inkatha Freedom Party | 8 | 7 | 0 | 17 |
| Other African | 2 | 0 | 0 | 0 |
| *Other* | 5 | 1 | 5 | 8 |

Table based on data reported in Reynolds (1994).

TABLE 1.2. *1999 Reported Vote by Race (percent)*

|  | Africans | Whites | Coloureds | Indians |
|---|---|---|---|---|
| *"White" Parties* | 3 | 81 | 40 | 34 |
| Democratic Party | 1 | 57 | 6 | 18 |
| National Party | 2 | 16 | 34 | 16 |
| Other White | 0 | 8 | 0 | 0 |
| *"African" Parties* | 95 | 5 | 60 | 30 |
| African National Congress | 82 | 5 | 60 | 30 |
| Inkatha Freedom Party | 11 | 0 | 0 | 0 |
| Other African | 2 | 0 | 0 | 0 |
| *Other* | 2 | 14 | 0 | 36 |

Table based on data reported in Reynolds (1999).

TABLE 1.3. *2004 Reported Vote by Race (percent)*

|  | Africans | Whites | Coloureds | Indians |
|---|---|---|---|---|
| *"White" Parties* | <1 | 74 | 20 | 18 |
| Democratic Party | <1 | 66 | 10 | 18 |
| National Party | 0 | 4 | 10 | 0 |
| Other White | 0 | 4 | 0 | 0 |
| *"African" Parties* | 86 | <1 | 59 | 36 |
| African National Congress | 81 | <1 | 59 | 36 |
| Inkatha Freedom Party | 4 | 0 | 0 | 0 |
| Other African | 1 | 0 | 0 | 0 |
| *Other* | 3 | 7 | 12 | 14 |
| *Refused* | 10 | 18 | 11 | 32 |

Table based on the Comparative National Election Project (CNEP) survey, conducted in September 2004.

insulated from competition by a captured constituency may behave irresponsibly, enriching themselves at the expense of the public and following policies at odds with the electorate – a worry echoed in the writings of South African political observers Giliomee and Simkins (1999) and Johnson and Schlemmer (1996). Horowitz (1985) speculates that census-style elections lead to a polarizing style of campaigning wherein raising the turnout of fixed constituencies replaces persuasion as the primary goal of parties. Ultimately, he suggests, this increases the chances of election-induced violence. Snyder (2000), echoing Huntington (1968), goes so far as to suggest that poor countries with ethnic divisions resist democratizing until political and social institutions capable of restraining the negative forces unleashed by elections have developed.

South Africa has yet to experience many of these reputed ills. Indeed, the ANC can point to numerous positive achievements during its first three terms of office: the aversion of civil war; the creation of an independent court system; the adoption of a constitution that enshrines civil and political rights; the expansion of basic services and the social safety net to populations grossly neglected by apartheid governments; and responsible fiscal politics and – until recently – an expanding economy (although one that still struggles to provide sufficient employment). At the same time, a thriving opposition is critical to the long-term health of any democracy, an outcome that will elude South Africa so long as party support is so clearly segmented by race.

While few observers of South African politics would dispute the aptness of the racial-census depiction of recent South African elections or its significance to the long-term health of South African democracy, explanations for the census remain elusive. What lies behind the polarization of voting in South Africa? In particular, why have African voters – who are about three-quarters of the electorate and therefore the driving force behind the census – remained loyal to the ANC, refusing even in small numbers to support the opposition?

The answer is surely not that the opposition parties are uninterested in African votes. It is true that South African opposition parties can subsist without the support of Africans. South Africa's electoral system could be described as very permissive proportional representation – there is one national list for the entire 400-seat legislature, making the threshold for representation very low and the upper bound on the number of parties nearly meaningless.[12] South African opposition parties can therefore earn enough votes from minority voters to guarantee themselves representation in the legislature. However, these parties have broader goals than simply warming benches: They want to influence policy and implement their agendas. They would like, someday, to command a majority and form a government. And they know that the sizeable African electorate is key to these goals. Winning even 15 or 20 percent of African votes would significantly alter the balance of power in the country. Hence, both the NP (until 2004) and the DA have had their eye on the African electorate, hoping to persuade at least a minority of these voters to cross over. The persistence

---

[12] See Cox (1997) and Sartori (1976) for discussions of electoral systems.

of the census fifteen years after the end of apartheid is a measure of the opposition's failure to achieve this objective. What explains this outcome?

IDENTITY VOTING?

The most obvious explanation is that elections in South Africa bear an unmistakable racial imprint because racial identities in South Africa are powerful, pervasive, divisive, and historically grounded in forty-plus years of apartheid and centuries of discrimination and segregation prior to that. Africans reward the ANC for liberating them from oppression and view voting for the party as a way of expressing, even celebrating, their identity and freedom. Given this heady brew of emotion and history, it is not surprising that the ANC captures the vast majority of the African votes.

Indeed, this sort of explanation, which emphasizes identity expression, is the reigning explanation for census style in political science. Building on the ideas of social psychologist Henri Tajfel, Horowitz (1985) locates the microfoundations of census elections in the identity attachments of voters. According to this viewpoint, individuals in divided societies connect their self-worth with that of their group. When the group is doing well, individuals in the group feel affirmed. When the group suffers, individuals experience a loss of personal prestige. In this context, voters see voting not as an act of choice, a careful weighing of options, but as a means of expressing identity, of declaring allegiance with their ethnic group. Identity expression through voting brings psychic benefits, whereas failure to vote with the group confers internally metered penalties. Voters do not use their votes to further self-interest. Indeed, they may actually vote in ways that work *against* their interests. Furthermore, their allegiance to their party, constructed as it is from the raw material of identity, is nonnegotiable. Voters become wedded to parties through an impenetrable species of partisanship, precluding persuasion as a viable campaign strategy. Elections become a mere counting of heads, a census of group size, with parties focusing on mobilizing the faithful rather than wooing converts. Numerous pathologies follow: locked out minorities, complacent and exploitative majorities, violence-ridden election campaigns, and so on. Altering this grim scenario requires nothing less than fundamental shifts in the identity attachments of voters.

While the identity voting perspective is associated most closely with Horowitz, it underlies the views of voting in divided societies promulgated by consociationalists like Arend Lijphart. Lijphart (1977, 1999) worries that voting in divided countries is inevitably rigid, leading to fixed electoral outcomes and the failure of majoritarian democracy. He recommends full-blown consociational solutions or, at the very least, institutions that take voting blocs for granted and incorporate as many players in the government process as possible ("consensual" democracy).[13] Horowitz's identity voting perspective

---

[13] See also Sisk and Reynolds (1998), Reynolds (2002), and Reilly and Reynolds (1999).

also resonates with a long line of work by American scholars that emphasizes prejudice as the key factor behind the reluctance of white voters to support African American candidates (Kinder and Sears 1981; Terklidsen 1993; Kinder and Sanders 1996; Mendelberg 2001).

The identity voting perspective informs various explanations for the racial census in South Africa. Johnson and Schlemmer (1996) suggest that racial attachments rather than rational policy preferences explain the stark pattern of polarization that emerged in the 1994 election. Friedman (2004, 2005) also advocates an identity voting perspective, suggesting that voters support the parties that can "best provide a vehicle for who they are," not those that reflect their policy preferences (Friedman 2004: 3). In the popular press, the reluctance of the African electorate to desert the ANC – even in the face of lukewarm economic performance, uneven service delivery, allegations of corruption, worsening unemployment, and a catastrophic AIDS policy – provide evidence that a noninstrumental, expressive logic drives South African voting decisions.

In short, according to expressive or identity voting perspective, it is the *identity attachments* of voters – especially African voters – that lies behind the racial census in South Africa. Africans became wedded to the ANC as the vehicle of African liberation, transformation, and representation. Their ties to the party, forged from this potent mixture, are impenetrable to other parties, generating a captured constituency for the ANC. And only through wide-scale identity change will the census pattern begin to erode. Given that identity change is, in most accounts, a slow process that occurs over generations, the identity voting perspective would see little prospect for change in South Africa.

However, while the identity voting perspective offers an intuitive explanation for the census-style outcome, racial identities are neither pervasive enough nor unique enough in South Africa to account for the country's voting patterns. Racial identities figure prominently in South Africa, but many South Africans (including a majority of Africans) privilege other identities more: those based on ethnicity or language, region, religion, and class. Although voting bears a stark racial imprint, patterns of identification in South Africa are blurrier (Mattes 1995).

Moreover, South Africa is home to many diverse political traditions. Although the ANC commands an impressive hold over African votes now, it is just one of many organizations and traditions that have flourished in the country at different periods of time. In the 1950s, the ANC competed with the Pan African Congress (PAC) for the allegiance of African supporters. During the 1970s, when the ANC was in exile and many of its leaders were in prison, the Black Consciousness movement swept through townships and motivated wide-scale political activity. In the 1980s, while ANC leaders negotiated with the National Party over the end of apartheid, the United Democratic Front (UDF) and the Congress of South African Trade Unions (COSATU) led the battle on the ground. And throughout all of these years of opposition to apartheid, many Africans – indeed, the majority of Africans – remained in rural areas, where their political allegiances, through coercion, loyalty, and lack of alternatives, remained tied to traditional leaders. In the closing days of apartheid and during the run-up to the first elections, the ANC emerged as the focal point for these diverse political traditions, but there was nothing pre-ordained about the party's ability to unify them under a single banner. Tensions within the party remained as different factions – with different goals and visions for the new South Africa – competed for favor.[14]

Reflecting these various traditions and organizations, Africans themselves are a politically diverse group. Policy preferences within the African population vary more than policy preferences across racial groups. Holding together this diverse population under a single banner has challenged the ruling party. While most Africans embraced the end of apartheid and the defeat of the National Party, euphoria about the ANC has not been uniform. African voters have wanted more than liberation; not all believed the ANC could deliver on its promises of peace and development; many remained loyal to other political traditions, viewing the party and its claim to the mantle of South African resistance with skepticism. Partisanship for the ANC amongst the African electorate has never been uniformly high: While the great majority of Africans vote for the party, many (in some periods, up to half) do not count themselves as ANC partisans. The ANC consequently had to work hard in its early campaigns to convince its "natural" constituency that it could contain the violence afflicting South Africa and induce social and economic change. In later campaigns, the party had to sell these same voters on its middle-of-the-road economic policies – which had done little to redistribute wealth to the great majority of Africans – and convince them that it had performed well enough to merit another chance in office. In short, the ANC has been engaged in active persuasion vis-à-vis the African electorate since it emerged as the predominant African political force post-apartheid. There was nothing natural or pre-ordained about the party's success in unifying the African constituency, even at the moment of its birth as a mass electoral party. The identity voting perspective, by viewing African support for the ANC as some kind of organic outgrowth of African racial attachments, obscures these diverse political traditions and the contingency of the ANC's hold on African voters.

CLIENTELISM?

If identity considerations do not underlie African support for the ANC, perhaps clientelism does? Clientelistic systems differ from programmatic ones on

[14] For excellent histories of African political movements in South Africa, see Tom Lodge, *Black Politics Since 1945* (New York: Longman, 1983); Tom Lodge and Bill Nasson, *All Here and Now: Black Politics in South Africa in the 1980s* (London: C. Hurst and Company, 1991); Anthony Marx, *Lessons of Struggle: South African Internal Opposition, 1960–1990* (New York: Oxford University Press, 1992). See also Peter Walshe, *The Rise of African Nationalism in South Africa* (Berkeley: University of California Press, 1971).

# Introduction

the basis of the nature of linkages between politicians and voters. Clientelistic systems revolve around contingent direct exchange: Politicians condition the provision of benefits on electoral support (only voters who vote for the party get the benefits; nonsupporters are excluded). In contrast, programmatic systems involve noncontingent, indirect exchange: Parties promise and provide benefits to voters regardless of whether they voted for the party (Kitschelt and Wilkinson 2007). Recent work by Chandra (2004), Posner (2005), and Fearon (1999) have noted a strong relationship between clientelism and ethnic politics: Where you see one, you very often find the other. Indeed, the ANC could use contingent direct exchange to maintain the loyalty of Africans in the face of political diversity and dissatisfaction, buying votes where it cannot otherwise win them. While it is difficult to rule out this explanation completely (clientelism is a notoriously difficult concept to measure as it manifests differently in different places[15]), there are strong reasons to believe that South Africa is not especially clientelistic.

First, political institutions and political history create infertile grounds for clientelism in South Africa. South African political institutions are textbook examples of constitutional engineering to mitigate clientelism: closed list proportional representation; a single national constituency; and parliamentarism with strong, nationally integrative parties. Politicians have no institutionally based incentives to pursue a personal vote (indeed, South African institutions have been attacked for severing the link between politicians and constituents), and competition is focused at the national level, between disciplined teams of politicians.[16] Moreover, South Africa's political history argues against clientelistic linkages. The ANC formed in the early twentieth century, long before Africans had the right to vote. During this time, it had to forge linkages with its supporters based on ideology and the struggle against apartheid, not the provision of benefits. When Africans earned the right to vote in 1994, they had no prior experience of exchanging support for private goods. This is not to say that "liberation" alone was enough to feed these voters. But it does suggest that their ties to the party were not of the "contingent, direct" sort associated with clientelism.[17]

---

[15] Kitschelt (2007) shows, for example, that in Japan clientelism is mediated primarily through businesses – especially "weak, politically biased business regulation that awards advantages to rent-seeking, ruling-party affiliated groups" (p. 302). In Italy, however, it is through public-sector employment, politicized public enterprises, and the social security system (pp. 301–302). Hence scholars of clientelism have tended to rely on a variety of indirect measures of the concept. The contributors to Kitschelt and Wilkinson (2007) provide many clever examples of this.

[16] An extensive literature has explored the link between clientelism and various (formal) institutions – especially those related to electoral rules and the relationship between the executive and legislative branches of government. On electoral institutions, see Carey and Shugart (1995), Ames (2001), Ramsayer and Rosenbluth (1993), and Cox and McCubbins (2001). On parliamentary versus presidential democracy, see Shugart (1999).

[17] South Africa thus provides a classic example of a dynamic noted by Shefter (1977, 1994; and see the useful review in Kitchelt and Wilkinson 2007, especially p. 17), who argue that where

Second, although South Africa's general economic situation (it is a middle-income country with large populations of desperately poor people) would seem to favor clientelism, the government has chosen to pursue economic policies that have reduced its ability to pursue clientelistic exchange. Clientelism tends to flourish precisely in countries like South Africa, where people are very poor yet the state is wealthy enough to engage in some level of redistribution. As discussed extensively in the literature, poor people find the immediate promise of a direct private benefit, even a very modest one, to be highly attractive.[18] However, too much poverty (such as is found in many of South Africa's neighbors to the north) may make full-fledged party-based clientelism difficult because parties remain undeveloped (and unable to monitor and enforce clientelistic bargains) and state coffers are too bankrupt to make vote buying, on any level, feasible (van de Walle 2007). Middle-income South Africa, with its legions of impoverished voters, is both rich enough and poor enough to support clientelism.

At the same time, while South Africa's general economic situation might argue in favor of clientelism, specific macroeconomic challenges the ANC has faced since taking power (and its responses to them) have reduced its latitude in pursuing expensive redistributive programs and/or using state employment to build a patronage machine. When it assumed power in 1994, the ANC inherited a fiscal mess. Real growth was flat or negative during the 1980s and early 1990s. The rate of job creation hit zero in the early 1980s and then went negative. By the end of apartheid, the budget deficit had ratcheted up to 10.8 percent of the budget and the total national debt to GDP (gross domestic product) ratio was 52.5 percent. The country also had crippling levels of foreign debt.[19] The ANC responded to this crisis by instituting fiscally conservative policies.[20] With the unveiling of GEAR (growth, employment, and redistribution) in 1996, it committed itself to lowering budget deficits,

---

social mobilization occurs prior to enfranchisement, parties organizing this mobilization (but still shut out of state office) have to build ideological links with their supporters that are not based on the delivery of material benefits. Once enfranchisement occurs, these established patterns of programmatic linkage inure the parties and the system within which they operate against the temptations of clientelistic exchange.

[18] The specific causal logic for this link is multifaceted and discussed in depth in Kitschelt and Wilkinson (2007), Lyne (2007), Medina and Stokes (2007), Calvo and Murillo (2004), Dixit and Londregan (1996), Magaloni et al. (2007), and Stokes (2005). Poor voters may have shorter time horizons/higher discount rates than richer voters, and they may be easier to monitor (so as to punish defection and reward support), especially if they are isolated and immobile in rural areas. Poor voters are also cheaper to buy off than rich ones: A bag of rice is unlikely to sway a wealthy voter but could be quite valuable to a poor one. Rich voters are also likely to have more diverse income streams and be less reliant on the type of good (for example, public employment) a politician has to offer in exchange for the vote. In sum, "programmatic parties are attractive only to voters who have enough assets (especially human capital endowments) to become entirely indifferent to clientelistic-targeted goods" (Kitschelt and Wilkinson 2007: 25).

[19] Statistics come from Gumede (2005: 81).

[20] See Gumede (2005) for an account of this time period.

# Introduction

streamlining the state, and privatizing state-owned businesses. In the process, the party initiated retrenchments in public-sector employment and fought upward pressure on government wages.[21] While GEAR successfully improved the fiscal situation of the country (South Africa's budget deficit fell to just over 1 percent for the 2002/2003 financial year),[22] it precluded wide-scale social spending programs like the National Solidarity Program (PRONOSAL) in Mexico or the Peruvian Social Fund (FONCODES) in Peru. It also reduced the party's ability to use the public sector to build a patronage machine. In 1995, South Africa had 1.27 million public-sector employees. In 2006, it had 1.08 million public-sector employees – a decline of about 4 percent (even as the population was increasing).[23] It has resisted demands for public-sector wage increases, generally keeping them below 6 percent (not always keeping up with inflation).[24] Its wage bill is much lower than other sub-Saharan countries, lower than most Latin American countries, and lower than lower middle-income countries in general.[25] In response to retrenchments and low salary increases, public-sector employees engaged in strikes in August 1999 and June 2007. The 2007 strike was particularly large, reportedly involving 800,000 workers in forty-three towns and cities across the country.[26] In sum, the ANC's macroeconomic policies – specifically its efforts to streamline the public service – suggest that it is not trying to use public-sector jobs as a means to build a patronage machine.[27]

---

[21] Addressing Parliament, Mandela explained the ANC's policies in this way: "Apartheid South Africa was overgoverned and oversupervised. The size of the public service had nothing to do with public service. Government is not an employment agency. Put in simple terms, we need to cut spending in personnel." Quote comes from Trevor Manuel's 1998 Budget Speech, delivered to Parliament on March 11, 1998.

[22] See Gumede (2005: 99).

[23] Data for 1995 from Müller et al. (1997); data for 2006 from RSA (2006, Annexure).

[24] Blade Nzimande, South African Communist Party General Secretary, quoted in Dixon (2007).

[25] Jobs are quintessential private goods. A politicized job allocation process – the provision of jobs in exchange for political support – is the hallmark of many clientelistic party machines. A bloated public sector and large government wage bill are therefore often taken as symptoms of clientelism (Alesina et al. 1998; Robinson and Verdier 2002; Gimpelson and Treisman 2002; Gibson and Hoffman 2007). This measure is far from ideal. The mere presence of a large number of public-sector jobs does not necessarily indicate a politicized allocation process (jobs may be allocated according to rational, merit-based criteria, not political support). However, it does speak to the *potential* for clientelism: If the public sector is large and government jobs lucrative and many, then parties have a nice pot of goodies to hand out to supporters. In contrast, a small public sector with relatively few jobs or poorly paying ones does not provide much of a clientelistic resource. South Africa's wage bill (compensation of employees as a percentage of government expense, or variable GC.XPN.COMP.ZS in World Development Indicators) was about 15% in 2005. This was significantly lower than other African cases. For example, Cote d'Ivoire was 38%, Benin was 25%, and even relatively wealthy Mauritius (with a per capita income nearly twice South Africa's) was 39%. It was also lower than lower middle-income countries in general (29% in 2004) and Latin America and the Caribbean (24%).

[26] See Dixon (2007) and Barchiesi (1999).

[27] The total number of jobs does not tell the whole story because the ANC pursued affirmative action programs as it was initiating retrenchments. White jobs were initially secured

Third, where the party has engaged in redistributive social spending, there is no evidence that it follows an obvious political logic. Although constrained by its conservative fiscal policies, the ANC has nevertheless attempted to address the massive social inequities that it inherited through a series of aggressive spending programs (initially gathered together under the aegis of the Reconstruction and Development Program [RDP] but continued as part of the government's general policies after the RDP phased out). These programs have focused on the provision of clean water, electrification, education, health services, housing, and social welfare. As of 2007, the government had provided access to clean water to 10 million, increased the number of children going to school by 10 percent, raised the annual number of people (mostly children) receiving social grants by about 8 million (from 3 million in 1999 to 11 million in 2007), approved more than 3 million housing subsidies, and built more than 1.8 million new homes.[28] Many of these programs have provided local public goods (clean water, schools) and/or private goods (social grants, houses) and could give the government significant resources for building a clientelist machine. As Magaloni (2006) demonstrates, the PRI used control over similar kinds of social spending to build an impressive punishment regime in Mexico (municipalities that supported the government received access to spending; those that supported the opposition were cut off). However, to date there is no evidence of any kind of punishment scheme operating in South Africa. The central government raises the lion's share of revenue and distributes it to the provinces, which are in charge of administering most development programs. Transparent formulas that take into account variables such as population, poverty, and the specific needs of different programs (for example, housing backlogs) determine the allocation of resources between provinces.[29] This would seem to leave little room for the central government to "punish" wayward provinces by denying funds. A cursory look at two areas – housing and

---

via a sunset clause negotiated by the NP at the end of its term. However, the sunset clause phased out by 1999, and the ANC began an aggressive effort to hire nonwhites into the public service, especially in management positions (RSA 2000). As whites left the public service, greater numbers of Africans (i.e., ANC supporters) could be hired. In 1989 the public sector was 34% white (Southall 2007), whereas in 2000 it was only 17% white (RSA 2000). Whites held 94% of all management positions (where management positions constitute around 2,300 jobs) in 1994 (Müller et.al. 1997) and 45% in 2000 (RSA 2000). Thus, while the size of the employment pie held steady (or decreased), the distribution shifted. These jobs – especially the well-paid management positions – represent an important political resource for the ANC. However, given the modest size of the public service, the fact that whites remain overrepresented, and the small overall pool of management positions, this resource in no way approximates true patronage machines such as seen in Italy and elsewhere.

[28] Figures come from a variety of sources: RSA (2005, 2007), Southall (2007), and Manuel (1998).

[29] For example, the allocation formula for the integrated housing and human settlement grant (a major transfer from the central government to the provinces to fund housing programs) reflects the housing backlog (50%), a poverty indicator (30%), and a population indicator (20%). See RSA (2005: 72). There are also formulas for determining who qualifies for housing subsidies (household incomes below R3,500). See RSA (2007: 67).

# Introduction

social grants – that due to their private good nature might be especially prone to manipulation – reveals no evidence of a punishment scheme. If the central government sought to punish provinces that have failed to vote ANC, then the Western Cape and KwaZulu-Natal would be its primary targets. However, delivery on housing and social grants (per capita) in these provinces is on par with provinces with similar socioeconomic profiles, suggesting that the central government has not attempted to deny funds or funnel them only to its supporters in these regions.[30]

Fourth, and anecdotally, there have been no reports in the press or elsewhere of vote buying or of efforts by parties to subvert the secret ballot process. Clientelism requires that parties have the ability to monitor voting on some level and convince voters that they know how they voted. If monitoring is not possible – or if voters believe that parties do not have enough information to target punishments effectively – then the clientelistic bargain breaks down. Case studies of classic machines discuss in great detail the methods parties use to insinuate themselves into the lives of voters. In these scenarios, it is common knowledge that parties monitor voting and that the secret ballot is not really secret (Chandra 2004; Stokes 2005). Thus, in clientelistic systems, one would expect discussions of vote buying and vote monitoring to be commonplace. In South Africa, however, the press, political analysts, and ordinary voters seem convinced that elections are free and fair and there are few, if any, stories about vote buying or vote monitoring.[31]

In sum, while South Africa's status as a middle-income country and its large populations of desperately poor people might make it fertile ground for clientelism, other factors (political institutions, political history) work in the opposite direction. Moreover, since assuming power the ANC has pursued

---

[30] Thus, as of 2005, the Western Cape had built 213,001 houses (.05 per capita) and disbursed social grants to 673,978 beneficiaries (.14 per capita). The per capita numbers are virtually identical to ANC-loving Gauteng, a province with a similar incidence of poverty. Along the same lines, KwaZulu-Natal looks very similar to the Free State. KwaZulu-Natal (where 36% of the population lives in poverty) constructed around .03 houses per capita and delivered .22 grants. Free State, with a similar poverty level, constructed .04 houses and delivered .20 grants. (Data on houses come from RSA 2005: 73; data on social grants come from RSA 2005: 57; data on poverty come from Leibbrandt et al. 2004: 19; and data on population come from Statistics South Africa 2006: 9–10). Virtually all of the money for provincial housing and social grants comes from the central government. If the ANC is punishing the Western Cape and KwaZulu-Natal for past political outcomes, it is not evident in these data. It is always possible, of course, that a more careful examination of less aggregated data could produce different conclusions. However, at least at this broad level, there is no evidence of the sorts of punishment regimes often associated with clientelism.

[31] One partial exception was the 1994 elections. In pockets of the country – most notably KwaZulu-Natal – the election was perceived as fraudulent (Johnson 1996). However, elections since 1994 have received high scores. Opposition parties, which are quite vocal in South Africa about problems they perceive in the electoral process, have rarely if ever suggested that the ballot process is not secret. There were also scattered reports of the ANC distributing packets of food to poor voters just prior to the 2009 election (not a tactic observed or at least reported on in prior elections), but no suggestion of *quid pro quo* for benefits provided.

economic policies that have reduced its ability to use state employment to build a patronage machine. Where it has initiated redistributive social programs, it has (it appears, anyway) based funding decisions on economic need (as determined by formulas) rather than political logic. As a result, there is little evidence of flourishing clientelism in South Africa.[32] This is not to say, of course, that South Africa could not evolve in the direction of clientelism. Kitschelt and Wilkinson (2007) wisely point out that institutions can be subverted and political history turned on its head. However, at the moment, at least, the ANC's success at cementing its position as a dominant party, and its ability to deter competition, reflect a strategy different from the ones used by the PRI and LDP, one that is not based simply on clientelism.

So if it is not identity voting, and it is not clientelism, then what does explain the puzzle of the racial census in South Africa? More specifically, why do African voters persist in almost uniformly supporting the ANC in spite of diverse identities and political attachments and in the absence of the material inducements? If neither racial identities nor some kind of binding or blinding partisan glue tie Africans to the ANC, and the party does not buy votes by making government benefits contingent on political support, then what does explain their loyalty? It is this puzzle that provides the focus of this book, and in the next section I will sketch out my answer.

## FRAMING THE RACE AND THE POLITICAL ORIGINS OF THE CENSUS: OVERVIEW OF THE ARGUMENT

I argue that racial-census elections in South Africa reflect the successful execution of a political strategy designed by the ruling party to discredit and delegitimize its primary competitors, the NNP and the DA. Central to my argument is the notion of *party labels or images* (terms that I use interchangeably). Party labels involve more than simply the name of the party (although party names often reflect labels).[33] Like party images, party labels refer to the party's "brand name," its reputation; the general ideology, values, or attributes associated with it; and the groups it is believed to represent. They convey "a great deal of information cheaply."[34] Party labels/images are both

---

[32] This is not, of course, to say that corruption is not a problem. The extent of corruption in the ruling party is a topic of great debate in the country, with some (mostly those in the ruling party) downplaying the issue and others (mostly in the opposition) playing it up (Southall 2007; Butler 2007). The recent legal travails of Jacob Zuma have further politicized the issue. However, corruption and clientelism – while perhaps correlated – are not the same. Corruption speaks to the use by politicians of public office and power for private gain. Clientelism concerns the relationship between parties and their supporters. While South Africa does not currently appear clientelistic, it may nonetheless have a problem with corruption.

[33] Thus, the National Party changed its name to the New National Party in 1997. This is a change of name, but not necessarily a change of label. The party was certainly trying to change its label, but it was not wholly successful, as I will show later in this book.

[34] John Aldrich. *Why Parties? The Origin and Transformation of Political Parties in America* (Chicago: University of Chicago Press, 1995: 49). Richard Rose and Ian McAllister. *The*

the independent and the dependent variables of this book: I begin by establishing that party labels/images influence mass voting behavior in South Africa. I then analyze the efforts of the white opposition parties – the NP and DP – to change their labels/images.

The NP and DP entered into the post-apartheid period with disadvantageous party labels or images. Because of their participation in apartheid, Africans in South Africa have tended to view them as "white" parties, out to protect and promote the interests of white voters, and have unsurprisingly refused to vote for them. The opposition parties, wishing to attract African votes, have attempted to alter their images through electoral campaigns and elite recruitment – efforts the ANC has fought tooth and nail, for as long as the ruling party's primary competitors are "white," then African voters have little choice but to keep supporting it, regardless of whether they enthusiastically endorse the party or simply view it as the lesser of two evils. Moreover, given its greater access to resources, both financial and human, the ANC has largely won the battle to frame the election and the opposition. The weakness of South Africa's opposition parties, and their lack of credibility in the minds of many nonwhite voters, are thus not organic outgrowths of social divisions but the result of a successful political strategy played by the ANC. While these parties inherited disadvantageous party images from the apartheid period, the *maintenance* of these images reflects the active efforts of the ruling party.

My argument begins with voters and then moves on to parties, tracing how the behavioral calculus of voters affects the types of strategies parties employ in their efforts at persuasion and the obstacles they face in the process. My focus is on South Africa's opposition parties and their success (or failure) at winning over African voters. But the ruling African National Congress (ANC) is the shadow player in this story: Its wily defensive actions explain the failure of the opposition parties as much as any shortcomings on their part. The weakness of the opposition is the strength of the ANC. The goal here is to explain how one feeds the other.

## Voters

I build on the pioneering work of South African political scientist Robert Mattes (1995, 2005) to argue that Dawson's (1994) "racial heuristic" approach offers the best explanation for South African voting behavior. South African voters, like voters everywhere, use party images as a cognitive shortcut to guide their voting decisions. Unlike countries where ideologies are well developed or class differences are strong, party images in South Africa are primarily racial in nature. Given the apartheid history of the country and the deep intertwining of individual and group destinies it produced, South Africans believe that

*Loyalties of Voters* (London: Sage, 1991). James M. Snyder and Michael M. Ting. "An Informational Rationale for Political Parties." *American Journal of Political Science*, 46(1), January 2002: 90–110.

the fate of their group is an informative and easily acquired predictor of their fate as an individual. They consequently evaluate parties based on the groups they believe the parties support and favor and the groups they believe the parties oppose. The image of the ANC differs substantially from the images of the NNP and the DP: while most Africans see the ANC as an inclusive party that embraces all racial groups, they view the NNP and the DP as decidedly "white." The origins of these beliefs are not hard to understand: The NNP ruled during the entire apartheid period, putting in place an artifice of racially defined set of policies that severely discriminated against Africans. The DP played the role of official opposition during this time, protesting many of the NP's policies, but doing so with decidedly conservative techniques that won it few allies in the anti-apartheid movement.

Importantly, beliefs about opposition party images have a massive impact on behavior. Africans who see the opposition as exclusive (i.e., white) are more likely to hold positive views of the ANC's performance and less likely to crossover vote or even to consider doing so. In contrast, Africans who have come to believe the opposition is inclusive are more likely to view the opposition as credible and trustworthy and also more likely to question the ANC's performance – perhaps because they are more open to the opposition's criticisms of it – and more open to alternative voting choices.

Hence, the problem for South African opposition parties is not that Africans overwhelmingly identify in racial terms (many do not), or that the strength of partisan attachments precludes alternative political choices (many Africans are independent of party affiliation), or even that Africans vastly prefer the policies of the ANC (the parties all put forth similar policies), but that Africans view them as "white." And because Africans view the opposition parties as white, they are less likely to see them as credible or trustworthy, to buy their criticisms of the ANC, or to support them at the polls. The challenge for the opposition is therefore one of *party label change*, to go from being seen as white to being seen as something more inclusive. This is a necessary, though certainly not sufficient, step to winning African votes. If the opposition parties convince Africans of their inclusiveness, they will gain credibility and trustworthiness in the African community and find a more receptive audience to their complaints about the ANC's performance. In this way, they might begin to build bridges to the African community.

## Parties

The second part of my argument focuses on the process of party label change and the challenges the opposition has encountered in bringing it about. Party labels have been sticky but not fixed in South Africa. The National Party (NP) and the Democratic Party (DP) began the post-apartheid period with solidly white images. Not surprisingly, Africans viewed the NP – the architect of apartheid – as a white party. And while the DP had hoped that its role as the official opposition during apartheid would earn it credibility amongst

TABLE 1.4. *African Impressions of the NP's Image (percent)*

|           | 1994 | 1999 | 2004 |
|-----------|------|------|------|
| Exclusive | 45   | 41   | 7    |
| Inclusive | 26   | 55   | 26   |
| Uncertain | 29   | 6    | 67   |

TABLE 1.5. *African Impressions of the DP's Image (percent)*

|           | 1994 | 1999 | 2004 |
|-----------|------|------|------|
| Exclusive | 16   | 34   | 13   |
| Inclusive | 34   | 13   | 23   |
| Uncertain | 50   | 53   | 64   |

African voters, these voters seemingly gave little credence to its claims to having "fought apartheid from within." Over the decade following the end of apartheid, beliefs about the opposition began to shift, although only in fits and starts, and not always in a clearly positive direction. Tables 1.4 and 1.5 summarize African views of opposition party images. Africans were asked whether the parties looked out for the interests of "all South Africans" (a response labeled in the table as "inclusive") or only those of a few groups ("exclusive"). By 1994, some change was already evident. Africans were most likely to call the NP exclusive (a "white" party), but fewer than half did so. In 2004, exclusive ratings of the NP had fallen to 7 percent. However, this did not mean that Africans had developed uniformly positive opinions of the party. Indeed, most had simply become "uncertain" about its credentials. The Democratic Party found itself in a similar situation. Over time, Africans became somewhat less inclined to see it as exclusively white. Indeed, only 13 percent of respondents held this view by 2004. However, rather than feeling positive about the party, they felt simply uncertain about it. Thus, while party labels have changed, this change has not been uniformly positive. By 2004, only about a quarter of African respondents viewed either the NP or the DP as inclusive.

If changing party labels is the cornerstone to persuasion, why have the opposition parties not been more effective at it? In the game of label change, opposition parties face a natural disadvantage: They lack control over policy and patronage, and therefore they can use neither as a means of signaling their support for new constituencies. Their efforts consequently center primarily on two other levers at their disposal: campaigns and the manipulation of leadership demographics, specifically, the recruitment of nonwhite politicians to their ranks. Yet, as I detail in Chapters 3–7, each of these options encounters difficulties, for as much as the opposition parties wish to transform their images, the ANC wishes to preserve them intact: So long as the

NNP and DA remain white, they are not credible competitors for the African vote. Hence, the party images of the opposition are the site of a major political battle in South Africa, one in which the opposition very often finds itself outgunned.

Popkin (1991) famously argues that campaigns matter. Voters are information misers, looking for handy clues to help them vote, and parties use their campaigns as a ways of providing these. By now we are all familiar with Popkin's Gerald Ford and the tamale example: By failing to husk his tamale, Ford unwittingly sent the signal to Latino voters that he was ignorant of their culture and not worthy of their vote. Politicians since Ford have been more careful, at least when eating tamales. South African opposition parties have also attempted to use campaigns as a way to communicate their transformation to the nonwhite electorate.

The National Party was the first to pursue image change through campaigns. According to Lodge (1994), the NP based its 1994 campaign on the premise that it was "new," that is, not the same party that had put apartheid in place (a few years later, it would make this claim formal by re-christening itself as the New National Party). It also argued that it deserved credit for dismantling apartheid, having set the process in motion by releasing Mandela and legalizing the ANC in 1989. Its efforts were most intense in coloured and Indian communities, where it not only championed its own transformed image; it also pilloried the ANC, charging that it was an African-only party. However, the NP also recognized and targeted African voters. Symbolic of these efforts was the party's federal congress a few months prior to the 1994 election. South African political scientist Hermann Giliomee observes that the old NP was gone from this campaign event: "[I]nstead of the all-white party faithfully singing Afrikaans songs like 'Sare Marais,' the two thousand delegates from all population groups chanted 'Viva FW' and swayed in unison to the strains of the workers' song 'Thotsholoza'" (Giliomee 1994: 57). The NP continued its efforts at racial transformation in its 1999 and 2004 campaigns, portraying itself as either a "brown" or "rainbow" party and trying to distance itself further from its apartheid roots.

The Democratic Party was slower to recognize the importance of party image. In 1994, it ran a campaign based only on policy and competence and was rousingly defeated at the polls (it won less than 2 percent of the national vote). In 1999, it focused on returning from the dead by courting the white vote. This campaign turned the party into the leader of the opposition, but it significantly alienated African voters. It tried to repair the damage in 2004, making a concerted effort to appeal to nonwhite, especially African, voters. In the words of DA Communications Director Nick Clelland-Stokes, it would "take on the ANC in its own backyard."[35] Just as the NP's 1994 federal congress bore witness to its transformation efforts, the DP (by then called the

---

[35] Quoted in Marianne Merten, "DA to 'Take on the ANC in Its Own Backyard.'" *Mail and Guardian*, January 9, 2004.

DA) showcased its Africanization at its manifesto launch in February 2004. The launch was held in Soweto, a bustling African township in Johannesburg. With African township music setting the mood, party leader Tony Leon faced a largely African audience, surrounding himself with black party leaders on stage. The party repeated this presentation at several other crucial campaign events like the introduction of its lists and its final campaign rally. In this way, the DP – like the NP – attempted to use campaign events as a mouthpiece to project a new image to nonwhite constituencies.

Opposition parties have encountered severe limitations to this strategy, however. South African campaigns have typically devolved into "he said/she said" situations. While the opposition parties portray themselves as "rainbow" and "Africanizing," the ANC counters by reminding Africans of these parties' apartheid roots and deep ties to the white community. And any missteps by the opposition are advertised broadly and widely by the ANC. Indeed, the nature of the opposition – whether it is white or Africanizing – has been a central theme in all recent South African elections and has grown in importance over time. In 1994, the ANC partially followed advisor Stanley Greenberg's advice to take the high road and focus on the future instead of the past. However, various party leaders, including Mandela, found it impossible to resist countering the NP's claim that it had ended apartheid and disputing its claims to be "new." And, perceiving that the high road had cost it votes in 1994, the party came out punching in 1999, taking advantage of the DP's overtures to white voters to portray it as racist and run by bigots. In 2004, with the DP (then DA) attempting to Africanize its image, the ANC's efforts to neutralize the opposition's transformation kicked into high gear. The racial profile of the DA was the third most frequently referenced topic in the campaign rhetoric of the major parties– discussed almost as often as unemployment and more frequently than the HIV epidemic. As hard as the DA fought to portray itself as "Africanizing," the ANC fought just as hard to keep its opponent in a little white box. Indeed, discussions of party images infected other, seemingly nonracial campaign topics like economic performance, with the ANC using the DA's image as a means for disqualifying its criticisms of the ANC's economic leadership. This he said/she said environment has simply increased African uncertainty about opposition parties (as evidenced in Tables 1.1 and 1.2) – it has not permitted the sort of wholesale label transformation necessary to win over new voters.

A second strategy the opposition has employed to change its image is the racial diversification of its candidate lists. As suggested by previous studies (Posner 2005; Chandra 2004), candidate characteristics play a central role in elections in divided countries. It is not difficult to understand why. Leadership change is a costlier and therefore more effective signal than mere campaign rhetoric. When it involves the upper echelons of power, it alters key decision makers in the party and, through this, beliefs about the types of actions the party is likely to pursue and which groups it will benefit. Furthermore, through the painful move of unseating party stalwarts with members of targeted groups, the party signals the seriousness of its transformation effort. During the post-apartheid period, the NNP and DA have made impressive efforts to Africanize their lists. The candidates of these parties were uniformly white at the end of apartheid. By 2004, more than 30 percent of their candidates were African and another large percentage was either coloured or Indian. Corresponding to these changes, Africans have slowly but surely revised their beliefs about the opposition parties in the more inclusive direction.

There is a glass empty/glass full aspect to these changes in candidate characteristics, however. For if candidate change is an effective way to achieve party label change, then why have opposition parties not taken it further? In particular, why haven't they placed Africans at the very tops of their lists, in the most prominent leadership positions available? Contrary to some arguments, the reticence of the opposition parties in pursuing more radical transformation relates less to racism or strategic blunder – the leaders of these parties are acutely aware that growing requires candidate change – and more to the challenges posed to small parties of recruiting high-quality candidates. South African voters clearly care about both race *and* quality (experience, credibility, trustworthiness) in assessing politicians. As a result, the opposition parties seek not just African candidates but *high-quality* African candidates. Filling the party ranks and hierarchy with black faces that are unknown, inexperienced, or disliked is unlikely to win black votes, but it will push out seasoned white politicians, reducing the party's human capital and jeopardizing its hold over white votes.

However, in their quest to bring on board high-quality African candidates, South Africa's opposition parties have faced daunting challenges. Assessing quality is notoriously tricky: Politicians do not come with obvious "quality meters." Parties therefore have two options for getting quality candidates: They either "grow their own," observing performance in low-ranking positions and only promoting the best, or they poach high-ranking individuals from other parties, taking their success in the other party as a measure of quality. Neither of these options works particularly well for small parties, as South Africa's opposition parties have learned to their detriment. They cannot grow their own because they lack a sufficient supply of low-ranking but electable positions. I show through an analysis of candidate career paths that the DP and the NP are no different from the ANC in placing newcomers relatively lower on their lists (indeed, if anything, they treat newcomers better than the ruling party). However, a low position on the ANC's lists has a far better chance of getting seated than a low position on an opposition list. As a result, opposition parties struggle to hold on to their candidates: Their candidate retention rate is typically half that of the ANC's, making the grow your own strategy highly inefficient. At the same time, these parties lose in the poaching game with the ANC: Anything they can promise to candidates in the ANC, the ANC can match. Poaching in South Africa is therefore a one-way street: Opposition parties lose candidates to the ANC but never gain them. All roads lead to Oz.

In sum, because of their size, South Africa's opposition parties have struggled to obtain a sufficient supply of high-quality politicians. As such, they share commonalities with opposition parties elsewhere in the world – including places without ethnic or racial divisions. Scheiner (2006) argues that the opposition in Japan faces difficulty in attracting high-quality candidates. The Japanese central state controls fiscal resources, allowing it to punish local governments controlled by opposition parties. This creates strong incentives for local governments to align with the ruling party as opposed to the opposition, making it difficult for the opposition to use local government as an arena in which to cultivate local connections and homegrown talent. As a consequence, opposition parties fail to attract a sufficient supply of high-quality candidates for higher office, which reduces their appeal in the eyes of voters. South Africa's opposition parties face a different but similar problem: They have political talent, but it is white. Their challenge is one of transformation, and the ANC's monopoly hold on African politicians makes this challenging. The parties must walk a treacherous path between being too concerned about quality (and therefore changing too slowly) and being too aggressive and seeing the collapse of their human capital.

The fate of the New National Party, which ironically folded into the ANC following the election in 2004, provides a telling illustration of this latter scenario. While there were many causes of the NNP's implosion, an important one was the loss of human capital following efforts to diversify candidate lists. The party made aggressive and early efforts to recruit nonwhite politicians – 30 percent of its candidates were African by 1999, with another large portion either coloured or Indian. Such rapid change created conflict within the party, which began hemorrhaging leaders during the post-1994 period, deeply damaging its traditional election machinery in the white community. At the same time, the quality of the new recruits – especially the African recruits – was not high enough to gain it support in African communities. As a result, the party lost more than it gained, finally throwing in the cards after very poor results in the 2004 elections. Rapid change of the wrong sort, that is, change that brought in unknown or disliked black faces, backfired. Voters were too smart for that: They were not just "counting heads" (per Chandra 2004), they also cared about quality.

Thus, while South Africa's opposition parties have the most to gain from candidate transformation, the ANC's monopoly over high-quality African politicians makes transformation a risky and challenging endeavor. Until the ANC loses its monopoly, the opposition's chances of bringing on board high-quality African politicians is limited, and so too, therefore, are its chances of bringing about fundamental changes in its party image. While this would seem to portend dim news for the prospect of persuasion in South Africa, the ANC will not be able to maintain its hold on African talent indefinitely. Internal party dynamics occasionally cause the party to spit out one of its own, as happened in 1997 with Bantu Holomisa (who went on to found the UDM) and, more recently, in 2008, when Mosiuoa Lekota, Mluleki George,

Mbhazima Shilowa, and others left the ANC to form Cope. Such conflicts create opportunities for existing opposition parties.

This brings us to a possible qualm about the focus of this book. One might reasonably ask if the white opposition parties are important enough to warrant so much attention. Surely change will come about from African entrepreneurs creating new parties – like Cope – that have clean slates and more appeal to African voters? While this scenario is certainly within the realm of possibility, the success of new parties is hardly a given. They have to create, from scratch, internal and external organizations. If they are splinters of the ANC, they have to build a reputation for themselves and define an issue space and identity separate from the ruling party. They need to raise funds as complete political outsiders without access to public campaign money. Indeed, many South African opposition parties, including, most recently, Cope, have floundered on these challenges. The DA, in contrast, has the advantage of experience, internal organization, a branch structure, fundraising networks, international connections, and, as a product of all these, access to considerable financial resources. It is not a foregone conclusion that the difficulties the DA faces in transformation – formidable as they are – are greater than those of organization faced by new parties. Moreover, any new opposition party will face some of the very same roadblocks faced by the white opposition since 1994: recruiting African talent and image control. Just as the ANC has used political framing to discredit the white opposition, it can use it to discredit other opposition parties as well. Indeed, during the 2009 election the ANC branded Cope as the "black DA," a party of elitists and "Polokwane losers" that offered no realistic alternative to the ANC. Negative framing may be particularly effective against the white opposition because of its past and the history of apartheid in South Africa, but it is a general tactic that ruling parties use against a variety of competitors. Hence, the DA may yet offer the most realistic alternative to the ANC, provided it can lose the "white" in its label and connect in a more meaningful way with the African electorate.

Another potential qualm about this book concerns the time period under study. Perhaps the first three elections after apartheid offer too short a period, or too unique a period, on which to base a study of census-style elections or single-party dominance: Any explanation advanced would be too particular to the immediate post-apartheid period to generalize to other moments in history or other cases. If the ANC holds on to power by discrediting the opposition on the basis of its role during apartheid, surely this strategy is temporary, a function of the very deep wounds apartheid inflicted on South African politics and society. To this I offer three rejoinders: First, most political strategies are temporary. If in the future the ANC moves on to other methods (perhaps developing a clientelistic machine to preserve its hold over power), its negative labeling strategy still helped it win four elections (twenty years of power), not a minor feat. Second, while apartheid may be unique to South Africa, almost every country that democratizes has some history of division or conflict in its past that can be exploited by parties in their competition with one another. Hence, the dynamics in South Africa may be more common than they seem. Indeed, I show in the conclusion that ruling parties in Israel and El Salvador – countries with mild to severe political divisions – used negative labeling strategies to discredit their opponents during the early decades of independence or democratization in their countries. Third, the factors that allow the ANC to use a negative labeling strategy against the white opposition – a monopoly hold over African political talent, greater visibility in the media, a deeper campaign chest than the opposition, and the use of clever campaigns – are not dependent on the amount of time that has elapsed since the end of apartheid. In sum, while aspects of the story told here are unique to the post-apartheid period in South Africa, the broader insights can be applied generally.

Finally, why South Africa? South Africa represents a tough case for an argument about the political origins of census elections. Given the history of colonialism, segregation, apartheid, the struggle against apartheid, and near civil war, South Africa would seem to offer plenty of material on which to base an argument about identity and emotion in politics. Indeed, it is safe to say that most people assume identity considerations drive South African politics. Moreover, in assuming that identity considerations drive South African politics, they conclude there is little to say about politics in this country: Africans represent the majority of the electorate; given apartheid and the rest of South African history, Africans care quite a lot about being African and vote for the ANC because it is the *African* National Congress; the ANC wins elections and will continue to do so until Africans no longer care about being African, which will probably be a very long time. The white opposition parties have no hope of ever winning African votes and can therefore be dismissed as historical footnotes, nothing more. Given this common view of the country, if I can convincingly make the argument that there is a *political* story behind the census in South Africa – where such a story seems relatively unlikely – then the general point that census-style elections reflect political dynamics as much as social ones strengthens all the more.

## BROADER IMPLICATIONS

Political scientists have often treated ethnically divided countries as a species apart from "ordinary" countries with their seemingly less troublesome political conflicts. They have viewed elections in divided countries as inherently problematic, in part because of their tendencies to produce census-like outcomes that freeze one party in power and the rest out (Horowitz 1985; Lijphart 1977, 1999). They have even gone so far as to recommend that ethnically divided countries not pursue democratization, for fear that the census would remove accountability from the ethnic majority party and destabilize the state (Snyder 2000). South Africa is perhaps the most spectacular, certainly the best known, of these census cases, but it is not the only one. As Horowitz (1985) and others have documented, census elections occur with some frequency throughout Africa, Asia, and parts of Europe. Prominent recent examples include Bosnia and Iraq, where ethnic and sectarian divisions have segmented electoral outcomes.

This book suggests that the origins of census elections rest not in identity, as is often assumed, but in politics. In South Africa, a particular set of beliefs about political parties drives the racial census. These beliefs originate in apartheid, but politics drives their preservation: the active and resourceful efforts of the ANC, through campaigns and the control of African political talent, to prevent its competitors from altering their images to become more credible in the eyes of African voters. While the story told here is a South African one, it suggests that, behind other census outcomes, there are political stories worth exploring.

This book also draws out the commonalities between South Africa and other cases of single-party dominance that occur in countries *without* ethnic divisions. As such, it questions the traditional divide between "ethnic" countries and nonethnic ones. The ANC, like ruling parties in Japan, Mexico, Israel, Sweden, and Italy, uses its size and position to enhance its power and emasculate its competitors, to create what Pempel (1990: 16) called a "virtuous cycle of dominance." The census in South Africa has as much to do with these machinations as with race. Indeed, race is a red herring, distracting our focus away from the real dynamics underlying South African elections.

At the same time, I diverge from most recent scholarship on single-party dominance, with its heavy focus on clientelism and patronage as central to explaining the roots and maintenance of dominant or hegemonic party systems (Magaloni 2006; Diaz-Cayeros et al. 2004; Scheiner 2006; Greene 2007; Arriola 2008).[36] Although earlier work highlighted the fragmentation and ideological extremism of the opposition or the cleverness of long-term ruling parties in adapting policy and strategy in the face of changing conditions

---

[36] Pempel (1990) offers a useful definition of dominance, identifying four dimensions: First, the party must win a larger number of seats than its opponents (but not necessarily a majority); second, the party must enjoy a "dominant bargaining position," i.e., it must "be in a strategic position that makes it highly unlikely for any government to be formed without its inclusion" (p. 3); it must be "at the core of a nation's government over a substantial period of time, not simply for a few years" (pp. 3–4); and it must be "dominant governmentally," i.e., it must carry out an historical project that gives shape to the national political agenda (p. 4). By these criteria, the ANC in South Africa is a dominant party. Magaloni (2006) further distinguishes between variants of single-party dominance, drawing a line between "hegemonic party" autocracy and "predominant party" democracy (also called "uncommon" democracies by Pempel). For her, the difference lies in the ability of the dominant party to unilaterally change institutions to further its power, which she measures as a two-thirds legislative majority (the threshold needed to change most constitutions) and/or unilateral control over electoral administration by the ruling party. South Africa, by these standards, would be borderline, but on the democratic side. The ANC has held a two-thirds majority over the legislature in one out of four elections (just missing it in two more) but does not have unilateral control over electoral administration (the Independent Electoral Commission is, as its name suggests, independent).

(Curtis 1988; Pempel 1990), recent explanations have shifted attention almost exclusively to clientelism. According to these accounts, clientelism reinforces single-party dominance by creating an asymmetry in resources and strategies available to incumbents versus oppositions, what Greene (2007) terms "hyper incumbency advantages." In essence, ruling parties with access to clientelistic spoils can make both policy promises and direct transfers of material benefits to supporters, whereas opposition parties compete only on policy. This asymmetry in available strategies puts the opposition at an automatic disadvantage: Any winning policy proposal it puts forward can either be adopted by the ruling party or compensated for with an exchange of clientelistic benefits that sweetens the deal for potential losers (Greene 2007). Moreover, it allows the incumbent to operate "punishment" regimes: Voters or regions that dare to vote against the incumbent can be penalized through the withholding of benefits. Provided the loss of benefits outweighs the gains to voting for a more preferred party, voters and regions continue to support the incumbent party even when they do not prefer its policies (Magaloni 2006; Diaz-Cayeros et al. 2004; Scheiner 2006).

Resource asymmetry may also have more subtle effects, ones that operate by weakening the opposition from within. Greene (2007) argues that, because the opposition faces a structural disadvantage that makes winning office unlikely, it can attract only candidates with extreme policy preferences who care more about ideological purity than holding office. Under the influence of such candidates, opposition parties adopt inflexible, niche positions that are unattractive to the majority of voters, further reducing their chances of winning and confounding coalition building amongst opposition parties. Arriola (2008) also links resource asymmetry with the failure of oppositions to coordinate into a united front. According to his account, creating robust electoral coalitions requires parties to solve a time inconsistency problem: They must credibly commit to a distribution of spoils prior to winning office. Parties can solve this problem if one can compensate the other with a transfer of wealth – an option that is unworkable when incumbents monopolize resources. Moreover, resource-rich incumbents can co-opt opposition parties in divide-and-rule tactics, preventing them from uniting against the dominant party (Magaloni 2006). In all of these accounts, the fractionalization and ideological extremism of oppositions identified as pivotal in earlier accounts of single-party dominance becomes endogenous to the party system, an indirect consequence of the asymmetry of resources between incumbents and oppositions.

Because clientelism provides a more reliable means than programmatic competition for incumbent parties to protect their hold on power, most recent work has seen it as a necessary condition for single-party dominance. To be sure, this literature has also identified other factors as important. Many studies highlight institutional facilitators to dominance, focusing particular attention on electoral rules like proportional representation (Pempel 1990), the single nontransferable vote (Kohno 1997), and mixed-member systems

(Magaloni 2006).[37] Malapportionment and fiscal centralization may also contribute (Scheiner 2006). Other studies note the frequent revision and manipulation of electoral rules by dominant parties, suggesting that it is not so much a particular endowment of rules that creates dominance, but rather the ability of parties to reform institutions in their favor – that is, dominance begets more dominance as incumbents rig the institutions to ensure their continued rule (Molinar 1996; Magaloni 2006). And authors working on semi-democracies note that incumbents in these systems often supplement clientelism with fraud and repression – especially when clientelistic resources dry up (Magaloni 2006; Greene 2007). However, most of these studies see institutions or fraud and violence as *supplemental* to clientelism, insufficient on their own to produce dominance.

But is clientelism the full story? Pempel (1990) argued that while the material bases of dominance are important, our focus on them should not be so exclusive that we ignore how dominant parties also use "symbolic manipulation" to perpetuate their rule, suggesting that ruling parties benefit from the polarization of the electorate, because "different blocs would find the theoretically plausible option of joining the opposition to be totally ludicrous ideologically" (Pempel 1990: 345). Moreover, polarization is not merely organic, an outflow of sociological difference, but actively cultivated by political parties to extend their rule. In particular, ruling parties use their control over public discourse to delegitimize the opposition, to place it in such an extreme ideological position as to make it "ludicrous" to most of the electorate.

With its almost exclusive focus on clientelism, most recent work on dominance has neglected Pempel's "symbolic" realm in favor of the material. Yet the South African case reminds us of Pempel's earlier wisdom. The ANC has won four sets of national elections with resounding victories. At the end of its current term, it will have ruled for twenty years with strong majorities. And while the party might eventually cultivate clientelistic relationships with segments of the electorate, to date it has achieved dominance *without* clientelism. This is not to say that there is no material base to ANC rule. The ANC, like political parties everywhere, uses material inducements to warm the hearts of voters, especially around election time. It is relatively cheap to make an impoverished and neglected group a little happier than they were before, and the ANC has been skilled and strategic in doing so. However, we must look beyond the exclusively material to understand ANC dominance. In particular, we need to understand how the ANC has won the battle to frame the image of the opposition in the electorate. As Lakoff (2004) demonstrates for American political parties, the ability to frame political discourse confers real political power. When framing removes the opposition as a serious option in the choice set of

---

[37] While these studies focus on different institutions, the arguments are similar: Electoral institutions that do not create incentives for the opposition to form a united front – or worse, induce opposition parties to compete with each other rather than the dominant party – create opportunities for the ruling party to divide and conquer its opponents.

voters, dominant parties no longer need to beg or bribe the electorate: They win by default. Framing therefore provides an alternative, often complementary, strategy to straight-up clientelism. And as few parties have the resources to buy all the votes they need to stay in power, it is a useful strategy indeed.

On a final note, this book initiates a discussion about the importance (and challenges) of two topics: first, how parties change their images; and, second, how oppositions in new democracies – especially those dominated by a single party – build credibility in the minds of voters. I view these topics as interconnected: Locked out opposition parties often need to change their images to establish credibility.[38] To complement my study of South Africa, I explore the relationship between image change and credibility in two supplementary cases: Israel and El Salvador. To gain credibility in the electorate, Herut (Israel's pre-eminent right-wing party post-independence and the predecessor of Likud) had to soften its reputation for being anti-democratic and dangerous; El Salvador's FMLN had to convince voters that it was not a terrorist or communist organization. In both cases, opposition parties faced a dominant party committed to preserving the status quo. The Israeli and Salvadoran cases also confirm the link between credibility and electoral success. In Israel, Herut was able to take power away from the dominant Labor party only after it gained credibility and legitimacy in the electorate; voters who might have been sympathetic to Herut did not vote for it because it was not in the realm of plausibility. In El Salvador, the ruling party ARENA continued to win elections even as the public soured on its neoliberal policies in part because the opposing FMLN lacked credibility.[39] As these examples make clear, when oppositions lack credibility, voters are stranded on the shores of the dominant party. They may not like it, but they have nowhere else to go. Indeed, battles over the credibility of opposition parties are often a central component of election campaigns in new democracies, with opposition parties attempting to establish their credibility in the eyes of the electorate and ruling parties hoping to destroy it.[40] Understanding when and how oppositions win

---

[38] I say *often* rather than *always* because sometimes the challenge for oppositions is one of overcoming obscurity and *building* a reputation rather than *changing* one.

[39] Beyond these cases, even in clientelistic Mexico, the credibility of the opposition played a role in the maintenance of single-party dominance. Magaloni (2006) and Dominguez and McCann (1995) document how a credibility gap between the dominant PRI in Mexico and opposition parties wed voters to the ruling party during times of economic downturn: Voters simply did not view opposition parties as credible contenders for the presidency and therefore continued to support the PRI even as their displeasure with the ruling party grew.

[40] Keefer (2007) and Keefer and Vlaicu (2008) highlight the importance of party credibility in new democracies and note the challenages parties face in cultivating credibility in these circumstances. I add to their discussion the observation that the difficulties of establishing credibility are often not evenly distributed amongst competitors. That is, there are often *credibility gaps* between parties in new democracies, where parties that have ruled for long periods of time have natural advantages vis-à-vis the opposition. These credibility gaps may be at least as important in explaining electoral outcomes as the overall level of credibility amongst parties in the party system.

this battle is crucial to our understanding how democracy consolidates, for without a coherent, credible opposition, elections lose their ability to generate accountability. It is to this end that I write this book.

PLAN OF THE BOOK

This book begins with voters (Chapter 2) and then moves on to parties (Chapters 3–7). Chapter 2 demonstrates that voters in South Africa use party images to inform their voting decisions: Africans who view the opposition as inclusive are less likely to support the ANC, less likely to have positive evaluations of the ANC's performance, and more likely to find the opposition credible and trustworthy. Chapter 2 argues that party images explain voting better than identity considerations, policy preferences, or performance evaluations alone. In addition to tracing the behavior of voters, Chapter 2 sets the stage for the remainder of the book. It demonstrates, through survey data, that party labels have not been fixed in South Africa. The remaining chapters of the book then explore the efforts parties have made to change their labels as well as the considerable challenges they have faced in this process.

Chapters 3–5 examine party campaigns in 1994, 1999, and 2004. These chapters demonstrate that persuasion attempts have been central to the campaigns of South Africa's opposition parties during most elections and also reveal that manipulating party images has been a central plank of these persuasion efforts. The opposition parties have gone to great lengths to portray themselves as new, reformed, transformed, and inclusive. At the same time, the ruling ANC has fought equally hard to keep these parties "white." Indeed, conflict over the nature of the opposition has formed one of the major fault lines running through all post-apartheid elections in South Africa. In this he said/she said environment, the opposition has typically found itself outmaneuvered by the ANC, which has greater campaign resources and ability to frame the election for its own purposes.

Chapters 6 and 7 consider a more potent means of signaling image change to the electorate: the manipulation of candidate characteristics. Chapter 6 demonstrates that the opposition parties have made large efforts to transform their candidate demographics and that these efforts have coincided with changes in popular beliefs about party images. Chapter 6 closes with a paradox: If candidate transformation is key to label change, then why have opposition parties not gone further in their efforts at candidate transformation? Chapter 7 picks up this question and examines the political barriers that opposition parties face in candidate change. It argues that, if the opposition parties replace their existing tried-and-true candidates with unknown or unpopular African candidates, they risk losing their existing votes without gaining new ones. Chapter 7 then traces the difficulties the opposition has had in attracting and retaining African political talent.

Chapter 8 generalizes the argument to other South African opposition parties, showing that the ANC has used image politics against three

*Introduction*  31

of its "African" competitors: the IFP, the UDM, and Cope. Chapter 9, the conclusion, considers the cases of Israel and El Salvador, showing that ruling parties in both of these countries used negative labeling strategies to discredit oppositions. Image politics and framing strategies are therefore not unique to the white opposition parties of South Africa but rather form part of the general repertoire of techniques used by ruling parties in other places. Finally, Chapter 9 uses insights from the South African, Israeli, and Salvadoran cases to speculate about the future of opposition politics in South Africa.

## 2

# Voters

Census elections like those in South Africa reflect the decisions of millions of individual voters. To understand the origins of the census, we must therefore begin with an exploration of individual-level voting behavior. The question can be framed as this: When an African voter chooses the African National Congress (ANC) over one of its "white" competitors (the New National Party or the Democratic Alliance), what explains her behavior? Is it the need to express her identity as an African? Is it general antipathy to whites and the parties that represent them? Or are her motivations more instrumental, a function of policy preferences and performance evaluations? If they are instrumental, what role, if any, does race play? And, perhaps most importantly, how do these factors interact with one another?

In addressing these questions, this chapter distills and tests three hypotheses from the general voting literature. The first hypothesis ("expressive voting") holds that racial voting results as voters use the ballot box to express their identities as members of racial groups. The second hypothesis ("politics-as-usual") explains racial voting through nonracial factors. It suggests that racial voters, like all voters, care what governments do and how well they do it. Convergence of voting behavior within racial groups occurs because group members share common policy preferences and performance evaluations – not a common identity. The third hypothesis ("racial heuristics") shares the instrumentalism of the second but gives race a more active role in explaining behavior. It suggests that, in a country like South Africa, where race acts as a good predictor for individual life chances, voters are likely to evaluate parties based on expectations about how they will treat different groups. Party images will consequently have a prominent racial component, and this component should strongly influence voting behavior. All three approaches can account for the aggregate pattern of the racial census. The goal of this chapter is to determine which, if any, best accounts for South Africa's racial census, and to explore interactions between them.

Although prior work has examined South African voting behavior in some detail, I make two important innovations in this chapter. First, I develop a novel operationalization of the racial heuristics hypothesis, based on party labels, that makes possible head-to-head tests with competing hypotheses. Second, I look at both crossover and uncertain voters, whom I take as sophisticated bell-weathers of future electoral change. This increases the range of variation in the data and permits richer inferences. Together, these innovations allow me to disentangle the evidence for and against the different hypotheses.

While uncovering the behavioral origins of the census is an important task in its own right, it also sets the stage for the remainder of this book. Different motivations at the individual level project different constraints and opportunities on the persuasion strategies pursued by parties. If identity concerns drive behavior, then parties hoping to win new voters must concern themselves primarily with breaking down old identity patterns and forging new ones. In contrast, if voters behave primarily out of a concern for policy and/or performance, then aspiring parties must look for windows of opportunity presented by unmet policy needs, situations where the ruling ANC stakes out a position at odds with its constituency or fails to deliver on promises made. And if voters use party labels as a heuristic to guide their decisions, then these labels – and their manipulation and transformation – become the lynchpin of persuasion. Different dynamics at the voter level predict different strategies at the party level, a point I will pick up on in later chapters of this book.

To preview the results, I find strong evidence that party labels are heavily racialized in South Africa and play a powerful role in shaping voting behavior: They correlate with African support of the ANC, uncertainty levels, and actual crossover voting. Furthermore, they correlate with Africans' perceptions about the credibility and trustworthiness of the opposition and evaluations of incumbent (ANC) performance, which in turn also correlate with vote choice. When Africans view the opposition as inclusive, they are more likely to find it credible and trustworthy, which may in turn open them to the opposition's criticisms of the ruling party's performance. However, when Africans view the opposition as racially exclusive, they tend not to trust it or find it credible. They are also more likely to credit the ANC with positive performance ratings. Thus, although voting looks like "politics-as-usual" on one level (voters do care about performance), on a deeper level their beliefs about performance are intimately related to their beliefs about party images. In contrast, I find little evidence in support of the identity hypothesis. Overt patterns of racial identification bear no relationship with voting. Furthermore, although partisanship is important in explaining voting, there are fewer South African partisans than racial voters. Altogether, these results suggest that *identity is not destiny*: Changes in the racial-census pattern depend not on altering patterns of identification in the electorate but on the ability of parties (particularly the opposition) to change their party labels.

## THEORIES OF RACIAL OR ETHNIC VOTING

Three general explanations have been put forth to explain racial/ethnic voting in South Africa and elsewhere: those stressing expressive motivations on the part of voters; those emphasizing policy preferences or performance evaluations; and those highlighting the informational role of race.[1] In this section, I situate each of these in the literatures on comparative ethnic politics, American racial politics, and South African elections.

### Expressive/Identity Voting

The expressive/identity voting framework sees voting as a means of expressing group allegiance. In comparative studies of ethnic politics, its most prominent advocate is Donald Horowitz, whose 1985 book *Ethnic Groups in Conflict* is still the benchmark for studies of ethnic voting. Building on the work of social psychologist Henri Tajfel, Horowitz argues that individuals in ethnically divided countries seek affirmation of self-worth through their identities as members of groups. Voters derive psychic benefits from supporting ethnic parties because the very act of casting a vote for an ethnic party is an affirmation of identity. Thus, voting is not an act of choice, based on a rational weighing of alternatives, but an expression of allegiance to a group. Voters do not use their vote to further self-interest. Indeed, they may actually vote in ways that work *against* their interests. Furthermore, their allegiance to their party, constructed as it is from the raw material of identity, is nonnegotiable. Patterns of partisanship are fixed, rigid. Elections become a rubber stamp for demographics, a mere "counting of heads." Although Horowitz has developed this logic the most thoroughly, it also lurks in most work on constitutional engineering in divided countries. Beneath Lijphart's recommendations for consociationalism (or at least consensual democracy), for example, suggest a fear that ethnic divisions inevitably produce rigid voting patterns and permanent majorities/minorities, which in turn auger in a series of negative consequences for democracy (see Lijphart 1977, 1999). Recent discussions of constitutional engineering (Sisk and Reynolds 1998; Reilly and Reynolds 1999; Reilly 2001; Reynolds 2002) share a similar (if unstated) set of assumptions: Because identity drives voting, divided countries must rely on the clever

---

[1] The second two explanations are both instrumental (as opposed to expressive) in nature. They view voting as *outcome* as opposed to *act* contingent. Voters cast a racial vote because they believe doing so will further their interests, not because the act of voting itself carries benefits. They are both therefore "rational choice" explanations for voting. They differ in the criteria voters use in making the voting decision: In "politics-as-usual" theories, voters look at policy promises (prospective criteria) or performance evaluations (retrospective criteria); in cognitive (or racial heuristic) explanations, voters consult party labels or party images to help predict what a party will do while in office. The difference revolves around voter uncertainty, *not* voter rationality: The cognitive/heuristic approach sees voters as uncertain about parties' policy platforms and/or performance records and how these predict the future behavior of the party if it wins office.

design of electoral institutions to contain the tensions and pressures elections inevitably produce.

The expressive voting perspective resonates with work by American scholars that emphasizes prejudice as the key factor behind white reluctance to support African American candidates. Thus, Kinder and Sears (1981) argue that "symbolic racism" best explains patterns of voting in Los Angeles in 1969 and 1973. Terkildsen (1993) offers experimental evidence suggesting that the racial prejudice of white voters prevents them from voting for black candidates. Kinder and Sanders (1996) test several explanations for the divergence of white and black opinions on policies such as affirmative action and conclude that racial resentment is most important, while Mendelberg's (2001) account of how parties use implict racial signals assumes that prejudice motivates white voters.

These explanations of racially polarized voting have seeped into explanations of voting in South Africa. Johnson and Schlemmer (1996) argue that that the racial-census outcome in South African elections reflects atavistic commitments to racial groups on the part of voters – not rational policy preferences. Friedman (2004: 3) concurs, suggesting that voter preferences are shaped by their assessments of which party can "best provide a vehicle for who they are," not an "instrumental choice between competing technical solutions to economic and social problems" (see also Friedman 2005). In the popular press, the reluctance of the African electorate to vote out the ANC – even in the face of poor economic performance – is given as further evidence that a noninstrumental, expressive logic drives South African voting decisions.

## Politics as Usual: Policy and Performance Voting

However, need race enter the picture at all? Abrajano et al. (2004) point out that racial voting and policy voting can be observationally equivalent if policy preferences are similar within groups and differ across them. In other words, a white voter might choose a white candidate over a black one not because she is moved to express her allegiance to whiteness, but because she likes the white candidate's policies better! Voting is driven not by identity but by interests, where interests manifest themselves in preferences over policy and general ideological dispositions. This perspective resonates with classic works on comparative ethnic politics by Hechter (1975), Bates (1974), and Rabushka and Shepsle (1972).

In the American literature, Sigelman et al. (1995) present experimental evidence suggesting that white voters care more about ideology than race: White voters avoid black candidates because they dislike their policies or ideological stances, not because they dislike blacks per se. Sniderman and Carmines (1997) also embrace ideological dispositions – as opposed to prejudice – as the root to white behavior. And Abrajano et al. (2004) argue that, although racial voting explains some racially polarized behavior in recent Los Angeles elections, policy preferences also matter.

In South Africa, Mattes (1995), Mattes et al. (1999), Mattes and Piombo (2001), and Bratton and Mattes (2003) argue that African voters overwhelmingly support the ANC because it is closest to them in terms of policy prescriptions and because they are happy with its performance. Whites, in contrast, dislike the ANC's policies and feel it has failed to deliver, and hence refuse to vote for it.

If these "politics-as-usual" perspectives are correct, then we need no special theory of racial or ethnic voting: The standard tools – namely, the spatial voting model of Downs (1957) or the performance models of Fiorina (1981) and Ferejohn (1986) – apply. Ethnicity/race plays no direct role in shaping behavior. Election campaigns may contain few overt references to ethnicity or race. Voters may not identify in clear ways with the groups in question. Yet behavior within groups is homogenous, thus fitting the "ethnic census" description.

### Race/Ethnicity as Information

The informational approach to racial/ethnic elections shares the instrumentalism of the "politics-as-usual" approaches. However, due to the presence of uncertainty, the link between interests and behavior is less direct. Downs (1957) and later Popkin (1991) argued that uncertainty induces voters to rely on "cognitive shortcuts" – easily acquired information that helps voters decide which options are most likely to benefit them in the future. Dawson (1994) applied this logic to a racial setting, arguing that racial divisions affect the types of cues voters privilege: If people believe group membership has a large impact on individual prospects, then group-based cues are likely to be informative and thus valuable to voters. Furthermore, it is easier to collect information on the impact of different electoral options on groups versus individuals. Voters therefore privilege group-based cues. Along similar lines, Chandra (2004) argues that ethnicity acts as an informational shortcut for voters in India[2] and Posner applies the logic to voting in Zambia.

In the South African context, racially based cues are likely to be highly valuable to voters. Alternative cues, standard in other electoral settings, are not completely reliable. Because democracy is relatively new to the country, ideological differentiation between parties (and amongst voters) is less than fully developed. Survey respondents frequently seem confused by questions

---

[2] Chandra's account diverges from Dawson's in that she suggests that certain innate properties of ethnicity make it uniquely attractive to voters as a source of information: Ethnic identity is often substantially more visible than other forms of identity – such as class – because it is encoded in names and physical appearance. Consequently, voters will inevitably use ethnicity as a shortcut in any low information setting. In contrast, Dawson suggests that it is only when individual prospects correlate with group prospects that group identity becomes a useful heuristic to voters. In other words, Chandra predicts the use of ethnic shortcuts whenever voters face informational deficits, whereas Dawson applies additional criteria.

about "left" and "right."[3] Furthermore, party labels do not consistently reflect these attributes. In survey responses, the ANC is generally to the "left" of its white opposition, perhaps reflecting its prior flirtations with socialism and its long-term association with the Communist Party. However, during its first ten years in office it pursued policies that aligned it with mainstream conservative economic policies – the same policies, more or less, advocated by the opposition. This has served to confuse and dilute whatever ideological differentiation might have existed between parties.

More importantly, racially based heuristics are informative in the South African context. Forty years of apartheid (and centuries of segregation before it) taught South Africans to link individual prospects to racial identity. Apartheid policies assigned individuals to racial groups and tied all significant rights, benefits, and opportunities to group membership. The ability to own land, to move freely around the country, to acquire occupational training and/or education; the right to vote and freely join political associations; the area where a person lived; the jobs he or she performed; the wages earned; a person's choice of spouse and sexual partner – all of these depended on racial classification. The state privileged whites over other groups, granting them the ability to own land, setting aside the best areas of the country for their exclusive occupation, reserving for them the top jobs, and providing them with first-world education, health care, and public amenities. In contrast, the state barred Africans from owning land, restricted their movement around the country, consigned them to live in overcrowded urban slums and barren rural reserves, prevented them from acquiring skills to obtain good jobs, legislated against their ability to organize collectively, and invested little in their education, health care, and public amenities.[4] In between whites and Africans, coloureds and Indians were "middlemen" minorities. They, too, faced restrictions on land ownership and residence and were not allowed to compete with whites for top jobs. The state invested less in their education and health care. At the same time, it took care to elevate them above Africans, designating better neighborhoods and schools for them and reserving better jobs.[5]

---

[3] As evidence for this, consider the following: When asked to place themselves on a left–right ideological scale in 1994, 38% of African respondents, 27% of coloured respondents, and 31% of Indian respondents claimed that they did not understand the question. Whites were much more likely to understand the question (only 6% said they did not), reflecting their longer experience with elections. By 1999, the numbers for nonwhites were better but still lagged well behind whites: 15% of Africans, 25% of coloureds, and 19% of Indians refused to answer the ideology question (the option of "do not understand" was not offered), whereas only 3% of whites refused. These data come from Idasa's 1994 survey and the *Opinion99* survey.

[4] Historical accounts of the apartheid and pre-apartheid periods are too numerous to discuss in any detail here. For a good basic history and comprehensive review, see Leonard Thompson, *A History of South Africa* (New Haven, CT: Yale University Press, 1990) or William Beinart, *Twentieth Century South Africa* (Oxford: Oxford University Press, 2001).

[5] For an account of coloured life under apartheid, see John Western, *Outcast Cape Town* (Berkeley: University of California Press, 1996). For an account of Indian life under apartheid,

Thus, the South African state drew sharp lines between racial groups, assigning racial identities to individuals and endowing them with separate rules, rights, and privileges. This classification was strict and nearly impossible to evade.

The legacy of these policies has been manifold. They have left behind a highly unequal society, one in which race continues to predict with a high degree of accuracy a person's prospects in life. According to a study of census data by researchers at the Centre for Social Science Research at the University of Cape Town, "the African group overwhelming [sic] dominates both the incidence and share of poverty" (Leibbrandt et al. 2004: 38). White per capita income was *more than eleven times higher* than African per capita income in 2001 – about the same disparity ratio as 1991. White incomes also greatly outpaced coloured (five times higher) and Indian (2.4 times higher). Thirty-five percent of Africans fell below the poverty line ($2 per day) in 2001, compared with 13 percent of coloureds, 3 percent of Indians, and 1 percent of whites. Only 60 percent of Africans lived in formal housing (compared with 89 percent of coloureds and 97 percent of Indians and whites), and only 78 percent had access to piped water (compared with 95 percent of coloureds and 96 percent of Indians and whites).[6] Apartheid also left behind a history of competition between groups, not just competition between whites and Africans but between Africans, Indians, and coloureds. In KwaZulu-Natal, Africans and Indians long fought over access to quality land in urban areas, sparking repeated riots throughout the twentieth century (Freund 1995; Gigaba and Marharaj 1996). In the Western Cape, land, housing, and jobs generated tensions between coloureds and Africans and coloureds and whites (Giliomee 1994; Western 1996). In this context, it is not surprising that many South Africans – of all colors – continue to tie their individual interests with those of their racial group (whether they identify actively with that group or not) and to believe that what is good for one group might be bad for another.

As surely as similar processes introduced the racial heuristic to Dawson's (1994) African American voters, apartheid introduced the racial heuristic to South Africa's. Given this history, Mattes (1995), Mattes et al. (1999), and Mattes and Piombo (2001) have argued that race acts as an information shortcut for South African voters.[7] Consequently, according to this viewpoint, the

---

see Bill Freund, *Insiders and Outsiders: the Indian Working Class of Durban 1910–1990* (Portsmouth, NH: Heinemann, 1995).

[6] Statistics come from Leibbrandt et al. (2004), who also show that inequality within racial groups has increased while inequality across racial groups has decreased – a finding also reported by Seekings and Nattrass (2002). If this trend continues, we would expect a decline in the usefulness of racially based cues in South Africa. However, as the earlier cited statistics clearly demonstrate, income, poverty, and access to basic services remain grossly unequal across racial groups.

[7] Why race and not ethnicity? Ethnic divisions certainly exist in South Africa, especially amongst Africans (who divide into nearly a dozen different distinct groups) and whites (with the historic split between Afrikaans and English speakers). However, life chances do not correlate heavily with ethnic identity, once race is taken into account. The differences *between* races swamp any differences *within* races. The apartheid state acknowledged and promoted

correlation between race and voting reflects the instrumental use of race as an informational cue, not the emotional attachment of voters to racially exclusive parties.

In sum, there are several plausible explanations for the correlation between racial classification and voting behavior in South Africa. Though distinct, they are often conflated. Thus, Abrajano et al. (2004) contrast "racial" explanations for voting with "policy" explanations and seem to use "racial" to mean either voting on the basis of prejudice or voting on the basis of racial cues. Similarly, Bullock (1984: 239) writes that it is "hardly surprising" that voters will vote for candidates of their same race and then suggests that some are motivated by racism while others may be using race as a cue. In both of these instances, authors do not distinguish between the expressive and informational accounts of racial voting. Mattes and his coauthors frequently combine various "politics-as-usual" stories with the race-as-information story (Mattes 1995; Mattes et al. 1999; Mattes and Piombo 2001 Bratton and Mattes 2003).

There is value to keeping separate different theoretical strands, however. They differ in key regards. They assign different roles to race in voting. The first and third stories give race active roles in voting, albeit very different ones. In contrast, the second explanation sees any correlation between race and voting as accidental. Furthermore, they differ on whether voting is primarily instrumental or expressive. The second and third explanations are both instrumental – they see voters as acting in accordance with their interests. In contrast, the first expects interest to play little if any role in voting. Indeed, according to this view of voting, voters may actually vote against their interests.

Finally, and most importantly, each approach projects different expectations for how and when a person might depart from the racial pattern. For the first approach, such a change would require either a change in identity or a reduction in prejudice or bigotry. In contrast, the second approach looks to more quotidian factors: The black candidate adopts the white candidate's policy positions and hence becomes more attractive to the white candidate's constituency. Or the white incumbent fails to deliver, and his color-blind supporters start shopping for alternatives. Finally, the third approach requires black candidates or parties to convince white voters that they can look out for their interests. Alternatively, race becomes a less useful heuristic or predictor

---

internal differences within racial groups, most especially through its homelands policy, which created separate rural "homelands" for most African ethnic groups, e.g., KwaZulu for the Zulu, Bophuthatswana for the Tswana, and so on. However, precisely because most of these homelands were ethnically homogeneous, ethnicity was not a point of competition within them. Furthermore, unlike colonial states elsewhere in Africa, the apartheid state did not give more rights and privileges to some ethnic groups over others; it did not, in other words, create an ethnic hierarchy. Life for the Zulu in KwaZulu was just as restricted and impoverished as life for the Xhosa in Transkei, especially when compared with the relative affluence of whites. Hence, apartheid tied individual interest to racial identity much more firmly than to ethnic identity. Since apartheid, little has occurred to change this. The ANC draws elites and votes from across African ethnic groups and distributes benefits accordingly.

of interests and voters turn to other shortcuts, or other types of information (ideology, for example) become more readily available (Dawson 1994). These are quite different paths to change and require divergent persuasion strategies on the part of politicians. For this reason, it is useful to keep the accounts separate. In the next section, I carry out a series of tests to see which, if any, of the stories best accounts for voting behavior in South Africa.

TESTS

In the analysis that follows, I introduce a new way to operationalize the heuristics story (a racial party label that acts as an information shortcut) that facilitates head-to-head tests with other hypotheses. I also complement simple bivariate breakdowns of the data with multivariate statistical analysis. In the statistical analysis, I look at three different types of voters: those who adhere to the racial pattern, those who cross over, and those who are uncertain about their vote choice. Focusing on this last category of voters is an important innovation. Uncertain voters represent an intriguing but understudied category of voter. Think of cross-racial voting as involving two steps: first, rejecting the party of "your" group and, second, accepting the party of the "other" group. Uncertain voters speak to the first of these steps, a necessary precondition to the second more important (but also more elusive) act of crossing over. Thus, uncertain voters may be harbingers of electoral change, the set of people most likely to challenge patterns of racial polarization in the future. Studying them provides a richer record of variation in behavior and may produce insights into the general causes of polarization in South African voting behavior.[8] Finally, I look beyond vote choice to attitudes that might be considered proximate causes of vote choice: evaluations of incumbent performance and beliefs about the credibility and trustworthiness of the opposition. While the data have their limits – being survey data from a single point in time, they cannot speak definitively to causation – the analysis that follows provides new clues on the correlates of racial voting in South Africa.

**Operationalizing Identity, Policy, Performance, and Shortcuts**

In this section, I provide a very simple first cut on the data, introducing the measures used to operationalize each of the main hypotheses, examining the distribution of responses across racial groups and reviewing prior work. I use four separate surveys: a 1994 survey conducted by Idasa (a South African research organization); a 1998–1999 survey called *Opinion99*, also conducted

---

[8] One possible qualm about using crossover voters is that they could represent uninformed and uninterested voters rather than voters on the fence. Though perhaps true in some electoral contexts, this does not appear to be the case in South Africa, especially for African voters. Instead, these voters tend to be *better educated* and *more informed* than their more committed peers.

by Idasa; the 2000 *Afrobarometer* survey; and a 2004 survey run by the Comparative National Election Project (CNEP).[9] The surveys vary in terms of which variables they contained, so unfortunately a somewhat piecemeal approach to the data is necessary.

## Identity

South African pollsters have attempted to solve the knotty problem of measuring the strength of ethnic and racial identification by asking questions about group belonging. Thus, in the 2000 *Afrobarometer* survey, enumerators asked the open-ended question: "Besides being South African, which group do you feel you belong to?" The 1994 Idasa survey asked, "In terms of culture, history, and language, do you consider you belong to a distinctive community (with its own distinctive culture and history)?"[10]

---

[9] The 1994 survey was nationally representative and interviewed 2,517 individuals (1,379 Africans, 664 whites, 423 coloureds, and 51 Indians) between August 26 and September 16, 1994. For more information, see Idasa (1994). The 1998–1999 survey (known as *Opinion99*) was conducted in four series. This chapter uses Series I, which involved 2,200 interviews and was in the field September 1–30, 1998 (1,776 Africans, 223 whites, 121 coloureds, and 80 Indians). See Idasa (1999c). The *Afrobarometer* survey conducted 2,200 interviews (1,560 Africans, 320 whites, 220 coloureds, 100 Indians) in July–August 2000 (see Cho 2002). The Comparative National Election Project (CNEP) conducted a nationally representative survey of 1,200 individuals (837 Africans, 113 coloureds, 67 Indians, and 183 whites) in September 2004. For a useful review of these surveys, see Appendix 1 in Collette Schulz-Herzenberg, A Silent Revolution: South African Voters during the First Years of Democracy 1994–2006. Doctoral thesis, University of Cape Town, South Africa, 2009.

[10] These are not ideal measures of identity. Respondents may under-report normatively undesirable identities. Furthermore, the questions do not allow for the possibility of multiple identities, per constructivist understandings of identity. And, given that identities are multiple, the survey may fail to tap into the identity most relevant to politics. There are good reasons to believe, however, that these problems are not terribly severe in the data used in this analysis. First, at least for Africans, racial identities are no more normatively undesirable than other common identities (ethnic ones, for example). Africans can view the assumption of a racial identity as a political statement *against* oppression, whereas professing an ethnic identity has sometimes been interpreted as buying into apartheid's "divide-and-rule" policies. Second, although the surveys did not explicitly "prime" respondents to think about identities relevant to politics, the nature of the other questions asked, their ordering, and the overall timing of data collection may have accomplished this accidentally. The 1994 Idasa survey was in the field about four months after the historical 1994 election. Per Eiffert, Miguel and Poser (2007), the proximity of the election most likely increased the salience of the national political arena in respondents' minds as they were answering questions. Furthermore, prior to answering the identity questions, respondents faced more than 100 questions about a great variety of political issues (partisanship, ideology, feelings about the opposition, feelings about certain candidates, etc.). Hence, the survey instrument itself primed respondents to think about national electoral politics prior to asking them about which identity most mattered to them. This arguably increased the validity of the survey questions as good measures of politically relevant identity. Thus, although the survey questions on identity are not perfect, their flaws are not so great as to make the data meaningless. I therefore turn to them as a first cut on the identity hypothesis.

TABLE 2.1. *Prevalence of Racial Identities in South Africa (percent)*

| Racial Identifiers | Africans | Whites | Coloureds | Indians |
|---|---|---|---|---|
| 1994 | 23 | 49 | 30 | 62 |
| 2000 | 30 | 12 | 45 | 61 |

*Source*: 1994 Idasa survey and 2000 *Afrobarometer* survey.

Mattes (1995) exhaustively analyzed the 1994 Idasa identity data, showing that less than one-quarter of African respondents believed they were part of a distinct racial community. As displayed in Table 2.1 (first row), around three in ten coloureds held this opinion, as did close to half of the white respondents and almost two-thirds of the Indian respondents. Thus, *racial identities were far less prevalent than racial voters*, leading Mattes to reject the identity voting hypothesis. The 2000 *Afrobarometer* survey shows a similar overall pattern (second row, Table 2.1). Respondents in this survey generated more than 141 different answers to the identity question, with racial identities frequent among them. However, only Indians listed racial identities more frequently than nonracial ones (with 61 percent naming a racial identity). The other three groups predominantly gave nonracial responses (Africans identified racially 30 percent of the time; whites, 12 percent; and coloureds, 45 percent). Thus, the surprising result of these surveys is that racial identities are *not* overwhelming in South Africa. And, perhaps even more surprising, they are least common amongst the two groups (Africans and whites) whose behavior is most polarized!

Partisanship provides an alternative window on identity. In his expressive approach to ethnic elections, Horowitz (1985) suggests that identity tends to create very strong bonds of partisanship. If we ignore for a moment the possibility that instrumental factors may also drive partisanship, then partisanship levels provide an upper limit on identity voters (it is difficult to imagine identity voters *not* being strong partisans, although not all partisans may be motivated by identity).

Here, again, the data caution against interpreting the racial census as purely a product of identity concerns. As Table 2.2 shows, after peaking a few months after the 1994 elections at 75 percent, African partisan attachment to the ANC never exceeded 60 percent. Indeed, at several points in the past decade, *independents have formed half or close to half of the African electorate*. And levels of partisanship are even lower for whites (see Mattes 2005). Thus, many Africans and whites who claim to be independent of partisan attachments nevertheless conform to the pattern of racially polarized voting, pointing once again to the conclusion that there is more going on in this story than simple identity voting.[11]

---

[11] For a thorough discussion of patterns of partisanship in South Africa, see Schulz-Herzenberg, A Silent Revoluation.

TABLE 2.2. *African Partisanship over Time (percent)*

| Date | ANC Partisans | Independents |
|---|---|---|
| 1994 | 75 | 11 |
| 1995 | 51 | 36 |
| 1997 | 51 | 37 |
| 1998 | 46 | 47 |
| 1999 | 53 | 41 |
| 2000 | 41 | 49 |
| 2002 | 54 | 22 |
| 2003 | 55 | 35 |

*Source*: Mattes (2005).

## Policy

In South African surveys two issues – unemployment and crime – emerge without fail as the problems South Africans view as the most pressing to their country. An *Opinion99* press release opined: "[I]n contrast to common wisdom, there is no lack of a national consensus with regard to priorities for government action. All South Africans are in general agreement over the key problems facing the country, despite differences of race, wealth, class or gender" (Idasa 1999d). Thus, differences in *issue importance* clearly do not drive racial polarization in South Africa.

Issue salience and policy preferences are not the same, however. While South African surveys have not asked direct questions regarding specific policy preferences, the *Afrobarometer* 2000 survey did ask a series of questions that tap into *hypothetical* policy differences. Generally, these questions asked whether a particular problem was best dealt with privately – by individuals or businesses – or publicly, by the government. Thus, the survey asked whether responsibility for reducing crime (providing jobs, helping farmers, etc.) fell to individuals, businesses, government, or some combination of them.

Analyzing these data, Bratton and Mattes (2003) find convincing evidence of differences between whites and Africans on some questions: Whites more commonly than Africans support fees for medical services, downsizing the civil service, and privatizing public corporations. Bratton and Mattes suggest that these opinions are rooted in self-interest: Whites support public-sector reform because they no longer control the state and are unlikely to benefit from its largesse, whereas Africans see the public sector as a key employer. Consequently, real economic differences produce a divergence in policy preferences. And perhaps, one might speculate, they drive polarization in the electorate.

The problem with this argument is that the policy preferences Bratton and Mattes measure rarely make it onto the radar screen of most South African voters. In Idasa's comprehensive, multiround pre-election survey in 1998–1999 (*Opinion99*) only one of Bratton and Mattes' topics (health care) emerged

TABLE 2.3. *Best Way to Create Jobs: Private Enterprise versus Government (percent)*

| | Africans | Whites | Coloureds | Indians |
|---|---|---|---|---|
| Best way to create jobs is through private enterprise (agree strongly) | 27 | 31 | 26 | 13 |
| Best way to create jobs is through private enterprise (agree somewhat) | 14 | 24 | 12 | 12 |
| Best way to create jobs is through government employment (agree somewhat) | 11 | 15 | 21 | 24 |
| Best way to create jobs is through government employment (agree strongly) | 49 | 24 | 40 | 48 |
| Don't know | <1 | 2 | 1 | 1 |
| Neither private enterprise nor government | <1 | 4 | <1 | 2 |

*Source*: Afrobarometer 2000.

as possibly significant, and even here only 14 percent of respondents listed it as a top priority. Civil service reform and privatization were not ranked at all. Indeed, in a separate publication Mattes has called these issues part of the "non-agenda," indicating their overall insignificance to South African voters (Mattes et. al. 1999). In 2004, these topics remained insignificant. Consequently, although opinions may be divided on these issues, voters do not see them as particularly important. It is therefore unlikely that they drive voting polarization.

But what of the other questions in *Afrobarometer* – those dealing with issues that South Africans *do* rank as important? Looking at preferences about employment policies (Table 2.3), certain racial differences are evident, if not overwhelming. Whites are the most likely to encourage a market solution to jobs (around 55 percent favor some role for private enterprise in job creation, compared with 41 percent of Africans, 38 percent of coloureds, and 25 percent of Indians). Africans are considerably more likely than whites to believe the government should create jobs (60 percent versus 39 percent). However, coloureds and Indians are at least (if not more) pro-government than Africans (61 percent of coloureds and 72 percent of Indians favor a public response). And furthermore, more than a quarter of Africans picked the most pro-market response in the survey, agreeing "strongly" that the best way to create jobs is through private enterprise (27 percent for Africans versus 31 percent for whites). In sum, although differences exist across groups in policy preferences about jobs, a stark African/white pattern of polarization is lacking. Policy preferences on crime display even less polarization: Overall responses across racial groups are very similar (Table 2.4).

TABLE 2.4. *Who Should Take Responsibility for Reducing Crime? (percent)*

|  | Africans | Whites | Coloureds | Indians |
|---|---|---|---|---|
| Government | 48 | 34 | 52 | 65 |
| Businesses | 3 | 5 | 2 | 3 |
| Individuals | 2 | 4 | 1 | 0 |
| Government and businesses | 27 | 22 | 26 | 14 |
| Government and individuals | 4 | 7 | 5 | 3 |
| Individuals and businesses | 1 | 4 | 1 | 0 |
| All three | 15 | 25 | 12 | 15 |

Source: *Afrobarometer* 2000.

Overall, these data provide little evidence that policy polarization drives the racial census in South Africa. Preferences over solutions to South Africa's major public challenges – unemployment, crime – display diversity within groups and only moderate divergence across them. In most instances, coloured and Indian responses register as more radical than African ones.

*Performance*

Mattes and Piombo (2001) argue that evaluations of government performance are a key factor driving South African voting behavior. Whites and Africans look at the same factors when evaluating performance (with some nuances) but draw quite different conclusions about them, with Africans approving of the ANC's performance and whites disapproving of it. Support for this argument is not difficult to find, although it does depend on which performance questions are used. I consider two: from the 2000 *Afrobarometer* survey, a question about how well the government manages the economy; and from the 1999 survey, a question about how well the national government is performing its job. The answers to these are summarized in Table 2.5.

Looking first at the narrow question regarding how well the government manages the economy, there are hints of polarization between whites and Africans. Far more Africans than whites give a positive response (32 percent versus 12 percent). Coloureds also give more positive responses than whites (26 percent). However, Indians display the most negative evaluations (only 9 percent believe the government manages the economy very well or fairly well). And overall, the tone of the responses is very negative: two-thirds of the most optimistic group (Africans) give negative responses to the question. Thus, although whites and Africans exhibit divergence on their performance evaluations, it would be difficult to argue that this divergence alone drives the racial census.

However, opinions on the *overall* performance of the government exhibit much more polarization. Here, three-quarters of Africans give positive responses, in contrast to less than 20 percent of whites. Coloured and Indian responses fall between the white and African extremes. Thus, more than

TABLE 2.5. *Performance Evaluations (percent)*

|  | Africans | Whites | Coloureds | Indians |
|---|---|---|---|---|
| *How well does the government manage the economy?* | | | | |
| Very well | 5 | 0 | 4 | 0 |
| Fairly well | 27 | 12 | 22 | 9 |
| Not very well | 39 | 24 | 35 | 12 |
| Not well at all | 28 | 63 | 38 | 79 |

*Source*: Afrobarometer 2000.

|  | Africans | Whites | Coloureds | Indians |
|---|---|---|---|---|
| *How well is the national government performing its job?* | | | | |
| Very well | 15 | 0 | 15 | 7 |
| Fairly well | 61 | 19 | 45 | 40 |
| Not very well | 23 | 40 | 19 | 27 |
| Not well at all | 1 | 40 | 21 | 26 |

*Source*: Opinion99.

other variables, general performance evaluations mimic the racial census.[12] Of course the *origins* of these different evaluations – *why* whites and Africans look at the same data and come up with different conclusions about them – are more obscure (more on this later in this chapter).

*Racial Heuristics*

The notion that racial shortcuts matter in shaping South African voting behavior is not new – Mattes discusses some version of this hypothesis in almost everything he writes. However, operationalizing and testing this story poses challenges. How does one capture a cognitive process in a survey? Mattes argues that South Africans exist in segmented information markets (they use different news sources, live in segregated communities, etc.) – consistent but indirect support for the theory. I offer another stab at the operationalization of racial heuristics by looking at party labels (or images).[13] Party labels operate as "brand names" for voters. They provide a great deal of information cheaply and easily (Aldrich 1995; Cox 1997). If the racial heuristics story is correct, then party labels in South Africa should have a prominent racial component.

The current party labels of the ANC, NP, and DP reflect both past and current politics. All three of these parties were active during apartheid – although in different capacities – and the image they brought with them into the new South Africa reflects in large part their role in the struggle against apartheid. This apartheid baggage has acted as a kind of "prior" about a party's image that voters update as new information becomes available. In the

---

[12] For a recent and comprehensive discussion of performance evaluations and vote choice in South Africa, see Schulz-Herzenberg, *A Silent Revoluation*.
[13] I will generally use the terms "party labels" and "party images" interchangeably.

following paragraphs, I review the baggage the ANC, NP, and DP brought with them into the post-apartheid period. I then use survey data to track how party images have changed over time.

### The Origins of the ANC's Party Image

A group of elite African lawyers founded the ANC in 1912 with the goal of working within the framework of the South African Constitution to reverse discriminatory legislation. By the 1940s, when it had become clear that the government would not respond to soft tactics, a new generation of more radical leaders, among them Nelson Mandela, Walter Sisulu, and Oliver Tambo, took over the party. Beginning in the 1950s, they initiated passive resistance campaigns, deepened the popular roots of the party, and aligned it with other political movements like the South African Communist Party (SACP). In 1955, the ANC, along with several other organizations, convened a "Congress of the People" to discuss options for opposing apartheid. During the Congress, a multiracial committee drafted a document that became known as the Freedom Charter. Among other items, the Freedom Charter listed a set of basic rights and freedoms belonging to all South Africans. It also put forth the nonracial ideology that was to inform the ANC from that point on, namely that: "South Africa belongs to all who live in it, black and white ... no government can justly claim authority unless it is based on the will of the people." In contrast to Africanism, which seeks to return South Africa to the control and ownership of Africans, or Black Consciousness, which opposes white rule by emphasizing a collective black identity, the "charterist" tradition initiated by the Freedom Charter endorsed multiracial cooperation to end apartheid and a multiracial future for South Africa.

The government of South Africa responded to the ANC's tactics by banning the party. Subsequently, the ANC switched from nonviolent passive resistance to armed struggle, forming a military wing, Umkhonto we Sizwe (Spear of the Nation), to carry out armed attacks. Massive arrests of party leadership in the early 1960s, including Mandela, drove the party underground and into exile, where it stayed for most of the next two decades. In the 1980s, it participated in the renewed apartheid struggle. In 1990, the National Party released Mandela and legalized the ANC, which quickly became the focal point of the anti-apartheid movement. The party was able to corral the diverse organizations that participated in the anti-apartheid movement (the Congress of South African Trade Unions, or COSATU, and the United Democratic Front, or the UDF) into a single front prior to the 1994 elections, which it won by a landslide.[14]

---

[14] For good histories of the ANC, see Tom Lodge, *Black Politics Since 1945* (New York: Longman, 1983); Tom Lodge and Bill Nasson, *All Here and Now: Black Politics in South Africa in the 1980s* (London: C. Hurst and Company, 1991); Anthony Marx, *Lessons of Struggle: South African Internal Opposition, 1960–1990* (New York: Oxford University Press, 1992).

The ANC's roots thus lay in the struggle against apartheid. It could (and did) claim with good cause to have a multiracial pedigree. In the Freedom Charter it had embraced a multiracial ideology. By aligning with the racially diverse South African Communist Party (SACP) in the 1950s, the ANC attracted a number of non-African leaders. The ANC's alliance with various trade union organizations like COSATU and its association with the multiracial UDF also diversified the ANC's leadership. Consequently, at the close of apartheid it had the most racially diverse leadership of any party in South Africa. Finally, by aligning with and absorbing these different political organizations (especially the UDF), the party inherited a vast grassroots network that reached out to numerous diverse communities, including coloured, Indian, and white ones.

At the same time, certain factors detract from ANC claims to multiracialism. The party originally formed not as a multiracial or nonracial organization but as an African one, committed to fighting for African rights. Indeed, it never dropped the word "African" from its name in favor of something more inclusive. Furthermore, while the ANC has officially embraced the Freedom Charter since the 1950s, periodic disagreements have erupted between factions of the party over whether it should focus more of its energy on Africans or stay committed to multiracialism (Chapter 3, on the 1994 election, discusses one of these incidents in detail). These disagreements cast doubt on the purity of the party's multiracialism. And, although the ANC's leadership has been racially diverse, top leadership roles have been monopolized by Africans. In almost 100 years of existence, a non-African has never been the leader of the ANC – or even a serious contender for this position.[15]

For these reasons, many non-Africans – especially whites, but also coloureds and Indians – have seen the party as more African than multiracial. One coloured student leader explained: "[I]n [coloured] people's minds, the ANC is an African organization."[16] Another observer noted: "Mandela was never too attractive to the conservative section of the coloured community. This section sees him as a leader of an African-led, black nationalist movement which is different from the UDF (United Democratic Front) that they were part of."[17] Roy Padyachee, a member of an ANC task force charged with wooing Indian voters during the 1994 elections, noted similar sentiments in the Indian community, suggesting that the ANC's perceived image was one of a "predominantly black political party."[18]

---

[15] Joe Slovo, who headed the ANC's military wing, Umkhonto we Sizwe, and ran training camps for soldiers while the ANC was in exile, was perhaps the most prominent white in the party during the apartheid period. Post-apartheid the party has had several whites, Indians, and coloureds in cabinet positions but never as president or deputy president.

[16] Eugene Paramoer, a coloured student leader active in the UDF in the 1980s, quoted in Cullinan (1995).

[17] Vuyani Boyce, an African teacher in the Cape Town township of New Crossroads. Quoted in Xayiya (1994).

[18] Roy Padyachee, quoted in Desai and Maharaj (1996) from a 1992 Leader article. In this case, "black" is being used in the sense of "African," not "nonwhite."

In sum, in spite of a long-term commitment to multiracialism and a diverse leadership, the ANC entered into the post-apartheid period with a somewhat ambiguous image in the electorate. On the one hand, the party portrayed itself as multiracial, pointing to its Charterist tradition and diverse leadership. On the other hand, its roots as an African organization and the dominance of Africans in its top leadership cast some doubt on these assertions, especially for non-African South Africans. For many, behind the multiracial rhetoric lay a party committed primarily to the advancement and protection of African interests.

### The Origins of the National Party's Image

Unlike the ANC, little ambiguity surrounded the National Party's inheritance from the apartheid era. For the greater part of the twentieth century, the National Party associated itself explicitly and exclusively with white (especially Afrikaner) causes. James Hertzog formed the party in January 1914 to promote the political and economic advancement of Afrikaans speakers and the segregation of racial groups. The Nationalists combined with the South African party in 1934 to form the United Party (UP), which put in place much of South Africa's pre-apartheid legislation regarding land rights, segregation, and industrial relations. Under the leadership of Dr. D. F. Malan, the party (then called the Purified National Party) splintered from the UP in 1934. The Purified Nationalists took up the cause of Afrikaners with renewed fervor, earning the endorsement of Afrikaner social and political organizations and large numbers of Afrikaner workers and farmers. During the 1948 election campaign, the party played to ethnic as well as racial fears, promoting even more drastic segregation of the races, or apartheid." Winning the 1948 election and all subsequent elections until 1994 allowed the Nationalists to implement their apartheid plans with few constraints.[19] Apartheid legislation guaranteed whites the best jobs and the best wages, set aside land for exclusive use by whites, gave whites educational opportunities and health care, and provided white entrepreneurs and farmers with extensive state support. It discriminated harshly against nonwhites while also encouraging divisions between nonwhite groups. As Hendrik Frensch Verwoerd, prime minister of South Africa from 1958 to 1966, explained: "Our motto is to maintain white supremacy for all time to come over our own people and our own country, by force if necessary."[20] Initially, the party was composed exclusively of Afrikaans-speaking whites, but by 1980 it had attracted the support of most English-speaking whites as well. Its leadership was entirely white. Thus, when it began negotiations with the ANC in the late 1980s, the National Party was

---

[19] The United Party (renamed the New Republic Party) took a majority of votes in the 1948 election. However, because of a rural bias in translating votes to seats, the NP was able to capture a majority of seats and win the election. The UP/NRP progressively shed voters from 1950 until it dissolved in 1977. See Thompson (1990) for more details.

[20] Quoted by Thompson (1990: 215–216).

unambiguously white, best known throughout the world for putting in place one of the most racially discriminatory regimes in history.

## The Origins of the Democratic Party's Image

Like the National Party, the Democratic Party entered the post-apartheid period as a "white" party, an image that had certain ironies, as the party viewed itself as the "lone voice" in Parliament to speak out against apartheid, as an inside-the-system agitator for change. The DP's origins lie in the Progressive Party, which formed in 1959 to protest the United Party's embrace of racially discriminatory policies.[21] The Progressive Party won only a scattering of votes: Between 1961 and 1974, its sole parliamentary presence was Helen Suzman, who represented the wealthy, white Johannesburg suburb of Houghton. Suzman used her considerable oratory skills to oppose racially discriminatory bills produced by the NP. She also drew attention to the implications of NP policy by personally investigating areas affected by apartheid – for example, visiting Africans who were moved due to "black spot" legislation or making a well-publicized tour of Robben Island.[22] While the Progressive Party – which became (successively) the Progressive Reform Party, the Progressive Federal Party, and, finally, in 1989, the Democratic Party – claimed to fight the system from within, it was a conservative party in many ways. The party did not endorse the ANC's use of violence. Until 1979, it pushed qualified franchise instead of universal adult suffrage. It chose to conform to the requirements of the Prohibition of Political Interference Act, which prohibited racially mixed parties. In doing so, it sacrificed a more diverse leadership.[23] Perhaps for these reasons, the DP entered the post-apartheid period without "struggle" credentials. As van Niekerk and Ludman (1999: 51) write: "Among black voters, the DP [has had] difficulty shedding the perception that because members of the party participated in the pre-1994 Parliament, even in opposition, they are 'apartheid-era leaders' and remain committed to protecting white privilege." Paulus Zulu said it more forcefully: "The DP has largely been a white party in spite of its protestations to the contrary. When the politics of non-participation was the principal strategy of the liberation movement, the DP happily participated in an all-white parliament and reaped the fruits of that participation for itself. Suddenly to expect the erstwhile disenfranchised voters to forget that easily is beyond imagination, if not political day-dreaming."[24] In sum, in spite of its role as the official opposition to the NP – and to its very great disappointment – the DP entered the post-apartheid period as a white party.

---

[21] For a general history of the Progressive and Democratic Parties, see Welsh (1994).
[22] Suzman (1993) provides fascinating detail of her role and experiences during this time.
[23] For a discussion of this period, see Behrens (1989).
[24] Quoted in Welsh (1994: 112).

## Tracking Party Images through Survey Data

Several recent surveys (the 1994 Idasa survey, *Opinion99*, and the 2004 CNEP survey) contain a question that taps into South Africans' views of the racial image of parties. For each major party the surveys asked: "Do you think that [party x] looks after the interests of all in South Africa or after the interests of one group only?" The response options were "All," "Only one group," and "Do not know enough about them." The 1994 survey followed this question with one asking respondents who identified a party as exclusive (looking out for the interests of only one group) to indicate which group they associated with it. By examining the answers to these questions, we can track how views on how party images vary over groups and over time.

Table 2.6 shows the responses by party and racial group for each of the three surveys (taken in 1994, 1999, and 2004) and reveals a fascinating picture of variation and change. There are large differences across groups in how parties are viewed, with polarization especially evident for whites and Africans. Across the three surveys, almost all Africans view the ANC as an inclusive party, representing the interests of all South Africans, whereas whites are much more likely (a majority in each survey) to see it as exclusive, representing the interests of one group only. Coloureds and Indians fall somewhere in between. The opposite holds for the DP and NP: Almost all whites see these parties as inclusive, whereas Africans are more likely to see them as exclusive. Again, coloureds and Indians fall in between.

Furthermore, when respondents found a party to be exclusive, they almost always perceived this exclusion in racial terms. Out of 1,722 total responses to the 1994 follow-up question, 1,383 responses (about 80 percent) gave a racial answer. Whites who see the ANC as exclusive strongly associate it with Africans (85 percent), as did coloureds (88 percent) and Indians (100 percent). Similarly, 78 (69) percent of Africans who see the NP (DP) as exclusive see it as white. In contrast, less than 200 responses gave an ethnic group, and only one respondent each named an ideological or religious group. Thus, racialized images of the parties are quite prevalent.

It is also interesting to note that images of parties are not fixed but change over time. The direction of this change is mostly in the inclusive direction, but the shape of the trajectory is hardly linear and varies across groups and parties. Thus, more whites viewed the ANC as inclusive in 2004 compared to 1994 (61 percent in 2004 and 52 percent in 1994). However, inclusive views of the ANC reached their nadir in 1999, when only 10 percent of whites saw the party in this way. Coloureds have also increasingly seen the ANC as inclusive (60 percent in 2004 and 46 percent in 1994). In contrast, Indians have actually moved in the opposite direction, coming to see the ANC as less inclusive over time.

Views of the opposition have also changed during the 1994 to 2004 period. Africans have decreasingly seen the NP as an exclusive party (45 percent in 1994, 41 percent in 1999, and only 9 percent in 2004) – a rather remarkable

TABLE 2.6. *Views of Exclusivity of Different Parties for 1994, 1999, and 2004 (percent)*

|  |  | Africans | Whites | Coloureds | Indians |
|---|---|---|---|---|---|
| ANC | | | | | |
| | 1994 | | | | |
| | Inclusive | 91 | 30 | 46 | 80 |
| | Exclusive | 3 | 61 | 34 | 12 |
| | Uncertain | 5 | 8 | 19 | 8 |
| | 1999 | | | | |
| | Inclusive | 98 | 10 | 41 | 23 |
| | Exclusive | 2 | 89 | 56 | 68 |
| | Uncertain | 1 | 1 | 3 | 9 |
| | 2004 | | | | |
| | Inclusive | 78 | 33 | 60 | 36 |
| | Exclusive | 5 | 52 | 23 | 40 |
| | Uncertain | 16 | 15 | 17 | 24 |
| NP/NNP | | | | | |
| | 1994 | | | | |
| | Inclusive | 26 | 79 | 65 | 71 |
| | Exclusive | 45 | 12 | 20 | 18 |
| | Uncertain | 29 | 9 | 15 | 12 |
| | 1999 | | | | |
| | Inclusive | 53 | 60 | 59 | 79 |
| | Exclusive | 41 | 28 | 27 | 11 |
| | Uncertain | 6 | 12 | 12 | 10 |
| | 2004 | | | | |
| | Inclusive | 23 | 44 | 34 | 24 |
| | Exclusive | 9 | 13 | 6 | 21 |
| | Uncertain | 67 | 43 | 60 | 55 |
| DP/DA | | | | | |
| | 1994 | | | | |
| | Inclusive | 34 | 60 | 33 | 41 |
| | Exclusive | 16 | 9 | 11 | 4 |
| | Uncertain | 50 | 30 | 56 | 55 |
| | 1999 | | | | |
| | Inclusive | 13 | 73 | 27 | 29 |
| | Exclusive | 34 | 16 | 15 | 20 |
| | Uncertain | 53 | 11 | 58 | 51 |
| | 2004 | | | | |
| | Inclusive | 26 | 72 | 30 | 46 |
| | Exclusive | 10 | 10 | 12 | 18 |
| | Uncertain | 64 | 19 | 58 | 36 |

*Sources*: Idasa 1994, *Opinion99*, CNEP 2004.

transformation when one considers the apartheid role of this organization. African opinions about the exclusiveness of the DP follow a less linear path, starting with around 16 percent in 1994, peaking in 1999 with 34 percent, and falling back to 10 percent in 2004. By far the most predominant trend for the opposition parties, however, is the growth of "uncertain" responses, especially amongst Africans, coloureds, and Indians. In 1994, these groups felt relatively certain that they knew who the NP represented (Africans were the least certain, but more than 70 percent still could classify the party). By 2004, majorities of all three groups gave uncertain responses. The DP started out relatively unknown in 1994. It was only a small party during apartheid, and many nonwhites had almost no experience with it or information about it during the first election. This probably explains why so many respondents were uncertain about it in the first survey. However, as knowledge about the party spread (by 1999, it was the major opposition party in South Africa), uncertainty about its image did not decrease. Indeed, Africans confessed to being *more* uncertain about the DP in 2004 than they were in 1994, after ten years of exposure!

In sum, party images in South Africa are racial in nature and highly polarized. The origins of these images lie in the apartheid period but they are far from static, having changed substantially since they were first tracked with survey data in 1994. In the next section, I evaluate the extent to which party images shape vote choice as well as attitudes and beliefs that shape vote choice. If party images matter in explaining outcomes, this offers direct support of the heuristics story.[25]

## Explaining Vote Choice

Simple breakdowns of the data have revealed that patterns of identification and policy preferences are far more heterogeneous than patterns of voting and therefore are unlikely, on their own, to explain it. In contrast, performance evaluations and party images mimic the polarization of the electorate and therefore offer more plausible explanations. In the following section, I look at

---

[25] Other interpretations exist, of course. One is that voters' evaluations of parties are simply *a more subtle measure of racial identification* – one that is more "politically correct" than admitting directly to a racial identity. If true, then the existence of racialized party images would support identity voting, albeit a fairly complicated form that involves lying on some survey questions and not on others. Although this possibility cannot be ruled out conclusively, a few factors suggest that – at least for Africans – images involve more than simply subverted racial identifications. First, as discussed earlier, African identities are not necessarily politically incorrect in South Africa. Furthermore, if holding an exclusive view of the opposition is somehow a substitute means of expressing a racial identity for Africans, then we would expect African identifiers to be a subset of those Africans who hold an exclusive view of the opposition. Yet this is not the case: In the 1994 Idasa data (the only data that asked both identity and party image questions), African identification is uncorrelated with holding an exclusive view of the two opposition parties. Altogether, the prevalence (and polarization) of racial images is not particularly consistent with an identity story for African voters.

how these latter two explanations fare head-to-head, after controlling for a variety of other factors that might influence vote choice, including socioeconomic circumstances and partisanship.

Because Africans are the best represented in the data and are the most numerous group in South Africa, I focus on their behavior. I look at three related dependent variables: African support for the ANC, African uncertainty levels, and African support for the NNP. These variables capture different steps in the process of crossover voting: leaving the ANC, examining different alternatives, and embracing an opposition party. They are measured in the survey through a question that asked: "If there were elections tomorrow, which political party or organization would you vote for?" Respondents were given a mock ballot and asked to indicate their choice ("do not know" was one of the options). I limit analysis to the 1998–1999 *Opinion99* survey because it includes questions on both performance and racial party labels (although unfortunately not on policy preferences or identification patterns) and offers the richest variation on African behavior: Of 1,776 African respondents, 188 claimed to support the NP, 221 claimed to be uncertain, and 1,301 professed support for the ANC.[26] Thus, around 23 percent of African respondents claimed to either be uncertain or to actually crossover vote. Together, these three responses account for 96 percent of all African responses.

As the dependent variable is binary, logit analysis is used in all cases. As basic controls, I included one or more measures for education (a "low" education measure that includes respondents that have not gone to high school and a "high" education measure that includes those that have some kind of post-matric degree), a measure for age, and a dummy variable for women. I also included a variable measuring political interest that asked respondents to indicate how often they follow what is going on in government and public affairs (higher values of this variable indicate *more* engagement).

Finally, I also control for ANC partisanship. Partisanship could matter one of two ways: First, it could soak up any variance explained by the independent variables of interest (party profiles, performance evaluations). This might occur if partisanship is *causally prior* to these factors (partisans adopt

---

[26] Two of the other surveys (Idasa 1994 and *Afrobarometer* 2000) do include questions on identity, and the *Afrobarometer* taps into policy preferences. These surveys are less ideal for studying crossover voting and uncertainty because they exhibit less variation in the dependent variable – few Africans claim to be either uncertain or to support the NNP. The likely reason for this is that these were in the field *after* the election rather than before (like *Opinion99*), and opinions and preferences had solidified. Nonetheless, the models in Table 2.2 can be replicated using these datasets. The results (in Appendix Tables 2.11 and 2.12) confirm the observations in the descriptive section: African identifiers are no more likely to conform to the racial voting pattern than nonidentifiers. In fact, there is some evidence that they are more likely to crossover vote (support the NNP), although this result appears only in 1994. Furthermore, controlling for holding an African identity has no effect on the party image variables, which remain robust across specifications. In addition, policy preferences over job provision bear no relationship to crossover voting or uncertainty. The results are contained in the appendix.

TABLE 2.7. *Logit Models of African Vote Choice (1998–1999 Opinion99 Survey). Standard Errors in Parentheses*

|  | Model 1: Support for the ANC | Model 2: Uncertainty | Model 3: Support for the NNP |
|---|---|---|---|
| Performance rating | .817 | −1.540** | .125 |
|  | (.431) | (.518) | (.536) |
| Believe DP is exclusive | −.196 | −2.978** |  |
|  | (.611) | (.809) |  |
| Believe NNP is exclusive | 3.719** | −1.031 | −3.358** |
|  | (.604) | (.796) | (.853) |
| ANC partisan | 3.026** | −.717 | −3.939** |
|  | (.582) | (.793) | (1.068) |
| Female respondent | −1.454** | .418 | 3.831** |
|  | (.547) | (.725) | (.755) |
| Age | .040 | .088 | −.500** |
|  | (.126) | (.145) | (.254) |
| Low schooling | .998 |  | −1.895** |
|  | (1.016) |  | (.983) |
| High schooling | −4.400** | 4.349** |  |
|  | (.713) | (.751) |  |
| Political interest | .530** | 1.086** | −.801** |
|  | (.251) | (.425) | (.344) |
| Pseudo $R^2$ | .85 | .89 | .86 |
| N | 810 | 820 | 1618 |

*Notes*: For models 1 and 3, all nonvoting responses (uncertain voters, refusals, abstainers) were eliminated from estimation. Higher values on the performance variable indicate *better* evaluations. Higher values on political interest indicate *more* political interest. For uncertain voters, low schooling perfectly predicts failure. For NP support, high schooling perfectly predicts failure.
\*\*$p \leq .05$.

negative evaluations of the opposition, positive evaluations of performance), which would cast doubt on the instrumental logic of the second and third hypotheses and suggest that it really is identity that drives voting. Second, partisans could behave differently than nonpartisans, placing less weight on performance evaluations and party profiles because their minds are already decided. This would suggest that the instrumental logic of the second and third hypotheses applies *only to nonpartisans*. Mattes and Piombo (2001) make a related argument when they suggest that the opposition's image matters only to that small group of African voters who are already disillusioned with the ANC.

Table 2.7 shows coefficient estimates and standard errors for each dependent variable. While the nature of this analysis is necessarily associational (survey data from a single point in time rarely speaks to causality), it nonetheless reveals several interesting patterns. Before examining the key explanatory variables, it is worth noting the significance of several of the controls: There is a noticeable gender gap in support for the opposition, with female respondents more likely to cross over than males. Age appears to matter for crossover voting – young Africans were more likely to support the NNP than older ones. Education plays a formidable though nuanced role: ANC and NNP supporters tend to be less educated (high schooling perfectly predicts failure to vote NNP), whereas uncertain voters tend to be better educated. Finally, political interest turns out to be an important variable. Both ANC supporters and uncertain voters tend to have high levels of interest, but not so NNP supporters. Altogether, ANC supporters tend to be men with less schooling but high political interest; uncertain voters tend to have high schooling and high political interest; and NNP supporters tend to be young females with low schooling and low political interest.

Turning to the performance and party image variables, a remarkably consistent story emerges. First, as expected, when Africans have negative evaluations of the ANC, they are less likely to support it (the coefficient on performance in the first model just misses significance at the .05 level). They are also substantially more likely to profess uncertainty. Second, party images also correlate quite strongly with voting patterns. Africans who believe the NNP is exclusive are far more likely to support the ANC than those who do not (and far less likely to support the NNP). An exclusive view of the NNP is also associated with a drop in uncertainty (although the coefficient is not well estimated), as does an exclusive view of the DP (note that multicollinearity may affect standard errors in equations with both variables). Thus, at least in this survey, *both* performance ratings *and* party images appear to correlate with African patterns of behavior.

The partisanship results in Table 2.7 also stand out. Not surprisingly, being a partisan of the ANC is associated with an increase in the probability of supporting the ANC and a decrease in the probability of supporting the NP. It does not, however, correlate with the probability of being uncertain, suggesting that even ANC partisans are capable of thinking of other options. More importantly, including the partisanship variable *has virtually no effect on the party image variables* – they are large and significant regardless of whether partisanship is in the specification. Performance evaluations are somewhat affected by the inclusion of partisanship – if the partisanship variable is dropped (results not shown but available from author), the performance variable is larger and better estimated for support for the ANC and support for the NP. However, even with partisanship in the equation, performance evaluations matter for two of the three models. Thus party image and performance evaluations matter *independently* of partisanship. This suggests that South African voting patterns are not simply a function of blind partisanship.

Finally, if the sample is split into partisans and nonpartisans (results in Table 2.13), party images matter more for independents, but they are not insignificant for partisans: In the NNP equation, the coefficient on the NNP party label is -3 for partisans and -4.3 for independents (both significant at

TABLE 2.8. *Fitted Values and 95 Percent Confidence Intervals for Models 1, 2, and 3 (African Probability of Supporting the ANC, of Being Uncertain, and of Supporting the NNP)*

|  | Probability of Supporting the ANC (Model 1) | |
|---|---|---|
|  | Positive Performance Evaluation | Negative Performance Evaluation |
| DP/NNP are exclusive | .96 (.90, .99) | .84 (.65, .95) |
| DP/NNP are inclusive | .48 (.24, .75) | .17 (.05, .40) |
|  | Probability of Being Uncertain (Model 2) | |
|  | Positive Performance Evaluation | Negative Performance Evaluation |
| DP/NNP are exclusive | .00 (.00, .01) | .06 (.01, .17) |
| DP/NNP are inclusive | .12 (.02, .31) | .70 (.43, .89) |
|  | Probability of Supporting the NNP (Model 3) | |
|  | Positive Performance Evaluation | Negative Performance Evaluation |
| NNP is exclusive | .00 (.00, .00) | .00 (.00, .00) |
| NNP is inclusive | .00 (.00, .00) | .01 (.00, .02) |

*Notes:* Fitted values and confidence intervals generated in Stata with *Clarify*. All control variables were held at their means.

the .05 level or above); in the ANC equation, the coefficient is 2.2 for partisans and 10.7 for independents (both significant at the .05 level or above); and for uncertain voters, the DP party label is around –4 for both groups (both significant at the .01 level or above). Thus, racial cues are not just important to that small category of voters who have already detached themselves from parties. They also appear to enter the calculus of more committed voters, which underlines their overall significance in explaining South African voting patterns.

To get a better sense of the impact of the performance and party label variables, Table 2.8 shows fitted values for four scenarios for each dependent variable: inclusive/exclusive views of the opposition and good/bad performance evaluations; controls were held at their means (estimates generated via *Clarify*: see King et al. 2000). For ANC support, the impact of these variables is formidable: In the best case scenario for the ANC (exclusive views of the opposition, positive evaluations), the probability of support was almost 100 percent. In contrast, in the worst case scenario (inclusive views of the opposition, negative evaluations), the probability of support was only around 17 percent. The impact on uncertainty was also large: When the opposition is seen as exclusive and performance is positively evaluated, uncertainty levels are nil; in contrast, when the opposition is seen as inclusive and performance is negatively evaluated, the probability of being uncertain is around 70 percent. For the NP, the impact was much smaller: In all cases except one, the probability of supporting the party was zero. In the best case scenario, it was only 1 percent. Although this seems like a miniscule effect, for the opposition parties it is important: Two percent of the African population is still a sizeable number of voters. Also, if different values of the controls are used (gender is set to female, political interest is set to minimal), larger effects result. Altogether, these results suggest that negative performance evaluations and inclusive opposition images loosen African voters from the ruling party, yet on their own they probably do not push them all the way into the arms of the opposition. They should therefore be viewed as *necessary* conditions to crossover voting but not *sufficient* ones.

In addition to showing sizeable effects, Table 2.8 also suggests that performance evaluations and party images *interact* in powerful ways. Changes in performance evaluations have the largest impact when the opposition is seen as inclusive: For the ANC, the effect of moving from a positive to a negative evaluation is more than twice as large when the opposition is judged inclusive; for uncertain voters, a negative evaluation increases uncertainty by around 6 percentage points when the opposition is viewed as exclusive, whereas the increase is closer to 60 percentage points when it is seen as inclusive. And for NNP support, performance evaluations only have an effect when the party has an inclusive image.

In sum, party images have a *direct* association with voting decisions: Africans who view the opposition as inclusive are less likely to vote for the ANC and more likely to either feel uncertain about their vote choice or to support the opposition. We can also consider *indirect* relationships – how party images work through secondary variables, which in turn also affect vote choice. Let us first look at performance evaluations. Table 2.9 shows the results of an ordered probit model for African respondents (again with the 1999 data) of performance evaluations. Intriguingly, *party images bear a strong association with performance evaluations*: Where the DP and/or NNP are viewed as inclusive, evaluations of ANC performance are less positive. Demographic variables also matter: Women are more likely to be charitable, as are older people and those with high political interest.

We can also consider the relationship between party image and two additional political attitudes that are likely to correlate with vote choice: African beliefs about the trustworthiness and credibility of the opposition.[27]

---

[27] For party credibility, respondents were asked: "Please tell me about how much of the time you can believe what the different parties say. If I come to a party you haven't heard of or you feel you do not know enough about, just say so. About how much of the time can you

TABLE 2.9. *Ordered Probit Model of African Performance Evaluations (1998–1999* Opinion99 *Survey). Standard Errors in Parentheses*

|  | Model 4: Performance Evaluations |
|---|---|
| Believe DP is exclusive | 1.148** |
|  | (.173) |
| Believe NNP is exclusive | .504** |
|  | (.179) |
| Female respondent | 1.13** |
|  | (.124) |
| Age | .090** |
|  | (.041) |
| Low schooling | −.283 |
|  | (.285) |
| Political interest | −.511** |
|  | (.071) |
| Pseudo $R^2$ | .35 |
| N | 820 |

*Notes*: Nonresponses eliminated. Higher values on the performance variable indicate *better* evaluations. Higher values on political interest indicate *more* political interest.
**$p \leq .05$.

Table 2.10 shows the results of several ordered probit models. Party image has a consistent, significant association across all specifications: Where Africans view the opposition as exclusive, they are less likely to find it credible or trustworthy. Using *Clarify* once again, we can unpack some of these coefficients. If a respondent views the NP as exclusive, her probability of believing she can trust it at least some of the time is only around 16 percent. However, if she sees it as inclusive, this probability rises to 70 percent. Similar results hold for the DP. The effects of party images on credibility are smaller but still important, especially for the NP: If a respondent views the NP as exclusive, she finds it credible only 38 percent of the time; if she sees it as inclusive, the probability rises to 78 percent. For the DP, the corresponding numbers are 18 percent and 25 percent. Several control variables are also significant: Women and older people are generally more willing to trust and find credible the opposition, whereas the opposite is true of respondents with high levels of political interest, and education has inconsistent effects (it decreases propensity to trust while elevating propensity to find credible). Almost all of the coefficients on

believe what [party x] says?" For party trustworthiness, respondents were asked: "Please tell me about how much of the time you feel you could trust [party x] to do what is right if it ran the government." In both questions, respondents were given a choice of the following categories: "Just about always," "Most of the time," "Only some of the time," "Never, almost never," and "Do not know enough about them." The "do not know" responses were dropped and ordered probit models run on the remaining data.

TABLE 2.10. *Ordered Probit Models of Africans' Views of the Trust and Credibility of the Opposition (1998–1999 Opinion99 Survey)*

|  | NP Trust | NP Credibility | DP Trust | DP Credibility |
|---|---|---|---|---|
| Party is exclusive | −1.509 | −1.083 | −1.361 | −0.218 |
|  | (19.97)** | (12.64)** | (8.49)** | (2.01)* |
| Female respondent | 0.703 | 2.228 | 1.289 | −1.958 |
|  | (10.47)** | (25.51)** | (9.62)** | (16.80)** |
| Age | 0.059 | −0.009 | 0.143 | 0.221 |
|  | (2.22)* | (0.32) | (3.41)** | (5.99)** |
| Low schooling | 0.280 | −0.775 | 0.250 | −1.439 |
|  | (3.60)** | (7.47)** | (0.79) | (5.08)** |
| Political interest | −0.152 | −0.356 | −0.678 | −0.543 |
|  | (4.03)** | (8.56)** | (9.24)** | (8.53)** |
| Psuedo $R^2$ | .21 | .46 | .54 | .42 |
| Observations | 1642 | 1639 | 808 | 805 |

Absolute value of $z$ statistics in parentheses. Higher scores on the trust and credibility levels indicate more positive evaluations of the trust and credibility of the party. Higher values on political interest indicate *more* political interest.
*Significant at 5%; ** significant at 1%.

the controls are smaller than the coefficients on the party image variables, once again suggesting the substantive significance of the latter.

These relationships tell an interesting story. Although Mattes and Piombo (2001) emphasize access to different sources of information as a primary reason for the divergence between white and African views of ANC performance, a political process is probably also at work.[28] In the context of a transitioning country with huge burdens from the past, there is great uncertainty about what the ANC can and should be held responsible for. One can make an argument – and the ANC does – that it inherited a mess that will take time to clean up. Hence, the very fact that the country has not disintegrated is indicative of high performance. An alternative argument – voiced by the opposition – is that the ANC has failed to deliver on growth, employment, and numerous other promises, and the overall economy is worse off than it was ten years ago. Both arguments are plausible. Which should voters believe? "Performance" models of voting often paint performance voting as a cognitively simple act: Voters consult a particular macroeconomic indicator (typically growth, unemployment, or inflation) and then return the incumbent to office if he has performed

---

[28] Mattes and Piombo argue that information markets in South Africa are racially segmented, so whites and Africans are exposed to different kinds of information. While this is true, it is not the full story. The credibility of information sources matters also. In particular, Africans are much less likely than whites to find messages from the opposition credible. It is not just that the markets are separate, but that even if exposed to the same message (as they often are during campaigns – not all information is segmented), the groups come to different opinions about it.

well or throw him out if he has performed badly. But this assumption of cognitive simplicity obscures a number of important questions: Which indicators should a voter consult? What is "good" performance? How much responsibility does the incumbent bear when performance is poor? These are especially vexing questions in a country like South Africa, where the incumbent party inherited an economy in shambles. In such a context, voters may legitimately struggle to assess the incumbent's performance.[29] Moreover, their reception to different theories might depend on the credibility and trustworthiness of the party making them, which in turn relate to how inclusive or exclusive that party appears to the voter. Hence, when the DP (and/or the NNP) is seen by an African as inclusive, this opens his or her mind to the viewpoint of these parties on ANC performance (that it was not so good), and together a poor performance evaluation and an inclusive view of the opposition detaches the voter from the ANC, opening him or her to the possibility of an alternative choice (even if not completely pushing him or her over to the other side).

CONCLUSION

The results presented in this chapter suggest that *racialized party images* play a critical role in shaping South African voting behavior: They interact with evaluations of the incumbent party's performance to associate strongly with African support of the ANC, uncertainty levels, and actual crossover voting. They also correlate with voting through several indirect channels, shaping performance evaluations of the incumbent and beliefs about the trustworthiness and credibility of the opposition. South African voting cannot be explained purely vis-à-vis politics-as-usual explanations: Performance evaluations matter, but they are intimately related to voters' beliefs about party images. While these results are correlational in nature, they are consistent with party images playing a central role in creating the racial-census pattern in South Africa, a finding that supports the racial heuristics hypothesis.

What about identity factors? Although it is possible that some South African voters behave as they do for reasons of identity, the results presented in this book caution against interpreting the overall pattern of polarized voting as driven primarily by expressive voting. Racial identities in South Africa have a surprisingly low prevalence and do not correlate with patterns of crossover voting. Many voters who conform to the racial pattern do not identify in racial terms, and many who conform to the pattern of racial voting are not partisans. Furthermore, controlling for partisanship does not eliminate the effects of the party image or performance variables, suggesting that these variables are not simply a function of political loyalty. Altogether, the evidence presented here weighs against the identity hypothesis.

The centrality of parties' images to voting behavior in South Africa has important implications for party strategies. Manipulation of party images is

[29] See also Stokes (2001).

likely to feature prominently in the campaigns of both the opposition and the dominant parties. Opposition parties, knowing that party images are central persuasion, should devote considerable effort to image transformation. The dominant party, in turn, is likely to fight hard to preserve party images as they are. And, in the long run, the erosion of the racial-census pattern will depend not on identity change but on decidedly *political* factors: the ability of each side to send credible signals to different constituencies about party images, the effectiveness of campaigns, and the success of different parties in recruiting politicians who are attractive to target constituencies.

## APPENDIX TO CHAPTER 2: REPLICATION OF TABLE 2.7 USING ALTERNATIVE SURVEY DATA

TABLE 2.11. *Logit Models of African Vote Choice (1994 Idasa Survey). Standard Errors in Parentheses*

|  | Model 1: ANC Support | Model 2: Uncertainty | Model 3: NNP Support | Model 4: Abstainers |
|---|---|---|---|---|
| African Identifier | .045 | −1.187* | .881** | −.404 |
|  | (.249) | (.610) | (.398) | (.562) |
| NNP is exclusive | .595*** | .791* | −2.087*** | −8.834* |
|  | (.219) | (.431) | (.469) | (.430) |
| Urban | −.147 | −.184 | .042 | −.410 |
|  | (.231) | (.361) | (.410) | (.434) |
| Female respondent | .670*** | −.568 | −.065 | .315 |
|  | (.218) | (.354) | (.397) | (.448) |
| Age | −.008 | .042 | −.004 | .320 |
|  | (.107) | (.172) | (.193) | (.207) |
| Low schooling | .000 | −.043 | −1.014 | .215 |
|  | (.313) | (.491) | (.767) | (.532) |
| Pseudo $R^2$ | .03 | .04 | .13 | .04 |
| N | 820 | 980 | 820 | 980 |

*Notes:* For models 1 and 3, all nonvoting responses (uncertain voters, refusals, abstainers) were eliminated from estimation. The survey did not include variables measuring political interest, performance evaluations, or policy positions, so these are not included in the specification. Of 1,379 African respondents, 933 (68%) indicated support for the ANC, 38 (3%) indicated support for the NP, 61 (4%) said they were uncertain, and 23 (2%) said they would not vote.
*$p \leq .10$; **$p \leq .05$; ***$p \leq .01$.

TABLE 2.12. *Logit Models of African Vote Choice (2000 Afrobarometer Survey). Standard Errors in Parentheses*

|  | Model 1: ANC Support | Model 2: Uncertainty | Model 3: NNP/DP Support | Model 4: Abstainers |
|---|---|---|---|---|
| African identifier | .063 | .971** | .115 | .548 |
|  | (.157) | (.422) | (.295) | (.381) |
| Policy preferences (job creation) | .005 | −.240 | .015 | .237 |
|  | (.055) | (.160) | (.106) | (.160) |
| Performance evaluation | .143* | .890*** | .023 | −.768*** |
|  | (.082) | (.269) | (.158) | (.255) |
| Urban | .458*** | 2.317*** | −.136 | .428 |
|  | (.142) | (.757) | (.276) | (.388) |
| Female respondent | .231* | −.333 | −.461* | .420 |
|  | (.141) | (.429) | (.280) | (.377) |
| Age | .002 | −.085*** | −.009 | −.002 |
|  | (.006) | (.028) | (.011) | (.015) |
| High schooling | −.069) | .677 | .151 | .755 |
|  | (.214) | (.498) | (.398) | (.484) |
| Political knowledge | −.065 | 1.059* | .036 | −.814** |
|  | (.152) | (.637) | (.298) | (.379) |
| Pseudo $R^2$ | .03 | .22 | .01 | .08 |
| N | 1295 | 1488 | 1295 | 1488 |

*Notes*: For models 1 and 3, all nonvoting responses (uncertain voters, refusals, abstainers) were eliminated from estimation. The survey did not include variables measuring views on the exclusivity of parties, so these are not included in the specification. Lower values of the policy preference variable indicate a more free-market perspective on job creation; higher values indicate preferences for government intervention in the job market. Higher values on the performance variable indicate better evaluations. Political knowledge is measured by whether the respondent can name the president. Of 1,560 African respondents, 1,088 (70%) indicated support for the ANC; 60 (4%) indicated support for the NP or DP; 25 (2%) said they were uncertain; and 31 (2%) said they would not vote.
*$p \leq .10$. **$p \leq .05$; ***$p \leq .01$.

TABLE 2.13. *Logit Models of African Vote Choice (1998–1999 Opinion99 Survey). Standard Errors in Parentheses. Split Sample: Partisans versus Independents*

|  | Model 1: Support for the ANC | | Model 2: Uncertainty | | Model 3: Support for the NNP | |
| --- | --- | --- | --- | --- | --- | --- |
|  | P | I | P | I | P | I |
| Performance rating | 1.396*** | 1.203 | -2.522*** | 5.450** | 1.060 | -.565 |
|  | (.533) | (2.075) | (.735) | (2.485) | (.721) | (.753) |
| Believe DP is exclusive | 1.363* | -6.035 | -4.113*** | -4.383*** |  |  |
|  | (.718) | (4.292) | (1.399) | (1.762) |  |  |
| Believe NNP is exclusive | 2.226*** | 10.745** | .279 | 1.522 | -3.046** | -4.294*** |
|  | (.697) | (5.502) | (1.317) | (2.012) | (1.292) | (1.270) |
| Female respondent |  |  |  |  | -.512 | 5.654*** |
|  |  |  |  |  | (1.235) | (1.339) |
| Age | .519*** | -2.208** | -.058 | .235 | -1.172*** | -.304 |
|  | (.201) | (1.061) | (.364) | (.293) | (.291) | (.268) |
| Low schooling | -.964 | 9.769 |  |  | 1.739 | -1.741 |
|  | (1.118) | (8.682) |  |  | (1.206) | (1.465) |
| High schooling | -4.196*** |  | 5.276*** |  |  |  |
|  | (.879) |  | (1.169) |  |  |  |
| Political interest | -.933** | 5.425* | 2.891*** | -1.746 | .430 | -1.849*** |
|  | (.456) | (2.901) | (1.113) | (1.128) | (.593) | (.760) |
| Pseudo $R^2$ | .88 | .93 | .95 | .44 | .33 | .85 |
| N | 609 | 198 | 614 | 203 | 1196 | 418 |

*Notes:* For models 1 and 3, all nonvoting responses (uncertain voters, refusals, abstainers) were eliminated from estimation. Higher values on the performance variable indicate *better* evaluations. Higher values on political interest indicate *more* political interest. High education was dropped in many specifications because it perfectly predicted success or failure.
*$p \le .10$; **$p \le .05$; ***$p \le .01$.

# 3

# The 1994 Campaigns

Chapter 2 established the centrality of racial credentials to persuasion in South Africa. It demonstrated that party images, which are rooted in the country's apartheid past, powerfully shape African voting behavior. The remainder of the book focuses on the process of party image change. If party images are the lynchpin to persuasion in South Africa, have the opposition parties attempted to change their images in a way that would make them more attractive to the electorate? If they have, what strategies have they used? And, finally, why have they not been more successful?

In this and the following chapters, I will show that the opposition parties in South Africa have understood the link between party labels and persuasion and made extensive efforts during the 1994–2004 period to transform themselves from "white" parties to multiracial ones. They faced daunting challenges in this process, however. For as much as opposition parties have wished to transform their images, the ANC has wanted to preserve them, thereby preventing the emergence of viable competitors for the African vote. The party images of the opposition have therefore formed a central battleground in South Africa's post-apartheid electoral landscape, one in which the ruling party has outplayed the opposition.

In this chapter, I focus on the campaigns of the ANC, NP, and DP during the first post-apartheid election, held April 27, 1994. The African National Congress (ANC), which inherited the liberation mantle from various organizations and movements involved in the apartheid struggle, emerged the clear victor, with close to 63 percent of the national vote and control over seven of nine provincial legislatures (KwaZulu-Natal and Western Cape eluded it). Its primary opponent at the national level (and nemesis from the apartheid era), the National Party (NP), won 20 percent of the vote and scored a majority in the Western Cape.[1] The DP, in contrast, won a mere 1.7 percent of the vote,

---

[1] The ANC also faced intense competition in KwaZulu-Natal and parts of Gauteng from the Inkatha Freedom Party (IFP). The IFP won control of the provincial government in Kwa-Zulu Natal and took about 4% of the vote in the Gauteng (much higher in select neighborhoods). I will discuss the IFP in greater detail later in the book.

far less than it had hoped. Exploiting a rich secondary literature, this chapter establishes three themes that recurred in later elections and figure prominently in the next two chapters of this book. The first theme concerns the *goal* of campaigns, whether they were focused primarily on mobilization or persuasion. The second concerns the *content* of the campaigns, specifically, the role played by race. And the third theme concerns the *effects* of the campaigns, especially on the party images of the major competitors.

I show that the major parties began their campaigns believing that voter loyalties were not set in stone. The NP and DP sought to move beyond their traditional white constituencies into the coloured, Indian, and African electorate, believing they could attract enough votes to offset white losses. Based on its own polling data, the ANC knew it could not take African votes for granted. It treated the NP as a credible competitor and worked hard to win over voters. The 1994 campaigns therefore involved more than just drumming up the party faithful and getting them to the polls. Even in this first post-apartheid election, when "liberation mania" was at its highest, efforts at persuasion – winning over new voters and defending existing voters against the encroachments of the other side – figured prominently in party efforts.

On the second theme – the content of the campaigns – I suggest that while parties emphasized standard politics-as-usual topics in their campaigns, going to elaborate lengths to lay out policy plans and debate competency, race lurked just below the surface. At issue were the racial images of the parties: Whose interests would they prioritize if elected to office? Policy promises and claims of competency were only credible when viewed through the lens of these images. Not all parties grasped the importance of party images at the outset of the election – but all had come to realize it by the election's close.

Finally, on the third theme, the effects of the campaigns were mixed. On the one hand, the National Party had only limited success in convincing Africans that it had truly moved away from its whites-only past. Only around a quarter of Africans saw the party as multiracial at the close of the campaign. Not surprisingly, the National Party failed to capture many African votes. On the other hand, the National Party did achieve a considerable degree of success at altering its image in the coloured and Indian electorate. These voters by and large bought the party's claims of transformation and a majority of them supported it, making the National Party the most diverse party in South Africa and giving it control over the Western Cape. The ANC was slower to realize the significance of party images during its campaign and focused more on policies and questions of competency, believing these would drive voter decisions. As a result, it had less success at image change with coloured and Indian voters, many of whom continued to view the ANC as an African-only party.

Hence, the legacy of the 1994 election was twofold. First, parties learned that they could not ignore race in their campaigns. In order to win votes, they had to pay attention to the racial component of party images, for these mediated how voters viewed policy and competence. Second, they also learned that manipulating their images was not a straightforward process: Simply saying they were transformed and being perceived as transformed were two different things altogether. These lessons would remain significant in elections to come.

PERSUASION AND MOBILIZATION

Kramer notes that party strategies come in two flavors: those aimed at trying to alter a voter's candidate preference (more specifically "the probability that if he votes, he will cast his ballot for a given candidate") and those aimed at increasing turnout (or "any alternation in the probability that he will vote at all, for either candidate") (Kramer 1966: 139). This first category of strategy – aimed at altering preferences – is a "persuasion" strategy. The second category – aimed at altering the probability of voting – involves "mobilization" (see also Cox 1999 for a similar breakdown).

In his seminal book on ethnic groups and conflict, Horowitz (1985) suggests that when ethnicity becomes politically salient, it pushes parties to abandon persuasion strategies in favor of those aimed at mobilization. His logic is intuitive and reasonable. He suggests that "the communitarian aspect of ethnicity propels group members toward concentrated party loyalties" (Horowitz 1985: 294). Attachment to an ethnic party, unlike attachment to parties based on shared policy preferences or other more shifting interests, is not susceptible to change. Thus, ethnicity creates very strong bonds between voters and parties that are unlikely to erode from election to election. This in turn induces politicians to give up on "defections from members of the other ethnic group" and to "solidify the support of its own group" (Horowitz 1985: 318). Furthermore, not only does ethnicity enhance the bonds of partisanship, reducing the probability of successful persuasion, it also lowers the cost of mobilization strategies because it makes supporters visible. As Horowitz writes: "[I]dentifying the voters of each party is a simple matter when ethnic and party identifications are synonymous" (Horowitz 1985: 326). As a result, parties focus all of their energies on mobilization and "turnout becomes all important" (p. 332). Elections become wars between parties to see who can most effectively mobilize supporters (often using violence, fear, and coercion in the process). Parties may also attempt to disenfranchise or otherwise bar the supporters of its opponents. This kind of politics can be deeply destabilizing: In addition to its abrasive style, it creates permanent winners and losers, complacency amongst some groups, and desperation amongst others. Horowitz captures this succinctly: "[T]he main features of the ethnic party system are readily summarized: stable parties, unstable politics" (Horowitz 1985: 348).

While this logic is intuitively plausible, is it correct? Does the ethnification of politics necessarily lead to the abandonment of persuasion strategies and the exclusive reliance on mobilization? Evidence from the 1994 South African campaigns would suggest not. All of the major contestants, including the ANC, NP, and DP, began their campaigns believing that the outcome of the race was up for grabs. Lodge (1994) notes that the ANC studied the

South African electorate for more than a year prior to launching its campaign in early 1994, investing substantial resources in opinion polls, focus groups, and imported experts (in particular, American pollsters Stanley Greenberg and Frank Greer).[2] From this research, the party learned that it could not assume it would win a majority. First off, surveys and focus groups revealed that the ANC's hold over the African vote was not absolute. In addition to the obvious (but regional) threat of Inkatha in KwaZulu-Natal, portions of the African electorate – in particular rural, less-educated women – appeared open to voting for the National Party (Lodge 1994: 28). Africans wanted more than "liberation": They sought material change in their lives. At the same time, they were unconvinced that the ANC could deliver. Years of protracted negotiation by the party had brought little in the way of real change yet had entailed significant disruption. Moreover, the ANC as an entity had been less visible on the ground to black South Africans during the crucial years of struggle in the 1980s than other bread-and-butter organizations like the United Democratic Front or COSATU. Many people had more immediate loyalties and direct links to these organizations than the ANC. While the ANC had united the anti-apartheid movement under a single banner in the period prior to the elections, tensions between constituent organizations simmered beneath the surface. The party struggled at times to hold its broad church together, make connections with a restive electorate, and convince voters that it was the rightful heir to the struggle.[3] Thus, if the ANC wanted African votes, it would have to work for them. It would be a mistake, as Greenberg put it, to think of the election as "only about mobilization and not about persuasion."[4] The ANC consequently devoted considerable effort to figuring out not just how to get Africans to the polls but also how to win them over.

The ANC's polling efforts also indicated that large numbers of colored and Indian voters did not feel particularly close to any party and were uncertain about their vote. Many others professed positive feelings toward the National Party and anxiety about a future under ANC rule. These attitudes surprised many in the ANC who had assumed these voters would automatically reward it for its role in the struggle, but they had concrete roots: Coloured and Indian voters feared they would be marginalized under an African government and would lose the limited (but real) benefits they had enjoyed during apartheid.[5] Although there was some internal debate – especially in the Western Cape – as

---

[2] Greenberg had been a scholar of South African politics prior to becoming a professional pollster. In 1992, he had helped to formulate Clinton's presidential campaign in the United States. Greer was a media specialist. Lodge's account suggests that Greenberg and Greer played a very significant role in shaping and guiding the ANC's campaign.

[3] For an incisive account of this period and leadership in the ANC during it, see Greenberg, Stanley. 2009. *Dispatches from the War Room: In the Trenches with Five Extraordinary Leaders*. New York: Thomas Dunne Books, St. Martin's Press.

[4] Greenberg was quoted in Mark Gevisser, "Clinton's Men on the ANC Campaign Trail," *Weekly Mail*, February 25–March 3, 1994, cited in Mattes et al. (1996: 127).

[5] Greenberg, *Dispatches from the War Room*.

to whether these voters should be courted, top ANC leaders like Mandela believed firmly that the ANC needed their support: Not only were they pivotal to certain regional races (coloureds are the largest group in the Western Cape), their votes would validate the ANC's claims to being multiracial.[6] Hence, after some hesitation, the ANC invested significant resources to winning the coloured vote. Eldridge and Seekings (1996) contend, on the basis of interviews with ANC strategists, that about 70 percent of the party's overall budget went to efforts aimed at the African electorate, and the remaining 30 percent went to non-African voters. In the Western Cape, the percentages were probably reversed.

For its part, the National Party believed it had a real chance at winning nonwhite votes. The party was especially confident about its chances in coloured and Indian communities. It began courting these votes in the early 1980s (if not before), when it introduced the Tricameral Parliament.[7] It cultivated links with coloured and Indian community leaders and politicians, incorporating them into the party as soon as racial restrictions were eased in the early 1990s. During this period, polls suggested high support for the party amongst these voters.[8] The NP also believed it could win over a small but meaningful portion of the African electorate and spent the three years prior to the election preparing itself to run against its past, hoping Africans would give it credit for ending apartheid.[9] An internal NP strategy document from the party's central office to the NP branches in February 1994 suggested that the party had the potential to draw African support: 15 percent of Africans named the party as their first or second choice, more than 60 percent said they harbored "no negative feelings" about it, and close to 30 percent actually said they "felt good" about the party (Giliomee 1994: 55). The NP hoped its affiliation with African politicians from apartheid structures would translate into meaningful support, especially in the rural areas (Giliomee 1994: 55).

Indeed, the National Party was so confident of its ability to win nonwhite votes that it at times ignored white voters in its campaigns, knowing that doing so risked losing them to conservative white parties like the Freedom Front. Most of the party's meetings in the Western Cape during the first three months of the campaigns were in held in coloured areas and by the end of the campaign "NP canvassers concentrated almost all of their energies on coloured voters" (Giliomee 1994: 64). Outside of the Western Cape, the party spent significant time in rural, African communities (Mattes et al. 1996: 133). In addressing conservative white voters, De Klerk repeatedly declared that apartheid was dead and would not return "in even one inch of the country," that a whites-only state (*volkstaat*) was a nonstarter, and that white right-wing

---

[6] Eldridge and Seekings (1996).
[7] Giliomee (1994).
[8] Giliomee (1994) cites a February 1992 poll that put coloured support for the NP at 66% (versus 6% for the ANC). A February 1994 poll showed a dip in NP (to around 47%), but this still greatly outweighed ANC support (which was around 17%). See Giliomee (1994: 54).
[9] Greenberg, *Dispatches from the War Room*.

violence was only a "dead-end" (Giliomee 1994: 64). Thus, the NP's gamble in 1994 was that it could make up for losses of whites to the right by currying votes in nonwhite communities. As for the ANC, the election would be at least as much about persuasion as mobilization.

The DP, which was probably the least known of the major parties at the outset of the election, also hoped to attract a multiracial constituency. According to DP analyst David Welsh, the party's aims were modest: It wanted to attract about 10 percent of the vote, preferably moderate voters turned off by what it perceived to be the bipolarity and extremism of the ANC/NP race (Welsh 1994: 111). It believed its history as the formal opposition during apartheid gave it an advantage over the NP and that a small but important segment of the nonwhite population – those who viewed themselves as liberals – would reward its history and policies with votes.

PARTY IMAGES AND THE ART OF PERSUASION

Given the centrality of persuasion efforts to campaigns, what form did these efforts take and when and how were they successful? As detailed in this section, issues, policy, and performance figured prominently in the campaigns of all of the major parties. At the same time, however, race – specifically the racialized images of the parties – formed a major election undercurrent. At issue was the profile of the National Party: Was it "new," as it claimed, or the unreformed monster that had created and implemented apartheid? Furthermore, in the Western Cape, where the race was most intense, the party images of both the ANC and the NP assumed central focus. Parties that paid insufficient attention to their images – the Western Cape ANC at first, the DP throughout its campaign – suffered at the polls. As important as images were, however, parties discovered that changing them was not simple. While campaigns presented opportunities to send signals to the electorate, signals intended for one community often had the unintended consequence of alienating a different community. The remainder of this section looks at the manipulation of images in the elections, paying special attention to the election in the Western Cape, which was especially competitive.

## The National Campaigns

Politics-as-usual concerns played a central role in the ANC's campaign. ANC advisor Stanley Greenberg advocated an issue-oriented future-focused campaign. He believed that the South African electorate was optimistic about the future and wanted to leave the bad days of apartheid behind. He also suggested that voters could not eat liberation, and the ANC would need to campaign on more than that if it wanted to win. When the party's initial campaign motto "Now is the Time" failed to spark much interest in African focus groups and raised the suspicions of coloureds, he had the party switch to the now famous "A Better Life for All." Focus group participants understood the imagery of the first slogan but wanted more than the end of apartheid and the assumption of political power. "A Better Life for All" more appropriately captured the mood.[10]

In keeping with the "A Better Life for All" message, the ANC centered its campaign on an extensive set of policy proposals, the core of which was the Reconstruction and Development Plan (or RDP). The RDP was a serious policy package. At 150 pages long, it itemized the ANC's plan for the future: how it would create jobs through public works; redistribute land through the courts and markets; build houses and provide clean water and electricity (a million new homes was the specific claim); improve health care access; put in place affirmative action programs; promote workers' rights; improve access to education; and, in general, reduce the concentration of economic power in the country. For the most part, the plan dealt with basic bread-and-butter issues: jobs, houses, schools, and services. According to Lodge (1994), many of the policies were on the vague side and few were very radical; in substance they did not diverge significantly from NP policies (Lodge 1994: 31–32). However, the plan was thorough and well researched and the ANC made a systematic effort to present it to the electorate, especially in its print media campaign.

The ANC also sought to convince the electorate that it had the skills to govern, often portraying a highly technocratic image in its print campaign. As Ken Modise, a marketing consultant involved in designing the ANC's advertising, explained: "Everyone knows the ANC was a highly effective liberation movement. But will it be an effective government? ... We had to be serious, to show people that we had the wherewithal to govern."[11] Lodge writes that "the restrained graphics, careful logic, and general seriousness of the ANC's propaganda successfully projected an impression of moral responsibility, social compassion, and intellectual sophistication" (Lodge 1994: 29). Eldridge and Seekings (1996: 525) describe ANC ads as "masses of grey print, summarizing the proposals in the RDP." According to Greenberg: "Even if you don't read or can't read the details you get the message: the ANC has a plan; it's serious."[12] Given the ANC's history as an anti-apartheid movement, its long years of being banned, and its lack of experience in government, the party believed that these efforts to establish credibility were essential.

The National Party also presented a set of redevelopment policies to the electorate, emphasizing the same sets of issues as the ANC. Indeed, the parties were fairly indistinct in the proposals they put forth. As Giliomee writes: "[T]he NP was at pains to stress that it was as eager as the ANC to provide jobs, houses and services to the people" (Giliomee 1994: 62). Giliomee suggests that the NP was more explicit than the ANC about using the market

---

[10] Greenberg, *Dispatches from the War Room*.
[11] Modise was quoted in Mark Gevisser, "Under the Pig's Hat, a Careful Strategy." *Weekly Mail*, April 15–21, 1994, p. 6. Cited in Mattes et al. (1996: 127).
[12] Greenberg was quoted in Gevisser, "Clinton's Men on the ANC campaign Trail," cited in Eldridge and Seekings (1996: 525).

to provide goods and reducing state intervention, but these differences were not a major point of contention in campaigns. The NP did emphasize what it believed was its primary strength – its long experience in government – and argued that the ANC was weak on these grounds. The ANC's plan was a "menu without prices," the party charged, and would bankrupt the country and lead to financial disaster (Gilliomee 1994: 61). In contrast, "the NP had the experience and ability to create order and economic prosperity out of chaos" (Gilliomee 1994: 62). Giliomee provides the example of an NP ad that proclaimed "The ANC makes promises; only the NP can deliver." The ad then contrasted the NP, which had built Africa's richest economy, with the ANC, which had "yet to run a township successfully, let alone a whole country" (Giliomee 1994: 62).

The Democratic Party believed its role as a longtime liberal voice during the apartheid years would earn it points with the electorate; hence this formed the backbone of its campaign message. According to Welsh (1994), it characterized itself as the voice of moderation and reason between two competing nationalisms and promised centrist, middle-of-the road policies. It also criticized the records of both major parties. According to party propaganda, the ANC had "no experience in the administration of a country," and the NP "was lousy in government [and] will be just as bad in opposition."[13] In contrast, it argued that it had a dignified record of fighting for human rights during apartheid and extensive experience as an opposition party. It was David to the NP's Goliath during the apartheid era and could play the same role vis-à-vis ANC post-apartheid.

In sum, all of the major parties employed standard "policy and performance" campaigns, trying to convince the electorate they had the ideas and ability to bring real change to South Africa. However, on another level, race – especially the racial images of the ANC and NP – formed an important subtext to the election. At the national level, a significant undercurrent of the race involved the NP's image – was it "new" – or the same party that had instituted forty years of apartheid? The National Party of course wished to sell the first version of itself, believing that this alteration in its label was crucial to winning African and other nonwhite votes. It repeatedly attached the adjective "new" to its name (later formally changing its name to the New National Party) and cultivated a new style at its campaign events. Giliomee observes that at the party's federal congress held a few months prior to the election, the old NP was gone: "[I]nstead of the all-white party faithfully singing Afrikaans songs like 'Sare Marais,' the two thousand delegates from all population groups chanted 'Viva FW' and swayed in unison to the strains of the workers' song 'Thotsholoza'" (Giliomee 1994: 57).

More controversially, the NP claimed that it deserved credit for the end of apartheid: "that the dramatic changes which South Africa had undergone since 1990 were all the work of the NP," that the NP had "destroyed apartheid

---

[13] Democratic Party, 1993, "Invest DP for Power and Peace." Cited in Welsh (1994: 111).

and liberated the country" (Giliomee 1994: 56). Complementing these claims, the party issued frequent and "fulsome" apologies to black audiences for the "heartache" caused by its policies (Giliomee 1994: 56). Giliomee suggests that "many blacks refused to dismiss these apologies as an election ploy" and that these moves counted a great deal with its recruits in the townships (Giliomee 1994: 57).

ANC strategists struggled early and often with the question of how to deal with race. Greenberg advocated that if the ANC were to attack the NP, it should do so on issues and policy, not the past, suggesting that even the "new, reformed" NP still did not care about Africans.[14] However, elements in the party disagreed with this strategy. Mattes et al. (1996: 127) indicate that there were pressures to bring the legacy of the past forty years into the campaign, to "wave the bloody shirt." One ANC strategist argued in 1993 that "emotions are crucial and apartheid must be deployed as an emotional issue – the NP-apartheid connection must be stressed."[15]

This strand of ANC thinking, although not dominant in the campaign, did assert itself from time to time. Lodge (1994) documents, for example, that in early February an ANC press release pictured a crowd of protesters with text reading "According to the NP you played no part in changing South Africa." In a double-page advertisement from the same time, Mandela in boxing attire stands by a pair of knocked-over boots (labeled "NP apartheid") while a ringside De Klerk yells "I did it, I did it." The text accompanying the ad read: "Judging from recent claims, the so-called 'New National Party' is looking remarkably similar to the old one. In their latest version of history they are the heroes that changed South Africa. ... Next thing they'll be telling us Apartheid never existed. The lesson of history is clear: those who deny the past, may never be trusted with the future."[16] Lodge also notes that local ANC ad campaigns sometimes diverged from the national message. For example, an ad from Lenasia (an Indian community in Gauteng) attacked the "National Party's dark history." Above portraits of apartheid leaders like Malan, Verwoerd, Vorster, Botha, and De Klerk, it asked: "Remember them?"[17]

ANC speeches were more aggressive about attacking the NP and De Klerk than its print campaign. At various points, Mandela attacked De Klerk as a "coward," a "weakling," and an "unstable person." He alleged that De Klerk had masterminded black-on-black violence to scare blacks away from the polling booth (Giliomee 1994: 60). He also characterized De Klerk as "a man who does not care about black lives."[18] Although these examples may not have been the norm, they nevertheless reveal that some elements of the ANC disagreed

[14] Greenberg, *Between People and Politicians*, p. 45.
[15] Quoted in Hen Marais, "Will the ANC Win?" *Work in Progress*, 88 (1993): 12. Cited in Mattes et al. (1996: 127).
[16] Quoted in Lodge (1994: 34).
[17] Example from Lodge (1994: 35).
[18] Quoted in Farouk Chothia, "Mandela's Many Faces," *Weekly Mail*, November 19–25, 1993. Cited in Matess et al. (1996: 127).

with Greenberg's exclusively forward-looking focus and sought to contest the NP's claims that it was new. Indeed, Mattes et al. (1996: 127) suggest that, without Greenberg and Greer, "the ANC would have run a negative campaign based on history and apartheid."

Disagreement over the focus of the campaign superimposed itself over an older and deeper divide in the party. As Eldridge and Seekings (1996) and Mattes et al. (1996) discuss in some detail, there was an ideological rift in the party between those who sought to deny the significance of racial differences (nonracialists) and those who sought to acknowledge and work with them (multiracialists). For the nonracialists, privileging racial categories – either by using race explicitly in campaigns or by developing separate structures and organizations for different groups – meant acknowledging apartheid's divisions. This was a step they resisted, even when it hurt them strategically. On the other hand, multiracialists felt the party *had* to pay attention to race, if only because the different groups that the ANC sought to unite had different backgrounds, interests, and fears. If the party ignored these, it would devolve into a purely African party. That is, in order to be multiracial, the party had to acknowledge race. This conflict in the party was nothing new: It was a strand of ideological debate since at least the Freedom Charter days of the 1950s.[19]

## The Western Cape Election

The various strands of debate in the ANC over the proper use of race in the campaign came to a head in the Western Cape election. Both parties wanted to win the province and believed they could. The Western Cape consequently became a major flare point in the battle between them. At issue was the coloured vote and how to capture it. Over the course of the campaign, the party images of both the ANC and the NP – in particular, whether they represented just one group (whites for the NP, Africans for the ANC) or many – emerged as central. According to most accounts, the NP understood the significance of its racial image to the coloured electorate early on, while the ANC denied it until late in its campaign, an error that probably contributed to its rout in the election.

According to Mattes et al. (1996), Eldridge and Seekings (1996), and Giliomee (1994), the Western Cape branch of the National Party employed aggressive, negative campaigning techniques against the ANC from the start. It sought to present its opponent as dangerous, communistic, and not in control of its own supporters, who were portrayed as violent and as having no regard for the rule of law. Giliomee provides the following example from the NP campaign:

The ANC is bad news for the country. The NP builds schools; the ANC disrupts schooling. The NP builds houses; the ANC breaks houses down. The NP stands for

---

[19] Marx, Lodge, and others.

peace and reconciliation; the ANC intimidates people. The NP builds hospitals; the ANC's supporters toyi-toyi in hospital corridors while people die inside.[20]

At times, the NP campaign veered into questionable territory, as when it published and circulated a "comic book" purporting to illustrate life under ANC rule. This piece of propaganda, which the Independent Electoral Commission (IEC) quickly banned due to its racist content, showed various disturbing images: African thugs preventing an old woman from going to church and a family dog transforming the militant phrase (associated mostly with PAC supporters) "Kill a Boer, kill a farmer" to "Kill a farmer, kill a coloured." According to Mattes et al., 80,000 copies of this comic book were printed – suggesting that the party intended to distribute it widely. The message conveyed was that the ANC would do little to prevent African thugs from running wild if it was elected to office.

The NP also played very effectively on coloured fears that privileges they had acquired over Africans during the apartheid period[21] would quickly be reversed by a vindictive ANC. It painted the ANC as a regional outsider, a party of blacks and Xhosas. As Anwar Ismail, a coloured NP politician, put it: "The Xhosas of Transkei and the ANC are the real settlers here. The ANC with its black profile and Communist cloak repels us."[22] Using similiar language, Marthinus van Schalkwyk (who would eventually succeed De Klerk as the head of the party) spoke of the ANC as a black organization that favored Xhosa speakers (Giliomee 1994: 63). This party, it warned, did not have the interests of the coloured population in mind: It would discriminate against them in allocating jobs and would not stand in the way of a violent redistribution of houses.

Events that unfolded just prior to the campaign period aided the NP in making these arguments. Giliomee notes that around this time, job advertisements began appearing in Cape Town newspapers requesting "Xhosa speakers," accentuating fears amongst coloureds that they would be discriminated against if the ANC came to power (Giliomee 1994: 65). Even more significant, in late 1993 African squatters took over houses built for coloureds in the Cape Town suburb of Delft. Around the same time, Africans in the Chesterville community (near Durban) invaded housing in adjacent Wiggins that had been set aside by the House of Delegates (the Indian chamber of the apartheid-era Tricameral Parliament) for lower income Indian families. Around 800 houses were involved in the Wiggins takeover – all newly built and ready to be occupied by their Indian owners. The impetus for the takeover was clear: Chesterville was overcrowded and new housing had been promised for years but not delivered. Chesterville residents also resented the racial designation of the houses: Why should Indians get them instead of Africans? This was especially difficult to accept given the liberalizing trend in the country at

---

[20] Die Burger, February 21, 1994, as cited in Giliomee (1994: 59).
[21] For a discussion of coloured gains during apartheid, see Gilliomee (1996: 96–97).
[22] *Rapport*, March 20, 1994. Cited in Giliomee (1994: 65).

the time. Whatever the motivation of the Africans, the takeover deeply upset the Indian community. Indian families had waited a long time for their houses and had invested savings in them. For the broader community, the takeover intensified fears about the implications of African rule. Indian communities in Durban (like coloured communities in Cape Town) bordered poorer, more densely settled African areas. In the past Africans had taken over Indian land and Indians had been victims of African mob violence. Indians – and coloureds – feared that an African government would do little to stop similar events from occurring in the future. Hence the Wiggins and Delft takeovers were scary omens, "a realization of the urban legend that Africans would take over the homes of Indians and whites in the new South Africa."[23]

The NP lost no time in taking advantage of these events. In Cape Town, it used full-page ads in newspapers to communicate messages like "Your house is not safe under the ANC" and "The ANC is not yet part of the government and already its supporters are taking houses which belong to legitimate owners" (Giliomee 1994: 62). In Durban, the NP blamed the ANC for the illegal occupation and suggested that the party had actively encouraged the squatters. It painted a grim picture of life under ANC rule, intimating that the party would condone the seizure of non-African property by Africans. It promised that land seizures would not be tolerated under its rule. Thus, the NP used events unfolding around the election to paint the ANC as a party of Africans that would not look out for minority interests.

The National Party also played up its own multiracialism. It used F. W. De Klerk, who was enormously popular with coloured audiences, to personify its reformed image (hiding Hernus Kriel, its actual Western Cape provincial premier candidate and a member of the old guard, as much as possible). It advertised the racial balance of its Western Cape lists, which included large numbers of politicians from the Tricameral Parliament days. In rallies, it surrounded De Klerk with coloured leaders and used their endorsements to bolster its claims that it was now a "brown" party.

In short, the NP went to great lengths to portray the ANC as a party of vengeful Africans while simultaneously offering an image of itself as a safe home for coloureds (in addition to whites, Indians, Africans). By and large, the party was successful at these tasks, especially the second one – a fact that was not lost to many in the ANC. As ANC media advisor Joel Netshitenzhe put it late in the campaign: "We have to acknowledge the National Party has been successful in presenting itself as a transformed multiracial party."[24] And it did this not by ignoring race, but by acknowledging its significance to the electorate it was courting.

However, it is also the case that the NP was much less successful at convincing Africans that it was a party for everyone. According to an Idasa survey in the field a few months after the 1994 campaigns (see Table 2.7 in Chapter 2),

---

[23] For an account of this incident, see Gigaba and Maharaj (1996: 225).
[24] Quoted in Gevisser, "Under the Pig's Hat."

around 65 percent of coloureds and 71 percent of Indians saw the NP as an inclusive party, one that represented the interests of all South Africans. In contrast, only around a quarter of Africans saw the NP as inclusive. While this result is impressive in its own way considering the apartheid past of the NP, the party clearly was less successful with African voters.

Although the reasons for this were complex (the party started on better footing with coloureds and Indians, having treated them better during apartheid; had difficulty accessing African areas; and faced an uphill battle in recruiting quality African candidates), the nature of the NP's campaign also contributed to its lower success at changing its image in the minds of African voters. To pillory the ANC, the NP often insulted ANC supporters, painting it as the party of blood-thirsty and violent Africans. This may have been an effective scare tactic for bringing coloured and Indian voters into its fold, but it also had the effect of alienating Africans. Thus, the very tactics that helped the NP to win brown votes may have lost it black ones. Campaigns offer the opportunity to send signals to the electorate, but signals do not always have the desired effect.

The ANC's responses to the NP's strategy were contradictory and reveal much not only about ideological debates within the party but also the challenges of knitting together multiracial constituencies. As at the national level, the ANC struggled to counter the National Party's campaign. After some initial hesitation, the ANC shifted its focus in the province from the mobilization of Africans to the persuasion of coloured voters. However, the party seemed conflicted on how to go about doing this. Eldridge and Seekings (1996) suggest that the ANC campaign evolved over time, partly in response to the NP's aggressive negative strategy. In the beginning, the ANC campaign resembled the campaign at the national level: focused on policy and competency. The ANC sought to impress on voters that it had a plan and the ability to implement it. Beyond advertising its multiracial candidate lists, it made few open acknowledgments about race or the particular needs and fears of non-African voters (Eldridge and Seekings 1996: 526). Indeed, Mattes et al. (1996: 129) note that "large elements of the ANC regional leadership ... suffered from a reluctance, amounting almost to hostility, to think seriously about ethnicity."

At times, the party also made significant blunders with regard to its effort to win over coloured and Indian voters. Lodge (1994: 39) notes that "early ANC public discourse did nothing to dispel the image of an organization of violent militancy: after Chris Hani's death, Winnie Mandela appeared in uMkhonto combat fatigues at a rally in Khayelitsha to urge the ANC youth to 'take the streets by storm and remain their until the fascist government was removed.' 'We want a revolution and we do not apologise to anyone,' Peter Mokaba exhorted at the same event." This did little to reassure anxious minority voters about the intentions of the ANC. Beyond this, the ANC also, at various moments, "cajoled and threatened" coloured audiences (Lodge 1994: 40). The most infamous of these was probably a speech (widely publicized) given by Mandela in February at Pochefstroom. During this speech,

Mandela called coloureds and Indians who voted for the NP "traitors of the revolution." In another incident, Boesak intimated in a public gathering that coloureds who voted for the NP acted against God's will. And ANC organizer Franklin Sonn lectured a coloured audience that "We must not make the same mistake as the brown community in Namibia. When they asked for houses, Nujoma asked: For whom did they vote?"[25] Overall, the party revealed (in Lodge's words) a "cultural condescension" to the very people it was trying to attract. At best it was tone deaf, at worst it was insulting.

The ANC also struggled to respond to housing takeovers in Delft and Wiggins. In both cases, it tried to reassure coloured and Indian voters that their property would be safe if it came to power. However, at the same time it was limited in how seriously it could condemn the actions of the squatters. As Gigaba and Marharaj (1996) show, the squatters and (in the Wiggins case) the organizations backing them were ANC supporters. Taking a hard stance against them risked alienating its core constituency. The ANC was also broadly sympathetic with the plight of the squatters, as Africans had been the most discriminated against during apartheid. And it opposed the whole notion that some urban spaces should be set aside for one group and not another. Hence, for strategic and ideological reasons, the party had difficulty coming down firmly on the side of the coloureds and Indians. While the NP could send an unambiguous signal of support to these groups, the ANC had to hedge its bets. This made it difficult for the ANC to convincingly reassure them that it had their best interests in mind.

Eldridge and Seekings (1996) suggest that, as the campaign period neared an end in the Western Cape, it became apparent to the ANC that its early efforts were not effectively countering the NP's negative campaign. Consequently, it shifted its campaign in the negative direction. It frequently attacked the NP's claim that it was new, connecting it to its apartheid past. Eldridge and Seekings (1996: 527) discuss two ads, sponsored by COSATU, aimed at doing this. The first showed a woman grieving over the coffin of a youth killed by the police in 1985. Accompanying the image was the text: "This is the Reality of 46 Years of National Party Rule … Don't Let Them Stain Your Hands with the Blood of Our Children." The second was a full-page ad that showed a cemetery of white crosses, each representing a fallen apartheid hero. The accompanying text read: "Now, on April 27 where are you going to put your cross? Stop the National Party. Vote ANC." The ANC additionally drew attention to Hernus Kriel, the NP's pick for provincial premiere, tying him to old-style apartheid-era politics. Eldridge and Seeking (1996: 528) also give the example of a pamphlet the ANC circulated that exhorted voters to "Beware of Kriel's 'new' NP" and showed Kriel restraining three dogs wearing collars that identified them as notorious African warlords. Although they were rumored to be involved in instigating violence, the NP had nonetheless put them on its lists. Kriel was also shown inviting into the Western Cape right-wingers

---

[25] Examples all from Lodge (1994).

and third-force members. Finally, at rallies the ANC called attention to the "racist" NP campaign and voters were asked to "Save the Cape from NP racism" (Eldridge and Seekings 1996: 528). Altogether, the ANC sought to keep the NP's image as white as possible.

At the same time, the ANC advertised more aggressively its multiracial list of candidates, especially the large number of coloureds, including Boesak, at the top. It campaigned heavily in coloured areas and brought in party heavyweights, like Mandela, to address coloured audiences. It placed large ads in newspapers, showcasing endorsements from prominent coloured community members. All told, by the end of the campaign, the ANC was focusing significant effort on its own image as well as the NP's.

However, it was probably a case of too little, too late: The ANC was never able to recover from its early blunders. Around two-thirds of the coloured electorate (see estimates in Reynolds 1994) supported the National Party in the election, handing it a majority. Alhough there were many reasons for this outcome, Eldridge and Seekings (1996) suggest that the ANC understood too late that coloured voters cared about more than just policy positions and competency. They also sought information on *whose interests the party would look out for if in office*, and the ANC's campaign did not sufficiently convince them that it would look out for theirs. As Eldridge and Seekings (1996: 537) put it:

The content of the Our Plan campaign was too academic and too broadly nonracial, notwithstanding efforts to reassure coloured voters in particular, in advertisements and at rallies. The constraints on ANC support in the Western Cape were not simply due to fears of ANC incompetence. Rather, they stemmed from the perceived association of the ANC with violence and its perceived neglect of the particular interests of coloured people, especially working-class coloured voters. The Our Plan campaign detailed the ANC's proposals for building houses and providing jobs, for example. But coloured voters might have asked "so what?" if an ANC government gave these to African and not coloured families? The strategy may have edged support upwards very slightly, but failed to challenge deep-rooted perceptions about the ANC.

Thus, perhaps because ideological blinders hindered it early in the campaign, causing it to make a number of strategic blunders, perhaps because on-the-ground conflicting interests between coloured and African communities prevented it from sending unambiguous signals, the ANC failed to sufficiently alter coloured perceptions that it was an African party. According to the 1994 Idasa survey, a few months after the election *less than half* of the coloured electorate viewed the ANC as inclusive. For the party of the Freedom Charter, the champion of the anti-apartheid fight, and successor to the United Democratic Front (UDF), this must surely have come as a surprise, and it cost it the election in the Western Cape.

It is interesting to note that the DP by and large stayed above the fray in the battle over racial credentials in 1994. As mentioned earlier, it saw itself as the voice of moderation and neutrality between two competing nationalisms, and it believed that this, along with its history of fighting apartheid, would win it support in nonwhite communities. After the smoke from the election had cleared and the votes were counted and the party had scored less than 2 percent of the overall vote, it did some serious soul-searching. One of the lessons it seemed to take away from the "disaster" (as Welsh 1994: 113 put it) was that (to paraphrase Horowitz), you can't ignore blood in a bloody election. Welsh (1994: 115) writes: "The DP's cerebral approach to politics, with its carefully worked out, rational policies, lacks mass appeal in a political system where calls to racial and ethnic 'blood' (even if concealed in the rhetoric of non-racialism) are the stock-in-trade of politicians on the stump." In other words, the DA believed it got trammeled because it had ignored race in its campaign. It would not make the same mistake again.

CONCLUSION

Each of the three central characters in this book – the NP, the ANC, and the DP – began the 1994 election period believing that voters could be won and lost through their campaign efforts. They learned several lessons over the course of the campaigns that would prove important in later elections.

The first was that, in their endeavors to win over new voters, they could not ignore race. Party images were key to persuasion – much as the analysis in Chapter 2 suggested. The National Party seemed to understand this from the outset and fashioned a campaign aimed at convincing nonwhite voters that it had transformed itself from an all-white party to a multiracial one. It also went on the warpath, portraying the ANC as an African-only party that would not look out for the interests of minority voters. Partially as a result of these efforts, the party that had engineered apartheid – a system that had discriminated against and displaced nonwhite South Africans – was able to convince close to two-thirds of coloured and Indian voters that it was inclusive and win a handsome majority in these communities. In contrast, the ANC struggled early and often with the question of race and how to deal with it. It committed itself to an official policy of fighting a positive campaign focused on the future and not the past and sought to minimize references to race in its campaigns, even in the Western Cape, where competition was the most intense. As the campaign period progressed and the success of the NP's strategy became more apparent, the ANC switched tactics. It began attacking the NP's claims of transformation and advertising its own multiracialism, especially in the Western Cape, where coloured voters seemed unconvinced by the party's policy plans and claims of competence. Thus, by the end of the campaign, both of the major parties had made party images a central component in their campaigns. In contrast, the DP did not discuss race in its campaign – a decision it later blamed for its failure to attract more than 2 percent of the vote.

In addition to learning the importance of party images to campaigns, parties also discovered that changing their images was not as straightforward as it might have seemed. As Popkin (1991) argues, campaigns present parties with the opportunity to send signals to the electorate. However, controlling the audience and interpretation of those signals is another thing altogether. The NP and ANC both learned that signals aimed at one electorate could poison relations with another. Hence, while the NP was able to persuade the majority of coloured and Indian voters of its transformation, it had much more difficulty with Africans – in part because the campaign tactics that brought it coloured and Indian voters did little to convince Africans that it would look out for their interests too. The ANC, for its part, struggled to find ways to indicate its "brownness" without alienating its African constituents. Judging by its poor performance in coloured and Indian communities, it largely failed at this challenge. Hence, while parties had come to recognize that changing party images was the key to persuasion, such transformation proved quite difficult – a reality the parties would continue to face in elections to come.

# 4

# The 1999 Campaigns

South Africa held its second post-apartheid elections on June 2, 1999. The African National Congress (ANC) dominated again, winning a healthy 66 percent of the vote. It captured outright seven of the nine provincial legislatures and increased its vote share in KwaZulu-Natal and the Western Cape, winning a plurality in the latter. This time around the ANC's major opponent in the national election was not the National Party (now the New National Party) but the Democratic Party, which took 9.5 percent of the vote. Indeed, the dramatic collapse of the NNP's support (from 20 percent in 1994 to around 7 percent in 1999) was one of the election's most notable departures from 1994. Also significant was the decline of the IFP in KwaZulu-Natal (down from 50.3 to 41.9 percent) and the rise of a new party, the United Democratic Movement, which won around 3 percent of the national vote, most of it concentrated in the Eastern Cape.

Unlike 1994, the 1999 campaigns of the two largest competitors (the ANC and the DP) conformed much more closely to Horowitz's description of "head-count" elections. The ANC focused most of its energy on African, coloured, and Indian voters (by and large ignoring whites). In African constituencies where it lacked a credible African challenger (the IFP or UDM), its campaigns leaned heavily in the direction of mobilization, suggesting that it did not take competition from the DP or NP seriously. Similarly, the DP prioritized the capture of minority (especially white) voters from the NNP, paying scant attention to Africans (at times making moves that would alienate them) – a strategic decision that would haunt it in later campaigns. In contrast to the ANC and DP, the NNP started its campaign with the goal of building a multiracial constituency and made frequent symbolic gestures to African voters. However, it had difficulty backing these gestures with concrete, on-the-ground campaigns in African communities. Furthermore, by the end of the campaign period, flustered by the DP's aggressive appeals to its home constituency, the NP reverted to a campaign aimed primarily at minorities.

*The 1999 Campaigns*                                                                          83

Unsurprisingly, race was at least as central to these elections as standard election topics like policy and performance. Both the DP and the ANC had learned lessons from the NP's use of race in 1994. The ANC ran a brilliant campaign to convince the African electorate that, in spite of setbacks, it continued to work to improve life in South Africa. Simultaneously, it sought to defuse criticisms of its performance record by portraying the opposition parties as white racists with no interest in African voters. The DP and the NP vigorously contested this portrayal, but their own battles over the white electorate lent validity to the ANC's claims. It was difficult for the DP to argue that it was not "really" a white party when it visibly focused so much of its campaign efforts on white voters; the same held for the NP. Thus, even though the ANC and the DP/NNP were not actively competing on the ground for the same sets of voters, they were engaged in skirmishes over the nature of each other's racial images.

These battles suggest that, even in this polarized election, parties viewed party images as critical to persuasion. If the ANC could ignore the NP and DP on the ground, it was because, as "white" parties, they lacked credibility with African voters. However, the attention paid to party images also suggests that parties viewed them as malleable – otherwise, why fight over them? Hence, although the 1999 campaigns conformed much more closely to Horowitz's expectations about party behavior in "mobilizing" elections, a closer look suggests parties did not see this state of affairs as permanent.

PERSUASION VERSUS MOBILIZATION

Party campaigns in 1999 were more closely bounded by race than they had been in 1994. Both the ANC and the DP focused on mobilizing the home base rather than pursuing persuasion across racial lines. In contrast, the National Party initially articulated a strong desire to move into African areas. However, it later backed away from this as it became clear that the DP was capturing the white vote, lending a certain degree of schizophrenia to its campaign. In this sense, these campaigns conformed more closely with Horowitz's expectations of party behavior in ethnic elections.

## The ANC

The ANC fought the 1994 election believing that the NP was a formidable opponent capable of capturing African votes. In 1999, it took racial boundaries as given. This is not to imply that the party took its African support for granted. Internal research had shown that it had work to do to convince the electorate that it had brought about real change in its first four years of government. Moreover, in areas where it faced a resourceful "African" competitor (the IFP or UDM), it fought fierce persuasion campaigns. However, in areas lacking such a competitor, the party focused more on mobilization: Its true persuasion task was convincing disgruntled Africans to vote, rather than abstain in protest. The ANC also devoted significant effort to winning over coloured votes in the Western Cape and (to a lesser extent) Indian votes in KwaZulu-Natal. In contrast, other than making reassurances to white capitalists, it by and large ignored white voters. The following section develops these points in greater detail.

### The Campaign for African Voters

The ANC's campaign tactics varied depending on whether it faced a viable African competitor. It fought intense persuasion campaigns in places like the Eastern Cape and KwaZulu-Natal, where an organized and resourceful African party challenged it. In contrast, its efforts focused much more on mobilization – specifically, raising registration rates – in areas where African challengers were weaker.

In 1999, the ANC faced two primary African threats: the ANC's traditional nemesis in KwaZulu-Natal, the IFP, and a new party called the United Democratic Movement (UDM). Bantu Holomisa (former leader of the Transkei) and Roelf Meyer (ex-member of the NNP) formed the UDM in 1997, and it quickly became a worrisome competitor to the ANC in the Transkei, an area of the Eastern Cape that had been a "homeland" during apartheid.

Unlike most of the ANC's other African challengers (the Pan African Congress, for example), the UDM had a concentrated organizational base in a sizeable African community. Holomisa used old homeland connections to unite dissatisfied bureaucrats downsized in ANC reforms and traditional leaders upset with ANC insistence on democratically elected local government.[1] Furthermore, UDM leaders had national stature: Holomisa and Meyer were both well-known politicians who had participated in the highest level of politics (Holomisa as an ANC member of Parliament and Meyer as a negotiator for the NP). These advantages of organization and visibility suggested that the UDM might be able to fill a political vacuum created by wide-scale African discontent with the ANC's performance since 1994, especially in the Eastern Cape.[2]

---

[1] Southall (1999c: 14–15).

[2] The Eastern Cape had many problems: crippling unemployment and poverty; infrastructure underdevelopment; and a bloated, inefficient bureaucracy left over from bantustan days. ANC attempts to reduce the provincial budget deficit resulted in layoffs of public-sector employees, delays in pensions and welfare grants, and deteriorating social services. The ANC also angered civil servants by moving the provincial capital from Umtata (in the Transkei) to Bisho (in the Ciskei) and alienated traditional leaders by pushing forward with local government elections in 1995. Consequently, by 1999 there was serious discontent in the province at many levels: amongst former members of the civil service, the chiefs, and ordinary voters. While the Eastern Cape's problems were not unique in South Africa (the Northern Province, for example, inherited many of the same issues), the Eastern Cape was the only province with an alternative African party organized and visible enough to challenge the ANC. For an analysis of this, see Southall (1999a: 18) and Lodge (1999a: 151–152).

Although the fraction of survey respondents reporting that they planned to vote for the UDM was never high,[3] the ANC responded to the new party with furious determination. Lodge (1999a: 118) notes: "[T]he aim of ANC planners was to maintain their organisation's 'undisputed representative' status." Consequently, the Transkei joined KwaZulu-Natal as the site of extensive ANC persuasion campaigns.[4] In both provinces, the ANC launched aggressive person-to-person canvassing efforts aimed at winning over and/or keeping African voters. It reinvigorated its branch structures and compelled them to canvass neighborhoods and knock on doors (Lodge 1999a). It also relied on the grassroots muscle of COSATU (the Council of South African Trade Unions, part of the ANC alliance) (Southall 1999b: 11). Prominent ANC politicians – Mandela, Mbeki, and Madikizela-Mandela – traveled throughout the contested provinces, stroking crowds with recitations of ANC achievements and pillorying leaders of opposition parties (especially Holomisa).[5] ANC politicians made well-publicized appearances to celebrate the extension of new services to communities (a road, a water pipe, a new school), using these opportunities to emphasize ANC success in delivery.[6] The ANC also favored the use of "road-shows," in Lodge's (1999a: 156) words "a slow motorcade of about fifteen vehicles in which political principals would ride in state while party workers would run alongside distributing leaflets and stickers."

In both provinces, the ANC targeted chiefs. Chiefs were unhappy with the ANC's efforts to introduce local elections in rural areas and had resources to cause problems: They controlled territory, making it difficult for party organizers to reach voters.[7] They also had considerable influence over public

---

[3] Idasa (1999a, 1999b) show it to range from around 4% to 16%.
[4] UDM also had somewhat of a presence in the shantytowns of Gauteng, although surveys put its support in the province as a whole at 2–5%.
[5] For example, during the weekend of January 10, 1999, the ANC held major rallies in the Eastern Cape towns of Peddie, Steytlerville, Engcobo, Port Elizabeth, Aliwal North, and Queenstown. During these rallies ANC "luminaries" highlighted ANC achievements and urged supporters to deliver a two-thirds majority result to speed up delivery. See EISA (1999a: 18). Winnie Madikizela-Mandela appeared at a rally in Flagstaff (Transkei) promising that the ANC would not rest on its successes but would push to improve its performance in the future. Mbeki conveyed a similar message in Peddie (Transkei) and Orlando (Gauteng). See Lodge (1999a: 118–120). Steve Tshwete poked fun at Holomisa at a meeting in Queenstown (Eastern Cape) and said the NNP was in "intensive care" at another meeting in King Williams Town (Eastern Cape). Mluleki George also addressed crowds in King Williams Town, calling the UDM "an organization of baboons." Nelson Mandela appeared at a rally in Idutywa (Transkei) and claimed that the UDM's leaders were cowards who had cooperated with apartheid. In the second half of May alone, 200 ANC rallies were scheduled, and Mbeki spent most of his weekends touring the province. See Lodge (1999a: 118 and 122).
[6] Thus Kadar Asmal opened a water scheme in Peddie (Eastern Cape) and Thabo Mbeki opened a new road from Centane to Butterworth (also in the Eastern Cape). See Lodge (1999a: 121). Mandela himself also engaged in some of this, opening a new group of classrooms in Zaku Heights (Transkei). See Lodge (1999a: 153).
[7] In the Transkei, for example, angry chiefs thwarted registration efforts and chased IEC workers out of their villages. See Dickson (1998).

opinion. Chiefs in KwaZulu-Natal had delivered the African vote to the IFP in years past. The ANC therefore focused on winning over IFP-aligned chiefs in KwaZulu-Natal and preventing chiefs in the Eastern Cape from defecting to the UDM. In the Eastern Cape, it vied with the UDM to put prominent chiefs in high positions on provincial electoral lists.[8] Top ANC leaders made repeated, public visits to chiefs to reassure them about their future in an ANC-led world.[9] In both provinces, ANC leaders played to tradition, emphasizing the wisdom of the elders and engaging in cultural ceremony.[10] Finally, and most brazenly, the ANC dramatically increased chiefly salaries a few months prior to the election.[11]

The type of campaign waged in the Eastern Cape and KwaZulu-Natal, with extensive visits by top ANC leaders, efforts to woo chiefs, repeated rallies and speeches, strategic openings of public works projects, and so on, was *not* repeated in provinces lacking major African challengers, even where sizeable numbers of Africans indicated dissatisfaction with the party and claimed to be independent. Instead, where the ANC lacked African competitors, it focused primarily on mobilization.

The party's mobilization campaigns aimed to increase the registration levels of African voters. The ANC had reason to believe that resource-poor African voters lacked the paperwork necessary to vote. The Electoral Act of 1998 required voters to obtain a special bar-coded identification document before registering. Survey research suggested that, as of July 1998, as many as 7 million voters (20 percent of the electorate) did not have these documents. Although it appeared that Africans were the most likely of the four racial groups to possess bar-coded IDs, millions of African voters still lacked

---

[8] Thus, Chief Phathekile Holomisa (nephew of Bantu Holomisa) figured prominently (number 16) on the ANC list, as did Chief Mwelo Nonkonyana (number 18). Both were high-placed and outspoken members of CONTRALESA (the Congress of Traditional Leaders of South Africa). Nonkonyana, as both a national organizer of CONTRALESA and the chair of the Eastern Cape House of Traditional Leaders, was regarded as a major coup for the ANC. See Southall (1999c: 14–15). Holomisa had been an ANC MP in the past but had attracted the ire of the party when he openly criticized its position on traditional leaders. All riffs were mended by 1999, however, when Holomisa became an important asset to ANC campaigning. See Mare (1999: 106).

[9] Thabo Mbeki paid a long visit to King Mpondobini Sigcau (the paramount chief of Mpondoland in Transkei) in the company of ANC MP Stella Sigcau, who is a kinswoman of the king; see EISA (1999e). Nelson Mandela also visited the king, decked out in beads and blankets and keen to stress the ANC's deference to tradition. See Lodge (1999a: 153).

[10] In speeches in rural areas Mbeki honored the elders of his Zizi clan, emphasizing kinship, family, and respect for elders. See Lodge (1999a: 119). When visiting with Zulu King Goodwill Zwelithini in KwaZulu-Natal, Nelson Mandela wore a leopard skin and paid homage to traditional leaders as spearheading the fight against colonialism. See Mare (1999: 106).

[11] In late March (1999), the provincial ANC government in the Eastern Cape announced pay increases for paramount chiefs (to R322,800) and headmen (to R7,997). See Lodge (1999a: 153). In KwaZulu-Natal, salary increases for chiefs came to an extra R20 million. The Zulu king's budget allocation from the provincial government is R12.2 million, while the national government provides him with an additional R400,000. See Mare (1999: 107).

them. Furthermore, a large fraction of the African electorate did not know the identity books were a prerequisite for registration. A further fraction did not understand that registration and voting were separate acts (during the 1994 elections, registration had not been necessary). Finally, many voters lacked information about where they needed to register: There were hundreds of registration points in some communities, and voters had to show up at the correct spot or they would be turned away.[12]

As the Independent Electoral Council (IEC) appeared unable to do much voter education prior to the election – overwhelmed as it was by the mechanics of registration – the task of ensuring that voters had the information necessary to participate in the elections fell to parties. After an initial round of registration (in late November 1998) showed low turnout in most areas of South Africa – including heavily African areas – the necessity of action became even clearer to the ANC. The party consequently invested significant resources in preparing the electorate – and specifically the African electorate – for the elections.

In urban areas, the party plastered townships with posters and pamphlets telling the population to register. Party representatives went door-to-door, reminding voters that they needed to register in order to vote and helping them to identify the correct place to do so.[13] By late November, the ANC had reportedly distributed 3 million leaflets and 2 million calling cards to the townships of Gauteng. Another million leaflets were distributed prior to the second round of registration (in late January 1999), and close to 11,000 volunteers from the party branches were trained to work as party agents and monitors at registration centers.[14] Major party leaders toured the townships and preached the virtues of voting.[15] COSATU (the Council of South African Trade Unions) got involved, calling on its members to "register in droves."[16] And Deputy Presidency Director General Reverend Frank Chikane urged church leaders to take a leading role in mobilizing their followers to register.[17] As one ANC leader explained, every effort was made to ensure that voters "get the message to register,"[18] and "it's an all-out campaign."[19]

The ANC also took the registration of rural Africans seriously. Lodge (1999a: 41) reports that "village electoral teams" assisted voters in obtaining identity documents in at least two provinces (North West and Northern). In the North West Province, where registration levels appeared low after the first round of registration in November 1998, the party introduced the "Votani Mawethu" campaign to assist the "very poor" in obtaining the requisite

---

[12] See Idasa (1998a).
[13] See Paton (1999a) and Cresswell et al. (1999).
[14] See Mdhlela (1999).
[15] See Tabane (1999a, 1999b).
[16] See Mdhlela (1999).
[17] See Tabane and Radebe (1999). Jacobson (1999).
[18] See Mdhlela (1999).
[19] See Jacobson (1999).

documentation (bar-coded identity books) to register.[20] During the course of the campaign, the ANC gave away free ID photos to at least 6,700 voters, most of whom were rural.[21] Party leaders also toured rural areas, requesting that people do their civic duty and register and vote in the upcoming elections.[22]

In some instances – particularly in rural areas where resources for mobilization were stretched – it was difficult to determine where the ANC's registration campaign ended and the Independent Electoral Council's began. In the Northern Province, the head of the IEC announced that chiefs would be paid R4 for every registration within their respective tribal authorities as an incentive for assisting with mobilization.[23] While there is no indication that the ANC was behind this program, it certainly benefited the party. In the North West Province, the party worked very closely with the IEC to raise registration levels – lending equipment in some cases and ANC vehicles in others.[24] This cooperation induced grumbles amongst leaders in opposition parties who felt that ANC "dominance" of the IEC would compel voters to support it.[25] Close collaboration between the IEC and the ANC drew criticism in the Northern Cape also, where IEC efforts to target young people and provide registration assistance to the poor resulted in accusations that the ANC and IEC were "birds of a feather" who were "working together to mobilise ANC support by subsidising voter registration."[26] The appointment of ANC people to high-level positions in the IEC added substance to the claims,[27] as did the controversial dismissal of the Kimberley's Local Electoral Officer (LEO) by the ANC-controlled municipal council, supposedly because councilors were unhappy with registration levels in African townships.

While the regions dominated by the ANC saw high levels of registration, levels lagged in the Transkei and KwaZulu-Natal, the two areas of South Africa in which the ANC faced an African party with an organizational presence on the ground. Did this lag represent a slackening of effort on the part of the ANC?

In the Transkei, where the UDM challenged ANC dominance, registration levels remained low after three rounds of registration and an apparently aggressive door-to-door campaign on the part of the IEC to reach voters.[28] While it is impossible to know exactly why registration levels lagged, there is some suggestion that ANC efforts to provide identity documents to Africans

[20] See Manson et al. (1999a).
[21] See Manson et al. (1999b).
[22] See EISA (1999a: 16).
[23] See EISA (1999e).
[24] See Manson et al. (1999a).
[25] Quote from a PAC representative, cited in Lodge (1999a: 41).
[26] See EISA (1999d: 16).
[27] Not to mention the fact that the Provincial Election Officer (PEO) was the wife of the Northern Cape's MEC for Health, and the deputy of the PEO was the son of the deputy speaker in the legislature. See Lodge (1999a: 52).
[28] With 100 vehicles reportedly involved, this was not a minor effort. See EISA (1999e: 2).

were lackluster. An official in the Department of Home Affairs accused the parties of not being fully engaged in its campaign to provide bar-coded IDs to voters and suggested that registration was slow because of a "lack of political will" on the part of parties and other stakeholders.[29] Another official, this time in the IEC, claimed that something had gone "terribly wrong" in the Transkei, and as many as a million voters were at risk of being disenfranchised.[30] In any case, while the ANC appeared to work very closely with the IEC and Home Affairs in other provinces, the relationship appeared more strained in the Transkei, with allegations that the party was not pulling its weight.

Registration levels also remained low in KwaZulu-Natal, even after three rounds of registration. There, as in the Eastern Cape, the ANC faced an African competitor (the IFP) for African votes. While there were reports of the ANC engaging in mobilizing activity in KwaZulu-Natal, it seems that the party's efforts were targeted to the regions of the province that it dominated – in particular, the urban townships. Areas in which partisanship was less clear, and areas dominated by the IFP (the rural areas, for example), do not appear to have benefited from ANC resources and efforts. This may partially explain the lower overall level of registration in the province.[31]

Thus, registration stayed sluggish in precisely the areas where the ANC faced competition from an African competitor. In contrast, when the ANC faced only the DP and NNP as major competitors, its mobilization efforts were intense. Once again, this shows that the type of campaign the ANC waged in African areas depended a great deal on the nature of its competition. Where it faced an African party, its campaign was heavy on persuasion and light on mobilization. Where it faced no African party, the opposite was true. This suggests that it did not consider parties like the DP and the NNP – "white parties" – to be true competitors for the African vote.

### The Campaign for Coloured and Indian Voters

The ANC *did* apparently believe the DP and NNP represented credible competitors for the coloured vote. These voters held the key to the Western and Northern Capes, where they are majorities, and had eluded the ANC in 1994. Consequently, the party pursued aggressive persuasion campaigns in coloured communities throughout these provinces.

As with African communities, the party focused on personal contact and extensive canvassing. Lodge (1999a) documents that party representatives toured the Western Cape in late 1998, before the campaigns officially began,

---

[29] See EISA (1999e: 13).
[30] See EISA (1999e: 13).
[31] Other explanations exist. First, Indians (who compose around 13% of KwaZulu-Natal's electorate) had very low registration levels. Second, there is some suggestion that both the IFP and the ANC refrained from extensive mobilization activity in order to maintain peace in a frequently conflictual province – mobilization in the past had often been carried out by the same enthusiastic youthful supporters who were responsible for some of the violence.

conducting "listening" meetings to discern issues and grievances deemed important by the community so as to better shape party strategy. By March 1999, ANC Western Cape provincial leader Ebrahim Rasool was able to claim that party representatives had visited every house in "strong to moderate ANC areas" (Lodge 1999a: 81). In addition, top ANC leaders – including Mbeki and Mandela – made numerous campaign stops in coloured neighborhoods to press the flesh with potential voters.[32] According to Lodge (1999a: 142), local speeches and printed media articulated policy goals that reflected coloured priorities (crime prevention over job creation). In the Western and Northern Capes, the ANC stacked provincial lists with coloured politicians that it had wooed from the NNP and made extensive efforts to downplay its African roots.

The ANC also aimed limited persuasion campaigns at Indians, particularly those in KwaZulu-Natal. Competition between the ANC and IFP split the African vote and drove up the value of Indian votes to both parties, but the small size of the group (and perhaps its suspected ambivalence toward the ANC) reduced its significance (Lodge 1999a). Consequently, the ANC made efforts to win over the Indian community (especially the Indian middle class), but these were less extensive than those geared at coloureds in the Western and Northern Capes or Africans in the Eastern Cape, Gauteng, and KwaZulu-Natal.

## The (Non)Campaign for White Voters

In contrast to its efforts in African, coloured, and Indian communities, the ANC ignored white voters. Lodge (1999a: 121–125) documents token attempts to reassure whites regarding some of their concerns – namely, that it would not use a two-thirds majority to re-write the Constitution, that it would not abandon its conservative macroeconomic program (GEAR), and that whites had a future in South Africa. At the same time, ANC representatives exhorted Africans to give it a two-thirds majority so that it would not be blocked in its transformation goals (thus contradicting its attempts to soothe whites on this issue). It ran a positive campaign – emphasizing its successes rather than addressing issues like crime and growth that worried the pessimistic and unimpressed white community. It typically avoided engaging the opposition on issues during publicity events and mocked white opposition parties and leaders – Mandela called the DP and NNP "Mickey Mouse" parties and Kadar Asmal referred to Tony Leon as a Chihuahua. The ANC substantially reduced its expenditures on advertisements in the print media – a key source

---

[32] Jacobs and Calland (1999: 18) write: "The regular presence of deputy president Mbeki at a series of high profile events in coloured areas in the Western Cape ... point to the seriousness with which the ANC views the battles for votes in the province. The visit on the Muslim festival, Eid, by Deputy President Mbeki to the controversial Claremont Mosque, as well as the holding of the ANC 8 January statement events at Athlone Staduim ... are testament to the ANC's response." Along similar lines, Lodge (1999a: 123) quotes ANC Western Cape Premier candidate Ebrahim Rasool as saying that "Thabo Mbeki has been down here and very, very close to the people."

of information for whites – and declined to engage in televised policy debates (Lodge 1999a).

It is instructive to look at ANC behavior in Gauteng, where the white vote could have been strategically valuable to the ANC had the party decided to pursue it. Lodge (1999a:148) notes that in Gauteng, "provincial leaders based their planning around the perception that the prospects for outright victory were 'marginal.'" The African constituency, though the largest in the province, is smaller than in most other provinces, and the white community is sizeable (around 25 percent). The smaller gap in size between the African and white communities in Gauteng makes the ANC more vulnerable to mood swings in the African community than elsewhere in the country. In late 1998, it appeared that many Gauteng Africans felt let down by the ANC and less inclined to identify with it or say they would vote for it if the election were held tomorrow. The ANC feared this would translate into votes for the UDM or high African abstention rates – both of which would open a door for the DP or NNP to take (or share) the province. As huge numbers of whites claimed to be independent – indeed many were looking for a new political home – recruiting from this constituency appeared to offer many possibilities.

However, the ANC made little attempt in Gauteng to woo white voters. It did not engage in door-to-door canvassing in the white suburbs or send motorcades into white neighborhoods. While township streets were plastered with ANC posters, white suburbs had relatively few. In mid-April the main road leading into Mamelodi township (near Pretoria) had ANC posters affixed on every available surface: lampposts, walls, street signs, and bus stops. In contrast, in Hatfield, a neighborhood around the University of Pretoria, one could walk for blocks without seeing a single ANC poster – and this was true in most white suburbs.[33] Lodge (1999a) lists several other observations backing this view: Although the party claimed to have distributed 12 million pamphlets in Gauteng alone, few of these made their way into white neighborhoods. The ANC did not host rallies in white communities or encourage whites to attend its rallies in African communities. Mbeki and other ANC leaders made relatively few visits to white communities in Gauteng, and when they did, their goals seemed to be to reassure the white business community of ANC intentions, rather than to woo white voters.[34] Finally, the party's nomination of Shilowa – an active member of both COSATU and the SACP – for premier emphasized leftist elements over moderate ones, not a move designed with white voters in mind. In sum, in contrast to 1994, the ANC in 1999 seemed satisfied to conduct its campaign within racial lines.

---

[33] Author observation based on field research in January–May 1999.
[34] Thus, rather than meeting with neighborhood groups or visiting churches (strategies in the Western Cape), ANC leaders met with business groups like the National Business Initiative and Investec.

## The DP

The ANC's decision to stick within the established racial contours of South African politics was mirrored by the decisions of the Democratic Party (DP). In 1994, the DP had hoped to build an enlightened multiracial constituency of committed liberals and failed in this regard. In 1999, it set its eyes on a larger and perhaps more practical prize: the capture of whites (especially Afriakaans speakers) from the NP. The party was quite candid about this turn, which it viewed as a temporary necessity to its longer term trajectory: First, it would conquer the white (and perhaps coloured and Indian) electorates; once this was accomplished, it would turn to the long-term goal of penetrating the African market, which it viewed as far more difficult. Tony Leon explained: "It took 46 years to get Afrikaner voters. After only four years, it is too soon for blacks to join in large numbers."[35] David Welsh, a member and chronicler of the DP, echoed this sentiment when he wrote: "It is difficult to be optimistic about the DP's or, indeed, any other minority party's ability to break into the African vote in the short to medium term, which may be as long as 10 to 25 years."[36] Thus, believing that the African vote was out of reach in the near term, and hoping to improve its showing over 1994, the DP concentrated its energies on minority (especially white) voters.

Evidence for this strategic turn abounds, much of it documented in Lodge (1999a), but it is clear in other accounts as well. First, there was the general tone of the campaign. The party emphasized *negative* trends in the country – high crime levels, poor economic growth – and harped on the leading party's performance in dealing with them. It railed against corruption and the accretion of power in the ANC, referencing the ANC's drive to achieve a two-thirds majority and the tendency of ANC representatives in parliament to "rubber-stamp" initiatives of the executive. It repeatedly criticized ANC leaders who were popular with Africans but unpopular with whites – Winnie Madikizela Mandela in particular. It fashioned its leader, Tony Leon, not as a compromiser or bridge builder but as a street fighter willing to get down and dirty in opposing the ANC. Party posters showed Leon with arms crossed and a surly expression on his face. The party called this "muscular liberalism" and accompanied it with the official slogan, "Fight Back." This message and approach appealed to pessimistic whites who felt they had lost significant ground since the ANC took power in 1994, but not to Africans, who were significantly more optimistic about trends in the country. Indeed, many Africans wondered what the DP felt it needed to "fight back" against, many cynically suggesting that it might be them. Thus, the DP's general tone – whether it meant it or not – most likely alienated African voters from the start.

The DP revealed its target constituency to be whites – particularly Afrikaners – in the realm of symbolic gestures as well. In one particularly

---

[35] Quoted in Welsh (1999: 98).
[36] See Welsh (1999: 98–99).

colorful incident, Tony Leon rode a white horse through Ventersdorp, the home turf of the right-wing Afrikaner Weerstandsbweging (AWB) – a gesture most certainly aimed at wooing conservative whites. DP campaign events assumed a distinctly Afrikaner feel – as one article put it, the party went from being one of "*verdomde liberaliste* (damned liberals)" to one of "*biltong, braaivleis, and boeremusiek.*"[37] Tony Leon (whom close associates called "*volkskeier,*" or people's leader, with some irony) gave speeches in Afrikaans – even though his command of the language was weak.[38] The DP also worked hard to bring on board Afrikaans-speaking leaders who could present an image of the party that would appeal to Afrikaner voters – much the same way that the NNP and ANC used coloured and Indian leaders in coloured and Indian communities. Hennie Bester, head of the DP on the Western Cape, is a good example of this. Barrell (1999a) attributes leaders like Bester with the DP's success in moving into Afrikaner communities: "He speaks the local white farmers' language, directly but softly and with the same Cape *brei* that purrs of [the local's] palate." In these various ways, the party attempted to signal its transformation from an elite English party to a party that embraced the Afrikaans-speaking electorate. The nature of these actions suggests once again that the target audience of DP persuasion efforts was Afrikaans-speaking whites, not Africans.

Moreover, the DP included on its lists several conservative whites who were bound to incite controversy in African constituencies. The Eastern Cape list, for example, included Tertius Delport, a notorious conservative who had defected from the NNP to join the DP. And the Gauteng list included Nigel Bruce, who, as the editor of the *Financial Mail*, had made colorful and controversial racist comments that did not endear him to African communities. In earlier campaigns, it is doubtful that such individuals would have been welcome in the DP, much less placed in prominent positions on party lists. DP representatives claimed that the party had not become more conservative; instead, conservatives like Delport and Bruce were moving leftward to the party (see Welsh 1999 for an example). Many observers voiced skepticism for this view (Lodge 1999a).

Finally, the DP's campaign techniques also suggested that its target constituency was middle-class whites instead of Africans. Lodge's (1999a) study of Gauteng reveals that the DP relied on telephones to reach voters instead of house visits, yet many African households lacked phones. Furthermore, DP efforts to visit townships were sporadic and half-hearted, even though the barriers to campaigning in townships were lower than they had been in 1994. And, just as the ANC placed the majority of its posters in African communities, the DP placed virtually all of its posters in white communities. Finally, the DP did

---

[37] *Biltong* is dried meat, a popular and traditional snack associated with Afrikaners. *Braaivleis* is a barbecue – a favorite form of get-together in South Africa, especially amongst Afrikaners. *Boeremusiek* – literally "farmer music" – is traditional music in the Afrikaans language. Quote from Barrell (1999a).
[38] See Barrell (1999b).

not hold major rallies in African communities and Tony Leon spent most of his time campaigning in non-African areas.[39]

If poaching white voters from the NNP was the DP's primary goal during the campaigns, entering the fray with the ANC and NNP for coloured and Indian voters formed an important secondary goal. Lodge (1999a) catalogs many of these efforts: The party launched its campaign in Durban (home of large concentrations of Indian voters), where Tony Leon told assembled supporters that KwaZulu-Natal represented its largest target audience. DP made particularly vigorous efforts in the Indian communities of Chatsworth and Phoenix, where the party aimed at stealing ground from the NNP and the Minority Front (MF). The party emphasized that ANC affirmative action policies were adversely affecting Indians and painted itself as the most able adversary to the dominant party. It also presented itself as a hard-liner on crime, an issue deemed highly important in Indian communities (Lodge 1999a). In the small Indian community of Lenasia (Gauteng), the DP played on Indian resentment about having to share schools with neighboring African squatter camps and the downgrading of a local hospital to a primary health care clinic – both undesired reallocations of resources initiated by the ANC (Lodge 1999a). In the Western Cape, the DP used similar tactics to woo coloured voters, arguing, for example, that "your skin colour still matters" and playing up its tough stance on crime.

Thus, in the realm of campaign messages, symbolic gestures, party lists, and campaign tactics the DP revealed its primary audience to be whites, coloureds, and Indians. In contrast, the DP did not make a concerted effort to attract African voters. Indeed, the DP's campaign, with its negative slant on the state of South Africa, its pugalistic stance toward the ruling party, its attempts to polarize Indian and coloured relations with Africans, and its recruitment of conservatives to its lists, largely *alienated* African voters. Prior to the onset of the campaigns (in September 1998), Africans gave Leon an average rating of 3 on a 0 to 10 point scale; by April, his rating had fallen to 2, below all other ranked leaders except Constand Viljoen, leader of the conservative Freedom Front.[40] The party that once saw itself as fighting apartheid from within appeared to have co-opted its old opponent's tricks in its efforts to win over the Afrikaner constituency.

## The NNP

The NNP contrived a fickle approach to the 1999 campaigns. NNP leaders repeatedly acknowledged the importance of making inroads into the African

---

[39] This is not to say that Leon spent no time in African areas. He made several well-publicized forays into African communities – events that produced nice photo opportunities of the DP leader surrounded by African children. For example, Leon visited the Charles Hurwitz Santa Tuberculosis Hospital in Soweto in April and used the opportunity to condemn the ANC's health policies. See Sepotokele (1999). Helen Suzman visited Soweto on Freedom Day and laid a wreath at the Hector Pietersen Memorial. See Powers and Tabane (1999). However, these visits were the exception, not the rule.

[40] Harris et al. (1999: 3–4).

community and sporadically attempted to follow up on this sentiment with concrete measures to attract African votes. The NNP's need to shore up evaporating white support overwhelmed its efforts to reach across racial divides, however. As tempting as the African vote was, NNP politicians feared going after it would result in losing existing supporters without gaining new ones, and the party veered schizophrenically between a truly multiracial strategy and one that focused only on minorities.

Throughout its campaign, the NNP made noises about the importance of pursuing a racially mixed constituency. As in 1994, NNP leaders viewed extending NNP reach into new areas as critical if the party were to flourish in the future. One of its very first moves was to change its name from the National Party to the New National Party. Accompanying this were claims about changing strategies. In September 1998, at a high-level party caucus, party leaders approved a document emphasizing, in part, an "inclusive (coalition) government" as the basis for its campaign (Lodge 1999a: 82). Johan Kilian, Gauteng leader of the NNP, explained that the party's primary goal was "to expand into new communities. The NNP "is not a white party" and "is not playing blood politics."[41] If the party looked only to white voters, it would be limited to 4 percent of the electorate by 2004.[42] Marthinus van Schalkwyk, who took over as leadership of the party after De Klerk resigned in 1997, spoke of its "dramatic modernization" and promised to "re-position" the party for the long term (Lodge 1999a: 131). In keeping with these sentiments, the party opted for a campaign message ("Let's Get South Africa Working") that it projected as constructive and positive – thus playing to African optimism instead of white pessimism. Campaign posters referenced Ian Smith in Zimbabwe, alluding to the folly of remaining a white party in a majority African country. Party leaders emphasized the racial diversity of its list, which was nearly half nonwhite. David Malutsi, an African, was elected deputy leader of the party. Party leaders frequently referenced the party's diversity. NNP leader in the Northern Cape, Pieter Willem Saaiman, proclaimed "Our party is the rainbow party for the province."[43] Moza Mayman Theron, also in the Northern Cape, announced that coloureds were "taking over" the NNP. He said: "It is the strongest party for coloureds and we are the rainbow nation." [44] Peter Marais, a popular coloured NNP leader, told a Cape Town audience that "the NP is the natural home of brown Afrikaners – you must stand up and be the boss."[45]

The NNP's approach therefore differed substantially from that of the DP. Nothing symbolized these differences more than the campaign stops of the party leaders at the height of the campaign period: While Tony Leon paid homage to Afrikanerdom by visiting the *Vrouemonument* (a statue

---

[41] Quote from Lodge (1999a: 131).
[42] Quote and statistic from Lodge (1999a: 131).
[43] See Turkington (1999).
[44] See Jaffer (1999).
[45] See ter Horst (1999).

commemorating Afrikaner women and children who died during the Boer War), Van Schalkwyk visited Sharpeville, the location of a 1960 anti-apartheid uprising (Breytenbach 1999: 122). The NNP attempted to use these differences to appeal to African voters, repeatedly accusing the DP of running a "whites-only" campaign. Marthinus van Schalkwyk claimed that the DP was leading "its small group of wealthy white supporters and the few right-wingers the party had gained down a whites only cul-de-sac in Houghton."[46] He reiterated this message while campaigning in the Northern Cape, asserting: "The DP is just a small white party which makes a lot of noise. They say 'fight back' – fight who and what?"[47] In these ways, the NNP tried to signal its departure from its all-white past.

Beyond the rhetoric, however, the NNP's attempts to pursue African voters were haphazard and ineffectual. Lodge (1999a) notes that the party relied heavily on the radio to get across its message instead of mounting a door-to-door campaign in the townships. When it was able to attract African politicians, they tended to be local-level politicians who had a beef with the ANC. Consequently, the NNP's African support was typically clustered around prominent local personalities. Finally, during the course of the campaign, the NNP's message became progressively more negative, harping on the danger of handing a two-third's majority to the ANC (posters read "Mugabe had 2/3's," a telling switch from the party's earlier admonishments about Ian Smith), rebuking the ANC for its performance since 1994 and drawing attention to the crime rate – tactics more likely to play well with whites versus Africans. In short, by the end of the NNP's campaign, a conventional appeal to minority voters competed with and overshadowed the party's more adventurous strategy of pursuing Africans.

The NNP's campaign in the Western Cape illustrates particularly well the contradictory tendencies in the NNP and how they interfered with the party's ability to run a consistent campaign. During the 1999 campaign, leadership of the NNP divided into two camps, one supporting Peter Marais and the other Gerard Morkel (who replaced Hernus Kriel as party premier). Both Marais and Morkel are coloured politicians, thus demonstrating the NNP's effort to put nonwhites in prominent positions. However, Marais and Morkel differed considerably in their beliefs about the proper course for the NNP to follow should it fail to win an all-out majority in the election: Align with the ANC, thus courting African votes and moving the party in the direction of a coloured/African alliance, or align with the DP, thus appealing to whites and preserving the current coloured/white alliance that ran the province (Breytenbach 1999). Marais favored teaming up with the ANC, Morkel with the DP. Conflict between the Marais and Morkel camps interfered with

---

[46] Quoted in Lodge (1999a: 130). Houghton is an old-money suburb of Johannesburg – one of the few neighborhoods that the DP (and its earlier manifestations) consistently won during the apartheid years.

[47] Quote from Lodge (1999a: 146).

the NNP's ability to run an organized campaign in the Western Cape, inducing many painful defections from the party leadership. Marais, a politician with deep roots in the coloured community, threatened repeatedly to leave the party for the ANC – disrupting NNP campaigning and sending mixed signals to the coloured electorate. At the same time, Marais' antics annoyed whites. In the end, the conservative Morkel camp won out and the NNP aligned with the DP – once again illustrating that, when push came to shove, the party opted for its traditional strategy of going after white votes rather than risking it for a chance at the much larger African electorate.

The rift between Marais and Morkel mirrored wider dramas in the party. Breytenbach (1999) argues that tensions over the proper course for the party – to pursue African support or stick with whites – dogged it from the early 1990s onward. For example, Roelf Meyer, who led the party during the post-1994 constitutional negotiations, had favored going after African votes. In contrast, Hernus Kriel, the first NNP premier of the Western Cape, pushed the party in a more conservative direction. Both Meyer and Kriel ended up leaving their positions of leadership in the party – Meyer to form the UDM with Bantu Holomisa and Kriel to retire. According to Breytenbach (1999), many hoped this would allow the party to pursue a more centrist strategy, with Meyer's departure placating unhappy whites and Kriel's diluting the party's exclusive image. However, the philosophical differences inherent in the Meyer/Kriel divide simply reasserted themselves in the guise of different leaders, as the Marais/Morkel conflict in 1999 illustrates.

In sum, although leaders in the NNP acknowledged the importance of pursuing the African vote, the party failed to follow through on its intentions. There were several reasons behind this decision. First, the party lacked organizational muscle on the ground in African communities, which made it difficult for it to launch an all-out attack, regardless of its intentions (Lodge 1999a). Second, fights within the party lent an air of schizophrenia to party actions. And finally, as the NNP dithered over its strategy, the DP was aggressively (and by many appearances successfully) pursuing the old NNP core of white voters, pulling away politicians, grassroot networks, and even the support of the Afrikaans press, which had solidly supported the NP for at least forty years (Breytenbach 1999: 122). While the NNP had shown, at previous junctures (like the 1994 election), a certain willingness to risk the white vote to pursue the brown and black ones, the swiftness of its electoral collapse in 1999 stunned party leaders and forced them to re-evaluate the "African" strategy they had embarked on. It was almost as if, coming up to the abyss and looking in, the party could not quite make the leap.

To conclude this section, 1999 campaign strategies diverged significantly from those in 1994. The ANC and the DP ran campaigns that largely stayed within racial boundaries, shoring up support from traditional constituencies. Except when faced with same-group competitors, their efforts focused on mobilization instead of persuasion. And while the NP initially attempted to run a campaign that bridged the racial divide, when it encountered rapidly defecting white supporters and little evidence of success in African communities, it abandoned this course. In this sense, the 1999 campaigns conformed much more closely with Horowitz's expectation that mobilization efforts will feature prominently in campaigns in divided countries.[48]

Why were the 1999 campaigns so marked by mobilization? In general, when do parties focus on the party faithful instead of reaching out to new voters? Based on the comparison between 1994 and 1999 and across different parties, two factors appear to drive party behavior: the size of their core and how anxious they are about its loyalty. A party with a large core constituency (like the ANC) resorts to persuasion only when it feels its hold over its core is threatened. Otherwise, it focuses on mobilization (for it can win solely on the basis of its core constituency). In contrast, a party with a small core constituency (like the NNP and DP) has the opposite response to threats: When it is confident about its home base, it can reach out to new constituencies; when its home base comes under attack, it must retreat from persuasion and focus on mobilizing its core. In 1999, the ANC felt threatened in only a few key areas (the Eastern Cape and KwaZulu-Natal). Elsewhere, it believed it had a lock on the African vote (in large part because the DP and NP could be discredited by branding them as white parties), so it focused on mobilization. The DP's aggressive move to take white voters from the NP – a move it made to survive – prompted the NP to turn away from its early efforts at persuasion (in 1994, when it was confident about its hold over whites, and in the beginning of 1999) and focus on the white vote. Hence, a large core and a confident party produces mobilization (ANC 1999); a small core and a confident party produces persuasion (NP 1994); a large core and a nervous party produces persuasion (ANC 1994); and a small core and a nervous party produces mobilization (DP 1999, NP 1999).[49]

CAMPAIGN CONTENT

In 1999, as in 1994, politics-as-usual topics featured centrally in campaigns. Even though they largely agreed on most issues, parties devoted significant time to developing policy positions and presenting them to the electorate. The ANC's performance was also the subject of much campaigning, with parties diverging sharply on whether the ANC's record was good or bad. However, race overshadowed these topics. Of central importance were the racial images of the opposition parties. The ANC sought to paint them as mired in apartheid

---

[48] Gavin Davis makes a similar conclusion based on newspaper content analysis from the 1999 campaigns. See Gavin Davis, 2004. "Proportional Representation and Racial Campaigning in South Africa." *Nationalism and Ethnic Politics* 10(2): 297–324.

[49] Davis (2004) provides an alternative explanation for party strategy. In his account, proportional representation (PR) rules induce parties to focus on mobilization over persuasion. While interesting and perhaps complementary to the account given here, this explanation cannot account for changes in strategies across elections when electoral rules stay the same, nor can it explain variation across parties in the same system.

thinking and interested only in protecting white interests. The DP and the NNP resisted these claims, arguing that they were evidence of the prejudicial, racialized thinking of the ANC. They also turned the same criticisms on each other. That the parties would invest energy in debating the opposition's image suggests two things: First, it indicates that they saw party images as critical to the persuasive efforts of the opposition (in particular, its ability to make headway with nonwhite voters). So long as the DP and NNP were seen as "white," they were not viable competitors for the nonwhite vote. Second, it suggests that the parties believed that the opposition's images were either ambiguous or had the potential to change. Otherwise, why enter into a public debate about them? Thus, although the lines of competition were clearly drawn along racial lines during the 1999 election, the parties behaved as if this pattern of competition was contingent on preserving the current status of the opposition's images. If the images changed, the patterns of competition could change, too. In the remainder of this section, I discuss first politics-as-usual concerns and then look more closely at the nature of racial campaigning.

## Policy and Performance

As in 1994, the ANC, NNP, and DP all presented extensive plans (manifestos) to the electorate, detailing the issues they believed were important and how they planned to deal with them. The ANC launched its manifesto at the end of March in an elaborate affair in Soweto that featured *kwaito* music and scores of ANC heavyweights. According to Lodge (1999a: 105), the manifesto was long (thirty-six pages) but unsurprising in content, emphasizing delivery, transformation, crime, corruption, jobs, and building a better Africa. It downplayed the government's neoliberal economic strategies (GEAR), devoting more time to more popular projects like infrastructure development and promising a better life for South Africans. The manifesto expressed support for the current Constitution, counteracting claims that the ANC planned to change it. As far as specific policies, the party promised better police conditions and tougher treatment of criminals. To stimulate job creation, it proposed regulating the private sector, redistributing economic power, increasing parastatal investment, and creating incentives for investment. It did not, however, endorse public employment (Lodge 1999a: 106). Lodge characterizes the entire package as somewhat left of center (and considerably left of the actual practices of the party in government).

The DP launched its manifesto, also quite long and detailed, at the end of March in Durban. Like the ANC, it emphasized crime, jobs, alleviating poverty, and stimulating growth (Welsh 1999 94–95). On crime, it endorsed policies very similar to the ANC. On job creation it diverged somewhat, continuing to argue (as it had in Parliament since at least 1997) against the government's labor policies (in particular, the Employment Equity Act) and in favor of more flexible ones (Welsh 1999: 93). The DP also opposed the ANC's affirmative action policies, believing that these were "re-racializing" South

Africa, and proposed reducing taxation and increasing privatization. On the topic of health, it took a more free-market approach than the ANC, emphasizing private supply of services rather than the expansion of state-supplied health care (Lodge 1999a). The NNP's manifesto converged significantly with that of the DP. Lodge characterizes these parties as being centrist or perhaps slightly right of center (Lodge 1999a: 108).

Altogether, the three parties agreed that the primary issues facing South Africa were jobs and crime. Differences did exist in their proposed solutions to these problems. DP and NNP policies were more market driven and envisioned a less extensive role for the state than those of the ANC, differences that emerged most clearly in labor market and affirmative action proposals. However, these differences were not terribly sharp. All three parties fell in the middle of the political spectrum. Furthermore, policy differences did not become the subject of extensive debates during the campaigns, perhaps because the points of contention were too small to be of much interest to the average voter. As Lodge (1999a: 134) writes: "[T]he disagreements were in the details – the differences often too complicated to project persuasively in the condensed messages of electoral propaganda." In any case, most observers of the election agreed that the election was not marked by significant debate over policy issues. Breytenbach (1999: 123) writes: "[I]t should not be forgotten that on macroeconomic policies and on the need to eradicate crime and violence from South African society, there were no serious differences between the government and any of the opposition parties to the right of the ANC." Hence, despite the emphasis given to issues, a sharp, principled debate over policies never emerged in the election.

In contrast, the performance record of the ANC did elicit diverging viewpoints. The ANC's term in office had failed to bring about the massive influx of foreign investment many in the administration had hoped for. Instead, the economy limped along with lower than expected growth. Unemployment, if anything, increased. The ANC also struggled to meet the promises it had made during the 1994 election, especially in the area of housing, and official crime levels ratcheted upward. Given this backdrop, it is not surprising that the South African electorate turned increasingly sour on the ANC during the year prior to the election. ANC internal polls and focus groups revealed a surly public, with Africans articulating despair with their personal situations and disgust with the flashy lifestyles of politicians.[50] Much of this unhappiness crystallized on the issues of jobs and crime. In both areas, the electorate felt the ANC was performing poorly. Seventy-three percent of respondents in the September 1998 Idasa survey cited job creation as one of the most important problems facing the country, but only 12 percent believed the government was

---

[50] For a lengthy discussion of ANC knowledge about and responses to the mood of the public in the period leading up to the 1999 elections, see Greenberg, Stanley. 2009. *Dispatches from the War Room: In the Trenches with Five Extraordinary Leaders*. New York: Thomas Dunne Books, St. Martin's Press.

handling the problem well or very well. Sixty-four percent similarly listed crime, but only 18 percent gave the government a positive rating in this area. Overall, the great majority of survey respondents (close to 80 percent) gave the government a negative performance rating on its management of the economy. Minority groups were the most negative, but Africans expressed strong reservations as well, with only 29 percent believing that the economy had improved over the prior twelve months.[51] Internal ANC polls suggested disgruntled African voters would not cross over to the NP or DP, but they might stay home in massive numbers, an outcome the ANC was keen to avoid.[52]

The opposition parties (especially the DP) attempted to use South Africa's lukewarm economic performance as a weapon against the ANC. Throughout its campaign, the DP adopted a stridently negative tone about the direction of the country and the ANC's reputed failures in putting it on a better path. The DP's primary slogan in the election was "Fight Back," by which it meant fight back against "crime, corruption, unemployment, unfairness, racism and power-abuse" (Welsh 1999: 97). It portrayed itself as a watchdog, as an aggressive and necessary opposition party that was ready to take to task the governing party for its failures – a job the NNP could not, or would not, do. The NNP, for its part, initially campaigned on a positive message, but by the end of its campaign had adopted the DP's negativity.

Rather than dodge criticisms about its record, the ANC decided to face them head-on, turning the election into a referendum on performance. Once again consulting Stanley Greenberg, it followed a two-pronged attack. First, it emphasized, over and over again, the positive outcomes it had achieved. Lodge (1999a: 118) writes: "[T]he essential message constituted an upbeat statistical litany of government achievement: 750 000 new houses, 500 clinics, clean water for three million citizens, electrification and telephones, as well as free health care for pregnant women and young children." This message was evident in ANC speeches, campaign slogans, and advertisements. Second, the ANC took pains to acknowledge shortcomings where they existed. Lodge (1999a: 120) provides several examples of ANC party leaders doing this. In a speech in the Eastern Cape, Winnie Madikizela-Mandela told a crowd that the "The picnic is over ... we are aware of our weaknesses." One ANC advertisement explained that "much work lies ahead" and another explained that "sadly we have found out that even some who fought for freedom have also become corrupt." Altogether, the party's message was that, although it had many great accomplishments, it understood that it had to do better and asked the electorate to continue working with it to make further gains possible. On the advice of Greenberg, it painted economic changes as a "work in progress" and pledged to keep "fighting for change."[53]

---

[51] See Idasa (1998b).
[52] Greenberg, *Dispatches from the War Room.*.
[53] Greenberg, *Dispatches from the War Room.*

In sum, the same record of performance received very different interpretations by the parties. The DP (and eventually the NNP) emphasized the negative aspects of the ANC term: rising unemployment, problems with corruption, crime, and so on. The ANC acknowledged problems but also pointed to its successes and promised to do better in the future. In this sense, the 1999 election resembled elections everywhere: the incumbent and its opponents debated the latter's performance record.

**Party Images**

In spite of the apparent focus on politics-as-usual topics and concerns, the debate over performance between the ANC and its opposition also had a racial subtext. If the ANC had been reluctant in 1994 to resort to negative (read racial) campaigning, its squeamishness was gone by 1999. The ANC took great pains to emphasize and highlight the "whiteness" of the opposition. In so doing, it sought to both de-legitimate the opposition as a viable competitor for the African, coloured, and Indian vote and discredit the opposition's complaints about ANC performance.

These tactics started prior to the 1999 elections. At the ANC's annual party conference held in December 1997, Mandela gave a speech that disturbed many South Africans, not in the least leaders of the opposition parties. In the speech, Mandela charged that the opposition parties "have chosen to propagate a reactionary, dangerous and opportunist position which argues that: a normal and stable democracy as been achieved; the apartheid system is a thing of the past; their legitimate responsibility is to oppose us as the majority party, thus to present themselves as elements of a shadow government which has no responsibility both for our past and our present; and consequently that they have ademocratic obligation merely to discredit the ruling party ..." (quoted in Welsh 1999: 93). What disturbed many about this speech was that Mandela seemed to view opposition itself as negative, or even reactionary. He also raised the specter of apartheid, suggesting that, because the opposition played a role in this, it therefore could not credibly criticize the ruling party. For many, this signaled the ANC's move away from the "high road" of its 1994 campaign, in which it largely avoided negative campaigning on the opposition's apartheid past.

In the 1999 elections, this line of attack continued. Welsh (1999: 93) writes that: "[T]he campaign itself was dominated by race.... The ANC, appearing to acknowledge that the DP offered the sharpest challenge, repeatedly accused it of being 'racist,' 'reactionary', 'opposed to transformation' and of 'clinging to minority privileges." The ANC's attack, though perhaps most fiercely leveled at the DP, also extended to the NNP. Examples abound. Mandela characterized both parties as "trying to protect the interests of right-wing whites"[54] and

---
[54] *Star* (1999d).

## The 1999 Campaigns

called them "cousins" who only wanted to use nonwhite voters to entrench white power. To a group of coloured voters in Johannesburg he suggested that "Van Schalkwyk despises the intelligence of the coloured people, he tells a lie because he wants to use them as voting cattle."⁵⁵ To a Northern Cape audience, he said: "Ask Tony Leon, ask Marthinus Van Schalkwyk, when they come to you: 'What have you as individuals done for our people? And they will evade the question.'"⁵⁶ Along similar lines, Winnie Madikizela-Mandela asked: "Who is Tony Leon in our struggle? Why is he always attacking strong black women like me?"⁵⁷

In the Western Cape, the ANC focused pointedly on the message that the NP was using coloured voters to entrench white privilege. It suggested that, although nonwhites were getting a chance for a better life in most parts of South Africa, they were being left out in the Western Cape because the ruling NP was bent on thwarting transformation.⁵⁸ In a pamphlet entitled "wat het die NP vir ons gedoen" ("What has the NP done for us?"), it accused the NP of spending disproportionately on whites, leaving coloured police underfunded and at the mercy of gangs and criminals.⁵⁹ In a campaign meeting, Ferlon Christians, a recent convert from the NNP, told a coloured audience that "The NNP is no party for bruin mense [brown people]." He claimed a white elite still ran the party and that the coloured NNP premier, Gerald Morkel, and his coloured ministers were simply "puppets" and "clowns" of the Broederbond. He asked:

Why are the waiters at the waterfront still white children, and not our children? Why do all the important jobs in the civil service still go to whites, and why are our children, who have got their matric, not good enough to fill those jobs?⁶⁰

Finally, the ANC cleverly attacked the DP's "Fight Back" slogan. In the Western Cape, the party printed up look-alike posters but changed the wording to "Don't Fight Blacks." Although the ANC was ordered to take its posters down, the move received extensive media coverage and became one of the most memorable moments in the entire campaign. ANC leaders further hammered home this message in interviews and speeches. Cameron Dugmore, the spokesperson for the ANC in the Western Cape, explained:

It's clear the ANC did not initiate a poster war and it is also clear that the DP has become the home of conservative, gun-toting elements who are responding to the essentially racist call of (DP leader) Tony Leon to fight back.⁶¹

---

⁵⁵ *Star* (1999e).
⁵⁶ *Star* (1999c).
⁵⁷ See Paton (1999b).
⁵⁸ See Heard and Paton (1999).
⁵⁹ See Lodge (1999a: 142).
⁶⁰ See ter Horst (1999).
⁶¹ See *Star* (1999b). Dugmore was responding to an incident in which a DP supporter, after being harassed by ANC members, pulled out a gun and fired a shot into the air, claiming that his leader told him to "fight back."

Gauteng premier-elect Mbhazima Shilowa, in a May Day rally on the East Rand, conveyed a similar sentiment when he said:

> There are those who want to continue with transformation and those who want to take us back. ... I hope that with the coming together of a conservative right-wing element in the DP, there is not some small town AWB member who sees "Fight Back" and "Fight Black."[62]

Although these quotes carefully speak of "conservative right-wing elements" instead of referring directly to race, the underlying message was that the DP's campaign, and the party itself, were deeply racist. Through this simple turn of words, the ANC reframed the election from being one about the ANC's performance to the whiteness of the DP.

Welsh (1999) suggests that the ANC's recasting of the election in a racial light was reflected in the media's coverage of the election. He argues that the English-language press, as well as the South African Broadcasting Company (SABC), bought into this message such that "the DP-as-rightwing became a kind of mantra whose mere repetition strengthened the perception in some quarters that the accusations were true" (Welsh 1999: 96). He references an internal SABC document leaked during the campaign that instructs journalists to suggest that the DP's campaign "made it unacceptable to the majority of Black voters," along with quotes from prominent journalists to back these claims.

The DP attempted to respond to the ANC efforts to portray it as exclusively white by pointing out the underlying racism of the ANC's claims, but it had difficulty doing so. Welsh (1999) summarizes much of the DP's argument. First, the DP contested the representation of its "Fight Back" slogan as racist. As put by Leon, "only those blinded by a bizarre racial bigotry could assume it was directed at any group" (quoted in Welsh 1999: 97). Instead, reiterated the party, the slogan was not aimed at blacks but at the many failings of the ANC: It attacked the ANC's performance, not its African constituency. Second, the DP argued that it did not shift to the right to attract white voters; instead, white voters shifted to the left, adopting the DP's liberal principals. As Errol Moorcroft, a DP Member of Parliament explained: "Having railed against liberalism for decades as a threat to their survival, many Afrikaners now identify liberalism as the guarantor of their future" (quoted in Welsh 1999: 96). Whites' attraction to the party was ideological, not racial, and the party had not sold its liberal soul to attract white votes. Third, the party claimed that it had expended between 60 and 70 percent of its budget targeting nonwhites and that its substantive message highlighted the unacceptability of the current income gap between the rich and poor in South Africa. It disagreed not with the ANC's goals (of alleviating poverty), but with its heavy-handed racially based methods (e.g., affirmative action, black empowerment). As

---

[62] *Sunday Times* (1999b).

Welsh (1999: 94) put it: "The DP's opposition to [the ANC's] social engineering was not animated by racism." Finally, it acknowledged that its efforts were strongest with non-Africans but argued that this was a short-term strategy. In the long term, its goal was to win over the African electorate; but before this could happen, it needed a larger legislative and electoral presence. Hence, easier votes first, harder votes second.

These arguments were a hard sell, however. The nature of the DP's campaign (the symbolic gestures aimed at whites, the inclusion of white conservatives on the lists, the campaign technology and style, the negative message, and pugilistic stance of the party leader) supports claims that it was prioritizing whites. This may have been a short-term strategy, but it lent credibility to the ANC's claims that the DP had picked up the apartheid mantle of the NNP. Furthermore, many of the DP's arguments were cerebral, whereas the ANC's response was visceral and simple ("Don't Fight Blacks"). This message was projected and repeated in the press and by voters in a way that the DP's messages were not. In this way, the ANC won the battle to frame the election. Reflecting this, Tony Leon's approval ratings amongst Africans declined over the course of the election.[63] Moreover, the DP's image became *whiter* over the 1994 to 1999 period: whereas 34 percent of Africans saw the party as inclusive in 1994, only 13 percent had this opinion in 1999 (with uncertain responses remaining roughly constant).

In sum, although parties devoted significant space to politics-as-usual issues (policy stances, performance records), race formed an important subtext to the 1999 elections. The ANC took pains to paint the opposition – especially the DP – as a reactionary white party whose heart and soul were still grounded in apartheid. The DP's campaign decisions made this claim more believable. The end result of this was that the DP was discredited as a viable competitor for the African vote. Furthermore, the ANC was able to shift the frame of the debate away from questions about its performance record. Because the DP was discredited as a viable opposition party, its critique of the ANC was also discredited, allowing the ANC to sell a different, far more positive story about its performance record. In this way, the debate about race enveloped the debate about performance. Finally, although much about the election followed predictable racial lines, the very fact that the ANC felt the need to harp on the DP's whiteness and its argument about performance suggests that the party was insecure about its long-term hold over the African electorate. Indeed, its internal polls and focus groups indicated that its hold on the African vote was not guaranteed; many Africans had deep concerns about the party and would need to be won over. Should that electorate develop a different view of the opposition, one that made it and its criticism of the ANC more credible, then the ANC might find itself in a much more competitive world.

---

[63] See Harris et al. (1999: 3–4).

## CONCLUSION

The 1999 election in South African brought a retreat from the racially bridging campaigns that marked the 1994 election. The ANC engaged in persuasion efforts vis-à-vis African voters only when faced with an organized, African competitor. Elsewhere, it focused on getting Africans to the polls. It ignored white voters. The DP, for its part, set its sights on wooing over whites from the National Party. Its efforts to attract African votes were perfunctory at best. Even the NP, which had initially courted the African electorate, backed away from this strategy in the face of collapsing white support. In short, the 1999 campaigns more closely resembled Horowitz's portrayal of mobilizing elections in divided countries.

This does not mean, however, that party images ceased to matter in the campaigns of the ANC and its opposition. Indeed, the party images of the opposition were as important as ever in shaping campaign strategy and content. On the one hand, the ANC viewed the opposition's images as secure enough in the short term to focus on mobilization. On the other hand, it engaged in a metacampaign aimed at preserving the opposition's image as it was: too white to be credible in the African electorate. The opposition parties contested the ANC's portrayals, but their own actions as they battled for control of the white electorate made the ANC's claims more believable. This was especially true of the DP. The DP had come dangerously close to oblivion in 1994, polling less than 2 percent of the vote. Party strategists believed African votes were out of reach in the short term, so they fought an aggressive campaign to ensure the survival of their party by taking white, coloured, and Indian voters away from the NP. They hoped that by building a solid base of supporters in these communities and a presence in the legislature, they would be better placed in the long term to move into the African market. In this, however, they made a strategic blunder. For in the process of courting white votes, they alienated Africans. Indeed, more Africans viewed the DP as exclusive in 1999 than had in 1994. The party succeeded in becoming the official opposition, but only at the cost of a more multiracial image.

# 5

# The 2004 Campaigns

On April 15, 2004, South Africa held its third post-apartheid national elections, which the ruling ANC won by a wide margin, taking almost 70 percent of the total vote and winning outright majorities in seven out of nine provinces. In the remaining two provinces – the Western Cape and KwaZulu-Natal – it won pluralities and quickly formed governments with coalition partners. As in 1999, the Democratic Party (now the Democratic Alliance) captured the most votes (around 12 percent of the total) of any opposition party, increasing its size by about 3 percentage points from the earlier election. ANC and DA gains came at the expense of the Inkatha Freedom Party (IFP), which saw support dip from about 8.5 percent in 1999 to 7 percent in 2000, and, more spectacularly, the New National Party (NNP), whose support fell from around 7 percent to under 2 percent (even in the Western Cape, the NNP's support evaporated). Two somewhat odd pre-electoral coalitions – one between the ANC and the NNP and the other between the DA and the IFP – seemed only to strengthen the hands of the ANC and DA. In terms of the smaller opposition parties, the United Democratic Movement (UDM) fell under 3 percent of the overall vote and also lost ground on its home turf (the Eastern Cape). A newcomer, the Independent Democrats (ID), led by Patricia de Lille, registered just under 2 percent of the overall vote but was stronger in the Western Cape (where it captured close to 8 percent of the vote). All together, the election mirrored earlier ones with the largest and second largest parties slightly concentrating their support at the expense of smaller ones.

As suggested by its meager polling results, the NNP's sun had set by 2004. Although formally independent (it would not officially merge with the ANC until after the election), it acted primarily as an auxiliary to the ruling party during the campaigns. It did not articulate original policy positions or play a major role in campaign discourse. Its principal job seemed to be to attack the DA. The DA, in contrast, solidified its position as the primary opposition party. I therefore focus on the campaigns of the DA and ANC in this chapter, looking at the targets of their campaign efforts and their strategies, as well as the contents of their campaigns.

In many ways, the 2004 elections represented a return to the persuasion-oriented efforts of 1994. After courting the white vote in 1999, the DA set its sights on the African electorate in 2004. In moves designed to attract African votes, the party distanced itself from apartheid and sought to convey a racially inclusive image. The ANC, for its part, also attempted to bridge the racial divide, making repeated and highly publicized forays into white communities in search of votes. More fundamentally, the ANC fought a defensive campaign aimed at neutralizing the persuasive efforts of the DA, which had become its primary opponent.

Central in these defensive efforts of the ruling party were repeated attacks on the DA's image. As hard as the DA tried to portray itself as Africanizing, the ANC – which had deeper campaign pockets and more exposure in the media – fought to keep its opponent white. Indeed, the DA's image assumed central focus in the campaign, vying with jobs as the second most frequently discussed topic by parties (ANC performance was the first) and beating out crime and HIV/AIDS. Moreover, although the DA received substantial coverage by newspapers during the campaigns, Africans were less certain after the elections about the party's image than they had been in 1994, when the party was relatively unknown. This suggests that the primary effect of the he said/she said battle of words between the ruling party and its opposition was simply *to muddy the waters*. The contradictory messages cancelled one another out, leaving the electorate just as confused (if not more) than it had been prior to the election.

Unlike Chapter 3 and Chapter 4, which rely primarily on existing studies to track campaign activity, in this chapter I make use of a dataset consisting of close to 1,200 newspaper articles clipped from nine newspapers in the eight-week period prior to the 2004 elections. These articles provide the basis for a narrative account of the elections, as well as a more systematic analysis of patterns and content of party rhetoric. In the next section, I discuss the dataset in greater detail. I then move on to look at persuasion versus mobilization in the strategies of the DA and ANC, the content of campaigns, and the debate over party images in them.

THE DATASET

While impressionistic analysis provides a fine sense of the flavor and texture of the campaigns, it is always open to the criticism that the researcher plays too heavy a hand in the shaping of the story that emerges. For this reason, I undertook content analysis of newspaper reports for the fifty-five–day period prior to the election (clipping began the fourth week of February and ended at the election on April 15). I culled articles from ten different dailies and weeklies: *Mail & Guardian, This Day, The Star, City Press, Sunday Times, Sowetan, Cape Times, The Financial Mail, Business Day,* and *The Sunday Independent*. Altogether 1,148 articles on the election were clipped, with an average of about 21 articles per day.[1] To economize on time, I selected a random sample of 400 articles for close analysis. (More details on the newspapers and sample are in the Appendix at the end of this chapter).

The goal of content analysis was to assess the nature of campaign strategies (persuasion versus mobilization) and the content of campaigns (race versus issues, policy, and performance). For both, I looked at reports of campaign *rhetoric* (specific quotes attributed to spokespeople officially associated with parties) along with campaign *activities*. Altogether, the sample of 400 articles yielded 218 observations of rhetoric and 71 campaign events. To assess campaign strategy, I looked at the flow of rhetoric between parties, what I call "rhetorical sparring partners" – Who did the ANC talk most about? Who did the DA talk most about? This gives a measure of the primary fault lines in the election and whether parties viewed one another as competitors. To the extent that the ANC viewed the DA as a true competitor, the election involved persuasion. I also characterized rhetoric according to whether it is bridging or bonding (were parties reaching across the racial divide or sticking with their primary constituencies)[2] and did the same for campaign visits (did parties visit only their home constituencies or did they also spend time in other racial communities?). To assess campaign content, I looked at the subject of party rhetoric – did it reference issues, policy, performance, race, or some combination therein? Which topics occurred most frequently? Were there differences across parties in patterns of rhetoric or did they converge?

Content analysis requires a clear set of rules for coding articles. In the case of this project, deciding when rhetoric involved race, issues, policy, or performance proved challenging. Some issues/policies have strong racial overtones (examples are affirmative action, "transformation," Black Economic Empowerment, land reform, and crime). Does mention of these policies constitute racial priming? Performance can also be turned into a racial issue (and this has happened with some frequency in the 2004 elections, as I will discuss later in this chapter). When the DA accused the ANC of poor performance, was this a racial slur (the implication being that Africans are incompetent)? Or was the party merely doing what opposition parties everywhere do – criticize the incumbent? The ANC often claimed the former about the DA's performance criticisms, while the DA argued the latter.

Furthermore, as Mendelberg (2001) shows, "racial" frames have varying degrees of subtlety. Parties often cue race with nonracial terms commonly understood by the audience and orator as racial. For example, when the ANC refers not to whites but to "former apartheid oppressors," is this racial or not? A racial word is not used, but South Africans understand the racial

---

[1] Many thanks to Jonathan Faull at Idasa for his help in organizing the South African end of this project. Any faults in interpretation are my own.
[2] I borrow this language from Davis, Gavin. 2004. "Proportional Representation and Racial Campaigning in South Africa." *Nationalism and Ethnic Politics* 10: 297–324.

significance: Apartheid oppressors were white. In another example, the DA addresses a largely black audience, it plays black music, and it surrounds its white leader with black faces as he instructs the audience on the numerous ways in which his party's policy will benefit them and communities with other people like them. Is this racial? The party uses the race of the audience to convey its point without direct reference to race. The DA speaks of its supporters in the townships, without calling them black or African. It avoids racial terms, but South Africans all know that township residents are largely African. The ANC talks of how the DA is a "right-wing party" that will not look out for the poor. "Right wing" is an ideological descriptor, but all right-wing parties in South Africa (with the possible exception of the IFP, which is sometimes thought of as conservative) are white. Hence, right wing might simply be a way of signaling race without actually using racial terms. There is no way to avoid judgment calls on these issues: They involve interpretation and subtly. Any coding solution is therefore necessarily arbitrary.

For the purposes of this book, I followed fairly conservative coding rules that will tend to *underestimate* racial rhetoric. They were as follows:

- A handful of policies were defined as explicitly racial policies and coded according to a racial frame. These are Black Economic Empowerment, Affirmative Action, and "transformation" more broadly. All of these involve the promotion of Africans (sometimes coloureds and Indians) and African interests in formerly white-dominated economic, political, and social institutions. In general, these policies came up infrequently in the 2004 election.
- Simple performance claims (e.g., the ANC has failed to deliver good growth) were not coded as racial, but counterclaims about performance that invoke a racial dimension (e.g., ANC claims that the DA is playing racial politics when it brings up performance) are coded as racial.
- Articles and rhetoric got a racial coding when they evoked explicit racial terms or terms with a very strong and commonly understood racial dimension. Altogether, the following terms were taken as indicating race: race, racial, nonracial, multiracial, rainbow, black, white, brown, coloured, Indian, African, apartheid, township residents, transformation, anti-transformation, and "former oppressors." Other terms with a plausible but deniable racial connection were not deemed racial. Examples are references to ideological position ("right wing") and economic groups ("the poor"). The racial terms were culled from articles during an initial experimental coding run that used a different set of articles from the 400 used in the random sample.
- The context of rhetoric, if not noted in the rhetoric, did not affect the coding of the rhetoric. If the DA spoke of its policies to a black audience but did not mention race or an explicit racial code word, its rhetoric was not coded as racial.

Coding did not force a decision between types of frames. Rhetoric could (and often did) have multiple frames. References to affirmative action, for example, were coded as being both racial and policy based. As mentioned previously these rules will tend to *underestimate* the extent of racial cue making by parties. In the following sections, I review campaign strategy (persuasion versus mobilization) and then move on to a discussion of the role played by race in the content of the campaigns.

PERSUASION AND MOBILIZATION

The ANC and the DA invested substantially more effort and resources in cross-racial persuasion in 2004 versus 1999. This was evident in their choice of campaign partners: The ANC formed an alliance with the (white) NNP and the DA with the (African) IFP. It was also clear in their campaign events (where they were located, their target audiences, the issues showcased during them) and the target and nature of their rhetoric (who they talked about and what they said). In contrast to 1999, when the DA focused on the white electorate, it actively sought African votes in 2004. It would, in the words of DA Communications Director Nick Clelland-Stokes, "take on the ANC in its own backyard."[3] This meant spending more time in African communities, listening to African voters, and fashioning messages that would appeal to them.

The ANC, for its part, also reached across the racial divide. While it devoted most of its campaign time and resources to African communities, it made periodic efforts to court whites. More importantly, while the ANC continued to publically deride the DA as an insignificant political force, it targeted most of its rhetorical attacks at the DA. This suggests that the DA had become the ANC's main competition and that the ANC took DA efforts to win African votes as a viable threat to its hegemony. Finally, when talking about their own parties, ANC and DA politicians avoided identifying them with specific racial groups, claiming instead to be multiracial and inclusive. In contrast, they castigated their opponents as racial chauvinists. The ANC was especially aggressive about portraying the DA in these terms, suggesting again that the goal of party behavior was not simply mobilization but persuasion: for the DA, persuading Africans to cross over; for the ANC, persuading them to stay loyal. I discuss each of these strategies in greater depth in the following.

## Campaign Events

Campaign events are a useful means for gauging a party's intentions. Time is a limited resource on the campaign trail, particularly the time of the party leader. Party leaders can only visit a limited number of venues each day. Major party events (the launching of the party manifesto, the unveiling of lists, the celebration of holidays) occur only a few times during the campaign period. Hence, campaign events provide a window into the priorities of the party, an indication of which groups and regions a party is focusing on.

---

[3] Quoted in Marianne Merten, "DA to 'Take on the ANC in Its Own Backyard'." *Mail & Guardian*, January 9, 2004.

By this measure, the DA had shifted strategies between 1999 and 2004. Whereas in 1999 it expended most of its effort on the white community (recall Tony Leon riding the white horse through Ventersdorp and visiting the *Vrouemonument*), in 2004 it had shifted some of its focus to Africans. It held major events in African areas: the manifesto launch in Soweto, the unveiling of its lists, and a final rally the day before the election to an African audience in Durban. It claimed to be engaging in extensive door-to-door campaigning in African areas (especially in Gauteng).[4] Leon made several well-publicized visits to African townships. In late March, he visited the tombstone of Hector Peterson in Soweto and laid a wreath for him, saying "[W]e must learn from the history of our nation so that we do not repeat it."[5] Leon often used these visits as opportunities to criticize the ANC's record of delivery to poor African communities and to highlight DA policies geared toward Africans. In late February he visited a crumbling hospital in the Gauteng town of Vereeniging, where he met with homeless unemployed Africans and listened to their frustrations on the slowness of ANC housing delivery and job creation. He also advertised the DA basic income grant policy.[6] At a rally in an East London squatter camp, Leon waived a copy of a fax sent from a local municipality, on ANC letterhead, that solicited funds from local business people, claiming it was strong evidence of "corruption in action."[7] Leon and Mangosuthu Buthelezi visited Thembisa (a township in Gauteng) and paid tribute to a woman who had been providing home care to hundreds of AIDS patients without government assistance. They used the opportunity to criticize the ANC's policies, accusing the government of neglect.[8] The overall message of these visits, explained by Hermene Koorts, DA Member of the Provincial Legislature (MPL) in the Gauteng, was to show that Leon understood the frustrations of ordinary South Africans:

While Mbeki says he knows of no one who has died of Aids, Leon has held Aids orphans in his arms. When President Mbeki flies around in a R600-million jet, Leon visits communities where unemployment is rife, and where Mbeki drives around in a six-car cavalcade, Leon talks directly to the victims of crime, trying to understand

---

[4] "Digging for Gauteng's Pot of Gold." *This Day*, March 31, 2004.
[5] Hector Peterson was a schoolboy who was killed on June 16, 1976 by the South African police during a protest against Afrikaans being used as a medium of instruction in black schools. His death sparked massive riots in Soweto that spread around the country. His tombstone is therefore an important symbol of the anti-apartheid struggle. For an account of Leon's visit, see "'Remember the Suffering.'" *The Sowetan*, March 23, 2004. Not everyone was impressed by his efforts. Peterson's sister, Antoinette Sithole, opined that "The DA is only coming now that we are approaching elections. The DA is obviously looking for something to gain and I don't for one, buy into their tactics." See Cecil Motsepe, "Tony Leon's Soweto Boo-Boo." *The Sowetan*, March 23, 2004.
[6] Caiphus Kgosana, "Grumbles about Empty Promises at DA Meeting." *The Star*, February 25, 2004.
[7] Christelle Terreblanche, "Tony Leon Accuses ANC of Corruption." *The Star*, March 19, 2004.
[8] Kristy Siegfried, "Leaders Laud Woman with Loads of Love." *The Star*, March 26, 2004.

their situation. It is a shame that the ANC has reduced communities like Vereeniging to such an advanced state of skepticism, but that will not stop the DA or Leon from trying to relate to and address the concerns of ordinary South Africans.[9]

The DA also emphasized its growing membership and branch openings in African townships.[10] It is unclear exactly how deep the DA's African membership was, but the party certainly attempted to portray it as growing.[11] Nick Clelland-Stokes explained:

> We've been able to win votes from the ANC and grow in black constituencies. We've committed enormous money and resources in identifying the things that black voters want and what they identify with. Until the launch of the campaign, Tony Leon has held 456 events in townships, squatter camps and rural constituencies. Not stage managed *imbizos* where selected people tell Thabo Mbeki he is great, but real, spontaneous information sessions.... We're going to fight this election on the terrain of the better life that the ANC promised 10 years ago. We'll be taking the fight to the ANC's own psychological territory.... We are spending a lot of money to communicate with black voters.[12]

A change was also apparent in ANC strategy. While the ruling party spent most of its time in African communities (Mbeki toured exhaustively during the month leading up to the election), the party also reached across the racial divide in search of new supporters. On one hand, it sought to preserve its links with white capitalists. Early in the campaign season, Mbeki reassured a high-powered group of businessmen that "there will be no rebellion among the masses of our people." In support of this claim, he argued (rather candidly) that poor South Africans trusted the ANC and therefore would not jeopardize investment in the country.[13]

More significantly (and a departure from earlier campaigns), the ANC also went after white votes. As Western Cape provincial leader Ebrahim Rasool explained: "We [the ANC] are not leaving any area uncontested, even the white communities. [They] are in need of a new dispensation, new politics. We will never be accused of not taking our message there."[14] Gauteng Minister of Safety Nomvula Mokonyane (also head of the provincial organizing and

---

[9] Hermene Koorts, "DA Rvives Hope Lost because of ANC." Letter to the editor, *The Star*, February 27, 2004.

[10] For example, DA election campaign spokesman Douglas Gibson claimed that "Since its formation in 2000 the DA has systematically increased its support among black communities. The DA youth leadership is predominantly black, a reflection of the growing support the DA enjoys among the black electorate." Douglas Gibson, "DA Offers Hope of a Better SA." Letter to the editor, *Business Day*, March 3, 2004.

[11] For a discussion of this, see Lodge (2003).

[12] Quoted in Paddy Harper, "DA Spin Machine Sells Slick Self-Confidence." *The Star*, February 22, 2004.

[13] Quoted in Mpumelelo Mkhabela, "Poor Won't Rebel – Mbeki." *City Press*, February 22, 2004.

[14] Quoted in Rapule Tabane, "ANC Targets Mlungu Vote," *Mail & Guardian*, January 23, 2004.

mobilization unit) echoed these sentiments, saying the ANC had failed in the past to communicate directly with whites but was altering its strategy in the 2004 election. He said "the focus on this campaign is to explain to them why they should vote ANC; why the ANC is their home."[15] In keeping with this goal, the ANC sent groups of politicians into white areas around South Africa to canvass door-to-door for white votes.[16]

Complementing these efforts, Mbeki also made a series of highly publicized visits to white communities during the campaign period. During these visits, which targeted both poor and affluent white neighborhoods, he shook hands, helped remedy small problems, and left behind surprised and delighted potential supporters. In early March, for example, he delivered the mail in several white neighborhoods in Pretoria. Along the way, he listened to complaints and promised help.[17] In mid-March, he visited the working-class white neighborhood of Rugby on the Western Cape, shaking hands, posing for photos, and promising to address eviction problems in the area.[18] In early April, he visited the white community of Kempton Park in Johannesburg, where he played with children and chatted with parents.[19] In a campaign speech in KwaZulu-Natal, Mbeki acknowledged that poverty had increased amongst whites in the ten years since 1994, and that it was a mistake by government not to pay attention to this.[20] And in an extensive interview a few days prior to the election, Mbeki explained his new understanding of South African whites:

Personally, I had not realized the extent of the poverty among the poor white sections of the white community.... The fact that on average the whites live better than the national average does not mean every white lives better and above the national average.... You can see the level of poverty and desperation...honestly, I hadn't understood it to that extent. But they actually share in the same mood as the black majority: confidence in the future and confidence in the government. Talking with the young whites, they also expressed surprise that the government actually cares about what they think.... They thought we didn't care, [they thought] they are a surplus population and we would ignore them.[21]

In addition to these high-profile visits, newspapers (especially those favorable to the ANC) reported flowerings of white ANC support in surprising places: poor, conservative Afrikaner towns like Christiana in the North West Province that more typically supported conservative right-wing parties but

---

[15] Quoted in Tabane, "ANC Targets Mlungu Vote."
[16] Xolisa Vapi, "ANC Chases Afrikaner Voters in Brixton with Koeksister Politics." *This Day*, February 23, 2004. See also Mariechen Waldner, "How to Catch a Boer for the ANC." *City Press*, April 11, 2004.
[17] Charles Phahlane, "Postman Thabo's Delivery a Hit in Pretoria." *The Star*, March 9, 2004.
[18] Sheena Adams, "Disbelieving Rugby Residents Jostle to Get 'Kisses for Free' from Mbeki." *Cape Times*, March 15, 2004.
[19] Rapule Tabane, "There Is No Secret to Our Success." *Mail & Guardian*, April 2–7, 2004.
[20] "FF+ Will Hold Mbeki to his 'Poor-Whites' Vow." *Business Day*, March 23, 2004.
[21] "The people have faith in tomorrow." Interview with Mbeki. *City Press*, April 11, 2004.

TABLE 5.1. *Campaign Events (All)*

|  | ANC | DA | Total |
|---|---|---|---|
| Bridging | 9 | 8 | 17 |
|  | (19%) | (35%) | (24%) |
|  | (53%) | (47%) | (100%) |
| Partially bridging | 8 | 6 | 14 |
|  | (17%) | (26%) | (20%) |
|  | (57%) | (43%) | (100%) |
| Bonding | 26 | 2 | 28 |
|  | (54%) | (9%) | (39%) |
|  | (93%) | (7%) | (100%) |
| Unclear/neither | 5 | 7 | 12 |
|  | (10%) | (30%) | (17%) |
|  | (42%) | (58%) | (100%) |
| Total | 48 | 23 | 71 |
|  | (100%) | (100%) | (100%) |
|  | (68%) | (32%) | (100%) |

*Notes*: The ANC column includes events where the ANC participated as part of the ANC/NNP team, and the DA column includes events where the DA participated as part of the DA/IFP team.

sought whatever benefits the ANC could extend.[22] These efforts to reach out to poor whites represented an important departure from the ANC's earlier campaigns.

While these events give a nice sense of the flavor of the campaigns, it is difficult to gauge whether they represent scattered incidents or a more systematic pattern. I therefore collected a record of campaign events from the 400-article sample detailed earlier, classifying each event according to whether it was bridging (reaching across the racial divide) or bonding (sticking within the party's traditional constituency). Mbeki's visit with voters in Rugby, a white working-class neighborhood in Cape Town, is an example of a bridging event. Mbeki's tour of the exclusively African Mamelodi township in Pretoria is an example of a bonding event. As shown by Table 5.1, of seventy-one total events held by the ANC and DA, twenty-eight (39 percent) were clearly bonding and thirty-eight (44 percent) were clearly bridging (the remainder could not be coded, either because information was lacking in the account or the crowd was mixed). Breaking down by party, about half of the ANC visits were bonding, whereas only 9 percent of the DA's fell into this category. If we look only at events in which the party leader participated (fifty-three events total for the two parties), bonding events were even less frequent – only about 30 percent

---

[22] See, for example, Tabane, "ANC Targets Mlungu Vote"; Dan Dhlamini, "AWB, FF Members Flocking to the ANC." *City Press*, February 22, 2004; Dan Dlahmini, "Members of the Volk Find Home in the ANC." *City Press*, February 29, 2004.

TABLE 5.2. *Rhetorical Sparring Partners*

| Target | Source | | | | | |
|---|---|---|---|---|---|---|
| | ANC | DA | NNP | IFP | ID | Total |
| ANC | 41 (57%) (41%) | 34 (44%) (34%) | 1 (4%) (1%) | 15 (63%) (15%) | 8 (38%) (8%) | 99 (45%) (100%) |
| DA | 12 (17%) (21%) | 31 (40%) (53%) | 9 (38%) (16%) | 1 (4%) (2%) | 5 (24%) (9%) | 57 (27%) (100%) |
| NNP | 0 (0%) (0%) | 2 (3%) (14%) | 12 (50%) (86%) | 0 (0%) (0%) | 0 (0%) (0%) | 14 (6%) (100%) |
| IFP | 9 (13%) (60%) | 0 (0%) (0%) | 0 (0%) (0%) | 6 (25%) (40$) | 0 (0%) (0%) | 15 (7%) (100%) |
| ID | 3 (4%) (19%) | 5 (6%) (31%) | 0 (0%) (0%) | 0 (0%) (0%) | 8 (38%) (50%) | 16 (7%) (100%) |
| ANC/NNP | 1 (1%) (11%) | 6 (8%) (67%) | 2 (8%) (22%) | 0 (0%) (0%) | 0 (0%) (0%) | 3 (4%) (100%) |
| "Opposition" | 5 (7%) (100%) | 0 (0%) (0%) | 0 (0%) (0%) | 0 (0%) (0%) | 0 (0%) (0%) | 5 (2%) (100%) |
| DA/IFP | 1 (1%) (33%) | 0 (0%) (0%) | 0 (0%) (0%) | 2 (8%) (67%) | 0 (0%) (0%) | 9 (1%) (100%) |
| Total | 72 (100%) (33%) | 78 (100%) (36%) | 24 (100%) (11%) | 24 (100%) (11%) | 21 (100%) (10%) | 218 (100%) (100%) |

of all events where the leader participated were classified as such. Less than half of the events involving Mbeki were directed exclusively at Africans. Only about 5 percent of the events involving Leon focused exclusively on whites.

## Rhetoric

We can also glean clues about party strategy by examining what they said and who they said it to. As parties are unlikely to speak about competitors they do not take seriously, we gain insight into patterns of competition by looking at references to competitors in speeches. To this end, Table 5.2 tracks the frequency with which parties spoke about each other (with 218 total observations of rhetoric). If parties were unconcerned with their opponents, most of their rhetoric would focus on themselves – not other parties – and the boxes along the diagonal of the table would be the most prominent. Alternatively, if parties were concerned with only same-race competitors, then the ANC would direct most of its rhetoric at either itself or the IFP, and the DA and the NNP would talk only about each other. The data in Table 5.2 contradict these expectations. It is true that the ANC directed most of its rhetoric at itself (a little more than half), but it is not true that it ignored the DA. In fact, *it directed more rhetoric at the DA than the IFP* – its historical nemesis in the African community. The ANC ignored the NNP – not a surprise, as they were coalition partners. For its part, the DA directed more rhetoric at the ANC than it did at itself (44 percent versus 40 percent) and almost completely ignored the NNP (only 3 percent of its rhetoric was directed at this party). Altogether, this suggests that the two largest parties – although currently representing different racial markets – had their eyes on each other, the DA because it hoped to woo away some of the ANC's support and the ANC because it sought to prevent the DA from doing so.

Further patterns emerge if we look at what the parties were saying about each other. When the ANC talked about itself, about seven of forty-one quotes (or 17 percent) were racial. Of these racial quotes, five involved rhetoric that referenced itself as a multiracial party ("bridging" rhetoric) and two involved rhetoric identifying itself as a party of Africans ("bonding" rhetoric). Thus, in forty-one instances of rhetoric about itself, only twice did the ANC paint itself as an exclusively "African" party. In contrast, when the ANC talked about the DA, fully half of its rhetoric was racial (six out of twelve instances) and all of it was bonding (i.e., it painted the DA as a racist or white party). For the DA, about a quarter of its rhetoric (eight out of thirty-one) about itself was racial. Of these, only two were bonding in nature. Hence, just as the ANC did little to paint itself as African, the DA did little to paint itself as white. When speaking about the ANC, the DA was very reluctant to raise race as an issue – only three out of thirty-four comments on the ANC (9 percent) did this. But all three of these comments painted the ANC as a bonding (African) party. Overall, both parties avoided explicit appeals to their "own" racial groups. When race entered their rhetoric, it was used either in a bridging fashion to reach out to groups across the racial divide or to paint an opponent as racist.

In sum, the data from this section are difficult to reconcile with parties motivated purely by mobilization. The DA teamed up with an African party, the IFP, almost certainly as a means to attract African voters. It directed most of its rhetoric at the ANC, not at white competitors. When it spoke of its own image, it almost always did so in bridging terms. Rarely – if ever – did it refer to itself as a white party. On the campaign trail, it spent most of its time in African areas.[23] Although preoccupied with its large African base,

---

[23] Further evidence of the bridging nature of the DA's campaign in 2004 comes from Davis (2005), who provides numerous examples of the DA's efforts to reach out to African votes. In terms of campaign posters, while the DA was not able to cover African townships as well as the ANC, it nevertheless made an impressive effort. On the main road between the African townships of Guguletu and Nyanga outside of Cape Town, there was one DA poster for every three ANC posters and most of the DA posters were in Xhosa (the language of most Africans

the ANC reached out repeatedly to white voters. It aligned itself with the National Party. When describing itself, it almost always did so in bridging terms. Very rarely did it claim to be an exclusively African party. It directed more rhetoric at the DA than the IFP, and about half of this rhetoric involved the DA's image. Thus, not only did the ANC reach out across the racial divide more than one might expect, it also displayed a certain amount of anxiety regarding the DA and its racial image. Such anxiety, more than anything else, suggests that the ANC did *not* believe that its African constituency was captured.

CAMPAIGN CONTENT

The 2004 campaigns covered a wide range of topics, including standard election fare like issue priorities, policy stances, and incumbent performance. Race formed an important undercurrent to much that was said, however. Responding to the DA's efforts to court African voters, the ruling party and its surrogates (including its coalition partner, the NNP) vigorously attacked the DA's image, contesting DA claims to Africanization and painting it as a right-wing white party whose apartheid-era leaders had no respect for or interest in African voters. The ANC also attempted to use the DA's whiteness to nullify its criticisms of ANC performance and question its policy proposals. Indeed, the DA's image figured nearly as centrally as jobs in the rhetoric of the parties during their campaigns. Thus, as hard as the DA fought to present itself as a newly reformed and multiracial party, the ANC fought just as hard to preserve its opponent's whiteness – and hence illegitimacy in the race for African votes. In this he said/she said environment, signals cancelled out, by and large leaving voters with substantial uncertainty about the true nature of the DA's image.

Issues and Policies

As in earlier elections, issues and policies formed an important arena of discussion. Table 5.3 breaks down rhetoric from five major parties into several categories: racial, nonracial identity, policy, priorities, and performance (see

---

in the area). In Imbali, an African working-class township outside of the KwaZulu-Natal city of Pietermaritzburg, 63% of the posters were ANC and 30% were DA. Along the main road leading into the Alexandra township in Johannesburg, there were forty ANC posters and twenty-two DA posters. These are scattered examples, of course, but they do suggest that the DA was investing significant resources in reaching out to African voters. Davis (2005) also notes that the DA spent R5.9 million on radio advertisements (compared with only R790,000 on print advertisements), outspending the ANC by more than R1 million. As many Africans get most of their political information via radio, this suggests an effort to reach African voters. Furthermore, R2 million of the money went to stations with a predominately black listenership. In contrast, the party spent only R1.3 million on stations with a predominately white readership.

# The 2004 Campaigns

TABLE 5.3. *Type of Rhetoric by Different Parties*

|  | ANC | DA | NNP | IFP | ID | Total |
|---|---|---|---|---|---|---|
| Nonracial Identity | 5 (7%) (56%) | 2 (2%) (22%) | 0 (0%) (0%) | 1 (4%) (11%) | 1 (5%) (11%) | 9 (4%) (100%) |
| Racial | 17 (24%) (41%) | 13 (17%) (32%) | 8 (33%) (20%) | 0 (0%) (0%) | 3 (14%) (7%) | 41 (19%) (100%) |
| Policy | 15 (21%) (36%) | 14 (18%) (33%) | 6 (25%) (14%) | 4 (17%) (10%) | 3 (14%) (7%) | 42 (19%) (100%) |
| Issue Priorities | 16 (22%) (31%) | 19 (24%) (37%) | 6 (25%) (12%) | 5 (21%) (10%) | 5 (24%) (10%) | 51 (23%) (100%) |
| Performance | 21 (29%) (31%) | 23 (29%) (34%) | 8 (33%) (12%) | 12 (50%) (18%) | 5 (24%) (7%) | 68 (31%) (100%) |
| Total | 72 - (33%) | 78 - (36%) | 24 - (11%) | 24 - (11%) | 21 - (10%) | 219 - (100%) |

*Notes*: Columns do not sum to total because quotes can have multiple subjects.

the appendix for a description of each of these).[24] Issues and policies were clearly important to parties: They named these in 42 percent of all quotes, enumerated them in manifestos, and reiterated them frequently throughout the campaign period.[25]

However, it would be difficult to argue that issues and policies generated the primary fault lines of the election. There was little principled debate between parties about the most important issues facing the country or how to deal with them. Table 5.4 shows the issues raised by parties and their frequencies.[26] At the top of the list were jobs, raised nineteen times by parties in

[24] Quotes can have multiple subjects and therefore can be counted several times in the columns – i.e., a single quote could have both a policy component and a performance component, which would cause it to be counted in both rows. Quotes can also have a subject other than identity, race, policy, issues, or performance. For this reason, the columns cannot be summed: There are seventy-two quotes by the ANC, but more than seventy-two quote categorizations because a single quote can have multiple categorizations.

[25] The parties identified their issues and laid out their policies in manifestos, which they launched in gala events early in the campaigns (most in late February or early March). Typically, the manifesto launches received significant attention in the media, where they were summarized and repeated many times. Parties also tended to reiterate their main points at speeches and other campaign events. Many also had websites where the complete manifestos were available. Hence, information about party issue priorities and policy stances was widely available – at least to those with access to newspapers.

[26] Quotes that mention issues can raise more than one issue. Therefore, the number of total issues in Table 5.3 exceeds the total number of quotes that mention issues in Table 5.1.

TABLE 5.4. *Issues Emphasized by Different Parties*

|  | ANC | DA | NNP | IFP | ID | Total |
|---|---|---|---|---|---|---|
| Jobs | 5 | 11 | 0 | 3 | 0 | 19 |
| Poverty | 3 | 6 | 1 | 4 | 1 | 15 |
| Crime | 0 | 13 | 0 | 0 | 1 | 14 |
| HIV | 1 | 8 | 0 | 3 | 2 | 14 |
| Services | 4 | 3 | 3 | 1 | 0 | 11 |
| Economic growth | 3 | 2 | 1 | 1 | 2 | 9 |
| Corruption | 1 | 2 | 0 | 2 | 0 | 5 |
| Economic inequality | 1 | 0 | 0 | 0 | 0 | 1 |
| Housing | 1 | 1 | 0 | 0 | 0 | 2 |
| Education | 0 | 2 | 0 | 0 | 1 | 3 |
| Gender inequality | 0 | 1 | 0 | 0 | 1 | 2 |
| Transformation | 1 | 0 | 0 | 0 | 0 | 1 |
| Foreign Affairs | 0 | 2 | 0 | 0 | 1 | 3 |
| Land | 0 | 0 | 0 | 0 | 1 | 1 |
| Other | 3 | 1 | 2 | 0 | 0 | 6 |
| Total | 23 | 52 | 7 | 14 | 10 | 106 |

*Notes*: Quotes can name multiple issues, so the number of issues named can exceed the number of quotes given in Table 5.1.

the sample, followed by poverty (fifteen times), crime (fourteen times), and HIV/AIDS (fourteen times). There were some minor differences in emphasis across parties. Both the DA and the ANC prioritized jobs. The ANC was more likely to raise poverty, the DA crime and HIV. The DA raised more issues than the ANC (fifty-two to the ANC's twenty-three) because when it brought up issues, it tended to name several all at once. In contrast, rhetoric from the ANC would discuss one or two issues at a time – usually jobs, poverty, and/or services. The NP, IFP, and ID registered fewer hits on issues (evidence of the DA's and ANC's domination of political discourse as covered by newspapers) but covered the same ground. In spite of these small differences, the overall picture painted by Table 5.4 is one of consensus: Parties more or less agreed on the issues facing the country.

Furthermore, on most key policy areas – especially the ones most central to the election – the DA and the ANC exhibited few differences. The DA had no arguments with the ANC's neoliberal macroeconomic policies, both parties supported privatization, both parties favored "get tough" criminal policies and proposed putting more police on the street (the same number, in fact), both parties had proposals for a basic (but limited) welfare net for the poorest of South Africa's citizens, and, perhaps most significantly, by the campaign period the ANC had converged on the DA's HIV policies (in particular, anti-retrovirals for all who are HIV-positive).[27] Indeed, leftist voices frequently

[27] For a good review of the government's efforts on HIV, see van der Vliet (2003). For an insightful discussion of the ANC's crime policies, see Gordon (2006).

criticized the ANC for being the DA in disguise.[28] As far as the other parties – none defined major alternatives to those posed by the DA or the ANC. The DA's alliance partner, the IFP, echoed the DA's positions, while the ANC's partner, the NNP, generally avoided saying much about specific policies. The ID, although quick to discuss issues, had few specific policy proposals.[29]

A few areas did exhibit differences between parties. Clear distinctions arose in prisoner sentencing laws (in an about-face, the DA allowed its MPs to support capital punishment while the ANC opposed it), black economic empowerment and affirmative action (the DA opposed both and the ANC supported). And, perhaps most prominently, the parties disagreed on labor market policies. The DA argued that greater investment and future growth depended on making the job market more flexible. In its view, Western European–style job protections and benefits were too costly for South Africa's developing economy. In a speech to Pretoria's Chamber of Commerce, Leon explained: "We have applied Rolls-Royce labour laws to a Volkswagen economy, and the results have been nothing short of disastrous."[30] The ANC – with its long history of trade union activism and alliance with COSATU – disagreed, arguing that the DA wanted to rob workers of the rights and protections they had fought hard to achieve. The ANC also attempted to put a racial spin on the debate, arguing that the DA's policies would benefit white capitalists at the expense of black labor.[31] The DA contested this characterization, arguing that a freer labor

---

[28] Thus, political analyst Dumisane Hlope, mourning the absence of "real" communist voices in the South African political scene, wrote that "All the parties are trumpeting liberal policies, with the only difference being the measure and the speed of implementation. ... I feel like I am being asked to choose from a pool of drivers, and yet the bus is one and the same. Hence, I miss communists. I am convinced that genuine communists have an alternative to the Gear policies. They have alternatives to privitisation and to the ANC's governments's social spending." See Dumisane Hlope, "A Real Communist Has My Vote." *City Press*, February 22, 2004. See also Devan Pillay, "Mirror, Mirror on the Wall, Is the ANC Tony Leon in Disguise?" *Sunday Times*, February 29, 2004.

[29] A useful review of economic policies is found in Robyn Chalmers, "Remedies Aplenty to Kickstart SA Economy." *Business Day*, March 18, 2004. For HIV/AIDS, see Hoosen Coovadia, "When Voting Is as Risky as Unprotected Sex." *Mail & Guardian*, March 19, 2004. Cooyadia opines: "If one is focused on the pandemic as a deciding factor, one may as well close one's eyes and make one's mark."

[30] "Leon Sets Sights on Labour Laws." *The Star*, March 11, 2004.

[31] For example, in a letter to the *City Press* editor, Pule Malefane, Gauteng ANC MPL and member of the South African Communist Party, wrote: "The DA should not exhibit its usual arrogance of white supremacy that suggests blacks cannot think – and you should only use them when you need them but then dump them after the elections. ... The DA wants workers to work as long as possible and earn as little as possible, arrive as early as possible and leave as late as possible. A vote for the DA is the end to a living wage, jobs and better working conditions, which the ANC together with progressive trade unions and employers built up over the past ten years and will consolidate after the elections. Workers must say no to wholesale privatization and labour market flexibility and vote ANC." Pule Malefane, "DA Doesn't Support Workers." *City Press*, March 7, 2004. See also the comprehensive attack by Zwelinzima Vavi, secretary general of Cosatu, in "DA Does Not Care for Workers or Poor," *Sowetan*, March 9, 2004.

TABLE 5.5. *Policies Named by Different Parties*

|  | ANC | DA | NNP | IFP | ID | Total |
|---|---|---|---|---|---|---|
| HIV policy | 5 | 6 | 0 | 2 | 1 | 14 |
| Increase police officers | 2 | 2 | 0 | 1 | 0 | 5 |
| Prison sentencing laws | 0 | 3 | 2 | 0 | 1 | 6 |
| Labor market legislation | 2 | 2 | 1 | 0 | 0 | 5 |
| Affirmative action | 2 | 1 | 0 | 0 | 0 | 3 |
| Privatization | 0 | 2 | 0 | 1 | 0 | 3 |
| Education policy | 2 | 1 | 0 | 0 | 0 | 3 |
| Economic policy in general | 2 | 2 | 0 | 0 | 0 | 4 |
| Foreign policy | 0 | 2 | 0 | 0 | 0 | 2 |
| Welfare safety net | 0 | 1 | 0 | 0 | 1 | 2 |
| Small business laws | 0 | 1 | 0 | 0 | 1 | 2 |
| Tax laws | 0 | 2 | 0 | 0 | 0 | 2 |
| Other | 2 | 3 | 2 | 0 | 1 | 8 |
| Total | 17 | 28 | 5 | 4 | 5 | 59 |

*Notes*: Quotes can name multiple policies, so the number of policies named can exceed the number of quotes given in Table 5.1.

market would create more jobs for more people and therefore would benefit the unemployed black masses.[32] In sum, in a few areas – most notably labor market legislation – parties offered divergent policies.

These policy differences were not central to the campaigns, however. Parties mentioned them sporadically in their rhetoric – usually when listing the full roster of their policies (e.g., in their manifestos) – but did not make them focal points for debate. Table 5.5, which shows the policies named by parties and their frequency, makes this clear.[33] HIV policy unambiguously dominated (fourteen mentions) – reflecting the pledges of all the parties to provide anti-retroviral medicines. Next in the list were crime-related policies. Prisoner sentencing laws – in particular the death penalty – was the second most common policy mentioned (six mentions, none from the ANC). Increasing police officers tied with labor market policies (five hits each) for third place. Affirmative action policy had only three mentions. Out of fifty-nine total policy mentions, only fourteen involved topics on which parties offered divergent prescriptions.

In sum, while policy and issues figured prominently in party rhetoric during campaigns, little of this discussion involved actual debates over priorities or solutions. Instead, parties identified the same set of problems and offered similar solutions to them. A few topics did engender principled debate, but they did not dominate election discourse.

---

[32] "Leon Sets Sights on Labour Laws." *The Star*, March 11, 2004.
[33] Quotes that mention policies can raise more than one policy. Therefore, the number of total policies in Table 5.3 exceeds the total number of quotes that mention policies in Table 5.1.

## Performance

In contrast, the ANC's performance record did elicit substantial attention from parties. It was the most frequent topic listed in Table 5.4, with 68 out of 219 party quotes referencing it. Moreover, unlike issues and policies, the parties diverged significantly in their views on this subject, with the ANC arguing that it had been successful on many fronts and the DA contending that the ANC had failed its mandate. In this sense, the South African campaigns looked like campaigns in countries without racial divisions, where incumbent performance is a frequent and central topic of debate. However, as in earlier campaigns, race and performance became conflated. The ANC attempted to deflect DA criticisms by branding the DA as white and questioning its credibility and motivations. Thus, race – specifically the "whiteness" of the opposition – penetrated even this politics-as-usual arena of campaign activity. In the following sections, I use examples of activities and rhetoric to further elucidate the debate over the ANC's performance.

The ANC painted a positive but nuanced picture of its performance during Mbeki's first term of office. It vigorously defended its record, pointing to successes in building houses and delivering services to areas that had been underserved during apartheid. At the same time, it did not overstate its successes and acknowledged the many challenges it still faced. It went to great lengths to demonstrate its desire to keep working to improve the lives of South Africans – most notably through a series of "walk-abouts" that involved President Mbeki spontaneously presenting himself in various communities, hearing out the complaints of their residents, expressing heartfelt sympathy, and promising to address them in his next term (sometimes, in a flourish of initiative, addressing them immediately).[34] Thus Mbeki addressed the (desperately poor) KwaMhlanga township in Mpumalanga: "We have tried a little bit but should make sure that after April 14 we try even more to address these problems. It would take us long to address some of them due to lack of resources but we will try."[35] In many instances, Mbeki went to extremes to put on a caring face, in one instance sitting on the floor of one household in the Eastern Cape, in another taking money from his pocket to give to a poor family.[36] All together,

---

[34] For example, two days after a Mbeki visit to Mamelodi, a Pretoria township, the executive mayor of the area convened an urgent meeting of the committee responsible for service delivery and then issued a directive to the credit control department to restore the supply of basic services (water, electricity) to the homes of pensioners. During Mbeki's visit, he had heard several complaints from pensioners about their services being turned off. See McKeed Kotlolo, "Mbeki Visit Has Tshwane Abuzz." *Sowetan*, March 8, 2004. In Limpopo, after one Jack Ramoadi of GaKgapane claimed that he saw no reason to vote because he found it impossible to access government grants, Mbeki ordered local officers to investigate the matter immediately. Selby Makgotho, "Crowds Besiege Mbeki in Limpopo." *Sowetan*, March 29, 2004.

[35] Mpumelelo Mkhabela "Mbeki on Harsh Soil in Election Walkabout." *City Press*, March 7, 2004.

[36] Sphiwe Mboyane, "Mbeki Puts on Caring, Human Face for Voters." *Business Day*, April 6, 2004.

the ANC conveyed the message that it cared deeply about the people of South Africa and was working hard to improve their lives – if it had not yet succeeded in all areas, this was only because of the depth of the challenges it faced and its short tenure in office.

Not surprisingly, the DA had a different view of the ANC's performance. It argued that the ANC had been in power for ten years, and during those ten years it had come up short in any number of areas: It had failed to create jobs and spur economic growth, it had mismanaged resources (spending money on foreign adventures rather than domestic ills), it had allowed corruption to blossom at all levels of government, it had seen crime spiral out of control, and, perhaps most damningly, it had sat on its hands, mouthing strange theories and advising home remedies while HIV/AIDS consumed generations of South Africa's workforce. The overall message the DA sent was that, aside from the fat cats who benefited from the ANC's patronage, ordinary South Africans had suffered under the ANC's reign: They were poorer, less likely to have a job, more likely to fall victim to violent crime, and sicker than they had been in 1994, when the ANC took power. The DA promised that it could do better. This message was iterated by the IFP, especially Buthelezi, who frequently attacked the ANC's record, most poignantly on the issue of AIDS.[37]

Thus, while issues and policies failed to generate substantial debates between parties, the ANC's performance was a central point of contention – evidence, perhaps, that South African politics are no different from politics in countries without a racial divide. However, although performance would seem to be a "nonracial" topic, in fact it often contained a racial subscript. The ANC argued that the blame for its poor performance record (if it had one) fell on the parties that had instituted (and collaborated in) apartheid: the NNP, the DA, and the IFP. Hence, it evoked apartheid when talking about current issues, a move aimed at keeping race salient amongst its supporters.[38]

---

[37] Thus, in a campaign speech in Durban, he accused Mbeki of wasting Parliament's time "flirting" with odd theories that questioned whether the HIV virus actually caused AIDS. He went on to say: "The South African people have the answer and must make their voice heard on April 14, because we just cannot have five more years of the same ambivalent, ineffective and negligent ANC policies. HIV/AIDS presents a national challenge as big as the one to defeat apartheid." "Buthelezi Berates ANC Over Its HIV/AIDS Policy." *The Star*, March 9, 2004.

[38] For example, facing a crowd in Mafikeng (NW Province), Mbeki claimed that the ANC would beat poverty, just as it beat apartheid. He said: "People used to say '*Die kaffers is lui*' (the kaffirs [derogatory term for Africans] are lazy). Our people have never been lazy; we are not lazy now." He then talked about the differences between white wealth and African poverty: "When you are in a helicopter and look down, you don't have to ask which one is a white suburb and which one is an African location. You can see it from the number of trees. That's what we inherited and that's what we must change." In this example, Mbeki raised the specter of apartheid in an emotional way (by referring to a derogatory belief) and then linked that with the ANC's current challenge of ending poverty. See Sue Blaine, "Mbeki Vows to Beat the New Enemy." *The Star*, March 12, 2004. See also, Mpumelelo Mkhabela, "Mbeki Faces Critics on Campaign Trail," *City Press*, March 14, 2004. The ANC also used this tactic to address concerns about its actions on HIV/AIDS. ANC KwaZulu-Natal Provincial spokesman Mtholephi Mthimkhulu argued that it was "hypocritical for those who are masquerading as

Furthermore, it deflected criticism of its record in two ways: First, it intimated that those criticizing it must think things were better under apartheid, indeed they must be yearning to return to apartheid; therefore, they must be racists. It turned this logic on Buthelezi after he suggested in Parliament that there was greater poverty in South African rural areas in 2004 than there had been ten years before.[39] Second, it argued that criticizing the ANC was tantamount to claiming that all governments headed by Africans were doomed to failure and that Africans were incapable of competent governance. Criticism of the ANC's record thus became criticism of Africans in general – a rather damning claim the party many times turned on the DA.[40] Indeed, the ANC used the same tactic in 1999 when it turned the DA's "Fight Back" slogan into "Don't Fight Blacks," thus equating the DA's criticism of the party with criticism of blacks in general. The following quote, from an opinion column in the pro-ANC newspaper *City Press*, demonstrates many of these points:

> Whereas many critical analysts believe and have always correctly argued that the government's policies have failed to deliver adequate basic services to the poor, it is another story altogether to take the DA's stance on government policies seriously. It is difficult to see the DA as representing anything other than traditional liberal cynicism and self-righteousness that induces paralysis and successfully hides a frightening racist agenda. This is an agenda that, at the very bottom, is based on the old belief that "black people cannot do anything right." Hence there must be a "fight back" strategy in place.... Behind the megaphone politics and the mastery of sound bites, coupled with the typical liberal arrogance of claiming to have "fought against apartheid" (interesting if service in the apartheid army and membership of the apartheid parliament was fighting against apartheid), is the DA's true nature. It is a party that stands for big business which will do anything to "fight back" against any encroachment on white privilege.[41]

To be sure, the DA invited attacks when it explicitly linked Mbeki to African rulers to the north – for example, in a Gauteng billboard that pictured Mbeki next to Mugabe. Ostensibly, the ad questioned Mbeki's decision not to

---

very concerned about HIV/AIDS, just for the sake of scavenging votes, when they did nothing when they were presiding over the so-called governments prior to 1994. ... What is usually not mentioned is that the first person with HIV was diagnosed in South Africa as early as 1983." Thus, the apartheid regime and the KwaZulu homeland government had done nothing to deal with it, and hence the DA and IFP should now stop using HIV/AIDS in their campaigns. See "HIV/AIDS 'used to scavenge votes.'" *Cape Times*, March 16, 2004.

[39] See response from Buthelezi in Mangosuthu Buthelezi, "But Life Was Worse in the Desert." Letter to the editor, *This Day*, March 3, 2004. See also comments by Gauteng Premier Mbhazima Shilowa in Khangale Makhado, "Shilowa Says Critics Have Short Memories." *Sowetan*, March 8, 2004. John Kane-Berman (head of the South African Institute of Race Relations) discusses this incident in "Political Mudslinging as Vicious as It Ever Was." *Business Day*, March 9, 2004. See also Anthony Johnson, "Looking Backwards and Forwards in the Run-Up to Elections." *Cape Times*, March 15, 2004.

[40] For an interesting analysis along these lines by a prominent African critic of the ANC, see Sipho Seepe, "Mbeki No Match for Leon." *Sowetan Times*, March 4, 2004.

[41] Console Tleane, "DA Reveals Its Racist Attitude." *City Press*, March 7, 2004.

condemn Mugabe, but it also evoked a general cultural notion/fear in South Africa (especially in the white community) that the ANC would turn out to be no different from other African-led regimes (all of which, according to this logic, have turned into corrupt dictatorships).[42] Voters did not need much help from the ANC to view the DA's portrayal of Mbeki through a racial lens.[43] The NNP also chimed in on this episode. Tom Classen, a NNP Provincial Member of Parliament in Gauteng, wrote in a letter to the *Star* (February 24, 2004) that "the DA has absolutely no qualms about vilifying the government, and in so doing stirring up racial hatred and thus polarizing the minorities from the majority."[44]

In sum, the performance of the ANC figured centrally in the election campaigns of the major competitors. Moreover, unlike issues and policy, the topic of the ANC's performance elicited real debate between the parties, with the ANC presenting a positive spin on its achievements and the DA arguing the opposite. It would be a mistake to believe that the centrality of this politics-as-usual subject signaled the decline of race in South African elections, however. Instead, questions of race and performance became fused as the ANC and its running mate, the NP, used the DA's "whiteness" to discredit its criticisms.

**Race and Party Images**

Race also entered into the campaigns in more direct ways as well. The DA's image in particular formed a central fault line of the election. In its efforts to penetrate the African electorate, the DA emphasized its inclusiveness, portrayed itself as Africanizing, and attempted to appeal to voters through its policy stances and criticisms of the ANC performance. In response, the ANC and its affiliates, including its coalition partner the NNP, launched vigorous attacks against the party, portraying it as mired in apartheid thinking and run by racial chauvinists. These contrasting views of the opposition party – Was it Africanizing? Was it racist? Was Tony Leon a man of the people? Was he a bigot? – merely served to muddy the waters for the electorate. At the end of the day, African voters remained highly uncertain about the DA and who it represented. This outcome, while perhaps not as ideal for the ANC as an unambiguously white opposition, nevertheless served the purpose of keeping Africans loyal to the ruling party by discrediting the only opposition party

---

[42] For a discussion of this incident, see Eddy Maloka, "More Subtle, but Racist All the Same." *Sowetan*, March 8, 2004.

[43] See, for example, a letter to the editor from Paseka Rakosa of Pretoria, "DA Must Approach Issues Differently," *Soweten*, March 11, 2004. This individual writes that the DA billboard comparing Mbeki with Mugabe confirmed "the perception held by many that the DA is a right-wing and a racist organization. This irresponsible behaviour of the DA and its leader is likely to lead to racial polarization in a society trying to build unity."

[44] Tom Classen, "Endorsing the DA is Wasteful." Letter to the editor, *The Star*, February 24, 2004. See also Tom Classen, "Stirring Up Hatred Will Not Gain Votes," Letter to the editor, *Sowetan*, March 4, 2004.

with sufficient organization and resources to seriously challenge it. In the following section, I develop these points in greater detail.

In keeping with its efforts to attract African votes, the DA followed a strategy similar to that of the NP in earlier elections. It attempted to minimize its role in implementing apartheid, clarifying Leon's duties during his youthful military service as a desk job, not active duty (in other words, he had not been brandishing weapons at crowds in the townships, carrying out covert operations in Namibia, or enacting legislation in Parliament). It resurrected the legend of Helen Suzman, the "lone voice" of opposition in Parliament during the dark years. Douglas Gibson, the party's number three man, went so far as to claim: "I am not responsible for apartheid and I don't think that I benefited from apartheid. Maybe someone can point out to me how I benefited."[45] Tony Leon, along similar lines, asserted that he was not a "guilty white."[46] In these ways, the party tried to distance itself from apartheid seats of power and responsibility. Of course, by talking in this way, the DA merely bought into the frame the ANC was using on it; by saying he was not a "guilty white," Leon looked like a guilty white. Gibson's claims that he had not benefited from apartheid seemed even more absurd and merely served to link the party and its leaders to the deplorable institutions of the past.

More fundamentally, the DA wished to convey the impression that it was rapidly "Africanizing." If it had been turned primarily to white voters in 1999, in 2004 its public emphasis was on courting Africans and blacks more generally. It aimed to "take on the ANC in its own backyard."[47] It conveyed this goal in numerous ways. It repeatedly described its candidate lists as black.[48] It held major events in African areas, where the crowd was primarily African (always described in the papers as such) and the party members on the stage with Tony Leon were various shades of black and brown. This was true of its manifesto launch in Soweto, the unveiling of its lists in Durban, and its final rally the day before the election. Typically these events were accompanied by loud township music and dancing and produced many pleasing photo opportunities. Leon also made well-publicized visits to African townships, where he hugged black people and (once again) had his photo taken.[49]

In keeping with this message, the DA never referred to itself as a white party and generally avoided the issue of race altogether other than to point out

---

[45] Quoted in Bryan Rostron, "But for the Accident of Pigment." *This Day*, March 8, 2004.
[46] Interview with Drew Forrest, *Mail & Guardian*, January 30, 2004.
[47] Quoted in Merten, "DA to 'Take on the ANC in Its Own Backyard.'"
[48] For example, at the launch of the DA's Western Cape provincial lists, provincial party leader Theuns Botha pointed out that half of the top ten names on the list were coloured and said "this list should finally shut the mouths of the prophets of doom who claim the DA is only for the white elite and the so-called right wing." Quoted in Nazma Dreyer, "DA Dares ANC/NNP Alliance to Name Their Candidates for Premier." *Cape Times*, February 25, 2004.
[49] For a typical article about DA efforts to reach African voters, see S'Thembiso Msomi, "The DA Bops to Afropop." *Sunday Times*, March 14, 2004.

its own growing inclusiveness.⁵⁰ It preferred to speak of issues and policies and to criticize the ANC's performance record. It rarely made direct allegations about ANC racial politics. In short, the party stuck to politics-as-usual topics or focused on its own image, which it portrayed as rapidly transforming.

The DA did not always stay on message, of course. It occasionally lashed out against the ANC's racial politics. In early March, Leon responded (on the DA website) to allegations by Mbeki (on the ANC website) that certain parties (unnamed) were using *"swaart gevaar"* (black fear) tactics to win white votes. Leon shot back: "The truth is that under President Thabo Mbeki, South Africa has abandoned the non-racial idealism of the rainbow nation and the politics of reconciliation. The president does not really care about reconciliation unless it happens on his own, racial terms. He refuses to listen to honest criticism and accuses those who disagree with him of racism and subversion." In other instances it targeted minority voters with messages that had racial overtones. It questioned Mbeki's desire for a third term (a billboard in Gauteng likened him to Mugabe) and his support for Haitian leader Jean-Paul Aristide. It brought up affirmative action in speeches to coloured and Indian audiences and ran a poster campaign in the Western Cape that used red and black colors (supposedly representing the black and red/communist threat) to draw attention to the alliance between the NNP and the ANC. Some of its leaders also made damaging gaffes, as when DA candidate for Western Cape Theuns Botha opined that the DA was "for the white elite."⁵¹ Probably worse was when a DA spokesman threatened legal action against the ANC, COSATU, and the SACP after a small number of their supporters shouted racist slogans outside a courthouse in protest of a recent series of violent attacks against farm workers. Although the DA was quick to condemn the ANC supporters, it said little about the violent actions of the white farmers – thereby missing an opportunity to reach out to Africans.⁵²

Damaging as these instances were, none of them represented main points in the party's campaign. Referring back to Table 5.5, out of fifty-two issues raised in DA rhetoric over the course of its campaign, only two referenced foreign affairs (which would include any mention of Zimbabwe or Haiti). Only one out of twenty-eight instances of policy-related rhetoric mentioned affirmative

---

⁵⁰ Quoted in Moshoeshoe Monare, "Whites Using *'swaart gevaar'* Tactics, Says Mbeki." *Sunday Independent,* March 7, 2004.

⁵¹ Botha said a number of odd (and damaging) "off-script" comments during the campaign. For example: "I feel about black people the same way I feel about white people. They will come second when it comes to the allocation of resources in the provinces." It's not entirely clear what he meant by that – possibly that coloureds would come out on top. And "I grew up in a *verligte* house. We never allowed our workers to call us *baas* and *miesies.*" He also suggested that the ANC was not announcing its premier for the Western Cape because it planned to put an African on top and coloureds would hate that. Such comments displayed (at best) insensitivity. They were unusual in the DA's campaign. See Hogarth, "Election Marred by Foot in Mouth." *Sunday Times,* March 14, 2004.

⁵² Msomi, "The DA Bops to Afropop."

action and only two mentioned foreign policy. Botha's comments were unfortunate, but they were not echoed by other party members. However, regardless of their centrality, they created ambiguity about the DA's true nature – ambiguity reinforced by the ANC's and NP's systematic attacks.

Concrete examples of such attacks abound. The ANC painted the DA as "right wing" and "white" and "racist," all words it used interchangeably to describe its opponent. Tony Leon was called a bigot and his service in the South African military was used against him. In late March, ANC spokesperson Smuts Ngonyama railed: "Leon was part of the propaganda wing of the South African Defence Force, which maimed and killed our people." He then intimated that Leon was using the same propaganda techniques in his election campaign.[53] The ANC placed the DA alongside the NNP as a major apartheid participant, obscuring differences between ruling party and opposition. At a meeting of COSATU shop stewards in mid-March, ANC MP Pallo Jordan attacked both the DA and the NNP, saying workers should remember the atrocities of apartheid (the Sharpeville massacre, the Soweto uprising) and which parties were responsible for them when casting their votes.[54]

Often the most vitriolic attacks on the DA were leveled by organizations affiliated with the ANC, rather than party heavyweights. For example, in a *City Press* opinion column, Nkululeko Kaizer Mohau of the Young Communist League described the DA as a "white racist" party, a "vocal representative of white business," and claimed it was "campaigning for a return to apartheid."[55] In an editorial in *The Sowetan*, Zwelinzima Vavi, general secretary of COSATU, segued from a critical discussion of the DA's labor policy proposals to a personal attack on Tony Leon. He wrote:

While many white compatriots chose to go into exile rather than get conscripted into the then-South African Defence Force (SADF), he was manning road blocks in townships, enforcing the apartheid regime's repression of black people through the state of emergency. How could workers entrust their freedom and democracy to someone with this track record?[56]

---

[53] "Leon Uses Army-Style Campaign Tactics, Says ANC."
[54] Chiara Carter, "'Back the ANC Despite Its Negatives.'" *This Day*, March 18, 2004. See also footnote 10.
[55] Nkululeko Kaizer Mohau, "The APF Misleads the People." *City Press*, February 22, 2004. The article was mostly aimed at the Anti-Privitization Forum, which had been critical of ANC privatization policies. Mohau argued that criticism of the ANC was equivalent to support for the racist DA, hence the APF was actually reactionary and counter-revolutionary.
[56] Zwelinzima Vavi, "DA Does Not Care for Workers or Poor." Vavi followed this up with an editorial along similar lines two weeks later in which he never mentioned the DA but spoke at length about not handing over power to those who "through their silence, condoned the suffering of the majority, or worse, actively participated in our subordination." These people, he says "did not raise a finger of protest" and therefore "can never truly protect or promote the basic freedoms enshrined in our Constitution." They understand "our needs" through surveys, not through actually living our lives; therefore, they should not get our votes. See Zweilinzima Vavi, "Vote in the Name of Struggle Heroes." *The Sowetan*, March 23, 2004.

The ANC's alliance partner, the NNP, also leveled vicious attacks against the DA. The leader of the NNP, Marthinus van Schalkwyk, at the launch of his party's manifesto, said that "the DA leadership was simply unwilling to leave behind the politics of fear and arrogance." He likened Tony Leon to former Rhodesian Prime Minister Ian Smith and warned that South African whites must not follow him down the path of alienation and marginalization.[57] In a later incident, van Schalkwyk attacked the DA's Western Cape provincial leader Theuns Botha as racist and right wing for having suggested that the ANC was delaying the announcement of its provincial premier candidate out of fear that naming an African premier would result in the loss of coloured votes.[58] He also suggested that the DA and the NNP had traded places – the NNP had become the liberal DP of earlier days, while the DA had become the "notorious NP of old."[59] To a crowd of coloured supporters at a rally at the Athalone Civic Center in early March, he suggested that the only way coloureds could keep white supremacists out of power was to vote for him.[60] Juli Kilian, NNP MPL in Gauteng, labeled the DA part of a "right-wing-opposition coalition" that would at best have no relevance and at worst would irresponsibly and immorally "lure minorities to the far-right fringes where they would have no influence or say."[61] In a particularly nasty attack, late in the campaign, van Schalkwyk told a group of coloured voters:

Parties like the DA, who describe themselves as "a party for the white elite," will never attract real support from any quarter except the right wing that is the focus of their efforts. This is because for them, coloured, and black and Indian South Africans are somehow less valuable, less experienced or less important.[62]

These comments framed the DA as racist and white, archaic, a throw-back from the past, a party by and for bigots.

Beyond these attacks by organizations affiliated with the ANC, Mbeki himself occasionally participated in the racial mudslinging, although he was careful in how and when he did this. In his weekly letter on the ANC website, he wrote that racial fear-mongering had long been a feature of "white politics." White parties used "*die swaartgevaar*" (black fear) and "*die rooigevaar*" (red fear) to scare white voters into supporting them. He suggested that recent

---

[57] Quoted in Edwin Lombard and S'Thembiso Msomi, "Leon 'the Ultimate Prima Donna,' Says Van Schalkwyk." *Sunday Times*, February 22, 2004.
[58] Nazma Dreyer, "Van Schalkwyk Confident He'll Stay on as Premier after 'Rightwinger' DA Candidate's 'Racist' Remarks." *Cape Times*, March 2, 2004.
[59] Comments from an interview with journalist Mariechen Waldner. See Mariechen Waldner, "NNP Still Alive, Says Korbroek." *City Press*, March 7, 2004.
[60] Bonny Schoonakker, "Battle Looms as Parties Vie for 'Cape Soweto.'" *Sunday Times*, March 7, 2004.
[61] Juli Kilian, "Opposition Irrelevant." Letter to the editor, *The Star*, March 17, 2004.
[62] Wyndham Hartley, "NNP Steps Up Bid for Cape Coloured Vote." *Business Day*, March 31, 2004.

DA allegations that the ANC planned to use its two-thirds majority to change the constitution were examples of this kind of politics.[63] Mbeki also attacked the DA's coalition partner, the IFP, using his website to accuse Buthelezi of entering into a "right-wing" coalition to protect white interests. He likened the DA/IFP electoral coalition to the pre-1994 relationship between the IFP and the apartheid government. He repeated these accusations on a popular Gauteng radio station (Yfm) and brought them up again while campaigning in Limpopo in late March.[64] At a different Limpopo rally during the same campaign blitz, he told crowds that De Klerk (former head of the NNP) was no different from the other apartheid leaders and had never cared about the lives of black people and then hit on the opposition in general, asking "Where were they during the liberation struggle?" Throughout, he characterized the DA as a party for white "right-wingers."[65] Similar attacks continued on into April.[66] A week before the election, DA strategy advisor Ryan Coetzee acknowledged the damage these sorts of attacks had on the DA:

> It takes time to build credibility. The ANC is running a defensive campaign that says at every opportunity the DA is racist. It cannot get any worse.[67]

The severity of the ANC's attacks, combined with their systematic nature, suggests that the DA was up against a very different opponent than the one the NP faced in 1994. In the earlier election, the ANC had officially committed itself to following the high road and mostly eschewed racial attacks on its opponent. This gave the NP more room to sell its "new and improved" image to the nonwhite electorate. In 2004, the ANC did not grant the DA this kind of maneuvering room.

As in earlier elections, the ANC avoided identifying itself as a "black" or "African" party. When speaking of itself, above all it emphasized inclusiveness. Thus, ANC Gauteng Premier Mbhazima Shilowa said: "This government is not a government for African people, it is a government for everyone and anybody who says that the light of freedom will only shine on African people is lying."[68] David Makhura, ANC provincial secretary in Gauteng, said that compared to the DA "the ANC is a vibrant movement steeped in a history of non-racialism. This is consistent in our messages and in our inclusive programmes."[69] The NNP followed a similar path, painting itself (as it had in

---

[63] Hartley, "ANC not Planning a Third Term – Mbeki."
[64] See S'Thembiso Msomi, Sabelo Ndlangisa, and Bongani Mththwa, "Mbeki, Buthelezi Savage Each Other in Poll War." *Sunday Times*, March 28, 2004. See also Mpumelelo Mkhabela, "Mbeki's Premier Promise to Limpopo." *City Press*, March 28, 2004.
[65] Ido Lekota, "'De Klerk Never Cared for Blacks.'" *Sowetan*, March 29, 2004.
[66] Ido Lekota, "ANC Attack on Shenge Continues." *Sowetan*, April 2, 2004.
[67] Rapule Tabane, "Squeeze + Spin = 30%." *Mail & Guardian*, April 7, 2004.
[68] Khangale Makhado, "Shilowa Says Critics Have Short Memories." *Sowetan*, March 8, 2004.
[69] David Makhura, "Ready to Market, not Ready to Govern." *This Day*, March 17, 2004.

TABLE 5.6. *The ANC/NNP and Racial Rhetoric*

| Source | Nonracial Rhetoric | Racial Rhetoric | Total |
|---|---|---|---|
| Other parties | 107 | 16 | 123 |
| | (87%) | (13%) | (100%) |
| | (60%) | (39%) | (56%) |
| ANC or NNP | 71 | 25 | 96 |
| | (74%) | (26%) | (100%) |
| | (40%) | (61%) | (44%) |
| Total | 178 | 41 | 219 |
| | (81%) | (19%) | (100%) |
| | (100%) | (100%) | (100%) |

Pearson chi2(1) = 6.0192 Pr = 0.014.

1999) as a "rainbow" party for all South Africans.[70] Thus, the overall ANC/NNP message was that the DA cared only about white interests, the IFP was a stooge (again), whereas the ANC (and NNP) were integrating and inclusive. Indeed, the very union of the white and black implied by the coalition (however ironic the partners) conveyed this message.

To get a sense of how systematic racial rhetoric was, it is useful to refer back to Table 5.3, which shows that parties brought up race as often as they brought up policy. It also shows that there were major differences in the originators and targets of racial discourse. The NNP and ANC mentioned race more frequently than their competitors and more often than all other topics except performance. In contrast, the DA emphasized policy, issues, and performance over race. Table 5.6, a simple breakdown of ANC/NNP as the source of the quote by whether the quote was racial, shows that the difference between these two parties and the others is statistically significant at the .01 level.

Furthermore, while the DA was less likely to originate racial rhetoric, it was more likely to be the target of it. Table 5.7 shows the nature of rhetoric directed at different parties. The DA accounted for 26 percent of total quotes but was the target of 44 percent of racial quotes (indeed, race was the most frequent topic of rhetoric directed at the DA). In contrast, only 27 percent of the racial quotes (but 45 percent of total quotes) focused on the ANC. Table 5.8, a cross tab of the DA as the target by whether the quote was racial, confirms the significance of this relationship.

Finally, if we disaggregate Table 5.1 into more specific topics of discourse (Table 5.9), we see that the DA's image nearly tied jobs as the second most important topic of discussion by parties in the election. Poverty, crime, HIV,

---

[70] Marthinus van Schalkwyk referred to the party this way at its manifesto launch in late February. See Waghled Misbach, "NNP Only Rainbow Party in SA." *Sowetan*, February 23, 2004. He repeated the comparison between the DA and Rhodesia in a later interview with journalist Mariechen Waldner. See Mariechen Waldner, "NNP Still Alive, Says Korbroek."

TABLE 5.7. *Type of Rhetoric about Different Parties*

|  | ANC | DA | NNP | IFP | ID | Other | Total |
|---|---|---|---|---|---|---|---|
| Identity | 7 | 1 | 0 | 0 | 0 | 1 | 9 |
|  | (7%) | (2%) | (0%) | (0%) | (0%) | (6%) | (23%) |
|  | (78%) | (11%) | (0%) | (0%) | (0%) | (11%) | (100%) |
| Racial | 11 | 18 | 5 | 2 | 2 | 3 | 41 |
|  | (11%) | (31%) | (36%) | (13%) | (13%) | (18%) | (19%) |
|  | (27%) | (44%) | (12%) | (5%) | (5%) | (7%) | (100%) |
| Policy | 17 | 17 | 3 | 0 | 1 | 4 | 42 |
|  | (17%) | (29%) | (21%) | (0%) | (6%) | (24%) | (19%) |
|  | (40%) | (40%) | (7%) | (0%) | (2%) | (9%) | (100%) |
| Priority | 20 | 13 | 4 | 2 | 6 | 6 | 51 |
|  | (20%) | (22%) | (29%) | (13%) | (38%) | (35%) | (23%) |
|  | (39%) | (25%) | (8%) | (4%) | (12%) | (12%) | (100%) |
| Competence | 50 | 7 | 3 | 2 | 1 | 5 | 68 |
|  | (51%) | (12%) | (21%) | (13%) | (6%) | (29%) | (31%) |
|  | (74%) | (10%) | (4%) | (3%) | (1%) | (7%) | (100%) |
| Total | 99 | 58 | 14 | 15 | 16 | 17 | 219 |
|  | (45%) | (26%) | (6%) | (7%) | (7%) | (8%) | (100%) |

*Notes*: Columns do not sum to total because quotes can have multiple subjects. "Other" includes references to "opposition in general," the ANC/NP coalition, or the DA/IFP coalition. Although quotes could have been about any South African party, *only the parties listed* were actually the targets of rhetoric in the sample.

TABLE 5.8. *The DA and Racial Rhetoric*

| Target | Nonracial Rhetoric | Racial Rhetoric | Total |
|---|---|---|---|
| DA | 40 | 18 | 58 |
|  | (69%) | (31%) | (100%) |
|  | (23%) | (44%) | (27%) |
| Other parties | 138 | 23 | 161 |
|  | (86%) | (14%) | (100%) |
|  | (78%) | (56%) | (27%) |
| Total | 178 | 41 | 219 |
|  | (81%) | (19%) | (100%) |
|  | (100%) | (100%) | (100%) |

Pearson chi2(1) = 7.8607 Pr = 0.005

and service provision all received less discussion. For a country with a devastating unemployment rate, tragic crime levels, and a raging AIDS epidemic, the centrality of the DA's image in rhetoric reveals the importance parties (especially the ruling party) placed on it.

TABLE 5.9. *Most Frequent Topics in Party Discourse in the 2004 Election*

|  | Frequency |
|---|---|
| ANC's performance record | 50 |
| Jobs | 19 |
| DA's racial image | 18 |
| Poverty | 15 |
| Crime | 14 |
| HIV | 14 |
| Services | 11 |
| Total instances of rhetoric | 219 |

## GETTING THE MESSAGE OUT: CAMPAIGN SPENDING AND MEDIA COVERAGE

If the ruling party and its opposition painted starkly different views of the DA's image to the electorate, which side was better able to get its message out? In this final section, I suggest that the playing field was far from equal for the two opponents: Although the DA had greater resources and received substantially more media coverage than any other opposition party, the ANC's campaign warchest dwarfed those of its competitors and it dominated media coverage as well. For these reasons, in the war of words between the ruling party and the opposition, the ANC was able to yell louder, more often, and longer, further weakening the DA's ability to use campaigns as a way to alter its image.

### Campaign Spending

South Africa's campaign financing laws shroud the amount of money parties raise and spend during campaigns. Some information about party resources is readily available: The Public Funding of Represented Political Parties Act 103, which came into effect on April 1, 1998, grants parties an allocation of funding each fiscal year that is public information. Furthermore, a handful of large companies have recently begun to make open contributions to parties. However, a large component of fund raising remains opaque: Legislation does not require parties to divulge how much private money they raise or whom they raise it from, and few – including the ANC and the DA – have opted to make this information available on their own volition. For this reason, any discussion of campaign finance is necessarily speculative.

However, based on the information that is available, the ANC appears to raise and spend significantly more money than any of its competitors, with the DA a distant second and the remaining parties trailing far behind. This is certainly true of the funding that is transparent to the public. Through the Political Parties Fund the IEC disbursed between R50 and R74 million each year between 1998 and 2004. It allocates this money according to the fraction of seats parties win in Parliament and provincial legislatures.[71] According to figures released from Idasa in 2003, that year's pot of R66.6 million translated into about R42.5 million for the ANC and about R7.1 million for the DA, with the remainder split by the eighteen other parties represented in Parliament.[72] Companies that make open campaign contributions (in 2004, sixteen corporations followed this route, most of them very large companies like Standard Bank, Liberty Group, Anglo Gold, Sanlam, etc.) also used a proportional formula to allocate funds between parties.[73] Hence, the ANC captures the lions' share of transparent party funding.

It also seems likely that the ANC raises significantly more money than its rivals from undisclosed private donors – both domestic and international. Allegations swirl each election period about the sources of its war chest – Lodge (1999a) reports rumors that the South African Chinese community contributed R20 million to the ANC's 1999 campaign and Islamic states another R60 million. Most donations are probably above board: companies, individuals, nongovernmental organizations (NGOs), and governments who donate without specific benefits attached or expectations of influence. However, critics of the party suggest a grayer zone as well. Robinson and Brümmer (2006) argue that some Black Economic Empowerment (BEE) companies act as conduits of funds to the ruling party. In requiring that companies be "BEE compliant" to win tenders or contracts from government and parastatals (per the broad based Black Economic Empowerment Act of January 2004), the ruling party has forced companies without BEE credentials (international companies, for example) to seek strategic partnerships with BEE firms, some of which, Robinson and Brümmer allege, are simply fronts for the ANC. The BEE firms then pass money (stock options, other resources) from the partnered firm to the ruling party. Not surprisingly, the ANC denies any allegations that it accepts money with "strings attached," and it is very difficult to ascertain how much money the party obtains through gray area ventures. In any event, such avenues of fund raising are not available to opposition parties. While the DA also raises private funds of undisclosed origin (it reportedly raised about R21 million from private funders in 2004),[74] and most likely has far greater success than other opposition parties, it is doubtful that it can come close to the ANC's level.

The ruling party's greater success in fund raising translates into a larger campaign war chest. In 1999, the ANC reportedly spent at least R100 million on its campaign whereas the DA spent perhaps R20 million.[75] The ruling party

---

[71] More specifically, 90% of the money is divided proportionally based on the number of seats held by parties in the national and provincial legislatures. The remaining 10% (the "equitable") portion is divided between the nine provincial legislatures based on the number of seats in each one. The parties in the provincial legislatures then divide the provincial allocations equally amongst themselves. See Steytler (2004: 61) for more details.
[72] Idasa. 2003. *Regulation of Private Funding to Political Parties* (Cape Town: Idasa).
[73] See Robinson and Brümmer (2006).
[74] See Robinson and Brümmer (2006: 14).
[75] Idasa (2003).

claims to have been forced to cut down on expenditures in 2004 – Lodge (2005) cites the more modest figure of R70 million – but even this scaled-back number was probably more than double the expenditures of the DA. And, in addition to actual campaign spending, the ruling party was better placed to exploit state resources during the campaigns. Although money alone does not determine the success of a campaign, the ANC's larger expenditures almost certainly allowed it to project its message more frequently and more broadly than its competition.

## Media Coverage

The ANC has also unquestionably dominated media coverage during South African campaigns, receiving greater attention in both the broadcast (radio, television) and print media during the run-up to the election. Amongst the opposition parties, the DA commandeered more attention than any other opposition party. However, it still fell well short of the ruling party. While this does not necessarily imply that the media is biased (as the opposition has at various times alleged), greater media coverage does provide the ruling party with yet another advantage over its competition.

The ANC's dominance of media coverage emerges clearly in the newspaper sample referenced earlier in this chapter. In addition to coding the rhetoric and campaign activities recorded in the articles, I also coded the number of times each article mentioned a particular party (results summarized in Table 5.10). In the 400-article sample, more than two-thirds of the articles mentioned the ANC, around half mentioned the DA, a quarter mentioned the IFP, and a quarter mentioned the NP. The average number of mentions of the ANC per article (for the whole sample, not just articles mentioning the party) was 3.3. The comparable number for the DA was 2.1, with the remaining parties dropping off considerably from there.

In a more extensive analysis of print and broadcast media, Davis (2005) reports comparable findings. Although it varied by station, television news coverage tended to devote around twice as much airtime to the ANC versus the DA, with the DA vying with the IFP for second place.[76] Coverage of parties by radio station also varied, but all stations devoted significantly more time to the ANC than any of the opposition parties. The radio station Yfm had perhaps the most equitable coverage, but it still devoted 32 percent of its time to the ANC, versus 24 percent to the DA and less for all other parties. Stations aimed at a largely African audience typically devoted more than twice as much attention to the ruling party.[77] Print media showed similar

---

[76] See Davis (2005: 234–235, Tables 12.1 and 12.2). Thus, data from the Media Monitoring project show that 31.7% of SABC coverage featured the ANC, whereas 16.3% featured the DA, 10.3% the IFP, 8.7% the NP, and so on from there. The same project showed that the independent channel E-TV devoted 47% of its airtime to the ANC but only 14% to the DA. Data from Media Tenor showed fairly similar results.

[77] See Davis (2005: 236, Table 12.3).

TABLE 5.10. *Media Coverage of Parties*

|  | Mean Number of Mentions of Party per Article | Number of Articles That Mention Party (percentage) |
| --- | --- | --- |
| ANC | 3.30 | 274 (.69) |
| DA | 2.08 | 204 (.51) |
| IFP | 0.93 | 102 (.26) |
| NNP | 0.84 | 102 (.26) |
| ID | 0.38 | 51 (.13) |
| Other | 1.42 | 115 (.29) |
| Sample Size | 400 | 400 |

patterns: Depending on the sample of papers surveyed and the group surveying them, coverage of the ANC represented about 41–42 percent of the total space of main news sections whereas coverage of the DA ranged from 16 to 20 percent and coverage of the IFP ranged from 10 to 16 percent.[78]

The uneven coverage of parties in the media does not necessarily imply bias, although both the ruling party and the opposition have made claims about the bias of various news sources in recent years. The ANC argues that the print media have resisted transformation and continue to favor white opposition parties, while opposition parties have alleged that the public broadcaster – the South African Broadcast Company (SABC) – has become dangerously intertwined with the ruling party and no longer represents an independent voice.[79] Refuting the ANC claims, Davis (2005) documents that South African print media transformed substantially over the 1994 to 2004 period. Most now have diverse readerships and editorial boards. During the 2004 campaigns, editorials tended to abstain from endorsements or support of the ruling party. Davis also finds little evidence in favor of the opposition's claim about the SABC: According to data collected by two different media monitoring projects, the SABC actually devoted less time to the ANC than E-TV, an independent television station. On the basis of this evidence, Davis concludes that the skewed coverage of the ANC represents not so much bias (an explicit attempt by the media to influence the election), but the fact that, as the ruling party, the ANC generates more newsworthy material than the opposition, and this results in greater coverage for the party across news media.

Regardless of their motivations, the South African media devote considerably more space, time, and attention to the ruling party. When taken into consideration with the ANC's greater ability to raise and spend money during elections, it becomes clear that the ruling party can saturate the electorate with its messages in a way that the opposition cannot match. In the war of words between the ruling party and the opposition over the image of the latter, this ability to project and saturate translates into a distinct advantage.

---

[78] See Davis (2005: 240, Tables 12.5 and 12.6).
[79] See Davis (2005) and Mbaya (2004).

## CONCLUSION: THE CHALLENGE OF IMAGE CHANGE THROUGH CAMPAIGNS

The 2004 elections saw the major competitors return to the persuasion-oriented strategies that marked the 1994 election. After focusing on the white electorate in 1999, the DA set out in 2004 to win African votes. In its efforts to do so, it adopted many of the tactics used by the NP in earlier elections: It distanced itself from apartheid; it fashioned its campaign events in a style designed to appeal to African voters and located them in African areas; it advertised the black and African leaders on its lists and made efforts to display them to the public at large; it aligned itself with an African party, the IFP; it designed policies and criticisms it hoped would draw African voters disillusioned by the ANC's performance; and it spent considerable time campaigning in African communities. In short, it attempted to portray itself as Africanizing. At the same time, the party failed to stay completely "on message," periodically making missteps the ANC used to hang it.

For as hard as the DA tried to sell its new image, the ANC – with its deeper pockets and greater media access – fought just as hard to preserve it. Although the ruling party often demeaned the opposition as insignificant, its patterns of rhetoric suggest otherwise. Along with its affiliates, the ANC routinely attacked the DA, countering the party's claims of transformation with apartheid imagery and allegations of racism. Indeed, the ANC referred to the DA more than any other party in the election, including its old nemesis, the IFP. And, although more standard election topics like policy and performance also figured centrally in party rhetoric, the DA's image vied with jobs as the second most common topic raised – beating out crime and HIV.

Moreover, as the competitors plied the electorate with radically differing stories about the DA's image, the end result was just muddied water: In spite of greater campaign coverage, African voters were more likely to profess uncertainty about the DA following the 2004 elections than they had been in 1994 or 1999. And, unlike 1994, when the DA was relatively unknown, the reason they were uncertain about the party in 2004 was not a lack of information in the media. Rather, voter uncertainty most likely represented genuine confusion about the nature of the DA's image. Was it a white party like the ANC said? Or was it transforming, as it claimed itself? The overall effect of the campaigns was simply to confuse voters as to the real nature of the party and its constituency – a result that almost certainly benefited the ruling party and its partners.

## APPENDIX TO CHAPTER 5: THE NEWSPAPERS

Research assistants in South Africa clipped election related articles for a fifty-five–day period prior to the 2004 election (clipping began the fourth week of February and ended at the election on April 15) using ten different dailies and weeklies: *Mail & Guardian; This Day; The Star; City Press; Sunday*

*Times; Sowetan; Cape Times; the Financial Mail; Business Day; The Sunday Independent*. Below is a brief synopsis of each of these papers.

## Daily Papers

*This Day*: A new (started in 2003) national daily with good political analysis and an excellent opinion/editorial page. The paper is generally progressive but even-handed. The parent company is Nigerian, giving the paper a slight pan-African bias.

*Business Day*: *Business Day* offers a pro-business, broadly pro-ANC critique.

*Sowetan*: This is the largest independent black-owned daily in the country. It is pro-ANC, with a latent African nationalism. It has a national distribution to urban centers but is mostly read in Gauteng.

*Cape Times*: Owned by Independent Newspapers, the *Cape Times* covers local Cape Town news and is the most general of the Cape Town papers.

*The Star*: Also owned by Independent Newspapers, *The Star* has some national distribution but is primarily a Gauteng (especially Johannesburg) publication.

## Weekly Papers

*Mail & Guardian*: The *Mail & Guardian* is the premier high-quality newspaper in South Africa that specializes in investigative reporting. It is based in Johannesburg but has a wide circulation, especially amongst the country's educated elite. Founded in 1985 by liberal journalists and initially run on a shoestring budget, it quickly developed a domestic and international following for its critical stories about the apartheid government. It was one of the first newspapers to target both black and white audiences. Now under the leadership of Ferrial Haffagee (ex-*Financial Mail* political editor), the first black female editor of a major paper in South Africa, it continues to offer extensive and often critical coverage of government activities.

*Sunday Times*: The *Sunday Times*, founded in 1906, is the largest weekly newspaper in South Africa. It covers a wide variety of topics and regularly does in-depth reports on political events and personalities. Its editor, Mondli Makhanya, was formerly with the *Mail & Guardian*.

*City Press*: This is the main "black" Sunday paper. Its editor, Mathatha Tsedu, was formerly with the *Sunday Times* and has a Black Consciousness background. The paper has traditionally been pro-ANC.

*The Sunday Independent*: This paper offers pro-business, liberal views and has a small, elitist but influential readership and a national distribution.

*Financial Mail*: This is a weekly magazine that includes good political analysis. It is broadly neoliberal and pro-business but is also pro-ANC.

The goal was to clip all election-related articles from all papers for all days the paper was available. In practice, the sample fell short of this. The clippers did a good job of clipping all of the articles from the days and papers they had, but they were not always able to get all papers for all days they were available. This happened for a variety of reasons: The paper did not show up in the office, the clipper forgot (or was unable) to buy the paper, the paper disappeared before it could be cut apart, and so on. In any case, it would seem that the actual sample of clippings was pretty random – at least with regard to the questions guiding my research. Altogether 1,148 articles on the election were clipped. On average, there were about 21 articles per day – though the number varied quite significantly from day to day. Almost all days had at least 10 articles. Of the dailies, articles came most frequently from *This Day* (17 percent of total), *The Star* (15 percent of total), *The Sowetan* (17 percent of total), and *The Cape Times* (19 percent). Of the weeklies, the *Mail & Guardian* (8 percent of total) and *City Press* (3 percent of total) accounted for the largest number of articles. Altogether, this represents a reasonably balanced, representative sample of newspapers.

# 6

## Can a Leopard Change Its Spots?

### Candidate Demographics and Party Label Change

The previous three chapters showed the many challenges South African opposition parties have faced in trying to use campaigns to alter party images. I now turn to an alternative method that parties have pursued toward this end: the manipulation of candidate characteristics. I argue that where the ideological reputations of parties are not well developed, candidate characteristics figure prominently in the formation of party labels. Changing candidate characteristics therefore offers parties a means to alter their party labels. This works through two mechanisms. First, a preference effect: Changing the decision makers in the party alters beliefs about the outcomes the party is likely to pursue. And second, a signaling effect: By unseating party stalwarts in favor of candidates with a different set of characteristics, a party sends a potent signal about its intentions.

I test these intuitions in the South African context. I show that parties (as well as journalists, pundits, and academics) frequently discuss the racial balance of candidate lists. Information about the racial balance of lists is therefore common knowledge and widely believed to be important. Using a new dataset that tracks the changing racial balance of the candidates of the ANC, the NNP, and the DA, I then demonstrate that the parties with the strongest incentives to change their labels – the "white" opposition parties – have indeed made extensive changes to their profiles since the end of apartheid. Starting out as exclusively white, these parties were at least 30 percent African by 2004. Finally, I examine whether these changes correlate with popular views of the images of parties. Although the data are noisy and far from conclusive, they show that as a party shifts in the inclusive (exclusive) dimension in terms of its candidates, popular impressions of the party generally follow suit.

Given the correlation between leadership demographics and party labels, this chapter closes with a puzzle: If changing leadership demographics is an effective way of bringing about label change, and parties want to change their labels, why have they not gone even further to "Africanize" their lists?

## CANDIDATES AND LABELS

Political scientists have traditionally seen party labels as ideological in nature and argue that voters use them as an informational device to distinguish between candidates. Whereas voters struggle to gather detailed knowledge about candidates, the label is widely known and understood, and hence imparts information about the likely policy preferences of candidates running on it (Downs 1957; Aldrich 1995; Cox 1997; Snyder and Ting 2002). Although this argument is prevalent and plausible, ideological positions are not always well developed: Ideologies can be incoherent, partially formed, or irrelevant, and parties may be young and not systematically associated with ideological positions. Under these conditions, the informational arrow likely runs in the opposite direction: from candidate characteristics to label. That is, voters make evaluations of what a party is about based on the candidates running on its slate: What are their reputations for honesty and competency? Where do they stand on certain issues? To what groups do they belong? This assumes that parties reflect the nature of the politicians that comprise them, their preferences, and the decisions that they make.[1]

While many different types of candidate characteristics might matter, group-based characteristics like ethnicity and race may be particularly relevant when voters believe that group identity is a strong predictor of candidate trustworthiness, credibility, knowledge, and behavior in office – the types of policies they will implement, how they will implement them, and, more basically, whom they will favor in the distribution of scarce resources. Group-based characteristics are also often highly visible, increasing their attractiveness as cues in low information environments. Empirically, examples of beliefs about group-based favoritism by elected officials abound, especially in Africa and parts of Asia. Chandra (2004) speculates that expectations of ethnic favoritism dominate in "patronage democracies" and demonstrates their prevalence in India. Posner (2005: 96) documents the pervasiveness of this belief in Zambia and other areas of Africa, writing that "it is widely assumed that [public officeholders] will use whatever resources they can control to build schools, clinics, and roads in their home areas and provide jobs for people from their ethnic group." Indeed, so central is the belief that the president will favor his own group that it has become "an axiom of politics" (Posner 2005: 99). Although both Chandra and Posner write explicitly about clientelistic or patronage-based systems, there is little reason to believe that beliefs about ethnic favoritism by elected leaders are limited to countries where these systems dominate: Favoritism can manifest itself in public policy development

---

[1] This observation generalizes to both candidate- and party-based systems. That candidate characteristics matter in the former is hardly contested (see Carey and Shugart 1995). The argument here is that candidate characteristics *also matter* in party-based systems when ideological party labels are undeveloped. Voters still need ways to distinguish between parties and are likely to look at candidate characteristics to infer something about the party as a whole.

and local public goods delivery just as surely as it does in handouts of rice or jobs on election day.

In situations where beliefs about group-based favoritism dominate, party labels become summary appraisals of the group characteristics of their members. If politicians favor members of their group, it follows that the larger the number and the higher the ranking of politicians from a certain group, the more likely the party will pursue the interests of that group and the closer the tie between the group and the party label. Chandra (2004) refers to voting based on this expectation as a "head count," explaining that "voters formulate preferences across parties by counting heads belonging to their 'own' ethnic category" (Chandra 2004: 83). Posner asserts even more simply that expectations about parties come from "the unprompted equation in people's minds of the party with the ethnic group of the party's president" (Posner 2005: 109). Whether voters add up all the group members in a party, or look only to the top rungs of the hierarchy, or perform some intermediate arithmetic, these examples suggest that candidate group characteristics will be a significant component of party labels. And, in a context of undeveloped ideologies and parties with little experience formulating and implementing policies, it makes sense that voters would look to the most visible members of the party to formulate beliefs about the party.

A powerful means for affecting label change therefore involves altering the demographic balance of candidates running on the party label. This affects party labels through two mechanisms. First, there is a *preference* effect. Altering the demographics of a party – particularly its leadership – changes the decision makers in the party and, hence, beliefs about the likely behavior of the party if in office. If voters all believe that politicians will favor their "own" group if in office, they should also believe that increasing the number of politicians from a given group will increase the chances that the party as a whole will prioritize the group's interests. A party that increases its representation of blacks, particularly at high levels, will become a "blacker" party.

Second, and less obvious, changing candidate characteristics produces a *signaling* effect: Bringing in new candidates means unseating old ones, and the more prominent the positions awarded to the new candidates, the more likely the individuals being unseated will have significant history and investment in the party. By unseating party loyalists, the party sends a costly – and therefore potent – signal about its intentions. Loyalists have invested years working their way up the hierarchy, have survived whatever sorting mechanisms the party uses to ensure its leadership is high quality, and presumably have skills that make them valuable. For these reasons, displacing them is a costly move, and one a party is not likely to make casually. In sum, altering candidate characteristics is a potent way for parties to manipulate their labels, and the higher up the party hierarchy the changes occur, the more powerful the effect. This is most likely to hold in countries where ideologies are poorly developed. But it may also hold for oppositions in more institutionalized systems – especially where they have long been out of power and have had few opportunities to develop reputations for policy implementation.

Posner (2005: 109 – 110) provides fascinating – if anecdotal – verification for these conjectures. He documents that Zambian party labels have been extremely responsive to changes in the ethnic background of party leaders. He tracks the history of the National Party (NP), formed in 1993. Its first leader was a member of a prominent Lozi family, so the party was initially seen as Lozi. When the torch passed to its second leader, a Tonga, the party label transformed from Lozi to Tonga, and with the ascension of its third leader, who hailed from the Northwest and was a member of the Kaonde tribe, the label changed once again. Similarly, the United National Independence Party (UNIP) started off as a Nyanja-speakers' party but transformed to a Tonga-speakers' party when the presidency was held by a Tonga-speaker and then to Lozi-speaking party with the arrival of a Lozi-speaking president. Although Posner's examples all originate in Zambia and display an unusual sensitivity to singular changes at the top of the party, the observation that party labels respond to changes in the composition of candidate characteristics is a general one that should apply to all cases where party labels reflect the individuals running under them. Hence, we should expect parties to exploit this avenue when attempting to change their labels.

## SOUTH AFRICAN CANDIDATE DEMOGRAPHICS AND PARTY LABEL CHANGE

The previous section makes two claims. First, party labels should respond to changes in candidate composition: As parties get "blacker" in terms of their candidate mix, so too, should their labels. And second, party leaders should be aware of this and seek to exploit it when attempting to bring about label change. This section uses data on the racial composition of party lists, public opinion research on views about the exclusivity of parties, and reports of campaign activity to evaluate whether these claims hold for South Africa. As previous chapters have argued, South African opposition parties have strong incentives to "Africanize" their images. To what extent have they tried to do this through altering their candidate lists? And has altering their lists affected popular views of their images?

To preview the results, I first show that the racial balance of party lists – especially the oppositions' – has been a frequent subject of campaign rhetoric. During campaigns, parties discuss (extol, condemn) the racial composition of their own lists as well as those of their opponents. The racial balance of lists is also a common topic of discussion amongst pundits, journalists, and political analysts. I then show that parties with the strongest incentives to change their labels – the "white" opposition parties – have made *extensive* changes to their candidate profiles since the end of apartheid. The National Party moved first, significantly Africanizing its lists by 1999. The Democratic Party moved second, with major changes not appearing until 2004. It is important not to overstate these changes: The candidates of these parties remain majority white or coloured and their top rungs of leadership are especially so. However, given their exclusively white starting point at the end of apartheid, their current levels of 30 percent or more African stand out. In contrast, the ANC, which began with almost perfectly balanced lists in 1994, has been slowly Africanizing – although its candidates remain, by far, the most racially representative of all South African parties.

Finally, I examine whether these changes match popular views of the exclusivity of parties – a proxy for the racial component of party labels. Although the data are noisy and far from conclusive, they generally show that as a party shifts in the inclusive (exclusive) dimension in terms of its candidates, popular impressions of the party follow suit.

## Campaign Rhetoric

The racial breakdown of party lists is a frequent topic of discussion in South Africa. Political analysts track trends in candidate racial demographics and parties characterize the nature of their lists and those of their competitors, providing head counts of different racial categories to voters. Hence, the racial composition of the leadership of parties is salient to both politicians and those who watch them.

Lodge (2004) notes that elections in South Africa are "as much about leadership and leaders" as they are about "programmes and manifestos."[2] Consequently, it is not surprising that political analysts and journalists focus considerable attention on lists during campaign periods, scrutinizing them along multiple dimensions. Lodge (1999a) devotes several pages to a careful accounting of the ANC's lists: the movement of incumbents up, down, or off of lists; the number and ranking of members of the Communist Party; the placement of defectors from other parties; charges of corruption or criminality against various candidates; the rise and fall of provincial factions; the gender breakdown of the lists; and – most relevant here – their racial composition. In 1999, Lodge – working with the Electoral Institute of South Africa (EISA) – provided a racial scorecard of the ANC's lists province-by-province, generally noting the party's efforts to have their candidate lists reflect constituency demographics. EISA coverage notes that "18 of the first 50 names in the national to national list belong to [non-Africans]"; therefore, "any 'Africanist' sentiments which exist within the ANC do not seem to have influenced the list process" (EISA 1999b: 5). Further, "African names appear in a third of the top 30 positions [of the Western Cape list], slightly more proportionately than the 20% African share of the provincial population," and "the 14 'non-African' names [of the Northern Cape list] also suggest a similar concern with racial representativeness" (EISA 1999b: 6). In contrast, "such preoccupations seem

[2] Tom Lodge, "Parties not People: An Opinion Piece." EISA *Election Update 2004* 3, 1 March 2004: 2.

not to have prevailed in KwaZulu-Natal" as "Indian names are absent from the first ten positions in the list for the KwaZulu-Natal legislature; and only nine out of 68 candidates listed are Indian, most of them in unelectable low positions" (EISA 1999b: 6).

This kind of racial score-carding is not limited to Lodge: Most EISA regional analysts in 1999 and 2004 provided some degree of running commentary on the racial breakdown of the ANC's lists – especially in those provinces where the party was courting non-African voters. In writing about the Northern Cape, Steve Robins noted that "the ANC in the Northern Cape appears to be acutely aware of the salience of ethnicity" as "five out of the six regional leaders [on the provincial list] are coloured."[3] He also devoted considerable discussion to the ANC's decision to place Manne Dipico, an African, on the top of the list, and the problems this might generate for the ANC's efforts to woo coloured voters. Commenting on the Northwest province, EISA analysts observed that the ANC regional list included "white Potchefstroom chicken farmer" Jan Serfontein – a move by the ANC "to reach or, at the very least, appease white farmers in the region."[4] And no discussion of Western Cape politics would be complete without an extensive analysis of the racial breakdown of the province's candidate list – see, for example, Calland and Jacob, EISA *Election Update 1999* 8, March 1999: 20–21 or Cheryl Hendricks, EISA *Election Update 2004*, 2: 35.

Race figured even more centrally – indeed almost exclusively – in discussions of the lists of the NNP and the DA. The NP's efforts to diversify its lists in 1994 and 1999 received lengthy commentary, some positive, some negative. Giliomee (1994: 57) noted that 40 percent of the party's National Assembly candidates were nonwhite by 1994 but bemoaned the fact that none of these were "political leaders of significance." Mattes et al. (1996), in an insightful discussion of the 1994 Western Cape election, observed that the top positions of the party remained white – only spots two and three in the top ten went to coloureds. Similar comments prevailed in 1999. In a discussion of Northern Cape politics, Robins (1999b: 14) noted that "the mostly white NNP candidate lists alienated a considerable number of black and coloured NNP members," which in turn "caused considerable damage to the party."[5] In contrast, Calland and Jacobs (1999:19) were more positive about the party's efforts in the Western Cape, noting that it was "fast becoming a largely coloured party, with a white-coloured leadership."[6] In 2004, coverage of the DP and its lists greatly overshadowed that of the NP, but when the NP's candidates did receive commentary, racial balance was the primary dimension of

---

[3] Steve Robins, "Northern Cape." EISA *Election Update 1999* 7, February 1999: 14.
[4] Andrew Manson, Neil Roos, and Jennifer Seif. "North West Province." EISA *Election Update 1999* 7, February 1999: 20.
[5] Steve Robins, "Northern Cape." EISA *Election Update 1999* 7, February 1999: 14.
[6] Calland and Jacobs, "Western Cape." In EISA *Election Update 1999*, No. 8, 12 March 1999: 19.

analysis. In an article that expended many paragraphs on the ANC's lists, dissecting them from multiple angles, the author finally got to the NP in the last few lines of the article. The central observation: Only one NP list was headed by a black person and, since losing David Malatsi, "there has been no black leader in its ranks with enough political clout to attract black votes."[7]

Political analysts have also frequently discussed the racial composition of the DP's lists, especially in 1999 and 2004, after the party became the largest opposition party. In 1999, a common refrain was that the party had become whiter by recruiting noted conservatives like Tertius Delport and Nigel Bruce and in the process losing valuable African candidates like Bukelwa Mbulawa (for a discussion of these events, see Lodge 1999a: 101–102). In 2004, comments focused on the party's efforts to Africanize. Cherry (2004: 7) noted that the party was making a "concerted effort" to bring on board more black candidates. Merten (2004) discussed efforts by the DP to alter its "white party" image by "ensuring its 2004 election candidates were selected on the basis of their representativeness of South African society, as well as merit." In a discussion of Mpumalanga's lists, Ndlangisa's (2004) only comment on the DA's lists was that they featured more black candidates than previous years.[8] Chalmers (2004) noted that "key black candidates remain high on the [DA's] list, in line with the party's bid to increase the number of votes it clinches in areas that have not traditionally been DA strongholds."[9] Other analysts were less laudatory: Nic Borain, an analyst at the HSBC, commented in a *Business Day* article a few days prior to the election that "The DA has to find black leaders who can articulate the DA's position in the black community" and suggested that it had yet to do this: In spite of prominent African leaders like Joe Seremane and Dan Maluleke and a "smattering" of other leaders around the country, all nine provincial leaders of the party were still white men.[10] In an article discussing the DA's hopes to "take on the ANC in its own backyard," Merten (2004) notes: "[A]s it stands, only a handful of its 54 MPs are black and the party lacks visible senior black public representatives." Others noted tensions produced by diversification. Tabane (2004d) discusses allegations by African DP candidates that the party was exploiting them, using them to get black votes but not advancing them fast enough.[11]

In sum, South African political analysts, journalists, pundits, and even ordinary citizens make frequent reference to the racial breakdown of party lists, charting how parties have pursued racial balance or racial change over time. Accompanying this narrative about race and leadership is a generally

---

[7] Hopewell Radebe, "ANC Women Beat Quotas on Poll Lists." *Business Day*, March 15, 2004.
[8] Sabelo Ndlangisa, "Mpumalanga List Surprise." *Sunday Times*, February 29, 2004.
[9] Robyn Chalmers, "Overlooked DA MPs Riding High on Party Electoral Lists." *Business Day*, March 15, 2004.
[10] Kevin O'Grady, Rob Rose, and Sphiwe Mboyane, "Vindication or the Scrapheap for Opposition DA." *Business Day*, April 13, 2004.
[11] Rapule Tabane, "DA Wracked by Racial Tensions." *Mail and Guardian*, March 12, 2004.

held belief that *candidate characteristics matter* – that voters understand enough about the racial characteristics of the lists to reward (or punish) parties for their actions and that parties – understanding that voters understand this – use the lists as a key way of signaling to the electorate. As Cherry (2004) put it: "[T]he makeup of [the parties'] candidate lists can reveal – at a superficial level, it must be conceded – the real extent of their transformation."

The statements of the parties themselves suggest that they also place significance on candidate characteristics. Although the ANC tends to place the most emphasis on nonracial aspects of its lists – especially gender – party leaders clearly believe racial balance is important and strategically emphasize it when courting minority votes. In 1994, when the regional leadership was formulating strategy in the Western Cape, Mandela himself pushed to diversify the lists to dispel doubts in the coloured community that the ANC was an African-only party. He exhorted his party:

> The ordinary man, no matter to what population group he belongs, must look to our structures and see that "I, as a coloured man, am represented. I have got Allan Boesak there whom I trust." And an Indian must also be able to say: "There is Kathadra – I am represented."[12]

Mandela also personally intervened to have a coloured politician – Allan Boesak – placed at the top of the provincial list as the party's premier-designate instead of African candidates Lerumo Kalako and Tony Yengeni – presumably because he believed coloured voters would be more likely to vote ANC if one of their own headed its lists.[13]

In 1999, the party continued to recruit coloured politicians in the Western Cape – overtly courting several in the NP (e.g., Peter Marais) it had previously spurned as apartheid collaborators. Ebrahim Rasool (ANC provincial premier designate) explained that the party had a "hunger for victory" and sought those who could help it achieve this. The party's lists reflected this philosophy: Coloured candidates dominated the top ten positions of the Western Cape lists and filled two-thirds of its total slots. African provincial leaders, previously dominant, had been rotated off the provincial list onto the national one.[14] ANC leaders used similar tactics in courting the Indian vote: When speaking to an Indian audience in Lenasia (Johannesburg), Mandela noted that Indians were the most represented group in government, with five ministers – Mac Maharaj, Kader Asmal, Jay Naidoo, Mohamed Valli Moose, and Dullah Omar – of Indian origin.[15]

In 2004, as the ANC moved in the direction of courting the "mlungu" (white) vote, it sent white (usually Afrikaans speaking) candidates like Sam de Beer (former education minister for the NP), Joggie Boers (also a former

---

[12] Quoted in Mattes et al. (1996: 122).
[13] Mattes et al. (1996); Eldridge and Seekings (1996).
[14] Calland and Jacobs (1999).
[15] Chetty (1999).

NP candidate), Derek Hanekom, Gerhard Koornhof, and Mary Metcalfe into white communities to play at "*koeksister* politics" (*koeksister* is a traditional pastry beloved in Afrikaaner communities). During one of these excursions, Joggie Boers exclaimed to an Afrikaans-speaking audience "Ek is 'n Boer in die ANC" ("I am a Boer in the ANC" – Boer is an Afrikaans term for farmer, and also means Afrikaner in general). At the same event, Koornhof quoted from the ANC's 1955 Freedom Charter, saying that South Africa belonged to all who lived in it – black and white.[16] Gauteng Minister of Safety (ANC) Novula Mokonyane explained that credible, prominent people like de Beer and Boers helped the party to dissuade whites of the misperception that the ANC was a black organization that cared for blacks only rather than a home for all South Africans.[17] Another high-ranking ANC official explained: "[On] the issue of race balance – we have to ensure there are Indians, coloureds and whites on the lists. It may seem like we are imposing this, but this is the criterion agreed to by ANC members."[18] In sum, the notion that candidate lists should be racially balanced to make the party attractive to non-African voters figures centrally in the ANC's philosophy.

The opposition parties lagged the ANC in using candidate demographics to court new constituencies, but by 2004 this had become an important component of their campaigns. Accounts of the first post-apartheid election (1994)[19] give little indication that the opposition parties engaged in overt advertising of their candidate demographics – perhaps because they were still by and large very white. However, by 1999, candidate demographics did enter into their campaigns, albeit in different ways. During that election, the NP utilized its nonwhite candidates (especially well-placed coloureds) to advertise its transformation to a "rainbow" party. For example, Pieter Willem Saaiman, the party's (coloured) leader of the Northern Cape, explained in a 1999 campaign event:

I am the most acceptable leader for the province. Manne Dipico [the ANC leader, an African] will always be seen as a person who represents only part of the people – it will take years before he can overcome that.[20]

He went on to proclaim the NP as "the rainbow party of the province." Coloured leaders in the Western Cape conveyed similar messages to the electorate.

In contrast, in 1999 the DP was not yet playing this game. If anything, its focus in this election was on promoting the *Afrikaans* speakers on its

---

[16] Xolisa Vapi, "ANC Chases Afrikaner Voters in Brixton with Koeksister Politics." *This Day*, February 23, 2004.
[17] Rapule Tabane, "ANC Targets Mlungu Vote." *Mail & Guardian*, January 23, 2004.
[18] Jaspreet Kindra, "'Too Many Pahads on the ANC List.'" *Mail & Guardian*, 21 November 2003.
[19] For example, Giliomee (1994), Welsh (1994), Mattes et al. (1996), and Eldridge and Seekings (1996).
[20] Turkington (1999).

lists – although this certainly was not overt. For example, the party recruited native son Hennie Bester to lead it in the Western Cape, a move Barrell (1999a) credits as allowing the party to move into traditional Afrikaans-speaking communities: "He speaks the local white farmers' language, directly but softly and with the same Cape Brei that purrs off [the local's] palate." The party also absorbed many whites – mostly Afrikaans speakers – from the National Party.

By 2004, however, both the NP and the DP placed great emphasis on their leadership profiles as evidence of their transformation and credibility as representatives of nonwhite communities. At the NP manifesto launch in Stellenbosch, Marthinus Van Schalkwyk proclaimed: "We speak in government with the voice of every community: coloured, white, black, and Indian.... There is no better proof of the strength of the NP than to stand here today looking out at the faces and the personalities of our party." He went on to showcase various candidates, including new recruits like John Mavuso (African), as evidence of the party's transformation.[21]

During his speech to launch the DA's candidate list (in Durban, mid-February), Tony Leon employed a similar strategy. He stated repeatedly that the DA's candidates would represent not just the party, and not specific communities, but "all of South Africa," and "all of the people." He also explained that the party's criteria for selecting candidates included "merit, first and foremost; integrity; diversity; and commitment to the party." The party, he said, sought to "achieve a list of candidates that is both effective and diverse." He then went on to showcase eight new candidates, at least six of whom were nonwhite. Fifteen or so additional DA politicians spoke that day, half of whom were nonwhite. Africans figured prominently on the speakers' list as well as in the group Leon touted. Thus, like the NP, the DA combined a verbal commitment to a diverse yet effective leadership that would represent all of South Africa with visual cues about its racial representativeness. Both parties – especially the DA – employed this strategy repeatedly at nearly all public events. Leon rarely appeared for major rallies, speeches, or other important campaign events without being surrounded by nonwhite DA candidates.

DA leaders spoke frequently of the need for its lists to "reflect South Africa." Thus, Communications Director Nick Clelland-Stokes explained: "We are going to have people who represent South Africa, quality people who are capable of providing solutions and change."[22] Leon echoed this sentiment in an interview, stating: "The lists should reflect South Africa. We don't want to go with an all-white team."[23] Theuns Botha, the leader of the party in the Western Cape, was more flamboyant in his expression. After explaining that

---

[21] Waghied Misbach, "'NNP Only Rainbow Party in SA.'" *Sowetan*, February 23, 2004.
[22] Marianne Merten, "DA to 'Take on the ANC in Its Own Backyard.'" *Mail & Guardian*, 8 January 2004.
[23] Drew Forrest, "I'm Not a Guilty White: Interview with Tony Leon." *Mail & Guardian*, Jaunary 30, 2004.

the first ten names of the DA's provincial list included five coloured candidates, he exclaimed: "This list should finally shut the mouths of the prophets of doom who claim the DA is only for the white elite and the so-called white wing." Botha also insinuated that the ANC/NP alliance had dragged its feet in announcing its candidate for provincial premier because it planned to put a black man in power and this would alienate coloured voters. Not missing a beat, ANC leader Ebrahim Rasool lodged a complaint with the IEC, accusing Botha of racism.[24] Finally, although the party generally avoided giving explicit racial head counts of it candidates (Botha was the exception), it frequently extolled the blackness of its youth leadership division, which it claimed was "predominantly black."[25]

In sum, the parties behaved as if they believed the racial profile of their candidates mattered – it had the power to alienate and the power to attract.

## Racial Balance of Lists

The last section established that – at least in terms of talk – South African parties have behaved as if they believe that the racial balance of their candidate lists is important. The general picture painted in the press and by the parties themselves is that the ANC is the most racially balanced party, while the opposition parties are slowly moving in that direction, gradually transforming their all-white candidate lists into more racially representative ones.

To what extent is the popular image correct? To evaluate this, I collected the full candidate lists for the ANC, NP, and DP for the 1994, 1999, and 2004 elections. Each party published between eighteen and nineteen lists for each election: nine "regional" lists (candidates for provincial legislatures), nine "regional to national" lists (regional candidates slated for the national legislature), and, for the ANC in all years and the DP in 1994, one "national" list (national candidates slated for the national legislature). The lists ranged from a dozen or so candidates to several hundred. Each party altogether put forth 500 to 800 candidates per election. Two researchers coded the race of each candidate on the basis of names. As white and coloured names are indistinguishable in South Africa, these two groups were coded together. Any conflicts in coding were subsequently researched and, if found impossible to resolve, the candidate's race was left as "uncertain." Fortunately this occurred in very few circumstances. The appendix at the end of this chapter has more details on the coding.

Looking at Table 6.1, the ANC's claims about racial representativeness appear grounded in reality. In 1994, the party displayed almost perfect racial balancing, with its candidate breakdown closely matching the racial breakdown of the South African population as a whole. It is also true, however,

---

[24] Waghled Misbach, "ANC Lodges a Complaint." *Cape Times*, February 26, 2004.
[25] See, for example, Joe Seremane (DA Chairperson and MP), "Nobody Cares What Azapo Says – It Has Nothing to Offer." Letter to the Editor, *The Star*, February 24, 2004.

TABLE 6.1. *The Racial Breakdown of the ANC's Candidates, 1994–2004*

|  | 1994 | 1999 | 2004 |
|---|---|---|---|
| Total |  |  |  |
| African | 553 | 669 | 636 |
| Indian | 67 | 43 | 39 |
| White/coloured | 166 | 146 | 123 |
| Overall Percent (all lists) |  |  |  |
| African | .70 | .78 | .79 |
| Indian | .09 | .05 | .05 |
| White/coloured | .21 | .17 | .15 |
| Overall Percent (national list) |  |  |  |
| African | .68 | .70 | .75 |
| Indian | .10 | .09 | .08 |
| White/coloured | .22 | .20 | .16 |
| Percent in Top 5 (all lists) |  |  |  |
| African | .78 | .74 | .79 |
| Indian | .01 | .04 | .04 |
| White/coloured | .21 | .22 | .17 |
| Percent in Top 10 (all lists) |  |  |  |
| African | .72 | .72 | .78 |
| Indian | .05 | .04 | .05 |
| White/coloured | .22 | .24 | .17 |
| Percent in Top Five (national list) |  |  |  |
| African | .80 | .60 | .60 |
| Indian | .00 | .20 | .20 |
| White/coloured | .20 | .20 | .20 |
| Percent in Top Ten (national list) |  |  |  |
| African | .60 | .80 | .80 |
| Indian | .20 | .10 | .10 |
| White/coloured | .20 | .10 | .10 |
| Percent in Top Twenty (national list) |  |  |  |
| African | .65 | .65 | .80 |
| Indian | .20 | .25 | .10 |
| White/coloured | .15 | .10 | .10 |

that between 1994 and 2004 the party pursued a gradual, bottom-up process of Africanization. In 1999, the top of its lists (especially the national list) underwent little change while the overall fraction of Africans on the lists increased. This suggests that the party was recruiting Africans at higher rates than the other groups but placing the new recruits in lower positions on the lists. In 2004, change had penetrated the top. However, changes were slow and mild, and at the end of the period the party still displayed impressive racial balancing.

Can a Leopard Change Its Spots? 153

TABLE 6.2. *The Racial Breakdown of the NP's Candidates, 1994–2004*

|  | 1994 | 1999 | 2004 |
|---|---|---|---|
| Total |  |  |  |
| African | 186 | 198 | 138 |
| Indian | 53 | 47 | 25 |
| White/coloured | 544 | 392 | 287 |
| Overall Percent |  |  |  |
| African | .24 | .31 | .30 |
| Indian | .07 | .07 | .06 |
| White/coloured | .69 | .62 | .63 |
| Percent in Top Five |  |  |  |
| African | .18 | .23 | .20 |
| Indian | .02 | .02 | .02 |
| White/coloured | .80 | .75 | .77 |
| Percent in Top Ten |  |  |  |
| African | .22 | .22 | .25 |
| Indian | .03 | .03 | .04 |
| White/coloured | .74 | .75 | .69 |

Table 6.2 shows the data for the NP. The NP pursued Africanization early and aggressively. Prior to 1994, the NP was 100 percent white. By 1994, it was almost one-quarter African and 18 percent of its top five slots were African – rather a remarkable change for the party that had designed and implemented apartheid! This pattern continued in 1999 when the NP increased the percentage of Africans on its list by 7 percentage points and decreased its percentage of whites/coloureds by a similar amount. This meant that more than 30 percent of the party's list in 1999 was African. Indians held constant at 7 percent both years. Furthermore, not only did the overall percentage of Africans increase, the percentage in the top five positions also increased and the percentage in the top ten held steady. In other words, not only was the NP bringing in more Africans, it was also putting them in its top positions, the ones most likely to actually get seats. In 2004, change leveled off and the party looked more or less as it had in 1999: A little less than a third African and a little more than two-thirds white, coloured, or Indian.

Table 6.3 shows the racial breakdown of the DP's candidates. The DP's initial efforts at Africanization were less aggressive than the NP's: Both parties started out with zero Africans prior to 1994 and while the NP had achieved nearly one-quarter Africans in 1994, the DP was only at around 14 percent. This pattern continued in 1999. While the NP's list was almost one-third African in 1999, the DP's was only 20 percent. Furthermore, while the DP did increase its percentage of Africans by 6 percentage points between 1994 and 1999, much of this change came at the expense of Indians. Finally, the top of

TABLE 6.3. *The Racial Breakdown of the DP's Candidates, 1994–2004*

|  | 1994 | 1999 | 2004 |
|---|---|---|---|
| Total |  |  |  |
| African | 51 | 143 | 137 |
| Indian | 36 | 39 | 15 |
| White/coloured | 287 | 527 | 243 |
| Overall Percent |  |  |  |
| African | .14 | .20 | .34 |
| Indian | .10 | .05 | .04 |
| White/coloured | .77 | .74 | .61 |
| Percent in Top Five |  |  |  |
| African | .18 | .12 | .19 |
| Indian | .02 | .03 | .04 |
| White/coloured | .80 | .84 | .76 |
| Percent in Top Ten |  |  |  |
| African | .19 | .18 | .25 |
| Indian | .01 | .03 | .04 |
| White/coloured | .80 | .78 | .70 |

the DP's lists actually became whiter over the same period. And, although the DP changed its overall representation of Africans, it still lagged far behind the NP. Hence, it remained a much whiter (or coloured) party than the NP and its attempts at Africanizing were more superficial.

In 2004, the DP/DA's strategy clearly shifted in the direction of Africanization. It increased the percentage of Africans on its lists from 20 to 34 – the largest change of any party in any election. This gave it a higher African percentage than the NP. Moreover, it also increased its African representation in the highest levels of its list – the top five slots. In 1999, these were only 12 percent African; in 2004, they were 19 percent African. Thus, while the DP initially lagged the NP in Africanization, by 2004 it had caught up and even surpassed it.

In addition to coding the race of each candidate, I also tracked their career paths, noting for the 1999 and 2004 elections candidates who had also been on a list in the election directly prior (so 1999 candidates that had also been on a 1994 list, and so on). Table 6.4 shows the racial breakdown of new candidates for each party for the 1999 and 2004 elections and provides another window into the recruitment patterns of the parties.

The data in Table 6.4 confirm the pattern of Africanization evident in Tables 6.1–6.3. All of the parties had more African recruits in 1999 and 2004 (percentage wise) than they had previously had on their lists. Thus, in 1999, ANC recruits were 84 percent African whereas the 1994 list (per Table 6.1) was 70 percent African. Similarly, the NP's recruits in 1999 were 39 percent

TABLE 6.4. *The Racial Breakdown of the New Candidates, 1999 and 2004*

|  | ANC | | NP | | DP | |
|---|---|---|---|---|---|---|
|  | 1999 | 2004 | 1999 | 2004 | 1999 | 2004 |
| African | 451 | 259 | 175 | 108 | 142 | 119 |
|  | (.84) | (.84) | (.39) | (.38) | (.22) | (.43) |
| Indian | 17 | 14 | 32 | 19 | 35 | 9 |
|  | (.03) | (.05) | (.07) | (.07) | (.05) | (.03) |
| White/coloured | 66 | 36 | 245 | 155 | 464 | 150 |
|  | (.12) | (.12) | (.54) | (.55) | (.72) | (.54) |
| Total New | 534 | 309 | 452 | 282 | 641 | 278 |

African, whereas its previous list was 24 percent – a substantial jump. The DP's African recruits in 1999 (22 percent) were the lowest of any party in any year but still represented a moderate jump over the previous list (14 percent). The most impressive jump belongs to the DP in 2004, whose recruit pool in that year was 43 *percent African* (versus 20 percent in the 1999 list). This suggests further confirmation that the NP's efforts at Africanization began *earlier* than the DP's – in 1994 and 1999, versus 2004 for the DP – but that by 2004 the DP had switched gears and was actively pursuing African politicians.

Altogether, the candidate data confirm party rhetoric: The ANC is the most broadly representative party in South Africa (in terms of its candidates) and the "white" opposition parties made substantial efforts in the decade after the end of apartheid to Africanize their lists. At the same time, the data also reveal the limits of these generalizations. While the ANC remains the most balanced party, it has made slow and subtle moves in the direction of Africanization. Furthermore, while the opposition parties made large changes in the racial balance of their candidate lists, they remain majority white (or coloured) parties: Their candidates by no means reflect the racial mosaic of the wider population. In other words, while they had traveled far, they still had a long way to go before they could claim to be real rainbow parties.

**Lists and Labels**

Have the oppositions' attempts at "Africanization" resulted in changes in popular views about party labels? Have Africans come to see these parties as less exclusively white? And has the gradual erosion of white and coloured representation on the ANC's lists resulted in changes in how these groups view the party? Finally, how have Indians responded to their diminishing representation on the lists of all three of the major parties? Insights into all of these questions can be gleaned by comparing data on views about the exclusivity/inclusivity of parties (for a full report on this variable, see Table 2.6) with shifts in candidate demographics (Tables 6.1–6.3). To facilitate comparisons, Tables 6.5–6.10 distill the most relevant information. (Note: Views of

TABLE 6.5. *African Impressions of the NP and Party Demographics*

|  | 1994 | 1999 | 2004 |
|---|---|---|---|
| Africans who see NP as exclusive* | 63 | 44 | 22 |
| Africans who are uncertain about the NP | 29 | 6 | 67 |
| African candidates on NP lists | 24 | 31 | 30 |

*Note*: All cells are percentages.
*Based only on those who had an opinion, i.e., uncertain responses eliminated.

TABLE 6.6. *African Impressions of the DP and Party Demographics*

|  | 1994 | 1999 | 2004 |
|---|---|---|---|
| Africans who see DP as exclusive* | 32 | 72 | 28 |
| Africans who are uncertain about the DP | 50 | 53 | 64 |
| African candidates on DP lists | 14 | 20 | 34 |

*Note*: All cells are percentages.
*Based only on those who had an opinion, i.e., uncertain responses eliminated.

exclusivity are calculated *based only on respondents who had an opinion* about the party. This eliminates "uncertain" responses, which are included in a separate row in the table).

Table 6.5 shows the change in African views about the exclusivity of the NP over time as well as the fraction of African candidates on the party's lists. As expected, the two correlate with each another: As the party increased its representation of Africans on its lists, fewer Africans saw the party as exclusive. Indeed, by 2004, only 22 percent of Africans with a clear opinion about the party believed it represented only one group. Uncertainty also increased over the time period (with a remarkable dip in 1999). Thus, as the NP diversified its lists, Africans either came to see the party as more inclusive or became more uncertain about it. Furthermore, if anything, the table *understates* the correlation: It only begins in 1994, *after* the largest changes occurred in both variables. Prior to 1994, the NP fielded only white candidates. And, as the agent of apartheid, it was almost certainly viewed as a whites-only party by Africans.

Table 6.6 shows the trajectory of African opinion about the DP from 1994 to 2004 as well as the fraction of the DP lists composed of Africans over the same time period. The relationship is less perfect but nevertheless exhibits the expected correlation. Between 1994 and 2004, the party significantly increased the percentage of African candidates on its lists – from 14 percent to 34 percent. Over that time, the fraction of Africans who saw it as exclusive diminished and uncertainty increased. Thus, as with the NP, as the percentage of African candidates on the list climbed, Africans either became more optimistic about the party's image or more uncertain. The change is perhaps not as large as the party might have hoped, but it is nevertheless in the correct direction. And, as with the NP, the most dramatic changes most likely occurred before the data series began – in the pre-1994 period when the party went from exclusively white to 14 percent African.

The major anomaly – if it is one – is the 1999 election, when Africans became quite negative about the DA's exclusiveness, even though it had marginally increased African representation on its lists. The difference between the DP and the NP is especially divergent and interesting. What was going on? First, recall from Chapter 4 that the NP's campaign in 1999 at least started on an inclusive note, whereas the DP ran on *swaart gevaar* (black fear) – or at least the ANC was successful at painting it as such. The DP's 1999 campaign was a sharp departure from its inclusive, liberal, "technocratic" campaign of 1994 when it was not very well known. For many Africans, their first real exposure to the party was in 1999, and it was negative. Second, as the previous section made clear, the DP's "Africanization" in 1999 was exceedingly superficial: Although its lists became marginally more African, the top slots of the lists actually became *whiter*. In contrast, the NP list change was much broader and deeper. Hence, it is not surprising that African respondents did not give great credence to the small increase in African representation on the DP lists between 1994 and 1999. In 2004, however, when the party made a much more aggressive change – both in terms of overall numbers as well as change at the top – and ran an inclusive campaign, Africans shifted their opinions of the party. This suggests that the overall fraction of list candidates is one of several indicators voters consult when forming opinions about parties. Voters may also look at the ranking of candidates and the most visible members and the general campaign behavior of the party.

Moving on to white and coloured impressions of the ANC: Has the relatively minor, yet nevertheless real, Africanization evident in the ANC's candidate lists translated into changes in the way groups view the party? Here the data are contradictory. On the one hand, between 1994 and 1999, both whites and coloureds became more likely to see the party as exclusive (i.e., African), a change that correlates with the biggest reduction in the fraction of these groups on the ANC's lists. On the other hand, between 1999 and 2004, when the Africanization of the ANC's lists continued, albeit at a slower pace, many whites and coloureds reversed their opinions and returned to seeing the party as inclusive (see Table 6.7).

Several explanations suggest themselves. First, although the ANC Africanized slightly between 1994 and 2004, it began the period with almost perfectly balanced lists and its lists were *still* the most representative of the broader South African population in 2004. It is possible that whites and coloureds began arriving at more realistic and empirically grounded impressions of the party as they came to know it better and fear it less. As Chapter 5 suggests, the ANC's 2004 campaign was substantially more "bridging" than its 1999 campaign, which may also have helped impressions. Second, although the party recruited at a faster rate than other groups

TABLE 6.7. *White/Coloured Impressions of the ANC and Party Demographics*

|  | 1994 | 1999 | 2004 |
|---|---|---|---|
| Whites who see ANC as exclusive* | 66 | 90 | 61 |
| Coloureds who see ANC as exclusive* | 42 | 58 | 28 |
| Whites who are uncertain about the ANC | 8 | 1 | 15 |
| Coloureds who are uncertain about the ANC | 19 | 3 | 17 |
| White/coloured candidates on ANC lists | 21 | 17 | 15 |

*Note*: All cells are percentages.
*Based only on those who had an opinion, i.e. uncertain responses eliminated.

(Table 6.4), it continued to recruit minorities, and these individuals were in many ways quite different from their predecessors. Although the ANC was "whiter" in 1994 than 2004, many of the whites on its early lists were old-guard anti-apartheid activists, typically members of the communist party – not individuals that ordinary white South Africans would count as "representative" of the white community (indeed, quite the opposite). In contrast, the recruits for 2004 include younger politicians, members of the technocratic elite, whose experience is in the post-apartheid era. They may not be "sons of the soil" in the sense of seeing themselves primarily as representatives of white interests, but neither are they old-guard communists. Whites might be inclined to give them more credit than their predecessors. Finally, because the data combine coloured and white candidates, it obscures relative changes between these two groups. It is possible, indeed even likely, that ANC recruitment of coloureds has declined less than recruitment of whites and may have even increased, especially in key areas like the Western Cape. If true, then changes in coloured popular opinion may in fact match changes in coloured representation. Unfortunately, the data do not allow this to be teased out.

Finally, we can analyze the effects of declining candidate representation on Indian impressions of the three parties. Here the results are all more or less as expected: As the parties have reduced their representation of Indian candidates, Indians have come to see them as more exclusive. Most Indians believed all three parties were inclusive in 1994. By 2004, half or close to half saw the ANC and NP as exclusive and around a quarter felt this way about the DP (see Table 6.8).

There is an interesting nonlinearity for both the DP and the ANC, which saw big jumps in exclusivity ratings in 1999 and a subsequent reversion (but not back to 1994 levels). This is perhaps explained by the large size of the decrease in Indian representation in these parties between 1994 and 1999: Both halved or nearly halved their level of representation. In contrast, change was very minor between 1999 and 2004; 1999 was also, of course, the election with the most negative campaigning, which may have had an effect (see Table 6.9).

TABLE 6.8. *Indian Impressions of the ANC and Party Demographics*

|  | 1994 | 1999 | 2004 |
|---|---|---|---|
| Indians who see ANC as exclusive* | 13 | 75 | 53 |
| Indians who are uncertain about the ANC | 8 | 9 | 24 |
| Indian candidates on ANC lists | 9 | 5 | 5 |

*Note*: All cells are percentages.
*Based only on those who had an opinion, i.e., uncertain responses eliminated.

TABLE 6.9. *Indian Impressions of the DP and Party Demographics*

|  | 1994 | 1999 | 2004 |
|---|---|---|---|
| Indians who see DP as exclusive* | 9 | 41 | 28 |
| Indians who are uncertain about the DP | 55 | 51 | 36 |
| Indian candidates on DP lists | 10 | 5 | 4 |

*Note*: All cells are percentages.
*Based only on those who had an opinion, i.e. uncertain responses eliminated.

TABLE 6.10. *Indian Impressions of the NP and Party Demographics*

|  | 1994 | 1999 | 2004 |
|---|---|---|---|
| Indians who see NP as exclusive* | 21 | 12 | 47 |
| Indians who are uncertain about the NP | 12 | 10 | 55 |
| Indian candidates on NP lists | 7 | 7 | 6 |

*Note*: All cells are percentages.
*Based only on those who had an opinion, i.e. uncertain responses eliminated.

In contrast, Indians actually became more optimistic about the NP's image in 1999 and did not turn negative/uncertain until 2004. This corresponds with a drop in Indian representation – albeit a very small one. It is also worth noting that, as the smallest group in South Africa, Indian respondents are the least numerous in surveys, and this adds a greater bracket of uncertainty to their responses (see Table 6.10).

Altogether, the data broadly confirm a relationship between changes in the demographic balance of party lists and party racial profiles: As parties included more representatives from a particular group, members of that group became more likely to view the party as inclusive. The relationship is strongest for the opposition parties, who have sought, with varying degrees of aggressiveness, to Africanize their candidate lists. The NP initiated this process earlier and was rewarded with earlier shifts in views about inclusiveness. After very superficial change in 1994 and 1999, the DP became more serious in 2004 and its party label followed suite. The ANC's image amongst coloureds and whites has been less consistently correlated with changes in its lists – it actually has grown more inclusive in the minds of these voters as it has moved slightly in the direction of greater Africanization. This may be due to the type of new whites and coloured candidates brought in, but it is difficult to know for sure. All three parties reduced their representation of Indians over the same time period, and, not surprisingly, Indians became more pessimistic about all of them.

CONCLUSION

In theory, at least, manipulating the racial balance of candidate characteristics should provide South African parties with a powerful means of effecting changes in their party labels. The ideological reputations of parties are still in formation in South Africa, so voters and parties look to candidate characteristics as a means of evaluating labels (not the other way around). By changing the racial balance of its candidates, a party sends a powerful signal. It alters its decision makers and therein alters expectations about its preferences. It also unseats party stalwarts, a costly and therefore powerful indicator of the seriousness of its efforts.

In keeping with these expectations, the racial balance of candidate lists has indeed played a central role in South African elections. Advertised by parties, discussed in the press, and tracked by academics, candidate characteristics are well known to voters. Moreover, the opposition parties have effected large changes in their candidate demographics since the end of apartheid, and these changes correlate with beliefs about the inclusiveness of parties.

However, while the opposition parties have made tremendous changes to the candidate profiles in the decade or so since the end of apartheid, they remain considerably less representative of the South African population than the ruling ANC – especially at top levels of leadership. Given the significance of candidate demographics to party labels, and the apparent desire of parties to change their labels, this leaves us with a bit of a paradox: Why have the opposition parties not gone further? Chapter 7 takes on this question.

APPENDIX TO CHAPTER 6: CODING LIST CANDIDATES

The goal of this part of the project was to code the race of all the candidates of the 1994, 1999, and 2004 lists of three parties, the ANC, the NNP, and the DP/DA. To do so, I relied primarily on *name*, although I also used provincial origin and in some instances (when the name was ambiguous) ran supplementary Internet searches for additional information on the candidate (photographs, resumes, family histories, associational memberships, and so on). Following are some notes on this process:

(1) I found that the reliability of names as a means of distinguishing race varied by race. Names were a very reliable means to distinguish African candidates from white and coloured ones. For example, two candidates from the ANC's 1994 list: LEWIS PAUL MUSAWENKOSI NZIMANDE and MELANIE VERWOERD. The first name is clearly African, the second clearly white or coloured. I also found that Indian names were usually distinctive enough to pick out. Some examples: RADHAKRISHNA LUTCHMANA PADAYACHIE and SHIRISH MANAKLAL SONI. One exception to this involved names that appeared Muslim, as these could indicate either coloured or Indian origins. For example, the name EBRAHIM RASOOL is a name suggestive of Muslim origins but could be either coloured or Indian. In such cases, I used provincial ties to decide race: Muslim names in KwaZulu-Natal were coded as Indian; Muslim names in the Western Cape were coded as coloured. Ebrahim Rasool was an ANC candidate in the Western Cape and hence was coded as coloured. The highest measurement error probably involved Indian names, and most often the miscoding involved coding Indians as white/coloured, and vice versa. This should not affect estimates of the percentages of African candidates, which were the most important to analysis. I coded the very small number of non-Indian Asian candidates as Indian, under the logic that "Indian" in South Africa is synonymous with Asian. This affected perhaps five codings out of many thousands. I could *not* use names to distinguish between white and coloured candidates. Very often these groups share surnames. Therefore, I grouped these two racial categories together.

(2) In looking at names, I looked at all provided names (first, last, middle). The general rule of thumb was that if there was an African name anywhere in the mix, the candidate was coded as African. Africans more often carry white or European names than whites carry African names, especially for this generation of candidates, all of whom were born during or before apartheid.

(3) During the initial coding, an "uncertain" option was available and coders were encouraged to use it when they felt they could not reasonably judge a name.

(4) All names were coded by two coders: one an American specialist on South African politics, the other a native of South Africa. After a very preliminary initial cleaning of the data to identify obvious key stroke errors (example, Marthinus van Schalkwyk of the NP being coded as African), the correlations between the two coders were at least .9 for the white/coloured and African categories and around .8 for the Indian category. Subsequent to this, remaining mismatches were identified and reviewed by both coders. After identifying any additional key stroke errors, Internet searches were used to resolve remaining conflicts. In many cases, we were able to retrieve biographical or photographic

information that allowed us to make a better decision. In other cases, we were able to get more information on a surname, allowing us to better code it. Where we were **not** able to resolve differences, we coded the candidate as "uncertain." This most frequently occurred between the coloured/white category and the Indian category.

# 7

## Why So Slow?

### *The Political Challenges of Candidate Transformation for Opposition Parties*

Given the importance of the transformation of candidate characteristics to party label change, why have South Africa's opposition parties not moved faster in transforming their lists and why, in particular, have they resisted changing the very top positions? In this chapter, I explore how party size affects the ability of parties to transform their candidate demographics, paying particular attention to the role that candidate quality plays in this process. I argue that small parties are especially sensitive to the quality of incoming candidates. Because they control only a small number of seats, any seats they take from existing members for new recruits are necessarily top-level seats, most likely filled with high-quality party leaders. To maintain overall candidate quality, small parties must therefore recruit only high-quality new candidates. At the same time, small parties face significant disadvantages in obtaining these candidates because they are neither able to grow their own nor poach them from other parties. As a result, the challenges of elite incorporation are more difficult for small parties. I argue that these intuitions hold regardless of the internal organization of the party and explain why the pace of candidate change has been slow for South Africa's opposition parties. I then evaluate several observable implications of this argument using the data on candidate career paths introduced in the previous chapter. I also explore the collapse of the New National Party shortly after the 2004 election and the role candidate transformation played in it.

### THE CHALLENGE OF ELITE INCORPORATION

In this section, I develop a theory about how party size affects the ability of parties to incorporate new elites. Chandra (2004) speculates that elite incorporation poses an "intractable" problem for parties: Although parties benefit from absorbing new elites, they risk paying high costs – the loss of existing party members unseated in the process. Chandra views the loss of old elites as a net negative and therefore sees the challenge of incorporation as one of bringing in new elites while maintaining the loyalty of old ones. However, as

I will argue in the following analysis, the net cost of losing old elites depends on an additional factor – *candidate quality*. Although candidate quality has long been recognized as an important factor in explaining electoral success in candidate-based systems (Jacobson and Kernell 1983; Green and Krasno 1988; Krasno and Green 1988; Jacobson 1990; Scheiner 2006), work on elite incorporation has largely ignored it. This omission is crucial, because the quality of incoming elites determines whether the loss of old elites has a net positive or negative effect for parties. If parties can replace outgoing elites with new candidates of equal or better quality, the net effect on the party is neutral or positive and the "intractable" problem of elite incorporation disappears.

Moreover, the size of the recruiting party (the number of seats it controls) mediates its sensitivity to the effects of candidate quality. Whereas large parties can give new recruits low-ranking seats previously occupied by rank-and-file (low-quality) politicians, small parties can create room only by unseating relatively high-ranking (high-quality) party elites. The average quality of outgoing elites is therefore higher for small parties. This means that elite incorporation will have a net negative effect for small parties unless they recruit higher than average newcomers. Unfortunately for these parties, their size also impedes recruitment: They lack enough low-level seats to "grow their own" quality candidates and have little to offer quality candidates from other parties. Small parties therefore face a catch-22: They are simultaneously more sensitive to the quality of recruits than large parties and less able to bring these recruits on board. Chandra's problem of elite intractability is therefore especially intractable for small parties, forcing them either to forgo candidate transformation all together or to risk jeopardizing the quality of their candidates in the process. I develop these points in greater depth in the following sections and also consider alternative accounts of the elite incorporation process.

## Candidate Quality

Candidate quality entails internal and external dimensions. Internal quality involves the skills and resources a candidate brings to the performance of the party within government: effort level, intelligence, experience in policy making, etc. Quality of this type is evidenced in behaviors like attendance and proposal rates, questions (in a parliamentary system), committee work, and so on. External quality involves the efficiency of the candidate in winning votes in the community: the percentage of community members he can attract to the cause of the party. Most previous research employing the concept of candidate quality (for example, Jacobson and Kernell 1983; Green and Krasno 1988; Krasno and Green 1988; Jacobson 1990; Scheiner 2006) has focused on external quality, and I follow this tradition in the analysis to come, leaving the internal dimension of quality untheorized at this point, although in reality it is also likely to be important.

External quality manifests itself in different ways in different communities. In South Africa, a central component of candidate quality involves connections to local communities. Lodge (2003) suggests that an active grassroots membership and visible and organized local branches are essential to winning votes in South Africa. "In contrast to wealthy industrial democracies," he observes, "in South Africa, face-to-face electioneering remains important, both for confirming active support among the ranks of the faithful and in soliciting favour from the uncertain and the doubtful." Recognizing this, both the ANC and the DA have made concerted attempts to encourage local volunteers and revitalize or establish branch structures. Along similar lines, scholars of the NP emphasize the strength of its local branch structures as central to its historical domination of white (especially Afrikaans-speaking) communities and suggest that its ability to build (or adopt) strong structures in coloured communities in the closing years of apartheid explain why it was able to capture so many coloured votes in early post-apartheid elections (Giliomee 1994; Breytenbach 1999). In this context, South African politicians who can tap into these resources are probably more effective at pulling votes from their communities than candidates who cannot.

Beyond local connections, credibility and trustworthiness also contribute to external quality, although these characteristics manifest themselves differently in different communities. Analysts of South African politics frequently note the importance of "struggle credentials" in winning African votes. Candidates who are perceived to have been part of apartheid structures (for example, councilors in local governments or Bantustan politicians) purportedly have less credibility with Africans than candidates who were part of the struggle against apartheid. Janet Cherry (2004), a senior analyst with South Africa's Human Sciences Research Council, writes:

Parties that were based in the "old apartheid divide" are making a concerted attempt to have more "black" candidates.... That many of these "black" candidates are the old regime's collaborators or may be considered to be "puppets" by the majority of ANC supporters, is seemingly of no consequence to them (although it may be, to the more discerning voter): superficially, the parties are seen to have a racially diverse list.[1]

Nomvula Mokonyane, Health and Safety Minister for Gauteng, echoed a similar sentiment when he contrasted the ANC's white candidates – characterized as "credible and prominent" – with the DA's inauthentic black ones. He explained: "We have not used discredited people like the DA has done, where it went into townships and used discredited people to target blacks."[2] Thus, it is not just putting black candidates on the list that matters. Also important is the *quality* of those candidates, in particular, whether they are tarnished with apartheid associations or not.

In coloured and Indian communities, "struggle credentials" have had a more ambiguous relationship to external quality – a fact the ANC has learned and

---

[1] Janet Cherry, "Elections 2004: The Party Lists and Issues of Identity." In *Election Synopsis* 1(3), 2004: 8.
[2] Rapule Tabane, "ANC Targets Mlungu Vote." *Mail & Guardian*, January 23, 2004.

adjusted to over time. In the early post-apartheid period, the ANC assumed that candidates with struggle credentials would appeal more to coloured and Indian voters than candidates with roots in apartheid-era structures like the Tricameral Parliament. It consequently made little effort to recruit Tricameral Parliament politicians to its lists, favoring instead candidates with ideological purity and a history in the struggle.[3] However, the party's relatively poor showing amongst coloured and Indian voters during the 1994 elections suggested it had miscalculated, misreading the sources of external quality in these communities. Unlike in African communities, "collaborator" coloured and Indian politicians were *not* uniformly suspect to their communities. Indeed, many had used the Tricameral Parliament to deliver concrete benefits (schools, housing) to their communities and had consequently built up loyal followings (Behrens 1989; Giliomee 1994, 1996).

By 1999, the ANC had become more pragmatic, actively recruiting politicians that it had previously tagged as tainted. In KwaZulu-Natal, the ANC semi-secretly aligned itself with Armichand Rajbansi's Minority Front, which joined the ANC as a coalition partner in KwaZulu-Natal after the election. Previously, the ANC had attacked Rajbansi, a House of Delegates politician, as an apartheid-era collaborator. In the Western Cape, the ANC's primary catch was Patrick Mackenzie, and local organizers associated with him. A former MP for Bontehewel (a large coloured community) in the Tricameral Parliament, Mackenzie has a strong following amongst coloured voters. In 1994, he was instrumental in helping the NNP to establish itself in the coloured community. The ANC hoped that by attracting him it would also attract his followers. With similar aspirations, the ANC recruited Mario Masher from the NNP and tried to recruit the biggest fish of all, Peter Marais, a former MP in the Tricameral Parliament and extremely popular in the coloured community. For months prior to the elections, rumors of Marais' imminent departure from the NNP to the ANC abounded (he ended up staying with the NNP). When questioned about the wisdom of recruiting these politicians, Ebrahim Rasool (the ANC's leader in the Western Cape) candidly explained:

---

[3] During the anti-apartheid struggle, the ANC and the organizations affiliated with it like the United Democratic Front frequently dismissed coloured and Indian politicians who participated in the Tricameral Parliament as collaborators and sellouts (Behrens 1989; Lodge and Nasson 1991). This attitude appears to have carried over to the initial days of the new dispensation, when – unlike the NP – the ANC favored UDF coloured activists like Allan Boesak, who was more well known and liked in the African community than the coloured one, over Tricameral politicians like Peter Marais, who had substantial supporters in coloured communities (Eldridge and Seekings 1996: 535–536). Similar decisions were made in the Indian community: The ANC prioritized struggle credentials in awarding its top spots over connections to the Indian community (Carrim 1996: 49). At one point, the ANC included the names of two prominent but controversial Tricameral politicians with large local followings (Dr. J. N. Reddy and Dr. D. S. Rajah) on its lists but was forced to remove them by outraged ANC activists (Desai and Maharaj 1996).

# Why So Slow?

We are reaching a stage of maturity about these issues in the ANC. There is a hunger for victory in the ANC and the organization will accept those that can help achieve that victory.[4]

Thus, principles gave way to expediency in the search for coloured and Indian votes. The ANC became willing to sacrifice ideological purity to get candidates with external quality – a testament to the importance it placed on this characteristic.

In short, external quality in South Africa – and probably elsewhere as well – involves the connections the candidate has to the community of voters: his visibility and perceived trustworthiness and knowledge within the community, his ability to mobilize grassroots networks and organizations to reach voters, and his reputation as a good representative (and provider) for the community. External quality manifests itself differently in different places and within a particular (racial, ethnic, class) community, and politicians vary in external quality – some are seen as credible, connected, knowledgeable representatives of the community, others are not. The higher the external quality of a politician, the more efficient she is in culling votes from her community.

### Candidate Quality and the Problem of Elite Incorporation

How does candidate quality affect the problem of elite incorporation? If the quality of the new candidate is equal to the quality of the candidate he replaces, then the net effect of the incorporation is neutral or positive: The party loses votes in its original community but gains enough votes in the new community to offset its losses.[5] In this sense, elite incorporation no longer poses an "intractable problem."

However, if quality is *not* equal – in particular, if the new candidate is of average or low quality and replaces an old candidate of high quality – the "intractable problem" re-asserts itself: The party risks losing more than it gains in the turnover. The party obtains a member from the desired community, but if that member is incapable of attracting votes, the party is worse off than it was when it started. In sum, *the net damage of replacement depends on the quality of the incoming recruits relative to existing candidates*, in particular, the efficiency of the old versus the new in drawing votes from their communities. If the new recruits are of high enough quality relative to the party members they are replacing, parties need not worry about the loss of their old candidates.

---

[4] Quoted in Calland and Jacobs, "Western Cape." In EISA *Election Update 1999* 8, 12 March 1999: 20.

[5] This holds constant the size of the communities represented by the old and new candidates. If the two candidates are of equal quality, but the new candidate comes from a larger community (presumably the case if the party is seeking to move into this community and certainly the case for white parties seeking to Africanize in South Africa), then the party can tolerate somewhat lower quality incoming politicians.

Comments by leaders of the DA suggest that they are well aware of the trade-off between recruiting and promoting nonwhites and losing the human capital represented by existing white members of the party. When asked shortly before the 2004 elections about the DA's quotas for blacks on its lists, party leader Tony Leon said: "The lists should reflect South Africa. We don't want to go with an all-white team, but if some white person has been incredibly active in building the party or raising money, they should not be discriminated against."[6] Along similar lines, Theuns Botha (DA leader of the Western Cape) explained that the large number of whites on the Western Cape lists reflected the party's need to retain "expertise."[7]

### It's Not Easy Being Small

Quality turns out to be especially important for small parties. Small parties have few electable positions. Only their top candidates – their long-term, highly experienced members – actually get seats. If they wish to change the demographics of their elected candidates, they must unseat these high-ranking, high-quality old members. In contrast, large parties have many electable positions and can replace members lower in the hierarchy and of more average quality. Hence, the average quality of politicians departing the small party is higher than the average quality of politicians departing the larger party. If we think of the replacing candidate as being a random draw from the population of candidates from the new group, and we assume that the average quality of the groups is the same, the large party is more likely to replace its existing candidate with one of similar quality than the small party and hence less likely to suffer from Chandra's "intractable problem."[8]

Small parties can avoid this perverse effect of their size by only seating high-quality members of the target group. However, in this also, small size has its disadvantages. Candidate quality, unlike other candidate characteristics, is difficult to assess. Politicians do not come with "quality" measures stamped on their foreheads. Furthermore, while visible characteristics like age and education might correlate with internal aspects of quality (performance on committees, drafting legislation, posing clever questions, etc.), their relationship to the appeal of the candidate within his or her community is likely to be weaker.

How, then, do parties assess quality and how do they ensure that they promote only the very best? Generally, candidate quality is best determined through observation, and there are two ways in which a party can observe

---

[6] Drew Forrest, "I'm Not a Guilty White: interview with Tony Leon." *Mail & Guardian*, Jaunary 30, 2004.
[7] Quoted in Booysen (2005: 134).
[8] This analysis (and that which follows) is written with a PR list system in mind (hence the frequent reference to ranking and lists). However, the same logic would apply to single-member districts – small parties are likely to be real contenders in fewer areas than large parties and thus have fewer electable positions to offer their candidates.

a candidate: either by putting her in a low-ranking position for a period of time and assessing performance, or by observing her career path in a different party. Indeed, both correlate with previous experience in government office – the primary metric employed by existing work to operationalize the concept of quality (Jacobson and Kernell 1983; Green and Krasno 1988; Krasno and Green, 1988; Jacobson 1990; Scheiner 2006). There are therefore two strategies open to parties to get high-quality candidates: They can *grow their own* or they can *poach*. Unfortunately for small parties, size impacts the success of both.

Consider the "grow your own" strategy. Parties often attempt to control quality issues by placing new candidates in low-ranking conditions and promoting only ones that perform well (Strøm et. al. 2003). However, size affects the success of this strategy. Large parties have the option of putting trial candidates in seated but low-ranking positions – local councilors, regional parliamentarians, or junior back-benchers – and observing their performance over time. Small parties, on the other hand, have a short supply of such positions and must either leave the candidate unseated (and therefore unhappy) or take the risk of placing them, untried, in a high enough position to obtain office. In other words, small parties do not have the reserve positions to make growing their own a viable strategy.[9]

Size also affects the poaching capacities of parties. What can a small party offer that a large party cannot? A relatively high-ranking spot on a small party's list might be less valuable (less electable) than a much lower spot on a large party's list. Furthermore, the large party can offer the candidate more opportunities to use her seat to influence policy. After all, being seated in a party that is permanently in opposition is usually not as valuable as being seated in the dominant party. Thus, anything the small party can do for the candidate, the larger party can do better. This all but eliminates the chances of high-quality candidates defecting from the larger party. Lower quality candidates, sensing a limited career path in the larger party, might be willing to defect, but the small party does not want these candidates anyway! Even more perversely, if by fluke or luck the small party does manage to "grow their own" high-quality candidate, the larger party has significant resources at its disposal to steal that candidate away. Indeed, the large party can poach promising but still uncertain candidates from the smaller party as a form of insurance. Poaching is a two-way street, and one that the dominant party is likely to monopolize.

In sum, small parties have strong incentives to seek only high-quality candidates but face significant obstacles in doing so, neither being able to grow

---

[9] The extent to which candidates in the party are driven by ideology/policy versus office might affect this trade-off. Policy-driven activists might be more likely to stick it out in unseated positions. This would suggest that issue-driven or policy-driven small parties – like the Greens in many European countries, for example – with cadres of ideologically driven candidates – might be better able to employ the "grow your own" strategy. In contrast, office-driven candidates might be more likely to abandon a small party as a lost cause. For related discussions, see Müller and Strøm (1999).

their own nor poach from the other side. As a result, these parties face an unattractive choice between forgoing candidate change altogether or engaging in highly risky turnover, firing their top members in favor of candidates from the target group of unknown (and almost certainly) lower quality. In the first instance, the party is stuck with its old (and losing) label. In the second, it risks sharp depreciation of its human capital. In short, it is not easy being small! Size is thus an important variable explaining the success of parties in changing their candidate mix: The "intractability of elite incorporation" is far more severe for small parties than large ones.

### An Alternative Hypothesis: Internal Party Structure

Chandra (2004) suggests an alternative explanation for why some parties are better able to alter the demographic balance of their candidate characteristics than others. Her analysis focuses on internal party structure. She argues that competitive (as opposed to centralized) rules for advancement tie the interests of existing elites to the incorporation of new ones. In essence, if old elites want to maintain their high position in the party, they must court the support of new elites. New elites in turn are attracted by the promise of advancement based on competition. In contrast, under centralized rules, advancement is based on appealing to party leaders, not by currying support from below. Top party leaders worry about being displaced by rising elites and depend on the support of loyalists to preserve their position, making them reluctant to pursue extensive incorporation of new elites even when it is in the interest of the party as a whole. For these reasons, Chandra concludes, parties with competitive rules for advancement will be better able than those with centralized rules to skirt the elite incorporation problem.

While Chandra's analysis is plausible, it implies precisely the sort of lengthy "grow your own" process that disadvantages small parties. Competitive internal selection procedures may well increase the attractiveness of a party to new elites by giving them a reasonable probability of moving up the party ladder with time. However, if moving up the ladder implies weathering several electoral seasons in progressively better but still unelectable positions (as it often does in small parties), talented newcomers may seek greener pastures. In other words, competitive internal selection procedures do not solve the problems created by being small. Chandra's analysis therefore best applies to large parties: Small parties are likely to struggle with the problem of elite incorporation *regardless of their internal structures*.

Furthermore, work by other authors suggests that internal structure actually works in the opposite direction. Norris (1996) argues that centralized party systems are *better* able to promote candidate diversification. Centralized systems – for example, those using proportional representation with large districts – generate higher incentives and fewer risks to diversification. She writes: "[I]n single member seats, local parties pick one standard bearer, and they may hesitate to choose candidates perceived as electorally risky. In

# Why So Slow?

contrast, there is a different 'logic of choice' with long party lists where selectors have an electoral incentive to pick a 'balanced ticket.' With a lengthy list of names, it is unlikely that any votes will be lost by the presence of political minorities on the list. But their absence may cause offense, thereby narrowing the party's appeal" (Norris 1996: 201). Norris suggests this logic lies behind the empirical regularity of higher legislative representation of women in highly proportional PR systems. In sum, the theoretical relationship between internal party structure and the ability of parties to pursue candidate transformation is not clear. In any case, small parties are likely to face bigger hurdles in this process than large parties.

## TESTABLE IMPLICATIONS

Several testable implications flow from the analysis in the preceding section:

First, because the quality of new recruits is unknown, while the quality of established party members is known and high, all parties face incentives to put new candidates relatively low on lists. In contrast, poached and returning candidates should place relatively high on lists.

Second, the first hypothesis is moderated for small parties: Because they are small and their electable positions are few and high, they must promise better spots or risk failing at their recruitment efforts. That is, they must balance their desire to sort candidates with their need to sweeten the package to compete with their larger rivals. The more they care about recruiting new candidates, the more difficult this balance becomes. As a result, the first hypothesis should hold most strongly for large parties.

Third, rank should influence retention patterns: A candidate will be more likely to return to a party's list in the subsequent electoral period if he/she is highly ranked in the first electoral period. There are two possible explanations for this. First, rank in the first period reflects the party's initial assessments of the quality of the candidate, and the better the initial assessment of quality, the harder the party works to keep the candidate around in the next election. Alternatively, candidates with low initial rankings decline to return to the list in the second period, either turning to nonpolitical ventures or seeking spots on other lists.

Fourth, large parties should be better able to retain their candidates than small parties. That is, the "grow your own" strategy, which implies candidates returning over repeated election periods, is more viable for larger parties.

Fifth, large parties should be more successful at poaching.

## SOUTH AFRICAN PARTIES

Earlier chapters discussed the ANC's success in winning elections. It is useful at this point to examine how this translates into control over provincial and national legislative seats. Just how much "bigger" is the ANC compared to its opposition? As Table 7.1 makes clear, the ANC has controlled close to five

TABLE 7.1. *Control over Seats by the ANC, DA, and NNP*

|  | 1994 | 1999 | 2004 |
|---|---|---|---|
| Seats in National Parliament | | | |
| ANC | 252 | 266 | 279 |
| DA | 7 | 38 | 50 |
| NNP | 82 | 28 | 7 |
| Seats in Provincial Parliaments | | | |
| ANC | 266 | 289 | 304 |
| DA | 12 | 35 | 51 |
| NNP | 82 | 38 | 7 |

*Sources*: Data come from Reynolds (1994, 1999a) and Piombo and Nijzink (2005).

times the number of seats of the NP and DA combined, and its dominance has grown over time. In 1994, the ruling party had 252 national seats and 266 provincial seats to hand out, allowing it to seat 518 candidates from its list. By comparison, the NNP could seat only 164 total candidates, and the DA (DP at that time), just 15. By 2004, the numbers had become even more lopsided: The ANC controlled 583 seats total. The opposition parties combined controlled 115. Although it is difficult to translate this into specific electability breakpoints on the lists (as explained in greater depth in the following section, the parties often draw national candidates from two lists), it is abundantly clear that party rankings are not created equally: Position 150 on the ANC national list, for example, is almost certainly an electable position, whereas position 150 on the DA (or NNP) list is most definitely not electable.

The ANC also dominated local and municipal elections. In 2000, it won 5,098 seats on municipal, local, and district councils. In contrast, the DA (which was the DP and NNP at the time), won 1,484. In 2006, the ANC won 5,718 of these seats and the DA 1,107.[10] While little analysis has been done tracing the career paths of local and municipal councilors in South Africa, it seems likely that the councils act as feeders to the national office (Scheiner 2006 documents a similar dynamic in Japan). Parties can use them as a low-risk way of evaluating talent, promoting the best to national office. If this is true, then the ANC's feeder pool supersedes the opposition's 5 to 1. These data on their own suggest that South Africa's ruling party should have a much easier time than its opposition in attracting, retaining, and promoting to higher office candidates of all color.

TESTS

To evaluate the implications delimited earlier, I employed the candidate career paths data discussed in Chapter 6 and its appendix. To review, I collected the

[10] Municipal/Local data come from the IEC website (http://www.eisa.org.za/WEP/souelectarchive.htm), accessed August 2, 2007.

TABLE 7.2. *Explaining Candidate Rankings, 1999*

| | Dependent Variable: Candidate Rank Percentile in 1999 | | | |
|---|---|---|---|---|
| | Pooled Sample | ANC | NP | DP |
| New candidate | −.1932*** | −.1990*** | −.2315*** | −.1716*** |
| | (.0136) | (.0201) | (.0246) | (.0384) |
| Poached candidate | .0166 | −.1928* | −.0363 | .1691* |
| | (.0639) | (.1121) | (.1559) | (.0944) |
| Age in 1999 | .0013** | .0004 | .0005 | .0026*** |
| | (.0005) | (.0010) | (.0010) | (.0008) |
| Male | .0332*** | .0003 | −.0067 | .1010*** |
| | (.0127) | (.0195) | (.0259) | (.0223) |
| African | −.0251*** | −.0121 | −.0563** | .0501* |
| | (.0123) | (.0252) | (.0245) | (.0268) |
| Indian | −.0038 | .0505 | −.0380 | .0110 |
| | (.0257) | (.0481) | (.0414) | (.0459) |
| Adjusted $R^2$ | .10 | .12 | .16 | .09 |
| N | 2193 | 846 | 636 | 711 |

*Note*: Dependent variable created for each ranked list for each party by dividing the candidate's rank by the length of the list and subtracting from one (*1 − candidate rank/ length of list*). Higher numbers indicate *better* list positions (e.g., 99th percentile would indicate the top positions on the list). Dependent variable ranges from 0 to 1. Reference categories are returning candidates and white/coloured candidates.
*Significant at 10%; ** significant at 5%; *** significant at 1%.

full candidate lists for the ANC, NP, and DP for the 1994, 1999, and 2004 elections. Each party altogether put forth 500 to 800 candidates per election. These candidates were allocated to eighteen to nineteen individual party lists (two regional lists per province and, in some cases, a national list) and given rankings on those lists. The race of each candidate was coded and the career path of the candidate was tracked from list to list. For 1994 and 1999, each candidate was tracked for the subsequent election to evaluate whether he/she returned to the same party, showed up on the list of a different party, or dropped out of the candidate pool altogether. For 1999 and 2004, the origins of each candidate were traced back to the previous election to evaluate if he or she had previously been on the list of the same party, the list of a different party, or was a new candidate. Throughout, the candidate's rank was also tracked. Finally, for data from 1994 and 1999, the age and gender of the candidates were identified using their personal identity numbers.[11]

As a test of the first and second hypotheses, I examined how new, returning, and poached candidates fared in terms of their list rankings. The results are displayed in Tables 7.2 (1999) and 7.3 (2004). The dependent variable for both is candidate rank percentile, which ranges from 0 to 1, with higher

---

[11] Personal identity numbers were available for these years, and gender and birth date were encoded in them.

TABLE 7.3. *Explaining Candidate Rankings, 2004*

| | Dependent Variable: Candidate Rank Percentile in 2004 | | | |
|---|---|---|---|---|
| | Pooled Sample | ANC | NP | DP |
| New candidate | -.2077*** | -.2445*** | -.2399*** | -.1348*** |
| | (.0135) | (.0192) | (.0264) | (.0358) |
| Poached candidate | -.1065** | -.2225** | .0230 | -.0438 |
| | (.0458) | (.0952) | (.2646) | (.0618) |
| African | -.0349*** | -.0106 | -.0315 | .0040 |
| | (.0139) | (.0260) | (.0280) | (.0314) |
| Indian | -.0088 | .0337 | -.0323 | .0167 |
| | (.0321) | (.0483) | (.0553) | (.0307) |
| Adjusted $R^2$ | .13 | .17 | .17 | .03 |
| N | 1654 | 801 | 454 | 399 |

*Note*: Dependent variable created for each ranked list for each party by dividing the candidate's rank by the length of the list and subtracting from one ($1 - candidate\ rank/\ length\ of\ list$). Higher numbers indicate *better* list positions (e.g., 99th percentile would indicate the top positions on the list). Dependent variable ranges from 0 to 1. Reference categories are returning candidates and white/coloured candidates.
*Significant at 10%; ** significant at 5%; *** significant at 1%.

numbers indicating better list positions.[12] The key independent variables are dummy variables for new and poached candidates, where returning candidates is the reference category. Controls include the age of the candidate at the time of the election, gender, and race for the 1999 specification and just race for the 2004 specification. I ran the specification both as a pooled sample and then split the sample by party. If the first hypothesis holds, new candidates should fair worse in the rankings than returning candidates; that is, the coefficient on "new candidate" should be negative. Furthermore, per the second hypothesis, the effect should be strongest for the ANC (the largest party) and weakest for the NP and DP.

The results strongly confirm the first hypothesis: In all specifications, the coefficient on new candidates is negative, well estimated, and consistent across elections. Parties place new candidates about 20 points lower in the percentile rankings than returning candidates. In contrast, poached candidates either do about as well as returning candidates (in 1999) or a little worse (in 2004), but not as bad as new candidates.

The second hypothesis received support in 2004 but not in 1999. In 1999, the greatest penalty for being new was actually paid by NP candidates – contrary to expectations. The lowest penalty fell on DP candidates, while ANC candidates were somewhere in the middle. In general, the differences between parties were not especially large. The 2004 results, in contrast, fall much

[12] Rank percentile was created by dividing the candidate's rank by the length of the list he/she was on and subtracting from one ($1 - candidate\ rank/\ length\ of\ list$).

closer to expectations. ANC candidates paid the most for being new – close to 25 points in their percentile rankings. DP candidates paid the least, about 10 points less than ANC candidates. NP candidates also paid less than ANC candidates, although the differences were slight. On the whole, these results make sense: The ANC has many electable spots to play with and can afford to place its new candidates low without risk of losing them. The DP, in contrast, must balance its desire to sort its new candidates with its need to put them high enough on the lists to keep them.

Also interesting are the differences in the treatment of poached candidates across parties. In both 1999 and 2004, the ANC treated its poached candidates much the way it treated its new ones: They were placed substantially lower than its returning candidates. This result is not difficult to explain. The ANC does not need to use poaching to get quality candidates because it can grow its own. Therefore, it can afford to treat them like any new candidate. In contrast, the opposition parties tend to treat poached candidates like returning candidates (or perhaps even better). For the DP and the NP, the coefficient on poached candidates is either insignificant or, if significant, positive. Poached candidates represent valuable commodities for these parties.

Turning to the control variables, age correlates with higher positions in 1999 (no data for 2004), although the size of the coefficient is not terribly large (ten extra years translates into around a 1-point increase in percentile rank). If age proxies for experience and quality, this makes sense. Male candidates also did better in 1999 (no data for 2004), although, again, the effect was very small (around a 3-point increase in percentile rank). This could also proxy for experience. Finally, all else equal, African candidates were at a slight disadvantage (around 3 points), which is surprising. Breaking it down by party, it appears that the ANC and the NP drive the negative results. The DP either does not treat Africans as different or gives them a slight advantage.

Altogether, the results provide strong support for the first hypothesis and partial support for the second: All parties place new candidates lower on their lists than returning candidates. However, the opposition (especially the DP) penalizes new candidates relatively less. Furthermore, the opposition tends to treat poached candidates better than new ones, whereas this is not true for the ANC. These results confirm the intuitions laid out earlier that small parties are less able than large parties to sort incoming candidates.

To test the third and fourth hypotheses, I looked at patterns of retention across parties. Table 7.4 shows retention rates over the 1994 to 1999 and 1999 to 2004 cycles (i.e., what fraction of 1994's candidates showed up on the 1999 lists, and so on). If the fourth hypothesis is correct, then the ANC (as the largest party) should have had greater luck holding on to its candidates than either of the opposition parties. We might also expect that, in the earlier period, the NP would have better retention rates than the DP, as it was by far the larger of the two parties. In contrast, after the DP surpassed the NP in 1999, the relationship would switch.

TABLE 7.4. *Retention Rates for 1994–1999 and 1999–2004 Periods*

|  | ANC | | NP | | DP | |
| --- | --- | --- | --- | --- | --- | --- |
|  | 1994–1999 | 1999–2004 | 1994–1999 | 1999–2004 | 1994–1999 | 1999–2004 |
| Africans | .40 | .56 | .12 | .12 | .02 | .10 |
| Indians | .39 | .53 | .29 | .09 | .11 | .11 |
| Whites/ coloureds | .44 | .56 | .26 | .25 | .18 | .13 |
| Overall | .40 | .56 | .23 | .20 | .15 | .12 |

*Note*: Figures reflect the percentage of all new or returning candidates in the category.

The results support these conjectures. As Table 7.4 shows, the ANC has been far better able than either of the smaller parties to retain candidates. During the first period, it was about twice as successful as either of these parties in holding on to its people. Furthermore, it improved its retention rates over time, while the other two parties have stagnated (or perhaps deteriorated) in their ability to hold candidates. Overall, the opposition parties have done quite poorly in retaining candidates.

It is also interesting to note that the ANC retains candidates across racial categories: It is as good at holding whites, coloureds, and Indians as it is at holding Africans. In contrast, the NP has been much better at holding white/coloured candidates than either of the other two racial categories (especially Africans). This was also true of the DP in the early period, when it failed spectacularly to keep Africans on board (only 2 percent of the 1994 cohort of African candidates returned in 1999). Interestingly, the DP in the later period improved its African retention rate while seeing its white retention slide – perhaps reflecting some purging of white candidates to accommodate new Africans on the lists. Finally, although the NP is relatively worse at holding Africans than candidates from other groups, it was still as good as or better than the DP at keeping them in both periods. In general, the NP outperformed the DP, in spite of the DP's ascension as the top opposition party during the 1999 election. This last result was not the anticipated finding, but otherwise the data support the fourth hypothesis: Bigger is better in terms of retention.

To further explore these results (as well as test the third hypothesis), I ran a series of logit models predicting whether a candidate who is listed in one election returns to the same party's lists in the subsequent election (poached candidates are dropped from the analysis). The results are in Table 7.5. In addition to the rank of the candidate and his or her party affiliation (ANC is the reference category), I also controlled for race, including some party-specific interaction terms, candidate age and gender. As a further test of the fourth hypothesis, I included a dummy variable for the Western Cape and interaction terms for DP and NP Western Cape candidates. The Western Cape is the only province in which the DA and NP have effectively challenged the ANC. During the 1994 to 1999 period, the NP unquestionably dominated

TABLE 7.5. *Logit Analysis of Returning versus Leaving Candidates*

|  | Dependent Variable: Probability Candidate Returns | |
|---|---|---|
|  | 1994–1999 | 1999–2004 |
| Rank of candidate in initial period | −.006*** | −.013*** |
|  | (.002) | (.002) |
| DP candidate | −1.222*** | −2.459*** |
|  | (.213) | (.222) |
| NP candidate | −.907*** | −1.860*** |
|  | (.182) | (.219) |
| African candidate | −.037 | .322 |
|  | (.217) | (.263) |
| White/Coloured candidate | .135 | .382 |
|  | (.202) | (.258) |
| African DP candidate | −2.283** | −2.70 |
|  | (1.038) | (.363) |
| African NP candidate | −.768*** | −.594* |
|  | (.300) | (.313) |
| Age of candidate | −.013*** | −.007 |
|  | (.005) | (.005) |
| Male candidate | −.049 | −.025 |
|  | (.123) | (.116) |
| Western Cape candidate | −.340 | −.269 |
|  | (.296) | (.286) |
| Western Cape NP candidate | 1.130*** | 1.118*** |
|  | (.391) | (.398) |
| Western Cape DP candidate | .157 | .128 |
|  | (.645) | (.472) |
| Number of observations | 1950 | 2156 |
| Pseudo $R^2$ | .08 | .19 |

*Significant at 10%; ** significant at 5%; *** significant at 1%.

the region. During the 1999 to 2004 period, all three parties vied for control. Hence, the ANC has not been the unquestioned dominant party in the Western Cape, and we might therefore expect the results to be different there. In particular, we might expect the opposition (especially the NP) to have an easier time retaining candidates in the Western Cape versus elsewhere in the country.

The results lend strong support to both the third and fourth hypotheses. The rank of the candidate on the initial list is a strong predictor of whether he or she will return on the next list: Candidates with less prestigious spots on the lists (higher numbers) were considerably less likely to return in the next election. There are two interpretations here: First, rank in the first period could reflect the party's initial assessments of the quality of the candidate and the higher the quality, the harder the party works to keep the candidate around in the next election. Alternatively, candidates with low initial rankings may decline to return to the list in the second period, either turning to nonpolitical ventures or seeking spots on other lists. Both factors are probably at work. Also of note is the importance of initial rank increases over time, with the coefficient more than doubling between the first and second periods. This could reflect parties' improved ability to assess quality in the later period.

The results also support the fourth hypothesis, confirming the more basic data on retention rates in Table 7.4. Being a candidate for one of the opposition parties has a heavy (and growing) negative impact on the probability of returning, as suggested by the simple bivariate tables earlier. The opposition (especially the DP) is *considerably* less likely than the ANC to keep its candidates. It is interesting to note that there is *no general racial effect*: The probability of returning is not statistically different for white/coloured, African, or Indian candidates. However, there are *party-specific* racial effects, especially in the first period, when Africans on either the NP or the DP lists were less likely to return than whites, coloured, or Indians on these lists, or Africans on the ANC lists.

Party-specific racial effects are clear in Tables 7.6 and 7.7, which show predicted probabilities and 95 percent confidence intervals for candidates of different races on different party lists.[13] In the first period, both of the opposition parties were considerably worse at keeping African candidates versus white/coloured ones (and the confidence intervals are not overalapping). The ANC was much better at holding on to Africans than either of the opposition parties, and it did just as well at holding on to whites and coloureds. Interestingly, these party-specific racial effects more or less disappeared by the later period: Relative to the ANC, the opposition had difficulty keeping candidates *across the board*, not just Africans. In Table 7.7 (more predicted probabilities with confidence intervals), the confidence intervals across races for both the DP and the ANC are overlapping, suggesting no racial effects. The NP's confidence intervals barely separate, indicating a small racial effect. Overall, the ANC performs much better at retaining candidates from *all* groups than either of the smaller parties – again, general support for the fourth hypothesis.

More support for the fourth hypothesis comes from the Western Cape variables. In the logit models, the NP/Western Cape interaction term is positive and highly significant for both years. Given the negative coefficient on the NP dummy variable, this suggests that the NP performs better (relative to the ANC) in the Western Cape than it does in the rest of the country. The DP/Western Cape interaction term is insignificant, which is not terribly surprising as the party has only very recently taken over the mantle of the NP in the province.

---

[13] Results were produced using Clarify. See King et al. (2000).

# Why So Slow?

TABLE 7.6. *Probability a Candidate on the 1994 List Returned in 1999 (95 Percent Confidence Intervals)*

| Party | Race of Candidate | |
|---|---|---|
| | African | White/Coloured |
| DP | .03 | .19 |
| | (.00, .14) | (.15, .24) |
| NP | .11 | .24 |
| | (.07, .16) | (.20, .28) |
| ANC | .40 | .44 |
| | (.36, .44) | (.37, .51) |

*Note:* Other variables held at means.

TABLE 7.7. *Probability a Candidate on the 1999 List Returned in 2004 (95 Percent Confidence Intervals)*

| Party | Race of Candidate | |
|---|---|---|
| | African | White/Coloured |
| DP | .09 | .12 |
| | (.05, .15) | (.09, .15) |
| NP | .11 | .20 |
| | (.08, .16) | (.16, .24) |
| ANC | .60 | .61 |
| | (.55, .64) | (.53, .69) |

*Note:* Other variables held at means.

Confirmation for this interpretation comes in Tables 7.8 and 7.9, which show predicated probabilities and confidence intervals. In the Western Cape, the NP is roughly similar to the ANC in its ability to hold candidates (in 1994, the predicted probability is higher for the NP while the opposite holds in 1994 but the confidence intervals overlap). In contrast, the gap between the parties is large in the rest of the country (with nonoverlapping confidence intervals). Thus, the ANC performs about the same in the Western Cape as elsewhere in the country (a little worse, but not in a statistically significant sense), whereas the NP does much better in the Western Cape. Given the traditional dominance of the NP in the Western Cape, these results are consistent with the size hypothesis: What matters is being large enough to credibly offer attractive positions to a wide variety of candidates. In the Western Cape, the NP was able to do this for these elections years, whereas it was not able to elsewhere in the country.

On a final note, general demographic variables have mixed effects. In the earlier period, age had a negative effect on probability of returning (not

TABLE 7.8. *Probability a Candidate on the 1994 List Returned in 1999 (95 Percent Confidence Intervals)*

| Party | Region | |
|---|---|---|
| | Western Cape | Rest of South Africa |
| ANC | .33 | .40 |
| | (.22, .46) | (.35, .45) |
| NP | .38 | .22 |
| | (.27, .50) | (.18, .25) |

*Note*: Other variables held at means.

TABLE 7.9. *Probability a Candidate on the 1999 List Returned in 2004 (95 Percent Confidence Intervals)*

| Party | Region | |
|---|---|---|
| | Western Cape | Rest of South Africa |
| ANC | .52 | .58 |
| | (.38, .65) | (.53, .64) |
| NP | .34 | .18 |
| | (.23, .47) | (.14, .22) |

*Note*: Other variables held at means.

surprising – older candidates are the most likely to retire). This effect disappeared in the second period. Gender had no effect in either period. The fit of the model improves over time, reflecting the growing impact of rank and party variables.

In sum, the data lend substantial support to the third and fourth hypotheses. Candidate rank, as anticipated in the third hypothesis, influences candidate retention patterns: A candidate is more likely to return to a party's list in the subsequent electoral period if the party ranks her highly in the first electoral period. Furthermore, the ANC has been consistently and substantially better at retaining its candidates than either of the opposition parties, a result that holds across all racial groups. The only place this result has *not* held is the Western Cape, where the ANC and the NP have been roughly on par at retaining candidates. All of these results are consistent with the prediction that big parties have an easier time retaining candidates than small parties and therefore are better able to pursue a "grow your own" strategy. The only results that are not consistent with this are that, although the NP outperformed the DP in retention in the 1994–1999 period (as expected, as it was the largest opposition party), the relationship did not flip in the 1999–2004 period, when the DP took over the role as lead opposition. This may be explained by the

TABLE 7.10. *New, Returning, and Poached Candidates in 1999 and 2004 (Percentages Sum by Column)*

|  | ANC | | NP | | DP | |
|---|---|---|---|---|---|---|
|  | 1999 | 2004 | 1999 | 2004 | 1999 | 2004 |
| Total New | 534 | 309 | 452 | 282 | 641 | 278 |
|  | (.62) | (.39) | (.71) | (.63) | (.90) | (.70) |
| African | 451 | 259 | 175 | 108 | 142 | 119 |
| Indian | 17 | 14 | 32 | 19 | 35 | 9 |
| White/Coloured | 66 | 36 | 245 | 155 | 464 | 150 |
| Total Returning | 318 | 481 | 182 | 166 | 58 | 89 |
|  | (.37) | (.60) | (.29) | (.37) | (.08) | (.22) |
| African | 217 | 376 | 22 | 30 | 1 | 12 |
| Indian | 25 | 23 | 15 | 6 | 4 | 4 |
| White/Coloured | 76 | 82 | 145 | 130 | 53 | 73 |
| Total Poached | 6 | 8 | 3 | 1 | 10 | 28 |
|  | (.01) | (.01) | (<.01) | (<.01) | (.01) | (.07) |
| African | 1 | 1 | 1 | 0 | 0 | 6 |
| Indian | 1 | 2 | 0 | 0 | 0 | 2 |
| White/Coloured | 4 | 5 | 2 | 1 | 10 | 20 |
| Total All | 858 | 798 | 637 | 449 | 709 | 395 |

continuing uncertainty over the two opposition parties and which one would consolidate strength over the long run: Candidates may have been reluctant (especially in the traditional Western Cape stronghold) to completely discount the NP even as the DP began its rise.

The fifth hypothesis contends that larger parties will be better at poaching than smaller parties. To test this, I looked at party switching between national/provincial election years as well as party-switching patterns amongst local councilors. Table 7.10 summarizes the national/provincial data, showing the breakdown of new, returning, and poached candidates by party for 1999 and 2004. In 1999, most candidates were new. In 2004, all parties had increased the percentage of returning candidates, but only the ANC had more returning candidates than new ones. For all three parties, poached candidates were only a tiny fraction of the overall candidate pool. The most successful poacher appears to have been the DP in 2004, when 7 percent of its candidates had come from other parties – a contradiction of the fifth hypothesis.

Looking more closely at the candidates who switched parties, it is clear that this was mainly a white/coloured phenomenon. Of the nineteen switchers in 1999, sixteen were white or coloured; of the thirty-seven switchers in 2004, twenty-six were white or coloured. And looking at the pattern of movement between parties (not in the table), the great majority of it occurred between the opposition parties (primarily the NP losing candidates to the DP), not between the opposition and the ANC. When this latter kind of switching did happen, it usually favored the ANC. Thus, in 1999, the ANC poached three candidates each from the DP and NP. Most were white. In the same year, the NP poached one African and two whites from the DP and the DP poached ten whites from the NP. In 2004, the volume of switching increased, but the pattern was similar. The ANC poached five white/coloureds and one African from the DP and two Indians from the NP. The NP poached only one candidate, a white/coloured candidate from the ANC. And of the DP's marvelous haul of twenty-eight candidates, all but one came from the NP. It did successfully recruit one African from the ANC – a Mr. Serake Leeuw of the Free State. However, this success was short lived as Mr. Leeuw stood as an ANC candidate in the local elections of 2005 and was elected ANC Mayor of Matjhabeng, a depressed municipality in the middle of the Free State goldfields.[14] In sum, most of the switchers were white or coloured, and most moved between the opposition parties. The ANC gained more than it lost to these parties, and over two periods only lost 1 African (out of a total of around 1,656 ANC candidates and 56 overall switches) to the opposition, and this proved very short lived. Therefore, although the opposition (at least the DP) *appeared* more successful than the ANC at poaching, this was largely illusory. Poaching from the ANC was not a viable means for the opposition to recruit candidates, especially African ones.

Until 2002, switching between election periods was the only form of party switching possible in South Africa. The Anti-Defection Clause of the Constitution (Schedule 2, Clause 23 A) penalized any politician who left the party on whose list he or she was originally elected with loss of office. New legislation (passed in June 2002, approved by the Constitutional Court in October 2002) altered this practice for local elections, allowing for two periods (fifteen days each) during a five-year term during which politicians might cross to a different party without penalty. Later legislation extended this to the national and provincial levels. In October 2002, floor crossings were permitted for local government councilors. In March 2003, the same option was opened for provincial and national Members of Parliament. And in 2004, municipal (local) crossings were once again permitted. Therefore, in addition to the switching between lists, we can also examine switching during the floor crossing periods.

Fortunately, the South African government (in particular, the Independent Electoral Commission, or IEC) compiled a record of all councilors who switched and which parties they left and joined.[15] The 2002 switching period was unusual in that it came on the heels of the dissolution of the Democratic Alliance (a coalition between the Democratic Party, the National Party, and the Federal Alliance) and a new alliance between the NP and the ANC. Hence it was dominated by DA politicians (who, in all likelihood, originally ran on

---

[14] Yolandi Groenewald. "Who Else Can We Vote For?" *Mail & Guardian*, 27 January 2006.
[15] Independent Electoral Commission, "2004 Floor Crossing – summary reports." Data found at http://www.elections.org.za/library1.asp?KSId=13&iKid=3, accessed 13 July 2006. Independent Electoral Council, "2002 Floor Crossing Results – Graphs." Data found at http://www.elections.org.za/library1.asp?KSId=13&iKid=3, accessed 13 July 2006.

an NP ticket) leaving the DA to return to the NP (around 340 did so). There was also zero defection between the NP and the ANC, probably because of their alliance at the time. However, these quirks aside, it is interesting to look at the flow of politicians between the DA (which was primarily the old DP) and the ANC. The DA/DP lost fifty-one candidates to the ANC during the floor crossing period and gained three. Using names as a metric for race, all three of the DA gains were white or coloured. In contrast, around twenty of the fifty-one losses were African.

Similar patterns pertain to the 2004 switching period (but no ANC/NP alliance this time, so switching between them was fair game). The DA lost 31 candidates to the ANC, with perhaps 12 of these Africans. The NP lost a whopping 195 candidates to the ANC, with close to 50 of them African. The NP also lost 55 candidates to the DP, with perhaps 9 or 10 of them African. In contrast, neither the NP nor the DA managed to steal a single ANC candidate.[16]

In sum, the floor crossing data show significant movement of candidates between the opposition parties (most of them white). Furthermore, when candidates flowed between the opposition and the ANC, it was a *one-way street*: Politicians left the opposition and went to the ANC. Very few made the opposite journey, and none who did so were African. Finally, somewhere between a quarter and half of the opposition's losses were African. Thus, the floor crossing data reiterate the main result from the analysis of list poaching: Luring African politicians from the ANC has not been a viable option for South African opposition parties hoping to increase the numbers of Africans on their lists. This suggests a modification of the fifth hypothesis: The largest party may not poach the most candidates overall (smaller parties may poach frequently from each other), but it will dominate any flow of candidates between itself and the smaller parties.

Altogether, the data on candidate career paths in South Africa suggest that the opposition parties have faced greater barriers and risks to candidate transformation than their much larger rival, the ANC. At the same time, they are the ones with the most to gain from the process. This might explain why the opposition parties have only gone part way in transforming their candidate demographics.

### EVALUATING ALTERNATIVE EXPLANATIONS: INTERNAL STRUCTURE AND CANDIDATE RECRUITMENT

Chandra (2004) develops an alternative explanation for the success (or failure) of parties in candidate transformation that posits that parties with competitive

---

[16] The March 2003 national/provincial crossing period was similarly disastrous for the opposition, which did not manage to take a single MP from the ANC, while losing many. The DP lost one of its most senior African politicians, Themba Sono (to the Independent Democrats). See Ferial Haffajee and Marianne Merton, "Floor-Crossers or Double Crossers." *Mail & Guardian*, 9 April 2003. See also Jame Myburgh, "Floor Crossing Adds New Muscle to ANC." *Focus* 30 2003.

rules for candidate advancement will have an easier time recruiting members from new groups than parties with centralized rules. How far does this explanation go in accounting for patterns of candidate change in South Africa? In particular, can it offer a competing explanation for why the ANC's efforts at Africanization resulted in lower candidate turnover (even amongst whites, coloureds, and Indians) than either of the opposition parties?

South Africa's Constitution does not provide details on how parties should select candidates; hence procedures are up to the individual parties to decide. Often these internal processes are not transparent to outside observers, although the degree of information available about them varies by party. Lodge (1999a) provides a comprehensive review of the ANC's procedures in 1999. The ANC produces three sets of lists: the national list (candidates decided by the national party leadership for the National Assembly), provincial lists (candidates chosen at the provincial level for the Provincial Assembly), and provincial to national lists (provincial candidates for the National Assembly). The procedure for generating the national list is highly centralized and involves no direct voting procedures. A National List Committee compiles lists of national nominations. These reflect in part the "most popular figures emerging from branch nominations nationwide" (Lodge 1999a: 89), but exactly how they reflect them is unclear as the results of the branch nominations are not made public. The national list also reflects ideological, racial, and political balancing and, according to Lodge (1999a: 95), is the result of "consensus politics within the National Executive." In any case, this component of candidate selection is on the centralized (vs. competitive) end of the spectrum.

Competition figures more centrally in the process that generates the provincial and provincial to national lists. Here, local branches submit lists of nominees to provincial list conferences, where delegates vote from amongst the hundreds of names put forward. This part of the candidate selection process is therefore quite democratic and incorporates local preferences. After this, however, the process becomes more opaque. The results of the provincial voting are never made public. Instead, they are reviewed by provincial executive committees (which can make changes) and then submitted to the National Executive (which can also make changes). The National Executive Committee produces a penultimate version of the lists, which is then vetted by the National List Committee to ensure that the candidates meet the ANC's internal criteria (candidates must be in good standing and have no history of discipline problems, corruption, or criminal convictions). ANC rules also require that at least 30 percent of incumbents obtain electable positions and a further one-third must be women. The party also has requirements for racial balancing and tries to keep at least some talented mayors in local office rather than automatically promoting them.

As a result of all of these various requirements, the final lists produced by the National List Committee could look quite different from the lists forwarded from the provincial list conferences – although, again, this is difficult to judge as the initial lists are not made public. Lodge (1999a) discusses several indications that national leadership has resisted interfering too much, preserving in large part the preferences that come up from the provincial level. In 1999, prominent ANC provincial leaders like Popo Molefe (Premier of the North West Province) and Ivy Matsepe-Casaburri (Premier of the Free State) were not at the top of their respective provincial lists – a result Lodge speculates reflected the preferences of the delegates at the provincial list conferences, not national leadership. Lodge also notes that national leadership has avoided removing regionally popular leaders from lists even when they have contradicted party requirements (for example, by being convicted criminals or charged with corruption). At the same time, there is substantial evidence that the ANC's top leadership manipulates the lists as it sees fit. The one-third rule on gender balancing alone most likely results in significant changes.[17] As one of the ANC's top strategists put it in an interview in November 2003:

> The entire list process is managed in such a way that after the people have voted a strategic political intervention is made that is not just aimed at ensuring the Indians are on the lists or the whites are on the list, but to ensure there is a gender balance because you need to have as a matter of principle at least 30% representation of women on the list. So, some of the people who are on the top there will have to come down. Then you have the issue of race balance – we have to ensure there are Indians, coloureds and whites on the list. It may seem as if we are imposing this, but this is the criterion agreed to by ANC members. We also have to ensure the geographical spread is represented. All the provincial lists will be studied to ensure all the criteria are met.[18]

What is more, centralized leadership reserves the right to disregard the first name on the provincial list and name a different person as premier – a move the party makes *after* elections. In any case, because the process is not transparent, it is difficult to evaluate how much the final lists reflect the preferences revealed by the initial, democratic stages of the process. At best we can probably judge the process "semi-democratic," a combination of competitive rules and centralized discretion.

Both the DP and the NP used provincial electoral colleges to compile provincial and provincial to national lists from nominations submitted by branches (after 1994, neither party compiled a purely national list). This suggests democratic elements to their candidate selection procedures, and indeed the DP has claimed at various points that its procedures are more democratic than the ANC's.[19] At the same time, as in the ANC, national and provincial leadership have discretion to manipulate the final lists. According to Kotz (2004), provincial NP leaders, in consultation with the national leadership,

---

[17] For a discussion of this with regard to the 2004 election, see Ferial Haffajee, "ANC Top Dogs to Rejig Lists." *Mail & Guardian*, 28 November 2003.

[18] See Jaspreet Kindra, "'Too May Pahads on the ANC List.'" *Mail & Guardian*, 21 November 2003.

[19] Roger Southall, "Eastern Cape Profile." In EISA *Election Update 1999* No. 5, p. 10. Andrew Manson, Neil Roos, and Jennifer Seif. "Northwest Province." In EISA *Election Update 1999*, No. 7, pp 20–21.

can intervene in around 10 to 20 percent of the candidatures – usually to move individuals up or down the ranking, not to remove/add them. In the DP, the ranking of candidates is determined by an internal (nontransparent) party procedure. Furthermore, subject to a two-thirds veto, party leaders can fill positions three, seven, and then every further seventh spot on the provincial list and every third spot on the national list – a practice that provides them with substantial leeway to make changes if they desire.[20] In an interview in late January 2004, Tony Leon explained that the quotas

> can be used to do a range of things – to advance representivity (sic), deal with skills shortages in Parliament ... Sometimes the leadership needs to intervene to undo the effects of local democracy, as when people get into voting blocs. But the leader's intervention is very slight; at the end of the day the local party will make most decisions.[21]

The ability of national leadership to intervene in the lists also permits the reinstatement of provincially unpopular politicians who do not get electable positions in the initial rankings – as when Leon intervened in March 2004 to move Raenette Taljaard, the DP's controversial shadow finance minister, to an electable position on the Gauteng list after her initial placement was low.[22] In sum, like the ANC, the DP and NNP appear to combine competitive procedures to generate nominations with centralized discretion to manipulate the final lists as necessary.

Given that there is no obvious ranking of the competitiveness of the parties – they all appear to fall somewhere in the middle of the centralized/competitive spectrum – it is difficult to attribute differences in their ability to transform their candidate demographics to differences in the competitiveness of their internal structures. Thus, the greater ability of the ANC to retain white, coloured, and Indian candidates while undergoing Africanization is probably not a function of greater internal democracy. Indeed, the opposite may be true – greater centralization may *facilitate* candidate transformation. Although the details of the process are opaque, South African parties appear to use centralized discretion to *increase* the diversity of their lists – a result more in line with Norris (1996) than Chandra (2004). The ANC's one-third requirement for female representation and its desire for racially balanced lists are two reasons why it purportedly alters the preferences that come up from the provinces. Similarly, the ability of DP leaders to fill set aside positions on lists allows it to increase the slots allocated to underrepresented groups. Hence, while the details of the candidate advancement process are no doubt important, their relationship with candidate change is ambiguous.

---

[20] For a good review of party procedures in 2004, see Dirk Kotz, "The Nomination Processes of Candidates on Party Lists." In EISA *Election Update 2004*, No. 7.
[21] Forest, "'I'm Not a Guilty White."
[22] "The Good, the Bad, and the Redeployed." *Sunday Times*, March 21 2004.

## A CASE STUDY: THE COLLAPSE OF THE NATIONAL PARTY

In August 2004, the NP ceased to exist as an independent political party, opting instead to fight all future elections under the banner of the ANC. In a moment of considerable irony, Marthinus van Schalkwyk officially joined the ANC and urged his colleagues and followers to do the same. While the full account of the collapse of the National Party and the myriad reasons behind it fall beyond the scope of this chapter, it is useful to look at one contributing factor – the diversification of the party's candidate lists and the blood letting of party personnel that followed.

As discussed in the previous chapter, the NP pursued an aggressive strategy of rapid list transformation during the post-apartheid period. Pre-1994, the party's candidate profile was 100 percent white. In 1994, it was about 70 percent white or coloured; in 1999 and 2004, this number had fallen to 60 percent. Between 1994 and 1999, the party began diversifying even the top ranks of its leadership. It elected David Malatsi (an African) to the position of deputy leader and placed coloured leaders at the tops of its lists in the Western and Northern Capes. In the Western Cape – the party's last remaining stronghold – it replaced old-guard NP leader Hernus Kriel with Gerald Morkel. As one observer put it, the NP realized that it "must have a person of colour at the helm" and consequently did away with the "last white governor" in Africa.[23] While various authors (Giliomee 1994; Mattes et al. 1996) have criticized the NP's transformation as not going far enough (especially given the shifts in the support base of the party), it nonetheless represented a dramatic change in a relatively short period of time. And, as the previous chapter demonstrated, the racial image of the party in the electorate moved with these changes: The NP went from being a pure white party (indeed, was there a whiter party in the world than the NP during apartheid?) to a brown or rainbow party.

As promising as these alterations in the image of the party were (at least with regard to its potential to capture nonwhite votes), candidate transformation also resulted in several less positive developments. First, the party faced challenges of quality. Although the party was able to exploit its connections to tricameral politicians to bring on board coloured and Indian candidates of high external quality (Giliomee 1994), its African candidates were of a more dubious sort. According to Giliomee (1994), the NP hoped to build a constituency around African leaders with a history either in the homeland structures or the black local authorities introduced in 1982. However, it discovered that few of these politicians had any credibility in African communities. Instead, they were "corrupt or inefficient and hamstrung by a lack of resources" (Giliomee 1994: 55). The ANC characterized NP African candidates as "warlords" responsible for violence in Cape Town's shack settlements (Eldridge and Seekings 1996). Even where the party was able to attract African candidates with followings, these followings tended to be very localized and

---

[23] See Bell (1997).

built around dominant personalities (Lodge 1999a). Thus, while the lists got less white, the African candidates on them lacked external quality.

At the same time, these candidates (as well as coloured and Indian candidates) displaced the traditional elite of the party, producing predictable tensions and squabbles. Calland and Jacobs (1999a: 22) describe events in the Western Cape, the province that underwent the most dramatic changes and also the heartland of the NP's support:

> Tensions in the NNP have apparently reached the status of open warfare, with MPLS openly clashing with MEC and senior party leaders.... In the latest incident, the NNP chair of the province's finance committee, Jean-Pierre Gerber, clashed with MEC for Agriculture, Lampie Fick, over the sale of state land. Fick wants to sell the provincial property to private developments. The finance committee [fought this]. Fick is a former Minister who served in the last apartheid government of FW de Klerk. He identified with the old guard in the party. Gerber, a former NNP youth leader, is identified with a largely coloured "liberal" block in the party.

Candidate diversification also resulted in a massive exodus of NP candidates – both new and old – to other parties. Many of its new brown recruits complained bitterly about not being promoted quickly enough, arguing that the party remained under the grip of a conservative, white, old-guard elite that exploited the new brown members for their potential to attract votes without handing over any real control or power. Frustrated with the perceived lack of change in the party, many left.

Thus, several prominent Indian leaders in the Durban area left the NNP for the Minority Front after the 1994 election in part because they were unhappy with their lowly positions in the party. In the words of one Indian organizer, Manna Naidoo, chairman of the NNP's Durban North region until shortly before the 1996 local elections, the system of candidate listing in 1994 was "so badly rigged that it only catered for the white Natal leadership and their friends." Similar problems plagued the NNP in the Western Cape. Patrick Mackenzie left the NNP for the ANC, claiming amongst his reasons the control of the Western Cape NNP by a "broederbond faction."[24] Given Mackenzie's large following in coloured areas, this was a significant loss to the party, especially as he took with him community organizers and branch leaders. Mario Masher, another coloured NNP leader in the Western Cape, also left for the ANC, claiming that right-wing elements and adherents of P. W. Botha were hijacking the party's policies and the Western Cape government.[25] In the Northern Cape, as well, African and coloured leaders protested their under-representation on the NNP's lists, claiming that old-guard white Afrikaners still controlled the party. Popular protests broke out in Kimberly over the whiteness of the party's leadership. Members of the party's Galeshewe branch argued that the old guard should hand over control

---

[24] Aranes et al. (1999). Of course, Mackenzie also left out of sheer opportunism, to "plug into where the real power is," as he candidly put it.
[25] See Nqayi (1999).

to up-and-coming nonwhite leaders who could bolster the party's popularity in coloured and African areas, and demanded the resignations of two local leaders, Jan Modise and J. J. Niemann, because of their involvement with the party during the apartheid period.[26] They called the election lists a total sham, explaining that "None of the black and coloured representatives were voted into office. It was an all-white affair and we were made puppets."

Coloured and Indian leaders were not the only ones complaining. African candidates also left the party, citing similar frustrations,[27] and even a handful of white politicians absconded to less white parties, citing their belief that white leadership had become anachronistic in South Africa. Pierre-Jean Gerber, the Western Cape provincial legislator who squabbled with NP MEC for Agriculture Lampie Fick, left for the ANC, as did Boetie de Wet, chairman of the NNP's Border Region branch in the Eastern Cape. Roelf Meyer – considered by many to be one of the most important younger NNP politicians and a prime negotiator during the CODESA talks – left the party in 1997 because he believed that it was not transforming itself deeply or quickly enough. With Bantu Holomisa he formed the United Democratic Movement (UDM), a party aimed explicitly at attracting votes across the color lines of South Africa.

In addition to politicians who left because the party had not changed enough, there was a flood of politicians leaving because it had changed *too* much. Many old-guard NNP politicians headed for the DP, the Federal Alliance, and parties to the right, in part out of "disaffection caused by the party's efforts to diversify its representation."[28] Thus, Tertius Delport, who had been part of De Klerk's cabinet, defected to the Democratic Party in the Eastern Cape, as did several members of the NNP's Western Cape leadership (Martha Olckers and Nic Koornhof). In Mpumalanga, Lucas Nel, a relatively high-ranking NNP leader, left for the Federal Alliance, prompting a "debilitating spate of resignations and defections" of senior NNP leaders angered when African candidates displaced them.[29] These are only a few examples: Throughout South Africa, the NNP bled white leaders to white parties in the run-up to the 1999 election.

All told, the NNP lost a significant number of politicians between 1994 and 1999, with a flood of defections in the months prior to the 1999 election. Almost every day from March through May, newspapers announced another

---

[26] See Robins (1999b: 14–16).
[27] Some examples are Maggie Ratsoma, Soshanguve (Pretoria) district chairperson of the NNP, who left for the ANC claiming: "The rightwingers are causing trouble in the party. They way they treated us (blacks) is like we had no political role." See Phanlane (1999). Reverend Muntu Absalom Nkosi, a senior member of the NNP in Mpumalanga and one of only three NNP legislators in the province, left for the UDM. Elizabeth Rapuleng, NNP organizer in Soweto, left for the Federal Alliance, after going public with her frustration that the NNP was a white party with "black mascots." See Ka'Nkosi (1999).
[28] See EISA (1999a).
[29] Thabo Rapoo, "Mpumalanga Province: Electioneering Head-Start for the Ruling Party." In EISA *Election Update* 2004, No. 2, p. 42.

switch.[30] This bloodletting had a predictably negative impact on the party. It compromised the party's electoral machinery. The NP's great strength in fighting elections had been its organization at the local level (Breytenbach 1999). Much of this was gone by 1999. Lodge (1999: 131) notes that the party "could no longer mobilize a large branch membership except where it could depend on the structures inherited from the old (coloured) Labour Party," and, of course, many of these had also left the party. The exodus of politicians also sent a negative signal to voters: Coloured, Indian, and African voters got the message that the party was not "really" transformed, while white voters came to see it as a lost cause. Moreover, while its candidates were fighting and fleeing, the strategic abilities of the party became compromised and its behavior more schizophrenic (Lodge 1999a).

Although these factors alone did not cause the NNP's fall from grace in the 1999 election (when it was eclipsed by the DP), they certainly contributed. Furthermore, the party's troubles continued after 1999. In the first floor crossing period for local councilors in 2002, it wooed back some of its candidates from the Democratic Alliance, but many stayed on. In the 2003 floor crossing period for national and provincial MPs, it sustained further losses. By the 2004 election, the party was significantly weakened, even in its heartland of the Western Cape. A few months after the election, it folded its cards.

CONCLUSION

In this chapter, I have proposed an explanation for the relatively modest pace of the opposition's efforts to transform its candidate demographics. As Chapter 6 revealed, such transformation is crucial to the opposition's efforts to win votes in African, coloured, and Indian communities – a fact well understood by the parties themselves. If candidate diversification is so critical, why have parties not gone further with it? In particular, why do their top rungs of leadership remain predominantly white? The explanation proposed here focuses on the challenges these parties face in recruiting high-quality politicians. On the one hand, small parties like the DA and the NP in South Africa are especially sensitive to the quality of incoming politicians. Because they control only a small number of seats, the average quality of outgoing politicians unseated by incoming recruits is high. To maintain candidate quality – essential for winning elections – these parties must therefore recruit high-quality new candidates. On the other hand, small parties face significant disadvantages in acquiring quality candidates. Unable to reward low-ranking trial candidates with seats, they struggle to keep their candidates, which makes "grow your own" strategies nonviable. At the same time, they fail in their efforts to recruit candidates from larger parties like the ANC, far more frequently suffering

---

[30] Note that the defection statistics cited earlier only include NP losses to the DP and ANC. The party also lost candidates to the Minority Front, the Federal Alliance, the Freedom Front, the United Democratic Movement, and other smaller parties.

losses of talent than gains. In sum, elite incorporation is especially intractable for small parties.

Using a dataset that tracks candidate career paths in the ANC, NP, and DA, I evaluated several observable implications of this explanation. The data showed that parties tend to place new candidates substantially lower on their lists than either returning or poached candidates – a finding in keeping with the notion that parties do not want to place candidates of unknown quality in their highest positions and instead seek trial periods during which candidate quality can be assessed. This was particularly true of the large ANC, which could pursue this policy without jeopardizing its retention of new candidates (it controls enough seats that even a relatively low position on its lists still gains election). In contrast, the smaller DA had to temper its desire to sort with its need to put newcomers high enough to give them a hope of getting elected. As a result, the penalty for being a newcomer was lower in the DA than it was in the ANC. The data also showed that candidates are indeed sensitive to their rankings: The lower the ranking, the less likely the candidate returned to the party. At the same time, holding rank constant, the ANC was far more effective at retaining candidates of all races than either the NP or the DA. Both of these parties – perhaps reflecting their long lists but short supply of seats – faced high levels of candidate turnover. The only place this was not true was the Western Cape, where the opposition parties have vied with the ANC for control. Here, the NP and the ANC were roughly on par in their ability to retain candidates – further evidence that size matters. Finally, the data revealed that the opposition parties have been singularly unsuccessful in poaching candidates from the ANC. Instead, all roads lead to the ANC, which has systematically stripped talent from the opposition in recent years.

In sum, the data show that the opposition has struggled both with growing its own candidates and recruiting candidates from the ANC. It brings in new candidates and places them in relatively high spots (at least compared with the spots given by the ANC). However, because the opposition parties control few seats, even these relatively high spots were not high enough to retain candidates. As a result, the oppositions' lists operate like a swinging door: huge numbers of candidates, few of whom get seated, and frequent change and turnover at all but the highest levels of leadership. The parties consequently fail to get the high-quality new candidates they need to make leadership diversification a winning strategy. And, as revealed by the chapter's case study, the recent history of the now-defunct NP neatly illustrates these dynamics: The party diversified rapidly up until 1999, but diversification produced significant internal problems in the party, with many nonwhites leaving because they felt they were not moving up the party hierarchy fast enough, and whites leaving because they sensed their loss of power. At the same time, many of the new recruits – especially the African recruits – were not of sufficiently high quality to bring in votes to offset white loses. As a result of these and other factors, the party's strategy became increasingly erratic and it lost support in both white and black communities. In a final ironic twist of fate, the party that had fought apartheid subsumed the party that had created it.

The analysis in this chapter points to a central and insufficiently recognized source of ANC power: its monopoly hold over quality African politicians. Opposition parties need to diversify their candidates to alter their apartheid-forged party labels. At the same time, pursuing candidate diversification willy nilly and filling lists with candidates who are unknown, untrustworthy, or lacking in credibility in their communities risks losing the parties more support than they gain (witness the fate of the NP). The ANC, by dint of its massive hold over seats, is able to retain its candidates, sort them, and promote the ones it deems valuable. If, by chance, the opposition manages to recruit a high-quality African politician – or one who shows promise of being high-quality – the ruling party can simply steal that individual away. In this way, the ruling party prevents the opposition from transforming itself into a viable competitor for African votes and preserves the racial census in South Africa.

# 8

# Negative Framing Strategies and African Opposition Parties

Thus far in this book I have focused on how the challenges faced by "white" opposition parties in transforming their apartheid-based party images contribute to racial-census elections and single-party dominance in South Africa. While the focus on the white opposition is appropriate when explaining the origins of the racial census in South Africa (after all, it is largely the failure of the white parties to attract African votes that drives this outcome), more is needed for a full explanation of ANC dominance. ANC dominance reflects not only the weakness of white or multiracial parties but also the failure of African opposition parties to mount successful challenges to ANC hegemony. It is therefore useful to consider whether image politics play the same role in weakening African opposition parties as they do for the white opposition. Have African competitors been hampered by problematic images? Has the ANC employed against its African competitors the same framing tactics and strategies that it has used so successfully against the white opposition? In other words, are image politics general to electoral competition in South Africa?

Many African parties in South Africa (the Pan African Congress [PAC], the Azanian Peoples Organization [Azapo], the United Christian Democratic Party [UCDP], and other microparties) lack fund raising capabilities and national branch structures. They are small, winning only a percentage or two of the vote and claiming a few seats in national or provincial legislatures. Many have debilitating internal divisions that prevent them from developing coherent strategies or revolve around a single leader. Few win votes outside of a narrow geographic or ethnic base. Indeed, many do not have discernible national aspirations, nor do they seek to play the role of leader of the opposition. For these reasons, the ANC has devoted little effort to fighting them. In my analysis of campaign rhetoric in the 2004 elections (see Chapter 5), I found virtually no references by the ruling party to most African opposition parties. The ANC simply has not taken these parties seriously enough to talk about them during its campaigns.

The Inkatha Freedom Party (IFP), the United Democratic Movement (UDM), and the Congress of the People (Cope) present exceptions, however.

While the IFP never captured significant support outside of its home base in KwaZulu-Natal, at its peak it controlled a majority of votes in KwaZulu-Natal and the KwaZulu-Natal government and nearly derailed the 1994 elections. As such, it has been the most significant "African" competitor to the ANC during the post-apartheid period. Its gradual weakening over the 1994 to 2009 period played an important role in solidifying ANC dominance, even if it did not influence the racial pattern of South African elections. The UDM also presented an important regional challenge to the ruling party, albeit a brief one. And most recently, Cope generated high expectations when it split from the ANC in late 2008, although its performance in the 2009 elections fell short of what its leaders and supporters had hoped.

While the factors limiting these ANC challengers are manifold, image politics played a central role in all three cases. Largely through its own making, the IFP entered the post-apartheid period with an image as a traditional/conservative Zulu nationalist party willing to use violence to further its own goals. While this image allowed the IFP to cordon off a core of support in the traditional rural areas of KwaZulu-Natal, it did not enable it to compete at the national level. Consequently, in the post-1994 period, IFP leader Mangosuthu Buthelezi attempted to broaden the appeal of the IFP by painting it as inclusive and reformed – an objective he failed to achieve, in part because the ANC sought to preserve the image of the IFP as it was in 1994 (violent, provincial). At the same time, the ANC was able to neutralize the positive aspects of the IFP's image by cultivating its own Zulu credentials and courting traditional African leaders. Thus, while the IFP failed in its bid to broaden its image, the ANC succeeded in making inroads into the IFP's core. The ANC used a similar strategy on the UDM, simultaneously adopting the UDM's "traditional" guise while also branding its leader, Bantu Holomisa, as an apartheid collaborator and fomenter of violence. Finally, the ANC also utilized a negative image strategy against Cope, successfully branding it as the "Black DA," a party of elitist "Polokwane losers."

Thus, far from being restricted to the white opposition parties, the ANC has used image politics to discredit a variety of competitors. By restricting the choice set of voters in this fashion, it has cemented its hold over power in South Africa.

THE INKATHA FREEDOM PARTY

In 1975, Chief Mangosuthu Gatsha Buthelezi, who had built a powerful support base in the KwaZulu Legislative Assembly after being been edged out of royal affairs in the late 1960s, resurrected from political obscurity a defunct cultural and political organization called Inkatha[1] and initiated a massive recruitment

---

[1] The full name of the movement was *Inkatha yeSizwe*, or National Cultural Liberation Movement, and it had originally formed in the 1920s to generate support for the Zulu monarchy.

drive within Zulu communities (Lodge and Nasson 1991; Hamilton and Mare 1994). Buthelezi sought a middle road between acquiescence and revolution, attempting to work within apartheid institutions to bring about change rather than use the more overt forms of resistance favored by other movements. He combined broad calls for African liberation (he opened Inkatha membership to all black South Africans in 1979) with more narrow goals of Zulu self-determination and hoped that his leadership of Inkatha would position him as a moderate intermediary between whites and blacks. Initially Buthelezi worked in concert with the ANC, adopting ANC colors, seeking (and getting) the support of ANC leaders in exile, and presenting Inkatha as the heir to the ANC (Piper 2002; Aitchison 2003; Hamilton and Mare 1994).

However, by 1979 tensions between the two organizations developed as each became less tolerant of the other and attempted to assert dominance over the leadership of the resistance movement. Inkatha quickly lost out to the ANC (and its affiliates, the newly formed United Democratic Front and Council of South African Trade Unions) and conflict devolved into a violent struggle over territory in KwaZulu-Natal, with Inkatha's stronghold in rural (more traditional) areas and the ANC/UDF's in the cities and townships (Piper 2002; Aitchison 2003). As ground war between the rival organizations built throughout the 1980s, Buthelezi sought rapprochement with the Zulu monarch, King Goodwill Zwelithini, and other traditional leaders, and increasingly presented Inkatha as an organization by and for Zulus. UDF leaders, in contrast, eschewed ethnic identifications, a neutrality Buthelezi attempted to turn against them by portraying the UDF and the ANC (and their supporters) as outsiders or Xhosa dominated (Piper 2002). In the struggle for ascendency, which left thousands dead, injured, or displaced and wreaked substantial property damage, most evidence suggests that Inkatha initiated more of the violence and suffered fewer casualties and that the apartheid state not only encouraged the conflict but also intervened on the side of Inkatha, providing funding as well as training support and not preventing attacks where it might have (Piper 2002; Aitchison 1993).[2]

With the release of Mandela in early 1990 and the beginning of negotiations between the ANC and the National Party (NP) over the form and substance of post-apartheid South Africa, the conflict between Inkatha and the ANC shifted to a new phase, even as the hostilities in KwaZulu-Natal raged unabated and spread to the townships of Gauteng (Piper 2002). Buthelezi felt marginalized by the cooperation between the NP and ANC and sought to force his inclusion into the negotiations by engaging in brinkmanship and the further politicization of the Zulu identity. He also converted Inkatha into a political party – the Inkatha Freedom Party (IFP) – in preparation for participating

---

[2] In the Natal Midlands area alone, there were 64 deaths during the 1980 to 1986 period, 1,810 deaths between 1987 and 1989, and 1,635 deaths between 1990 and 1992. Much of this violence involved stunning brutality, as people were stoned, raped, clubbed, beaten, sjamboked, tortured, and burned Statistics from Aitchison (1993).

in elections. Hostilities peaked in early 1994, when King Zwelithini called for the secession of KwaZulu-Natal from South Africa and Buthelezi threatened to boycott the election. Mandela refused to delay the election, and Buthelezi finally – one week before voting was to start – agreed that the IFP would participate (Piper 2002, Hamilton and Mare 1994). The IFP won the election in KwaZulu-Natal, taking just over half the vote to the ANC's 32 percent. While substantial irregularities marked the election, civil war was averted, and Buthelezi assumed the premiership of the province.[3]

Following the 1994 election, hostilities between the ANC and the IFP diminished considerably. Mandela included Buthelezi as a deputy prime minister in the Government of National Unity and appointed him Minister of Home Affairs, posts Buthelezi continued after the 1999 election. Political violence dropped precipitously and was minimal by 2004.[4] At the same time, as conflict between the parties fell away, the IFP's dominance of KwaZulu-Natal also ebbed. In 1999, it took 42 percent of the provincial vote to the ANC's 40 percent. In 2004, the ANC superseded the IFP, taking 47 percent of the vote to the IFP's 37 percent. And in 2009, the route was complete when the ANC took 64 percent of the provincial vote and the IFP took a little more than 20 percent (and just 4.6 percent of the national vote) – a significant defeat of a party that once planned to lead the country.

The causes of the IFP's failure to convert itself to a national player and its slow decline at the provincial level are manifold and (one can speculate) include resource constraints (the IFP lacks the ANC's access to state resources and receives far less state campaign funding than the ruling party while at the same time does not have the wealthy constituency of the DP), the lack of a vibrant national branch structure, the difficulties of building a national party from a provincial base in a political system that grants provinces few autonomous powers (provinces raise few of their own revenues), and the challenges of competing in an increasingly urban environment from a base that is largely traditional and rural. In addition to these factors, image factors also played an important role.

The IFP entered the post-apartheid period with an image shaped by its history of competition and violent conflict with the ANC. During the 1980s and

---

[3] On the voting irregularities, the IFP's success surprised many as several pre-election polls had placed the IFP and ANC much closer together and some polls had even suggested that the ANC would win the election. When the IFP won the provincial election, many South Africans believed that the outcome must have represented a back-room deal between Buthelezi and Mandela, brokered to ensure peace. However, others have suggested that, while fraud was ubiquitous, it may not have substantially altered the result of the election, that is, that the election was basically an accurate poll of public preferences. According to this argument, it was the pre-election polls, not the election results, that were wrong: Many IFP supporters distrusted the survey enumerators and either refused to answer the survey questions or did so dishonestly. See Johnson (1996) for a discussion of these points.

[4] In 1994, more than 1,000 people died in political violence. By 1999, the number had dropped to 82. In 2004, it was less than 20. See Piper (2005: 148).

1990s, when competition between the parties was most intense, Buthelezi increasingly appealed to Zulu nationalism in his effort to gain ground in KwaZulu-Natal and a seat at the negotiating table. He frequently referenced (and exalted) the history of the great Zulu nation, associated Inkatha with the royal Zulu institutions, and presented Inkatha as a Zulu organization.[5] Inkatha's support base was in the rural areas and traditional leaders (who still controlled these areas) provided its organizational backbone. At the same time, Inkatha engaged in substantial acts of violence in KwaZulu-Natal and (later) Gauteng – sometimes with covert support from the apartheid regime. As a result, at the time of the first post-apartheid election most South Africans viewed the IFP as a tradition-bound, rurally based, exclusively Zulu party willing to foment violence to further its own ends. In a 1994 survey conducted by Idasa, 53 percent of all respondents (56 percent of Africans) viewed the IFP as representing the interests of one group only (Zulus). In the same survey, 34 percent of all respondents (67 percent of Africans) named the IFP as the party most associated with encouraging violence. And 25 percent of all respondents (40 percent of Africans) gave the IFP as the party most associated with working against law and order. No other party was more associated with violence and working against law and order.[6] Many Africans probably also viewed the IFP as an apartheid collaborator, especially as information about its relationship with the NP emerged through Truth and Reconciliation Commission hearings.

Inkatha's image both helped and hurt it. On the plus side, its strong association with the Zulu ethnic group and traditional institutions won it a resolute core of voters in rural KwaZulu-Natal (and urban areas with migrants from rural KwaZulu-Natal) that loyally supported it at least until the 2009 election (Piper 2005). On the negative side, rural KwaZulu-Natal voters represented a limited (and probably diminishing) constituency; Inkatha could never be a nationally competitive party on the back of this group alone.[7] Buthelezi tried sporadically to use the IFP's "traditional" credentials and image as the party of chiefs to cultivate a national constituency of conservative, rural, tradition-bound Africans (a sizeable group) but ultimately did not invest much energy in this direction.[8] And the IFP's image as violent and reactionary and the rumors

---

[5] Piper (2002, 2005) convincingly argues that this was a strategic move by Buthelezi, driven by the exigencies of competition with the ANC. Buthelezi always had national aspirations for Inkatha, and when times were good "it presented itself as a black, national, conservative-liberal, anti-apartheid organization using peaceful tactics to bring about change" (Piper 2005: 150). However, when competition with the ANC got difficult (and Inkatha was losing), he would fall back on appeals to Zulu nationalism and violence as a last resort. The 1980s and 1990s were a time when competition with the ANC was intense hence the frequent use of ethnic rhetoric and symbolism.

[6] See Chapter 2 for more details on the 1994 survey.

[7] Interestingly, there is evidence that a substantial minority of white NP supporters in KZN voted for the IFP in the 1994 provincial election as a way of counteracting ANC strength in the province. See Johnson (1996) for further discussion. However, these voters alone could hardly give the party a national standing and they would prove fickle in later elections.

[8] See Lodge (1999: 127).

of its collaboration during apartheid certainly did not win it votes beyond that minor segment of its constituency engaged in (and profiting from) promoting conflict.

As Buthelezi had always had national aspirations for himself and the IFP, he increasingly came to see the IFP's image as a liability and began efforts to change it soon after the 1994 election (Piper 2005). Zulu nationalist rhetoric subsequently disappeared from the IFP's public discourse and the party backed away from the violent tactics that it had used in the past, instead presenting itself as a liberal democratic party for people of all races and ethnic groups (Piper 2005: 151). During the 2004 election, the IFP tailored its message to new supporters, not its core group, emphasizing policy and criticizing the ANC on delivery rather than focusing on identity issues. The goal was to frame the IFP "as the party with the better policies and leadership to address these issues," a party to be taken seriously as a national leader, not a provincial throw-back (Piper 2005: 157). It also employed campaign techniques designed to reach a broad audience outside of rural KwaZulu-Natal, holding rallies and sending Buthelezi around the country, rather than focusing exclusively on door-to-door canvassing in its traditional strongholds (Piper 2005). Piper (2005: 156) dissects the visual symbolism of the IFP's manifesto, observing that the cover of the manifesto "presented Buthelezi as a benign yet accessible grandfatherly figure, welcoming of women and people of all races." He stands "head and shoulders above others in the photograph; his protective and inclusive stance in relation to a group of younger women of all races; and his old world yet funky dress style, as revealed by the words, 'It's Cool Man,' inscribed on his braces." Piper notes that "this imagery is precisely the opposite of public perceptions of the IFP as a Zulu traditionalist" Piper (2005: 156). Piper (2005) also recounts a campaign question-and-answer session in which Buthelezi tried to distance the IFP from its past and demonstrate its commitment to diversity. In response to the question "What would you say to those who perceived the IFP as a Zulu party?" Buthelezi responded by pointing out the IFP's communications spokesperson, Suzanne Vos, using her as an example of the IFP's gender and racial diversity. Finally, Buthelezi entered the IFP into an electoral coalition with the Democratic Alliance, signaling his desire to build bridges to opposition voters. In sum, the IFP attempted to leave behind its problematic apartheid-era image as a violent, atavistic Zulu organization and re-engineer itself as a modern, inclusive liberal democratic party with a plan to develop South Africa.

The IFP failed to accomplish this goal, however; its transformation was incomplete (Piper 2005). As indicated earlier, about 53 percent of the respondents in the 1994 Idasa survey believed the party was exclusive, 17 percent saw it as inclusive, and 31 percent did not know. In 1999 (with the *Opinion99* survey), responses were similar: 56 percent saw the party as exclusive, 22 percent saw it as inclusive, and 22 percent were uncertain. In 2004 (after the IFP's concerted campaign efforts), the percentage seeing the party as exclusive dropped significantly, all the way to 18 percent. However, still only 26 percent saw it as inclusive. The big change was in the number of respondents who were uncertain about the party: 56 percent fell into this category.[9] Thus, rather than convincing a large percentage of the electorate that it had changed, the party's efforts merely succeeded in increasing voter uncertainty about its label.

Several factors hindered the IFP's efforts at image transformation, some internal to the IFP and some external. Piper (2005) suggests that the party's internal culture has made convincing change difficult: The party is built around the person of Buthelezi, who perhaps has less crossover charm than party strategists believe. Moreover, many of its leaders are traditionalists who remain entrenched in the "politics of patronage and intrigue" and have little tolerance for open debate. More open-minded liberal members of the party tend to leave, often for the ANC.[10] As a result "the IFP is simply not an organization conducive to liberal-democratic politics" (Piper 2005: 152). It is difficult to dress a wolf in a sheep's clothing.

At the same time, the ANC made an active, if subtle, effort to cast doubt on the IFP's transformation and remind the electorate of the IFP's past, particularly its role in fomenting violence. These efforts were not especially evident in the earlier elections. Lodge (1994) suggests that the ANC largely stuck with the high road in 1994, focusing on its forward-looking policy message rather than dwelling on the past. Consequently, its efforts at negative framing were limited (and voters most likely needed little help in seeing the IFP as a violent party in 1994, as violence was still ubiquitous at that point). Even in 1994, however, the ANC ran a national advertisement in the last days before the election contrasting the ANC's proposals for "jobs, housing, education, peace and security" with "poverty, unemployment and oppression" in IFP-NP–ruled KwaZulu-Natal. Here the ANC portrayed itself as the party of peace, the IFP as party of oppression and apartheid collaboration. In 1999, explicit negative framing efforts by the ANC also appear to have been limited – most likely because the IFP was a coalition partner and the ANC was hoping to encourage a merger (Lodge 1999a: 121). However, by 2004, when the ANC and the IFP were no longer in coalition, negative framing tactics became more pronounced.

The ANC efforts in 2004 were twofold: First, the ruling party said much by saying nothing at all. Throughout most of the campaign, the ANC spoke little of the IFP, ignoring it as it ignored most other opposition parties. The rhetoric database for the 2004 election (see Chapter 5) has a total of 218 quotes, 72 from the ANC. Only 9 of these ANC quotes made any reference to the IFP (with one additional reference to the DA/IFP coalition). Second, when the

---

[9] This shadows the movement of African public opinion about the DA and NNP: Fewer respondents saw these parties as exclusive by 2004, but many shifted simply to feeling uncertain about them, rather than seeing them a completely inclusive.

[10] While the IFP has not suffered the massive outflows during floor crossing periods that the DA experienced (see Chapter 7), it still has lost more to the ANC than it gained. In 2002 it lost seven to the ANC and gained seven from the ANC. In 2004, it lost twenty-five to the ANC and gained only two back.

ruling party did make reference to the IFP, it did not engage it on substantive issues: Of the 9 references the ANC made of the IFP in the rhetoric database, *none* referenced policy, competence, issues, or priorities. Rather, one made Buthelezi an apartheid apologist (a quote from ANC Pallo Jordan responding to Buthelezi's comments that poverty in rural South Africa was worse than it ever had been, saying Buthelezi was "happier feeding on oppression"),[11] and the remainder all spoke of the IFP's campaign strategy, with particular focus on violence and intimidation. A typical example of this occurred in late February, when ANC safety and security spokesperson in KwaZulu-Natal Bheki Cele said: "The trend seems to be that wherever there are political blockages and incidents of violence, it is the IFP who [incite] the ANC." To this the IFP's KZN spokesperson Blessed Gwala responded: "The most recent activities of violence have been caused by the ANC, who are attempting to discredit the IFP in the eyes of the public."[12] Another example occurred a few weeks later at a pre-election debate when senior ANC MP Pallo Jordan accused the IFP of provoking violence, including a threat to use arms against a presidential *imbizo*. Musa Zondi, IFP spokesperson, responded that violence emanated from both sides, not just the IFP. He also urged the media to be sensitive when reporting and not to characterize drunken brawls and criminal activities as instances of ANC-IFP violence.[13] A few weeks later, after IFP supporters carrying spears and sticks and throwing stones prevented Deputy President Jacob Zuma from entering a hostel in the Johannesburg area, ANC Gauteng Provincial Secretary David Makhura accused the IFP of being "hellbent on obstructing free political activity and instigating violence as a means of creating no-go areas."[14] The remainder of examples from the rhetoric database follow similar lines. Of course, many of the incidents of violence/intimidation did occur – the IFP (or IFP supporters, anyway) gave the ANC ample material with which to make its claims. However, as Piper (2005: 18) explains: "[T]he ANC was determined to make as much mileage as it could out of the incidents that did occur." Moreover, the ANC presented the violence as originating solely in the IFP and probably gave the party leadership more credit for orchestrating events than it deserved.

Thus, when the ANC publically discussed the IFP – which was infrequent – it almost always used a violence frame to do so, reminding voters of the infamous past of the party and refusing to engage it according to the new terms Buthelezi was trying to introduce. Moreover, the press picked up on this framing of the election, devoting more discussion to the role the IFP played (or did not play) in generating violence than it did to the party's policy plans or

---

[11] Quoted in John Kane-Berman, "Political mudslinging as vicious as it ever was." *Business Day*, March 9, 2004.
[12] Quotes from Vicki Robinson, "Weary of warfare." *Mail & Guardian*, February 27, 2004.
[13] Charles Phahlane, "IFP-ANC debate over who is provoking pre-poll violence." *The Star*, March 2, 2004.
[14] Themba Wa Sepotokele, "ANC slams intimidation by IFP followers in Gauteng." *Cape Times*, March 16, 2004.

substantive criticisms of the ruling party (Piper 2005). The overall message was that the IFP was irrelevant at best and threatening, violent, stuck in the past, at worst. In response, IFP leaders attempted to counteract the message by urging peace and pointing out the ANC's role in generating conflict but eventually stopped because they realized they were simply playing into the ANC's hands and confirming their negative framing efforts (Piper 2005).[15]

Compounding this, the IFP had far fewer campaign resources than the ANC. In 2004, IFP national spokesperson Musa Zonda complained that the IFP could only afford 60,000 posters whereas the ANC put up 1.8 million posters in KwaZulu-Natal alone (Piper 2005). The IFP had limited cars and a limited travel budget, whereas the ANC's pockets were incomparably deeper. And the ANC, as the ruling party, got far greater coverage in the media than the IFP (Davis 2005). These discrepancies in resources meant that the ANC could broadcast its message and framing farther and wider than the IFP. It is not surprising, therefore, that the IFP had difficulties selling the electorate on its image change.

Even as the IFP struggled to convey an image that would allow it to compete more favorably for votes outside of rural KwaZulu-Natal, the ANC sought to re-frame its own image in ways that would make it more attractive to the IFP's core constituency. Beginning in the early 1990s, the ANC began to cultivate its Zulu credentials, to convey the message that "being Zulu did not mean being Zulu nationalist, and that the ANC was a home for Zulu people too" (Piper 2002: 17). ANC leaders conveyed this message using the usual techniques: declarations of the importance of Zulu identity by prominent (Zulu) ANC leaders, the use of traditional Zulu dress by ANC leaders, and the hosting of Shaka Day rallies (Piper 2002). The ANC used similar tactics during the 1994 elections in KwaZulu-Natal. Lodge (1994) describes a rally in Durban in October 1993 "which began with the Kushisha Impepho ceremony to call down the blessings of the ancestors on the 60,000-strong multitude, and after ninety minutes of prayer, song, and dance, Mandela appeared in royal leopard-skin regalia" (Lodge 1994: 36). He addressed the crowd in English and Zulu and praised a long list of tribes, chiefs, and kings who had fought colonialism and apartheid (Lodge 1994). Such demonstrations continued in 1999. When visiting with Zulu King Goodwill Zwelithini (who had left the IFP), Nelson Mandela once again donned a leopard skin and paid homage to traditional leaders as spearheading the fight against colonialism (Mare 1999: 106). Perhaps more important than the rhetoric, the ANC made a strict policy out of creating ethnically balanced lists (Butler 2007) and placed Zulu Jacob Zuma in the position of deputy president to Mbeki in 1999 and then elected him party leader in December 2007. In April 2009, during the same election that saw IFP support collapse almost completely, Zuma – who was fond of wearing "100% Zulu Boy" t-shirts during the campaign and

---

[15] One is reminded of Lakoff's argument in "don't think of an elephant!"

singing in his native language – became the first non-Xhosa African president in South Africa.

In addition to cultivating Zulu credentials, the ANC also sought to portray itself as a party that respected tradition and traditional leaders. Traditional leaders provided the organizational muscle of the IFP in KwaZulu-Natal and also played a role in the UDM's rising popularity in the Eastern Cape during the late 1990s. In 1999, the ANC engaged in an all-out effort to woo traditional leaders in the Eastern Cape and KwaZulu-Natal. As documented in Chapter 4, it put prominent chiefs in high positions on provincial electoral lists, sent top leaders to make repeated and highly public visits to prominent chiefs, played to tradition, and increased chiefly salaries a few months prior to the election.

Thus, not only did the ANC skillfully use the negative aspects of the IFP's image against it, the ruling party co-opted those aspects of the IFP's image that worked in its favor. It employed both positive and negative labeling strategies to fatally weaken a key opposition player.

THE UNITED DEMOCRATIC MOVEMENT (UDM)

The ANC responded in a similar fashion to the United Democratic Movement (UDM) and its leader, Bantubonke Holomisa. Holomisa joined the ANC in 1994, from somewhat controversial origins. Unlike most of his contemporaries, who had their beginnings in the antiapartheid movement, Holomisa was a career officer in the Transkei Defense Force (TDF), the military wing of the Transkei (Bantustan) government. After quickly moving up the TDF career ladder, Holomisa staged a coup against Transkei Prime Minister Stella Sigcau in 1987. From 1987 until 1994 (when he joined the ANC), he was the head of state of the Transkei. Although initially popular in the party, Holomisa made several missteps that eventually resulted in his expulsion in September 1996. In May 1996, he testified in front of the Truth and Reconciliation Commission (without, apparently, first vetting his statements with ANC higher-ups) and accused ANC Cabinet Minister Stella Sigcau of accepting a bribe from casino magnate Sol Kerzner during her time as a minister in the Transkei Cabinet. The accusation was just a small part of Holomisa's testimony, but the press picked it up and the incident proved embarrassing to the ruling party. When Mbeki censured Holomisa for his actions, Holomisa responded by issuing further accusations against high-ranking ANC members. Holomisa then walked out of an ANC National Executive Council disciplinary committee, calling it a "kangaroo court." Shortly thereafter, Mbeki expelled Holomisa from the party.

Holomisa then joined forces with former NP member Roelf Meyer to launch the UDM in 1997. The UDM hoped to capture the Eastern Cape (building on Holomisa's Transkei connections) as well as establish a national presence as a truly multiracial alternative to the ANC, NP, and DP. Sensing a potentially lethal adversary, the ANC responded with a fierce election campaign in the regional strongholds of the UDM (see Chapter 4 for more details). As part of this campaign, it went to great ends to play up its "traditional" image, courting chiefs and other local dignitaries. It also sought to discredit Holomisa. In a document entitled "The Rise and Fall of Bantu Holomisa" (issued by the ANC Department of Information and Publicity in May 1997 and published in the *New Nation*), the ANC smeared Holomisa's background, emphasizing his links with apartheid-era security forces and intimating that he had participated in counterinsurgency efforts. "While hundreds of thousands of patriots joined the liberation struggle," the article contended, "Bantubonke Holomisa was climbing up the ladder of a bantustan army, under the tutelage of the apartheid SADF." It also alleged that corruption in the Transkei intensified under his rule, questioned his willingness to team up with shady characters like Sisfiso Nkabinde and Lucas Mangope, and suggested that he was an opportunistic troublemaker without plan or ideological anchor.[16] In short, the article made a thorough attempt to discredit Holomisa and thereby neutralize any threat posed by the UDM.

The ANC's efforts – combined with the significant organizational challenges faced by the UDM – resulted in the party burning out before it built a mass following at the national level. In its debut election in 1999, the UDM managed to capture a little over 3 percent of the vote, most of it in the Eastern Cape. In 2004, its national support fell under 3 percent. In 2009, it dropped below 1 percent of the national vote and Cope surpassed it as the official opposition in the Eastern Cape.

THE CONGRESS OF THE PEOPLE (COPE)

The 2009 election saw the debut of a new party, Cope, formed in late 2008 by ANC leaders disgruntled by the battle between Jacob Zuma and Thabo Mbeki for control over the leadership of the ANC. Before discussing Cope and the 2009 election, I will first give an overview of the succession crisis and the rise of Jacob Zuma.

### The Succession Crisis and the Rise of Jacob Zuma

Leadership succession often creates challenges for dominant parties, and the ANC is no different. Mbeki's anointment as the president of the ANC in 1997 followed significant jockeying within the party between Mbeki and competitors like Cyril Ramaphosa and Tokyo Sexwale. Both Ramaphosa and Sexwale were popular in the party, had lengthy and luminous careers in the struggle, and could count on substantial grassroots constituencies.[17] Mbeki's ascension

---

[16] African National Congress, Department of Information and Publicity, "The Rise and Fall of Bantu Holomisa." First printed in the *New Nation*, May 30, 1997, accessed online September 11, 2007 at http://www.anc.org.za/ancdocs/misc/holomisa.html.

[17] Ramaphosa once headed the National Union of Mineworkers (NUM) (a precursor to COSATU), served as secretary general of the ANC, and led the ANC delegation during the

required the party to manage the ambitions of these competitors in a way that did not damage party unity. The ANC's solution was to release Ramaphosa and Sexwale to lucrative private-sector careers in Black Economic Empowerment (BEE) firms. This "deployment" allowed Mbeki to assume power without close rivals (winning the internal ANC election for president of the party in December 1997 at the ANC National Conference in Mafiking and taking over as President of South Africa after the 1999 election). It also provided golden parachutes to his competitors and ensured that their careers remained tied to the ANC, thereby significantly reducing the chances that they would pursue careers in other parties. In this way, the ANC used the private sector as a pressure valve to release tensions generated by leadership succession without producing an exodus of disgruntled party elites who might then fill the seats of opposition parties (see Butler 2007: 41 for related discussion).

The succession of Mbeki proved much more difficult. At the same 1997 ANC National Conference that saw Mbeki elected president of the party, ANC delegates chose career ANC politician Jacob Zuma (who had served as the national chairperson of the ANC as well as the chairperson for the party in KwaZulu-Natal) as deputy president. In June 1999, following the 1999 national and provincial elections, Zuma was appointed deputy president of South Africa, a post he continued to hold after the 2004 elections. As Mbeki had served as deputy president under Mandela, it was widely believed that Zuma would succeed term-limited Mbeki as president of the ANC (to be anointed at the 2007 ANC National Conference) and then president of South Africa (after the 2009 election returned the ANC to power). Zuma did succeed Mbeki, but the process that put him in power derailed early from established ANC precedent, tore the ruling party in two, and at times seemed to threaten the very survival of South African democracy.

Problems began for then–Deputy President Zuma during Mbeki's first term in office and reflect events that occurred even earlier, beginning with a November 1998 multibillion rand arms deal. In late 1999, opposition parties began raising questions about the procurement process in the arms deal and in September 2000, the auditor general recommended a forensic audit. In November 2001, Schabir Shaik, director of Nkobi Holdings (which had won a R400-million tender in the deal), was arrested and charged with corruption. As Shaik was an advisor to Zuma, his arrest raised questions about Zuma's role in the arms deal. In August 2003, Bulelani Ngcuka, the national director of public prosecutions alluded to "prima facie" evidence of Zuma's corruption but declined to prosecute the case because he believed it was not winnable. Zuma quickly countered that Ngcuka's allegations were a plot by Mbeki to remove him by trying him in the court of public opinion. He accused Ngcuka of being an apartheid spy (a subsequent investigation found

---

negotiations with the NP prior to the first democratic election in 1994. Sexwale spent time on Robben Island alongside Mandela and was highly respected in his role as premier of Gauteng during the first ANC administration.

no evidence of this) and claimed that Ngcuka had abused his office during his investigation. In July 2004, Zuma's effort bore fruit when the public protector charged Ngcuka with improper conduct and he resigned. Zuma's problems were far from over, however. During the Shaik trial (concluded in June 2005), Judge Hilary Squires found evidence of a corrupt relationship (or "mutually beneficial symbiosis") between Zuma and Shaik, who had made payments totaling R1.2 million to Zuma and had solicited a R1-million bribe from a French arms dealer on Zuma's behalf.[18] Mbeki called on his deputy president to resign and when Zuma refused, arguing that he had not yet been tried or convicted of any crime, Mbeki "released" him from his duties and the National Prosecuting Authority (NPA) formally charged him with corruption October 11 2005.[19]

Zuma's dismissal might have signaled the end of the story had deeper dynamics within the ANC not been in play. By the summer of 2005, a year into his second term as president of South Africa, Mbeki had earned the enmity of powerful actors within the ANC. Over the course of his tenure, Mbeki substantially increased the powers of the central government over the provinces (interfering, for example, in the selection process of provincial leadership) and the executive branch over Parliament (in the eyes of many, Parliament had simply become a rubber stamp to the president's highly powerful and influential cabinet) (Southall 2007; Butler 2007). Mbeki's ostensible goal in strengthening the central state, the presidency in particular, was to increase the developmental capabilities of the South African state (Southall 2007). But in the process he stifled debate and competition within the party and ran roughshod over provincial-, parliamentary-, and branch-level actors, creating significant discontent (Butler 2007; Ndletyana 2007). Moreover, Mbeki's fiscal policies – his commitment to keeping deficits and inflation low and his pro-business stance – and the trade-offs they entailed with regard to development goals and labor had alienated those within COSATU and the SACP who had hoped to see more expansionary policies. According to his detractors, Mbeki had come to represent the black elite, the empowered, the business classes.[20] And, at least in some quarters, the growing dominance of Xhosa politicians in Mbeki's cabinet amplified concerns – usually so carefully managed by the party – that non-Xhosa leaders did not get the respect they deserved (Butler 2007: 42).

Growing discontent with Mbeki and his autocratic leadership style crystallized around the person of Jacob Zuma. To those already suspicious of the president, Ngcuka's allegations of corruption but decision not to try Zuma in a court of law (where he could defend himself), Mbeki's dismissal of Zuma,

---

[18] Squires, J. Judgment for "The State versus Schabir Shaik and 11 others," Case Number CC27/04, 31 May 2005, The High Court of South Africa, Durban and Coast Local Division Durban.
[19] See Southall (2007) for a general review of these events.
[20] For a fascinating account of voter anger at ANC politicians see Atkinson (2007).

and the new decision by the NPA to charge him smacked of a purge. Zuma thus became a focal point for anti-Mbeki sentiment, drawing in support from provincial and branch leaders (especially in KwaZulu-Natal, Zuma's home), COSATU, the SACP, and the ANC Youth League, who saw him as the champion of the poor and dispossessed.[21] For his supporters, the issue was less Zuma's guilt or innocence of the corruption charges and more Mbeki's purported use of them to eliminate a rival. At the same time, while powerful elements of the party cohered around Zuma, other important players (namely, the Cabinet, other supporters of Mbeki's fiscal policies) remained loyal to Mbeki. And thus sprouted the seeds of a major battle.

With these strong currents mixing the waters around Mbeki and Zuma, Mbeki's June 2005 dismissal of Zuma assumed epic proportions. In a stinging defeat to Mbeki that signaled the extent of Zuma's support, 3000 delegates at the ANC's National General Council meeting ruled that Zuma should be allowed to continue as deputy president of the party (even though he had been forced to relinquish his role as deputy president of the country) and vowed to support him as he faced corruption charges. The General Council ruling was significant because it represented one of the first time rank-and-file ANC members had stood up against the will of top leadership.[22] It also foreshadowed events to come.

Bolstered by the support of the party, Zuma began conducting a shadow campaign for the presidency, using the 2006 local elections as means to rally his supporters and demonstrate his grassroots appeal (Southall 2007). Ironically, even as evidence of his popular support – especially among the young and poor – grew, the legal net around Zuma tightened. In February 2006 he was charged with the rape of the daughter of a family friend. Although he was eventually acquitted, Zuma's "sexually irresponsible behavior" alienated liberal and business elites as well as the socially conservative members of the ANC (Southall 2007: 17)[23] but did not deter huge rallies of his supporters outside the courtroom where he was being tried. Meanwhile, the corruption case plodded along. The case was struck from the roll in September 2006 after the prosecution's application for a postponement was dismissed, but the NPA continued to gather evidence against Zuma. In a temporary setback

---

[21] The support of COSATU and the SACP is interesting because Zuma was not an insider to either of these organizations. Instead his roots were in KZN provincial government. Butler (2007: 48) explains that COSATU viewed Zuma as one of the few members of the Mbeki Cabinet not "tarnished" by association with Mbeki's neoliberal policies.

[22] Blade Nzimande. 2006. "Red Alert: ANC National General Council: An Important Turning Point." *Umsebenzi Online*, South African Communist Party website. Accessed July 31, 2009. http://www.sacp.org.za/main.php?include=pubs/umsebenzi/2005/no38.html

[23] Among other salacious details (the age of the woman, her apparent mental instability, the fact that she was the daughter of a friend), many South Africans were appalled that Zuma had knowingly had unprotected sex with an HIV-positive woman and were unimpressed with his explanation that he had reduced his risk of contracting the disease by taking a shower afterwards. See Jenni Evans and Riaan Wolmarans, "Timeline of the Jacob Zuma rape trial." *Mail & Guardian*, March 21, 2006.

for the government, the Durban High Court ruled that raids by the NPA on Zuma's properties and those of his attorney were unlawful and that materials obtained in the raids (some 93,000 documents) could not be used in a trial. The NPA appealed the Durban court's ruling to the Supreme Court of Appeal (SCA) in August 2007, and in November of that year the SCA overturned the Durban court, ruling that the searches had been lawful, and dismissed Zuma's legal team's efforts to block the NPA from gaining access to documents held in Mauritius. Finally, it seemed, the government was ready to take Zuma to court – even as spokesmen for the ANC Youth League, the SACP, and COSATU continued to voice strong support for Zuma and accuse Mbeki of a witch hunt, and even as evidence of his popular support at the grassroots level grew.

Meanwhile, Mbeki struggled to find a new "heir" – a candidate for the ANC presidency he could endorse (who would continue his policies) that the rest of the party would also support. Mbeki had replaced Zuma with Phumzile Mlambo-Ngcuka (previously the Minister of Minerals and Energy) as deputy president. Media reports painted Mlambo-Ngcuka as a competent, even skilled, technocrat.[24] But she was not particularly well known at the grassroots level, lacking the visibility of many other top ANC leaders. Moreover, her husband – former Director of Public Prosecution Bulelani Ngcuka – soured her to Zuma supporters, who could not help but see a conspiracy behind Ngcuka's prosecution of Zuma and his wife's subsequent rise to power. Not helping matters, Mlambo-Ngcuka was linked to a series of high-visibility corruption scandals. Altogether, she had too many strikes against her to make for a viable presidential candidacy. Other Mbeki favorites – the controversial Nkosazana Dlamini-Zuma (Zuma's former wife, no less!), for example – also lacked widespread support. Mbeki thus had a problem. Unfortunately, his solution to the problem – to stand for a third term as president of the party – did little to assuage the situation. It raised serious questions about his intent – did he plan to step down as president of the party when a new president took control of South Africa? Or would he stay on, "ruling from the grave" and making the new president his "puppet?" Was this a bid to gain time to groom a successor or was it a power grab?[25] Predictably, views on this subject fell sharply along the existing Mbeki/Zuma divide.

This was the backdrop to the December 2007 National Conference of the ANC. The conference, held in the Limpopo town of Polokwane (formerly Pietersburg), began badly for Mbeki. One newspaper article described it as "open rebellion."[26] The crowd heckled Mbeki and the conference chairman Mosiuoa "Terror" Lekota, booed pictures of Mbeki's cabinet, and periodically broke into raucous renditions of Zuma's signature song *Umshini Wami*

---

[24] See "Report card: Cabinet ministers from A to G." *Mail & Guardian*, 21 December 2007.
[25] See Vicki Robinson, "ANC chiefs meet on Mbeki third term." *Mail & Guardian*, May 4, 2007.
[26] "Rebellion at Polokwane." *Mail & Guardian*, 17 December 2007.

(translated from the Zulu: "bring me my machine gun"). As the ANC has traditionally valued discipline and respect for party leadership, the behavior of party delegates spoke to a significant breakdown of norms within the party as well as the depth of conflict between camps. In the run-up to the conference, Mbeki gained the endorsement of four provinces (Eastern Cape, North West, Limpopo, and Gauteng) while Zuma took the other five plus the Youth League and the Women's League (both of which have the voting weight of a province). COSATU and the SACP also backed Zuma. The results of voting therefore surprised few: Zuma resoundingly defeated Mbeki for the presidency, taking 2,329 votes to Mbeki's 1,505, and Zuma-associated candidates also took all six top cabinet positions. Several Mbeki cabinet members failed even to get spots in the eighty-six–person NEC. By late January 2008, Zuma had appointed two of his supporters to chief whip and caucus chairperson in Parliament, tightening the link between party leadership and parliamentary leadership and weakening Mbeki's ability to push through legislation in his remaining year and a half in office. A changing of the guards had occurred.

Perspectives on the events of Polokwane vary. On the upside, Mbeki' fall signaled the defeat of party leadership by back-benchers, branch leaders, and others in the party who had felt side-lined and marginalized by the Mbeki administration. As the new Deputy President Kgalema Motlanthe explained in an interview: "Polokwane would not have happened if a monopoly of ideas by a few was not evident."[27] In this sense, it signified the revitalization of the party, the triumph of internal democracy, the ability of the party to prevent ossification from within. Had Mbeki prevailed in spite of the popular discontent and anger leveled at him within the party, how long could it have deterred the exit of disgruntled leaders? Polokwane may have also allowed the party to defuse some of the mounting anger of the masses against a party elite that was often seen as more interested in its own self-enrichment than the well-being of the common people.[28] This was certainly what Motlanthe hoped for when he said: "The ANC must go back to the masses and restore its credibility among them and their faith in it."[29]

On the other hand, the beneficiary of the ANC's internal revolution – Jacob Zuma – represented a somewhat ironic choice to lead the party. Southall (2007) and Butler (2007) note that the surge of support for Zuma represented less an endorsement of his specific leadership qualities, experiences, and plans than a rejection of Mbeki. Although Zuma had not been convicted of a crime at the time of Polokwane, the allegations of corruption and rape at the very least suggested a history of poor choices and unsavory associates. And although party elites might have sold Polokwane as a triumph of the masses, Zuma is a consummate ANC insider. Once in office, he moved quickly to assuage fears

---

[27] "ANC must go back to the masses." *Mail & Guardian*, 12 February 2008.
[28] Atkinson (2007).
[29] "ANC must go back to the masses.'" Of course, it is also worth noting that Polokwane represented shifting power relations between members of the elite, not the arrival of a new set of leaders drawn from the masses.

amongst business leaders that he would not pursue a radicalization of policies and indicated that he would keep Trevor Manual, Mbeki's minister of finance and widely credited for the fiscally conservative policies that have stabilized South Africa's economy.[30] Indeed, Zuma and his associates repeatedly emphasized that the Zuma/Mbeki conflict was one of personalities, not policies.[31] While this might have reassured some (namely big business), it is unlikely to present a long-term solution to mass discontent over the slowness of economic change in South Africa and the rise of a new African elite that seems disconnected from the "the people."

Moreover, although Zuma resoundingly defeated Mbeki at Polokwane, the leadership question was far from settled. Zuma was president of the party, his rival, Mbeki, president of the country – an arrangement bound to create tension.[32] And not two weeks after the close of Polokwane, the NPA indicted Zuma on sixteen charges of racketeering, money laundering, corruption, and fraud, with a court date of August 14, 2008. This raised a whole new round of questions: Would the court case conclude before the 2009 elections? If not, could the court try an acting president? If convicted, would Zuma step down? Zuma's supporters responded to the news of the charges against Zuma with bellicose promises of blood in the courtroom.[33] They also questioned whether South Africa's courts could deliver a fair judgment. A spokesperson for COSATU explained: "[I]t does not matter who the judge is, we do not believe the judiciary will be able to be objective."[34] Once again, they saw the charges as fabricated by Mbeki as part of a last-ditch effort to stay in power. The NPA's timing – so soon after Mbeki's defeat – did little to dispel this impression. COSATU claimed that the timing of indictment had the "hallmarks of vengeance, deep-seated anger and frustration by the NPA and whoever else is behind this."[35] Somewhat threateningly, the organization also suggested that

---

[30] Michael Hamlyn. "Manuel not concerned over future fiscal policy." *Mail & Guardian*, January 10, 2008. Dan Perry. "Zuma's charm offensive in Davos." *Mail & Guardian*, January 27, 2008. Michael Hamlyn. "Zuma Takes Charm Offensive to the JSE." *Mail & Guardian*, January 31, 2008.

[31] Michael Hamlyn. "The ANC Is Not Divided." *Mail & Guardian*, January 11, 2008. "ANC Must Go Back to the Masses'" *Mail & Guardian*, 12 February 2008

[32] "Zuma vs Mbeki: Battle lines drawn." *Mail & Guardian*, 23 December 2007.

[33] COSATU's KwaZulu-Natal provincial secretary Zet Luzipho warned: "[P]eople are now angry. ... This time there will be blood spilt in the courtroom." Mariette le Roux. "Zuma Backers Put SA Judges on Trial." *Mail & Guardian*, January 12, 2008.

[34] "COSATU condemns Zuma indictment." *Mail & Guardian*, 29 December 2007. Two of South Africa's top legal scholars, retired Chief Justice Arthur Chaskalson and prominent attorney George Bizos, were so concerned about these comments by COSATU that they issued a statement defending the South African judiciary and demanded that the involved parties allow the system to do its job. They wrote: "[P]utting pressure on the courts by making serious allegations of partiality, uttering threats of massive demonstrations, and expressing opinions in intemperate language are harmful to the judicial process, to our constitutional democracy and to our country's reputation." "Let the courts decide on Zuma, say top legal minds." *Mail & Guardian*, January 5, 2008.

[35] "COSATU condemns Zuma indictment."

"workers will not allow the NPA and whoever is handling them to abuse its power in this matter."[36] ANC Youth League President Fikile Mbalula accused Mbeki of orchestrating the indictment from "behind the scenes," allegations both the NPA and Mbeki firmly denied.[37] The NEC also weighed in, questioning the NPA's handling of the case.[38]

Months of legal wrangling over the case against Zuma and increasingly aggressive rhetoric from the ANC and affiliated organizations followed Polokwane. Zuma's lawyers launched an appeal of the SCA's decision regarding the September 2005 NPA raids to the Constitutional Court. In late July 2008, just before the trial was scheduled to begin, the Constitutional Court upheld the legality of the warrants, dealing a serious blow to Zuma's defense.[39] Meanwhile, Zuma's lawyers had also filed an application with the Pietermaritzburg High Court asking the Court to set aside the National Director of Public Prosecution's (NDPP) decision to prosecute him, arguing that the decision was unconstitutional because the NDPP had failed to seek representations from him before reversing the earlier decision not to prosecute. Judge Chris Nicholson was assigned to the case, promising a judgment on September 12.[40] As the attorneys battled out technicalities in the courts, Zuma supporters in the ANC launched repeated verbal attacks on the court system and judges, arguing that they were biased, even "counter-revolutionary," and that Zuma could not get a fair trial.[41] Julius Malema, ANC Youth League (ANCYL) leader, along with the MK Military Veterans' Association (MKMVA), pledged mass action on behalf of Zuma, promising he would be president "whatever the judgment."[42] Throughout August and early September, thousands gathered around the Pietermartizburg High Court in a show of support.[43] In the face of increasing tensions, the ANC began discussing a

---

[36] "Let the courts decide on Zuma."
[37] Giordano Stolley. "Zuma charges: NPA denies political interference." *Mail & Guardian*, January 2, 2008.
[38] "ANC stands by Zuma despite cCharges."
[39] See Nic Dawes. "Court's giant blow to Zuma." *Mail & Guardian*, August 1 2008. As a side drama, in May 2008 the Constitutional Court lodged a complaint with the Judicial Services Commission (JSC) accusing Cape Judge President John Hlope of trying to influence the Constitutional Court's decision over the raids. In September, the Johannesburg High Court found that the Constitutional Court judges had violated Hlope's rights when they made public statements about the alleged interference. Zuma supporters used these events as pretext for questioning the impartiality of the court system. As of July 2009, the JSC had yet to rule on the case. See Giordano Stolley. "Hlophe accused of Zuma interference." *Mail & Guardian*, May 30, 2008. See also "Court decides in Hlophe's favour." *Mail & Guardian*, September 26, 2008.
[40] See Sam Sole and Adriaan Basson. "Zuma's lawyers open new front." *Mail & Guardian*, June 27, 2008.
[41] Matuma Letsoalo, Mandy Rossouw, and Sello S Alcock. "ANC boss accuses judges of conspiracy against Zuma." *Mail & Guardian*, July 4, 2008.
[42] Mandy Rossouw. "Rolling action for Zuma." *Mail & Guardian*, July 28, 2008.
[43] Niren Tols, "JZ's backers are like bad songs ..." *Mail & Guardian*, August 10, 2008. Giles Smith. "Sit-ins and picketing in KZN." *Mail & Guardian*, September 2, 2008. "Cops to beef up security for Zuma's court appearance." *Mail & Guardian*, September 10, 2008.

potential "political" solution to Zuma's problems; business leaders, reportedly fearful of further destabilization, also began expressing support for such a plan. Potential "political" solutions included a plea bargain by Zuma, amnesty in exchange for information on the arms deal, or possibly a change to the Constitution prohibiting a criminal trial against an acting president.[44]

Surprising many, and momentarily ending calls for a political solution, Judge Chris Nicholson ruled that the NDPP's decision to prosecute Zuma had been unlawful because it should have allowed Zuma to make representations before it decided to recharge him. Nicholson set aside the charges but stressed that the finding was a procedural point and did not relate to Zuma's guilt or innocence. More explosively, Nicholson also argued that he found evidence of political interference on the part of Mbeki's government, that Mbeki had encouraged the heads of the NPA to pursue prosecution of Zuma for political reasons. Almost immediately, Zuma supporters in the ANC began calling for Mbeki to resign.[45] On September 21, 2008, after the ANC NEC indicated that it would no longer support him in Parliament, Mbeki resigned (followed by several members of his cabinet). Shortly thereafter, the ANC appointed Kgalema Motlanthe as interim president.[46]

Undeterred by intense pressure to drop the case, the NPA appealed Nicholson's ruling. In January 2009, the Supreme Court of Appeal, led by Judge Louis Harms, found in favor of the NPA, arguing that Nicholson's interpretation of the Constitution was mistaken and the NDPP had had no obligation to hear Zuma's representations before charging him. The SCA further argued that Nicholson had overstepped his bounds when he had implied a political conspiracy against Zuma orchestrated by Mbeki. The charges against Zuma were therefore once more reinstated.[47] A court date was set for August 2009, raising again the specter of Zuma returning to court as president. Zuma's lawyers pledged to pursue all legal options, including an appeal to the Constitutional Court and a bid for a permanent stay of proceedings. Once again the NPA faced pressure to drop the case,[48] and in mid-March rumors began to surface that the NPA intended to do just this. Finally, on

---

[44] Mandy Rossouw and Rapule Tabane. "Business wants a political solution." *Mail & Guardian*, August 22, 2008. "Deal? No Deal!" *Mail & Guardian*, August 22, 2008. Richard Calland. "Creating a case to bend the law." *Mail & Guardian*, September 12, 2008. Sipho M. Pityana. "A 'political deal': Let's consider the options." *Mail & Guardian*, September 12, 2008.

[45] "Round one to Zuma." *Mail & Guardian*, September 12, 2008. Chris McGreal. "Mbeki fights for survival after Zuma's showdown." *Mail & Guardian*, September 15, 2008.

[46] Mandy Rossouw. "ANC dumps Mbeki, moves to heal 'rift.' *Mail & Guardian*, September 20, 2008.

[47] "NPA confirms correspondence from Zuma's lawyers." *Mail & Guardian*, January 13, 2009.

[48] Thus ANC Youth League President Julius Malema called on the NPA to "save the country" by dropping the charges and also warned that there were "dark forces" at work against Zuma, implying that the judges on the SCA had been influenced in their finding in favor of the NPA. See "Malema: NPA must drop Zuma charges." *Mail & Guardian*, January 15, 2009. ANC Secretary General Gwede Mantashe echoed Malema's comments to a crowd of Zuma supporters, saying that dark powers were using the Zuma case to destroy the ANC. Tolsi, Niren. "Mantashe: Zuma's prosecution is an attack on ANC." *Mail & Guardian*, February 4, 2009.

April 6, 2009 (just a few weeks prior to the election), Mokothedi Mpshe, acting head of the NPA, announced that all charges against Zuma were being dropped in light of evidence that the legal process had been tainted. Mpshe cited taped telephone conversations between the former head of the Scorpions, Leonard McCarthy, and former head of the NPA, Bulelani Ngcuka, in which the two purportedly conspired to manipulate the timing of the Zuma charges in December 2007 (presumably to strengthen Mbeki's position). Mpshe emphasized that dropping the charges did not amount to an acquittal but that the legal process had been too compromised to continue the case.[49] Opposition leaders, journalists, and other political observers raised important questions about the NPA's decision, but by then the die was cast.[50] Zuma supporters proclaimed the innocence of their leader and the ANC entered into the final weeks of the 2009 electoral campaign with the leadership question finally settled.

### The Formation of Cope and the 2009 Election

The ANC did not survive the Zuma-Mbeki leadership crisis unscathed. One important consequence of the battle between the two leaders was the formation of a new political party, the Congress of the People (Cope). In what follows, I will discuss the formation of Cope, its campaign, the outcome, and the causes for its limited success, paying particular attention to how "image" issues prevented Cope from having a wider appeal.

Shortly after Mbeki resigned from the ANC, former ANC defense minister Mosiuoa "Terror" Lekota issued an open letter to the ANC, arguing that the party was moving away from its founding principles like the rule of law, internal democracy, and respect for political institutions. In early October, Lekota made the divorce formal, leaving the party and alluding to the formation of a new movement.[51] Joining him were his former defense deputy Mluleki George and several other middle-level ANC cadres; shortly thereafter, former Gauteng premier Mbhazima Shilowa also threw in his hat.[52] Lekota and Shilowa had big ambitions for the party, claiming "we are not going to build a small party – we

---

[49] "Mpshe: Zuma decision not an acquittal." *Mail & Guardian*, April 6, 2009. "NPA drops corruption charges against Zuma." *Mail & Guardian*, April 6, 2009.

[50] Some suggested the allegations of interference were weak; others questioned how Zuma's legal team, which had given the NPA the recorded conversations, had come to possess them in the first place, noting that possession of the tapes (whose origins were never explained) might have been a criminal offence; finally, many argued that the proper response for Mpshe would have been to continue the case against Zuma but also to seek to prosecute McCarthy and Ngueka. Richard Calland. "The high price of political solutions." *Mail & Guardian*, April 27, 2009. "Trengove: Zuma decision 'tipping point.'" *Mail & Guardian*, April 16, 2009.

[51] Mandy Rossouw, "Lekota serves 'divorce papers' on ANC." *Mail & Guardian*, October 8, 2008.

[52] Both Lekota and Shilowa had impressive "struggle" credentials. Lekota joined the ANC in 1990 after being a prominent leader in the UDF. He was elected to the party's executive in the 1990s. Shilowa helped form COSATU and became its general secretary in 1993.

are building a giant party."⁵³ In early November, they announced the name of the new movement – the Congress of the People (Cope) – and registered it as a political party with the IEC. In mid-December, Cope held its first party congress in Bloemfontein (some 4,000 delegates attended), announcing Lekota as party chairperson and Shilowa as his deputy. Also in December, Cope won ten out of twenty-seven seats in by-elections in the Western Cape.⁵⁴ In late January, it launched its election manifesto to some 300,000 people in Port Elizabeth.

Cope did not significantly distinguish itself from the ANC on the basis of macroeconomic policy.⁵⁵ Indeed, it explicitly supported Mbeki-era policies like GEAR and the use of state spending to create a security net for the poor (not surprising as the founders of Cope left the party in protest over tactics, not policy). Instead Cope promised to improve the implementation of policy, specifically to increase accountability and reduce corruption and cronyism, which it claimed were preventing the government from achieving its goals.⁵⁶ The party also raised questions about the ANC's affirmative action and Black Economic Empowerment policies, suggesting that both programs had admirable goals but, as currently implemented, unintended consequences like "nepotism and cronyism in the public service, exclusion of minorities from the public service and using race as a sole criterion of employment."⁵⁷ BEE, according to Lekota, shifted wealth to a small number of well-connected blacks while leaving the vast majority of South African citizens impoverished. Cope sought to preserve the goals of these programs – to rectify the ills of apartheid – while improving their implementation.⁵⁸ Cope endorsed reinstating the Scorpions (the National Prosecuting Authority's elite crime-fighting unit tasked with investigating corruption and organized crime). The centerpiece of Cope's policy proposals, however, concerned electoral reform. The party endorsed the adoption of a mixed-electoral system that would combine elements of proportional representation with the direct election of some candidates (presidents, mayors, and provincial premiers), arguing that the selection of top leaders, as well as their removal, should be left to the voters rather than party bosses.⁵⁹

---

[53] Quote from Shilowa from "Meet the COP: Dissidents finally settle on party name." *Mail & Guardian*, November 7, 2008.
[54] The ANC had missed a filing deadline and did not contest several of these seats, which almost certainly helped COPE.
[55] Susan Booysen. "The ANC and COPE: Fleeting phenomenon or substantive opposition?" EISA South Africa Election Update #2, March 2009.
[56] Paul Simao. "Cope unlikely to alter economic agenda." *Mail & Guardian*, December 7, 2008.
[57] COPE publicity statement from mid December 2008, quoted in "Cope clarifies position on affirmative action." *Mail & Guardian*, December 18, 2008.
[58] "Cope clarifies position on affirmative action." *Mail & Guardian*, December 18, 2008. Georgy, Michael. "Cope: Affirmative action misdirected." *Mail & Guardian*, March 13, 2009.
[59] Dawes, Nic. "Reform the X." *Mail & Guardian*, January 18, 2009. "Cope: South Africans must elect their president." *Mail & Guardian*, January 30, 2009.

Beyond specific proposals, Cope pledged to defend the court system, the Constitution, and the rule of law (which it argued were under attack by the Zuma contingent in the ANC) and to de-politicize the public service by ending the practice of deploying comrades to high-ranking government positions.[60] It invoked the nonracialism of the ANC's charterist tradition, stating it would be a party for all South Africans, regardless of race, religion, or language.[61] The general image the party sought to portray was summed up by a Cope supporter at the January manifesto launch: "Cope is more like the ANC that my father joined."[62] It was the disciplined party of Mandela, Tambo, and Luthuli, not the corrupt and disrespectful party of Zuma and Malema.

Cope thus sought to portray itself as the more moral, moderate choice to an ANC that had departed from its original path. Underlining this contrast, in late February Cope selected the relatively unknown Dr. Mvume Dandala to be its presidential candidate. Dr. Dandala was the general secretary of the All Africa Conference of Churches (AACC); he had also been the presiding bishop of the Methodist Church in Southern Africa and the president of the South African Council of Churches. While not a complete newcomer to politics (he had been involved in the anti-apartheid struggle and had used his church positions to advocate for social and religious change), he was known more as a church man than a politician. As a press was quick to point out, he stood in "stark contrast" to Zuma: "Where Jacob Zuma is essentially an autodidact, Dr. Dandala has degrees from Cambridge University, as well as honorary degrees from The University of Transkei and from the Cameroons. Whereas Zuma has several wives, Dandala has but one. Dandala publicly took an HIV/AIDS test. Zuma famously took a shower."[63] And of course, "squeaky-clean" Dandala did not have corruption charges hanging over his head.[64] Dandala thus personified the message Cope was selling to the electorate.

However, the selection of Dandala reportedly induced (or reflected) tensions within Cope. Many had assumed that Lekota would be Cope's presidential candidate: He had moved first to break from the ANC, he was the party's leader, and he had stature in the electorate. The party claimed that it had chosen Dandala because he was not tainted with a past in the ANC, whereas Lekota was a party insider and loyal Mbeki man. But newspaper reports saw Dandala's selection as evidence of a power struggle between Lekota and Shilowa, speculating that Dandala's selection was driven by Shilowa and his supporters in a move against Lekota.[65] After an initial period of silence,

---

[60] "Cope: Public service should be depoliticized." *Mail & Guardian*, December 11, 2008. "Lekota says Cope won't tolerate cronyism." *Mail & Guardian*, February 24, 2009.

[61] "Battle lines drawn for 2009 poll. *Mail & Guardian*, December 16, 2008.

[62] Anonymous Cope supporter quoted in "'Cope is like the ANC by father joined." *Mail & Guardian*, January 24, 2009.

[63] For the shower reference, see footnote 4. "Cope's new leader in stark contrast to Zuma." *Mail & Guardian*, February 24, 2009.

[64] Mandy Rossouw, and Mmanaldi Mataboge. "How terror lost Cope." *Mail & Guardian*, February 27, 2009.

[65] Rossouw and Mataboge. "How terror lost Cope."

Lekota endorsed Dandala and attempted to dispel rumors of conflict within the party, but the shadow of "leadership divisions" dogged the party throughout the entire campaign period.

In spite of an enthusiastic beginning, a lot of hype and coverage in the media, optimistic predictions that Cope could capture as much as 40 percent of the ANC vote, and a ruling party facing an unsatisfied electorate with a risky candidate, by March Cope's campaign appeared to be flagging. Media reports following Dandala on the campaign trail suggested a luke-warm reception in many communities – voters either did not know him or were not impressed with him or his party – and surveys showed Cope's support hovering in the single digits.[66] In contrast, the ANC's campaign gained momentum as the election approached and polls showed it close to a two-thirds majority. Results for the April 22 election therefore surprised few: The ANC took almost 66 percent of the vote (down from close to 70 percent in 2004) and won outright majorities in eight out of nine provinces.[67] Cope captured a modest 7.4 percent, better than any other new opposition party in post-apartheid South Africa (the Independent Democrats failed to get 2 percent of the vote in its maiden election in 2004; the United Democratic Movement topped out at 3.4 percent in 1999), but well below the aspirations of its leaders and supporters. It did best in the Northern Cape, the Eastern Cape, and the Free State, where it replaced the DA as the official opposition. The DA, in its best showing ever, won almost 17 percent of the vote and a majority in the Western Cape. The IFP saw its support collapse almost completely (down to just 4.5 percent of the national vote and 22 percent of the KwaZulu-Natal vote), and the ID and UDM also suffered losses, both falling below 1 percent of the overall vote.

Why was Cope not able to capitalize more on the excitement greeting its founding days and the general difficulties faced by the ANC and its leader, Jacob Zuma? Cope's performance reflected its own unique challenges as a new party and the decisions it made in dealing with them, as well as smart strategic moves on the part of the ANC. In the end, the party had difficulty convincing the electorate that it represented more than simply "Polokwane losers." Moreover, Zuma's ANC successfully portrayed itself as the champion of the poor and dispossessed and its rival as the "black DA" – the elitist Mbeki rump of the ANC that had ignored the common voter in its quest for self-enrichment.

As a new party, Cope faced formidable structural challenges. It had a mere six months in which to constitute itself, select a leadership team and presidential candidate, organize its membership and branch structures,

---

[66] Mmanaledi Mataboge. "On the train with Mvume Dandala." *Mail & Guardian*, April 1, 2009. "Dandala tours Soweto." *Mail & Guardian*, April 9, 2009. Ed Cropley. "Cope struggles to win support." *Mail & Guardian*, April 16, 2009.
[67] Although the ANC won just about the same percentage of votes in 2009 as it did in 1999, there was nonetheless an important shift in its support base. In 1999, the IFP took 8.6% of the vote. In 2009, it took 4.5%. Assuming most of those IFP votes went to the ANC (almost all of them in KwaZulu-Natal), then the ANC lost votes elsewhere in the country.

craft a message, raise money, and sell itself to the electorate. Raising money proved especially difficult. As with all new parties in South Africa (or parties without representation in the legislature), Cope received no state-funded campaign money. Moreover, given its formation in late 2008, it had little time to cultivate private donations. Hence, its leaders were quite frank about their resource constraints and how they hampered the party's ability to run a campaign.[68] Cope also faced challenges related to leadership. As already noted, reports of leadership squabbles surrounded the party almost from its inception. Cope leaders repeatedly claimed that these were inventions of the press and ruling party but could not dispel the image of a party divided from within. Moreover, Cope leaders seemed to expect an exodus of cadres from the ANC to swell its ranks – after all, roughly 40 percent of ANC delegates had voted for Mbeki at Polokwane. Yet many defections never materialized. Several times Cope leaders would announce that a certain comrade had defected to Cope, only to have that comrade deny the rumor and stay in the ANC.[69] The ANC delayed releasing its lists until late in the campaign period, perhaps as part of an effort to avoid Cope defections.[70] It also sought to keep Mbeki supporters loyal by placing them well on the lists.[71] In the end, the ANC probably suffered far fewer high-level defections than Cope originally hoped (and planned) for.

As a result of resource constraints and leadership distractions, Cope was slow to set up branch structures and launch a formal campaign. In early March, analysts noted that "they [Cope] aren't in the public eye. They aren't on radio, lampposts or television nearly enough."[72] Indeed, the party only unveiled its election posters in mid-March, a mere five weeks before the election.[73] Cope was especially invisible in the townships and villages. It failed to hold the big rallies and run the door-to-door campaigns that are especially effective in reaching African voters, focusing instead on "the rich, educated, and opinionated."[74] Given its late start and its inability to pull away a large

---

[68] Mandy Rossouw and Mmanaledi Mataboge. "No campaign, no votes." *Mail & Guardian*, March 2009.

[69] For example, in February Cope announced that Frank Chikane, top Mbeki aide, was the top contender to be Cope's Gauteng premier. Chikane denied he was a Cope member and declined nomination. Similar confusion surrounded Sello Moloto (Limpopo premier) and Fish Mahlalela (Mpumalanga health minister). (Moloto did eventually defect). See Mmanaledi Mataboge. "Who's hot, who's not." *Mail & Guardian*, February 22, 2009. See also Thebe Mabanga. "Party poopers." *Financial Mail*, February 20, 2009. And Phumzile Mlambo-Ngcuka (Mbeki's deputy president) was rumoured for months to be "about" to take a prominent position in the party, but she never did.

[70] Mandy Rossouw. "MPs sweat over jobs." *Mail & Guardian*, February 22, 2009.

[71] Thebe Mabanga. "Party poopers." *Financial Mail*, February 20, 2009. Matuma Letsoalo. "Last chance saloon for Mbeki-ites." *Mail & Guardian*, January 30, 2009.

[72] Quote from Markinor executive director Mari Harris. In Mandy Rossouw and Mmanaledi Matoboge. "No campaign, no votes." *Mail & Guardian*, March 6, 2009.

[73] "Cope unveils election posters." *Mail & Guardian*, March 13, 2009.

[74] Rapule Tabane. "How Cope lost it." *Mail & Guardian*, April 24, 2009.

contingent of ANC leaders, it is hardly surprising that the party had difficulty hosting massive rallies and plastering townships with posters.

Cope also made strategic blunders. South African political analysts have suggested that the morality message did not play well to a South African electorate mostly concerned with bread and butter issues.[75] Moreover, given the confusion surrounding Zuma's trial and Zuma's argument that he was the victim, not the criminal, issues of who was right and who was wrong may have been difficult for voters to adjudicate. If the morality message did not play well, then the choice of the clean but little-known Dandala probably also hurt the party.[76] In the realm of policy, Cope's decision not to differentiate itself from Mbeki's ANC may also have been a strategic error. Its argument that it would pursue the same policies as the ANC but implement them better was too abstract a point, as was its promise to reform the electoral system. Finally, Cope's early comments about Black Economic Empowerment may have alienated the middle-class African voters it was reaching out to with its campaign tactics and moderate policies.[77] Altogether, Cope's message seemed limp.[78]

Finally, Cope suffered from an almost structural image problem: As a splinter party formed by individuals who had been prominent leaders of the ANC, Cope had difficulty offering too much criticism of the ruling party's past. In essence, in criticizing the ANC, Cope leaders were criticizing themselves – a challenging conundrum they never quite resolved.[79] Moreover, Cope was "top heavy with leaders too easily dismissed by their association with Mbeki, and the worst failings of his leadership."[80] And, as Cope was formed after Mbeki was forced out of the ANC, it could be dismissed as the final fallout of Polokwane: It was formed from the "Polokwane losers," the people who had aligned themselves with the wrong (Mbeki) side of a leadership battle.[81]

---

[75] "Cope faltering, ANC going strong." *Mail & Guardian*, March 14, 2009. "'Parties failed to push the Zuma factor.'" *Mail & Guardian*, April 21, 2009

[76] Rapule Tabane. "How Cope lost it." *Mail & Guardian*, April 24, 2009. "'Parties failed to push the Zuma factor.'" *Mail &Guardian*, April 21, 2009

[77] Hence, in December, the Black Lawyers Association (BLA) announced that Lekota's views on affirmative action represented a threat. BLA president Andiswa Ndoni said: "Cope seems determined to reverse the few gains made by black people on account of these policies in order to attract white votes. This is short-sighted and out of step with the aspirations of black people and the equality provisions in the Constitution." See "Black lawyers say Lekota a 'threat' to empowerment." *Mail & Guardian*, December 17, 2008.

[78] Of course, hind-sight is twenty twenty. It is possible that the same message might have been attractive to voters had other factors (resources, ANC strategy) not intervened.

[79] Susan Booysen. "The ANC and COPE: Fleeting phenomenon or substantive opposition?" EISA South Africa Election Update #2, March 2009. Booysen suggests Cope attempted to deal with this by focusing its criticisms on the short term: "[W]hat had gone wrong in the period since the ANC had started deviating from the ideals of the liberation movement, roughly equated with the run-up to December 2007" (p. 3). This was a difficult distinction to make.

[80] Nic Dawes. "Saving Cope – the breech baby." *Mail & Guardian*, March 7, 2009.

[81] Susan Booysen. "The ANC and COPE: Fleeting phenomenon or substantive opposition?" EISA South Africa Election Update #2, March 2009. Emsie Ferreira. "Cope launches battle to gain votes." *Mail & Guardian*, December 11, 2008.

In this sense, Cope could be branded as a party of discontents and sore losers, Mbeki-ites left out in the cold.[82]

Added to these difficulties, the ANC ran an intelligent campaign. As in the past, the emergence of a clear challenger motivated the ruling party and concentrated its energies. With a reported campaign war chest of R200 million, it moved early and extensively.[83] In November, it had posters up and was sending out the troops to go door-to-door, a four-month head start on Cope.[84] Zuma addressed massive crowds in rallies throughout the campaign season, at times bringing on stage a frail Nelson Mandela. The final election rally, held in Johannesburg, anticipated a crowd of 400,000 people and filled two stadiums. Stadiums in the eight other provinces were connected via live satellite link.[85] In smaller events, the ANC used celebrities to portray itself as hip to the urban youth and professional and business organizations to reassure the middle class. In the poorest neighborhoods, it reportedly distributed bags of food.[86] The party also increased the deficit to fund social spending, raising old age pensions by R50 a month and extending the child support grant to fifteen-year-olds (funding an additional 600,000 children). By the end of 2009, more than 13 million South Africans were expected to receive a grant of some sort. In short, the party pulled out all the stops.[87]

Moreover, while the press pondered the unsavory nature of Jacob Zuma and the corruption charges hanging over him, the man had a widespread following amongst ordinary South Africans, especially the young and poor. As one reporter put it: "Unlike the scholarly and aloof Thabo Mbeki, who habitually quoted Shakespeare or phrases in Latin, Zuma can dance. He is charming and charismatic and comfortable in his own skin."[88] Whereas Mbeki had an elite upbringing and education in Britain, Zuma was the son of a domestic worker and policeman in rural KwaZulu-Natal. He frequently danced and sang his trademark song, *Umshini Wami*, at rallies, to the euphoric delight of his fans. Popular songs like *Msholozi* (Zuma's praise name) by Izingane zoMa extolled his praises.[89] He had particular appeal in KwaZulu-Natal, where his traditional face scars and multiple wives marked him as an authentic man of the people.[90]

---

[82] "Polokwane losers" was a term used extensively by the press. For an example, see Nic Dawes. "Saving Cope – the breech baby." *Mail & Guardian*, March 7, 2009. Rapule Tabane. "How Cope lost it." *Mail & Guardian*, April 24, 2009
[83] "ANC spends R200-million on election campaign." *Mail & Guardian*, April 17, 2009.
[84] Mondii Makhanya. "ANC's election campaign a triumph of getting down and funking it up." *The Sunday Times*, April 4, 2009.
[85] "ANC spends R200-million on election campaign." *Mail &Guardian*, April 17, 2009
[86] Makhanya. "ANC's election campaign a triumph."
[87] "An election year budget." *Mail & Guardian*, February 13, 2009.
[88] David Smith. "Jacob Zuma the chameleon brings South Africans joy and fear." *Mail & Guardian*, April 20, 2009.
[89] Niren Tolsi. "The cult of Zuma." *Mail & Guardian*, March 6, 2009.
[90] David Smith. "Jacob Zuma the chameleon brings South Africans joy and fear." *Mail & Guardian*, April 20, 2009.

Finally, as in the past against other opponents, the ANC did a brilliant job of framing the election, casting itself in a positive glow while negatively branding its opponent. William Gumede of the *Mail & Guardian* writes that the ANC:

> [S]uccessfully framed the 2009 election as a face-off between well-off blacks and whites on the one hand and the poor black majority on the other – rather than on an examination of the government's record in power. ... Zuma successfully portrayed himself as "poor," identifying his personal marginalisation by former president Thabo Mbeki with the marginalisation of the poverty-stricken masses. He successfully distanced himself from the failures of the ANC government in the minds of poor voters, blaming them on Mbeki. Throughout the election campaign, his strategists portrayed his camp, which now dominates the ANC, as an almost different party.[91]

Thus, Zuma turned the corruption charges against him from liability to benefit by framing himself as the victim of an elitist and autocratic regime. He also associated the failures of the ANC with Mbeki, such that with Mbeki purged from the party, the ANC could reinvent itself as a new populist party. Moreover, as Cope had clear ties to Mbeki, the ANC could then paint Cope as the repository of the elitist, autocratic bad-old ANC, "a rich black and white cabal which opposes the interests of the poor." Perversely, Cope, the new party, assumed the ruling party's image liabilities. It gave the ANC the ability to claim credit for its prior successes (the expansion of the welfare safety net, the extension of services to many communities throughout the country) while simultaneously distancing itself from its failures. The ANC also drew analogies between Cope and the DA. A Cosatu booklet distributed in January 2009 called Cope the "Black DA"[92] and Zuma told a rally in November that the Cope leaders ("dissidents") who had celebrated their divorce from the ANC were at the same time celebrating a new marriage to the Democratic Alliance.[93] Finally, as noted by Booysen (2009), the ANC made "pervasive" efforts to brand Cope as "illegitimate and virtually treasonous in its dissent and digression," suggesting that it was a party of "opportunism, sore losers, and the dissident's rejection of processes of ANC internal democracy."[94] In these ways, the ANC simultaneously legitimated itself, disassociating from the failures of its past while de-legitimating Cope. Zuma's ANC became the true torch carrier for the party's most venerated traditions (egalitarianism, populism, struggle), while Cope represented the failures of the Mbeki years (elitism, authoritarianism, corruption). Voting for Cope, the ruling party suggested, was analogous to voting for the DA. The ANC thus framed its opponent in

---

[91] William Gumede. "The power of the poor." *Mail & Guardian* April 25, 2009.
[92] Miranda Andrew. "Cosatu vows to spread anti-Cope booklet." *Mail & Guardian* January 28, 2009.
[93] "Ngonyama resigns from the ANC over 'disrespect.'" *Mail & Guardian* November 13, 2008.
[94] Susan Booysen. "The ANC and COPE: Fleeting phenomenon or substantive opposition?" EISA South Africa Election Update #2, March 2009, p. 2.

a way that questioned its legitimacy and credibility, as it had with previous challengers like the IFP, UDM, DA, and NNP.

In sum, Cope's performance in the 2009 elections must be placed in the context of the various forces arrayed against it. It faced all of the standard challenges of a new party, organizational and resource based. It got off to a late start and never achieved much of a presence in the townships and small towns. It ran on a message (morality) that, in retrospect, seems to have had little appeal to voters and chose a candidate that few voters knew. It did not offer much of a policy alternative to the ANC. Cope also faced many of the problems other opposition parties have encountered in the past. Even as an ANC splinter party, with intimate connections to ANC insiders, and even in the context of crisis within the ruling party, it had trouble drawing candidates away from the ANC. Moreover, it had a difficult image problem to overcome: It had to convince voters that it was the "good" part of the ANC – the ANC of Mandela and Tambo – not simply the ANC of Mbeki and those who followed him to their ruin at Polokwane. In trying to make this argument, it faced a ruling party with very deep pockets that began its campaign early and saturated the country with its message; a ruling party with a candidate that appealed to many voters, especially poor voters, who make up the majority of the country; a ruling party that adeptly framed the election in a way that confirmed its own legitimacy while casting doubt on its opponent. In this environment, we should perhaps be impressed that Cope did as well as it did.

## CONCLUSION

The ANC has used negative framing strategies and image control methods not only to discredit the "white" opposition of South Africa but also to neutralize parties with greater claim to African credentials. To be sure, these methods represent only part of the diverse menu of techniques the ANC has at its disposal as a ruling party. Most notably it has also focused on delivery, expanding the social safety net; building houses, schools, and hospitals; extending the power grid and clean water supply; and using its affirmative action policies to open opportunities for the African middle classes. It has also run effective positive campaigns about its own successes, which are many. Moreover, opposition parties have contributed to their own difficulties in South Africa: Few have unblemished pasts that cannot be used against them, many have made missteps in their campaigns, giving fodder to the ANC's efforts, and most face challenges with message control. Every time IFP supporters disrupt ANC meetings or rallies, they contribute to the image problems of their party. However, the ANC has exploited these missteps to the fullest extent possible, using them to disqualify opposition parties as legitimate contenders to power in South Africa, to remove them, as it were, from the choice set of African voters. And with the choice set thus constrained, these voters continue to support the ruling party, even when the safety net does not extend to them, even when they are still waiting for the house that has yet to be built, and even as service provision in their area continues to deteriorate. As such, strategies of image control and negative framing constitute a powerful "soft" technique for holding on to power that complements more resource intensive methods. They shield the ruling party from low levels of voter discontent, which is very useful, because no party can put a chicken in every pot that needs one.

# 9

# Conclusion

*South Africa in Comparative Perspective*

While the beginnings of South Africa's racial census lie in its past, in the effects apartheid had on voters' beliefs about race and destiny and the reputations parties forged during this period, the enduring imprint of race on elections reflects current politics, in particular the ruling party's ability to use the powers and benefits of office to frame elections and prevent opposition parties from transforming the uncompetitive party images they inherited from apartheid into ones that would give them broader appeal in the electorate. By keeping these parties "white," by preventing them from evolving in a more multi-racial direction, the ANC has rendered them toothless.

In this final chapter, I consider two additional cases: El Salvador and Israel. I show that dominant parties in both countries used image control and negative framing strategies to discredit their opponents and fortify their own hold on power. The power of the frame, the ability to shape how the electorate views the opposition, is thus a *general* tool that dominant parties use to continue their rule. While much current research has focused on resource-based strategies for control (especially clientelism), the case material from El Salvador, Israel, and South Africa all point to the importance of broadening our understanding of the repertoires of dominance. Dominant parties most certainly depend on their monopoly over resources to maintain power. At the same time, they cannot buy off all of the voters all of the time. An important additional tool is the ability to frame elections in favorable terms, to project their own legitimacy and credibility while simultaneously questioning the legitimacy and credibility of their opponents. Indeed, we might consider the strategies of dominance as a hierarchy, from the relatively inexpensive framing methods discussed in this book, to the more costly and difficult to implement clientelistic practices highlighted in earlier work, to the risky and destructive use of violence by regimes that have no other options (Robert Mugabe of Zimbabwe, for example). When dominant parties can maintain power through framing, they are likely to do so, resorting to more expensive or risky strategies only when necessary.

Israel and El Salvador also help to establish the ways in which oppositions have slipped the noose of dominant party framing. In El Salvador, the militant group turned political party Farabundo Martí National Liberation Front (FMLN) successfully contested its negative label by building a reputation for successful management at the local level and running a presidential candidate with no ties to its guerilla past. In Israel, historically discredited Herut toned down its rhetoric, pursued alliances with more moderate parties, and responsibly participated in a government of national unity. In both cases, once opposition parties cultivated more favorable images, they were able to take advantage of ruling party weaknesses and missteps to win elections.

In the final section of this concluding chapter, I discuss the future of electoral politics in South Africa. When might the racial census disappear? When might ANC dominance erode? Utilizing insights derived from the study of Israel and El Salvador, I speculate on hypothetical paths away from the census. I also discuss the significance of the birth of Cope for the opposition as a whole. I conclude that the true impact of Cope may have less to do with the immediate number of votes it wins from the ANC and more to do with how it changes the nature of political competition in South Africa. As the first nonwhite opposition party to win substantial votes throughout South Africa, Cope alters the landscape of elections. No longer is opposition to the ruling party a strictly white/black affair; not all opponents can be dismissed through racial tactics. The de-racialization of opposition in turn enhances the credibility of criticisms from other opposition parties, notably the DA. It also generates possibilities for coalitions and alliances, particularly at the local level, that could help opposition parties gain credibility and legitimacy. In short, the rise of Cope could lead to the normalization of opposition in South Africa, reducing the ability of the ANC to single-handedly frame elections. And this, eventually, could end the era of ANC dominance and racial-census elections in South Africa.

BEYOND SOUTH AFRICA

To what extent is the strategy of saddling your opponents with sticky and problematic labels one that parties – particularly dominant parties – have used in other settings? In other words, is the negative labeling strategy a general political tactic of ruling parties everywhere or is it somehow unique to South Africa? To explore this question, I consider two additional countries, Israel and El Salvador. Both were ruled for lengthy periods of time after independence or democratization by a single party. In Israel, Labor (or Mapai) dominated politics for more than three decades after the country gained independence in 1948. In El Salvador, right-wing ARENA won four presidential elections (one before full democratization, three after) before finally losing to the FMLN in 2009. In both countries, as in South Africa, negative framing strategies figured prominently in the tactical repertoires of the ruling parties. Israel's

Mapai successfully discredited its primary opponent on the right, Herut, by portraying it as an irresponsible, fascist party that would destroy Israeli democracy. El Salvador's ARENA preserved its hold over the presidency in part by branding the FMLN as an unreconstructed communist organization with terrorist tendencies. Both Israel and El Salvador, like South Africa, had past histories of civil conflict. The extent of civil conflict varied across these cases, from full-fledged civil war in El Salvador, to apartheid in South Africa, to milder political tensions between co-combatants in a war of independence in Israel. Nonetheless, these lines of division became the basis for exclusion and delegitimization in the new regimes. Image politics and negative framing strategies are therefore not unique to the ANC's treatment of the white opposition parties of South Africa, although they may be especially common (or effective) in post-conflict societies undergoing democratization.

In all three cases, negative framing tactics co-existed with and complemented resource-based strategies of dominance. Israel's Mapai operated a well-documented patronage machine through the Histadrut, an encompassing labor union and service provider for Jewish workers. ARENA of El Salvador exploited a large resource gap between itself and its competitor, the FMLN. Many previous studies of single-party dominance, most recently by Magaloni (2006), Scheiner (2006), and Greene (2007), highlight the use of such techniques. However, as is clear in both cases, dominant parties complement resource-based strategies with softer methods of image control and election framing to neutralize their opponents. With the voters' choice set limited by the successful play of these strategies, far fewer resources need to be expended to keep the electorate loyal.

In addition to revealing the generality of image politics and negative framing strategies, these cases highlight a few additional points. First, opposition parties often make the task of ruling parties easier by giving them material on which to run negative campaigns, facilitating their own downfalls through strategic missteps and errors. Ruling parties then amplify these errors and use them to hang the opposition. Second, party images are not set in stone. Even powerful ruling parties sometimes cannot prevent their opponents from reversing their images. Once this happens, as Mapai in Israel and ARENA in El Salvador found to their detriment, it becomes much more difficult to maintain a hold over power. This sounds out a positive note for the opposition in South Africa, suggesting that if it can successfully contest its current labeling in the electorate, it will have a good chance of improving its performance at the polls.

## Israel

Israel's Labor Party dominated Israeli politics for more than four decades, beginning in the pre-state days of the Jewish settlement of Palestine and continuing until 1977, when it was finally excluded from government by a coalition led by its long-term rival, the right-wing Likud. While there were many sources to Labor's dominance, the party's success in branding Likud's predecessor – Herut – as a dangerous and irresponsible organization bent on destroying Israel's democracy figured centrally. This strategy weakened a key rival for power, ensured Labor's centrality to coalition formation, and facilitated its hold on power. It was only after Herut constructed a more favorable image in the electorate by moderating its rhetoric and behavior, building alliances with more centrist parties, and participating in the Government of National Unity (formed during the Six Day War of 1967) that it was able to offer a credible alternative to Labor. In 1977, when internal conflicts weakened Labor, Likud outflanked it on questions of nationalism, and economic development reduced the efficiency of its patronage machine, voters defected en masse to Likud. The Israeli case thus demonstrates the power of branding and the liability of a negative image. It also shows how, with skill and luck, oppositions can re-engineer their image in ways that allow them to compete more favorably in the electorate. In this section, I first review the history of Labor in Israel, discussing the sources of its dominance and paying special attention to the negative framing strategy it used to great effect on its primary opponent, Herut; I then discuss how Herut turned its image around.[1]

Mapai (the Palestine Workers' Party) formed in January 1930 in the Jewish settlement of Palestine. It quickly established its leadership in the settlement as well as in the world Zionist movement. After Israel became a sovereign state in 1948, Mapai won a plurality in the country's first election and formed a coalition government with David Ben-Gurion as prime minister. In the following seven Knesset elections (until 1977, when it was defeated for the first time), Mapai (or one of its successors) captured a plurality of votes, participated in every government that formed, and controlled the premiership.[2] In contrast, its closest rival, the right-wing Herut (which later became Likud), typically took less than half of Mapai's vote.[3] For these reasons, Mapai is

---

[1] I am grateful to David Forman-Barzilai for his advice on this section; all errors remain my own.
[2] In 1965, Mapai and the leftist Ahdut Avoda merged to form the Labor Alignment, which then became the Israeli Labor Party, which then combined with Mapam to form the Alignment, and finally the Labor Party. For simplicity, I will follow the example of most of the literature on Israeli parties and refer to the left in Israel interchangeably as "Mapai" or "Labor."
[3] Israel has a highly proportional electoral system (one large district for the entire country) and supports a large and fluctuating number of parties that form three basic blocs: the leftist bloc, the rightist bloc, and the religious bloc. In the leftist bloc, Mapai was joined by Mapam and Ahdut Avoda (its "immediate" rivals) as well as the Communist Party (Maki), which was excluded from all coalitions. As noted earlier, Mapai, Mapam, and Ahdut Avoda eventually formalized their relationship in the Alignment. The rightest bloc consisted of the largest party, Herut (also called the Revisionist Party) and two more moderate "liberal" parties, the General Zionist (later Liberal) Party and the Progressive Party. In 1965, Herut and the Liberal party combined to form Gahal, which later (combined with some additional smaller parties) became Likud. The primary party in the religious bloc was the National Religious Party (NRP). In addition to the three major blocs, there were small parties devoted to the representation of Arab interests. Until 1973, the left bloc of parties varied between 61 and 71 seats; the right

considered a classic example of a dominant party (Pempel 1990; Shalev 1990; Aronoff 1990).

Mapai's dominance had many sources, several originating in Mapai itself. Mapai had a charismatic leader, Ben-Gurion, who commanded great loyalty amongst wide sections of the Israeli public. The party came of age and assumed political leadership during "the heroic epoch of pioneering and the successful struggle for national independence." It was viewed within the world Zionist movement as "the most active and creative force in settling immigrants and reclaiming (literally and figuratively) the land of Israel," as "the pioneering vanguard of Zionism" (Aronoff 1990: 263). After independence, with Israel facing antagonistic neighbors and threatened invasions, Mapai continued to present itself as the protector and champion of the Israeli nation. Mapai's role in the Zionist struggle to establish and defend the state of Israel thus endowed it with a deep reservoir of legitimacy for the Israeli public.

Mapai also made astute institutional investments and innovations. Central amongst these was the Histadrut, an all-encompassing labor organization and service provider for Jewish workers. The Histadrut, established in 1920 by the labor parties that later merged to form Mapai, operated as "the executive arm of a clientelistic party machine" (Shalev 1990: 92). Before independence, it functioned as a "state in the making;" after independence, it was a "state within the state" (Beilin 1993 32). It provided for many of the basic needs of workers: wage bargaining, health care, defense, schools, unemployment assistance, pension funds, old age homes, sports associations, and so on. The Histadrut also owned or was affiliated with large, labor-intensive business enterprises in construction and industry and through these controlled a significant number of jobs.[4] As a result, the Histadrut simultaneously wore "the hats of union and boss" (Shalev 1990: 107). It not only provided welfare benefits, it also controlled jobs. By establishing and maintaining hegemony within the Histadrut, Mapai captured significant resources with which to build a powerful and extensive patronage system. As a result, "not only could the party provide workers with an uplifting role in national rebirth, but it did so alongside many eminently practical activities addressed to their present and future security in Palestine and their immediate material interests" (Shalev 1990: 96). Combined with its success in integrating successive waves of immigrants, delivering solid economic growth throughout the early 1970s, and performing well in various regional wars and skirmishes throughout the 1950s and 1960s, Mapai's ideological and organizational strengths reinforced each other and gave the party significant resources for perpetuating its dominance (Aronoff 1989, 1990).

---

bloc, between 21 and 39 seats; and the religious, 15 to 18 seats. Before the mergers that created the Alignment and Gahal, Mapai took 32–38% of the vote to Herut's 7–14%. See Beilin (1993), Aronoff (1989), and Shalev (1990) for discussions of the Israeli party system.

[4] Shalev (1990: 106) estimates that, by the early 1970s, half of all economically active Histadrut members were dependent to some extent on the labor organization for their livelihood.

At the same time, Mapai's strength also reflected the comparative weakness of parties on the right – the Liberal party, which represented business interests, and the more radical Herut. The weakness of these parties stemmed in part from structural sources. Shalev (1990) argues that there was only a "limited and fragmented socioeconomic basis" for mobilization on the right: Organized labor provided for many of the security (economic and otherwise) needs of the middle classes, cutting into the right's natural constituency. Moreover, capital itself was internally divided and lacked effective organization and leadership.

Not all of the right's problems were structural, however. Politics factored in also. Beginning in the pre-independence days of the Jewish settlement, the Revisionists (which later became Herut) faced a significant image problem. Herut had a "persistent public image as an untrustworthy, irresponsible, and therefore illegitimate political organization" (Levite and Tarrow 1983: 301). Levite and Tarrow locate the sources of this image problem in the tactics and decisions made by the Revisionists/Herut at critical moments in the past and the strategic exploitation of these responses by Mapai to brand its opponent as dangerous, irresponsible, and anti-democratic.

The conflict between Labor and the Revisionists, Mapai and Herut, goes back to the period prior to the establishment of Israel, with tension and confrontation continuing during the struggle for independence and the early years of statehood. Labor, led by Ben-Gurion, and the Revisionists, led by Vladimer Zeev Jabotinsky, vied for ascendency within the Jewish settlement of Palestine and for control over the international Zionist movement. The world views of the two political movements differed substantially: Labor was universalistic and social-democratic; it emphasized egalitarianism, pioneering, and the settlement of Palestine. The Revisionists were more militant, militaristic, and nationalistic (Aronoff 1989). The Revisionists created a rival trade union to the Histadrut, the National Federation of Labor (NFL), and a right-wing militia Irgun Zvai Leumi (also known as Etzel or IZL) that vied with Labor's military organization, Haganah; they also pulled out of the World Zionist Organization (WZO) and formed the New Zionist Organization (NZO). Tension between the two movements went deeper than rival ideologies and organizations. In 1933, a prominent labor leader was murdered and three members of an extreme fraction of the revisionists were charged (but not convicted) of the crime – an event that remained salient in Israeli politics for decades (Aronoff 1989). Neither the NZO nor the NFL proved successful, and the Revisionists found themselves isolated from the key institutions of Zionism and the legitimacy and resources they conferred. This left Labor in an undisputed position of power and deprived the Revisionists of playing an active role in the establishment of the institutions that would become the Israeli state (Levite and Tarrow 1983; Aronoff 1989, 1990).

A decade later, as the Jewish settlement attempted to gain independence from Britain, conflict between the two movements again flared, verging at points on civil war. Haganah, Etzel (led by Menachem Begin, who had succeeded Jabotinsky and would go on to lead Herut), and Lechi (also known as the Stern Gang after its leader, Avraham Stern) united to resist the British but had different styles and strategies. While Haganah followed a policy of restraint and moderation toward the British, Etzel and Lechi were more extreme and clandestine, at times verging on terrorism. Begin and Stern resisted subordinating their groups to the elected (Labor-led) government of the Jewish settlement. This resistance reached full bloom and nearly induced civil war in an incident known as the *Altalena* affair. The *Altalena* was a ship commissioned by Begin to bring arms and ammunition to Israel. Ben-Gurion, who was in the process of creating the Israel Defense Forces (IDF) out of the various militant groups, demanded that Begin turn the armaments over to the IDF. Begin refused, prompting fears that he planned to use the arms to launch an armed revolt and coup. Tensions between government troops and Etzel soldiers escalated, a gun battle broke out, and government troops sunk the ship, killing Etzel soldiers in the process. Civil war was averted, but tension on both sides remained.[5]

Tension between the Revisionists (now Herut) and Mapai re-surfaced frequently during the early years of Israeli statehood, finding expression in clashes between Begin and Ben-Gurion. The most prominent of these occurred in 1952, over reparation payments from Germany for property lost by Jews during the Holocaust. Ben-Gurion had opened discussions with Germany about reparations, believing the resources could aid Israel's development. However, resistance to the payments ran deep in Israeli society, a sentiment that Begin attempted to use to discredit Ben-Gurion. While the Knesset debated the issue, Begin addressed a crowd gathered nearby, referencing the *Altalena* affair, evoking Holocaust imagery, and promising "This will be a war of life and death.... Today I shall give the order: Blood!" (Aronoff 1989; Beilin 1993: 75). The crowd then marched to the Knesset, pushing through police barricades, throwing stones, and breaking windows. Ben-Gurion called in the army to restore order, hundreds were arrested, and Begin was barred from the legislature for three months.

By taking the Revisionists out of Zionist organizations like the Histadrut and the WZO and engaging in repeated, sometimes violent conflicts with Mapai, Revisionist leaders Jabotinsky and Begin established their party as a right-wing, more militaristic alternative to Labor and Mapai. They also isolated it and contributed to its marginalization. Ben-Gurion in turn exploited Herut's history to brand it as a dangerous, irresponsible, fascist organization that would destroy Israeli democracy. In doing so, he delegitimated Mapai's most significant adversary, facilitating Mapai's hold on power. Indeed, some view this as "one of Ben Gurion's greatest political achievements," as "a brilliant political strategy" (Levite and Tarrow 1983: 300).

Levite and Tarrow (1983) and Aronoff (1989) show that Ben-Gurion's efforts at discrediting the Revisionists date back to the very early days of the

---

[5] This recount of the *Altalena* affair and the German reparations incident borrows heavily from Aronoff (1989) and Beilin (1993).

conflict between the parties. Aronoff writes that "during bitter rhetorical exchanges, Ben-Gurion called the revisionists fascists, referred to his rival Jabotinsky as 'Il Duce' [Mussolini's title] and compared him to Hitler [prior to the Holocaust]" (Aronoff 1989: 20). Ben-Gurion used the departure of the Revisionists from the WZO and the Histadrut to suggest that they had moved beyond legitimate Zionist politics, that they were even anti-Zionist (Aronoff 1989; Shalev 1990). These efforts at delegitimation continued into the early years of the Israeli state. Levite and Tarrow write: "In countless public and private appearances and in letters written and speeches made over the years, Ben-Gurion warned of the overwhelming danger to the state and nation posed by Herut and its leader, Begin" (Levite and Tarrow 1983: 302). After the German reparations incident, Ben-Gurion castigated Begin as having tried to destroy Israeli democracy (Aronoff 1989: 21). He left the Knesset whenever Begin rose to speak and refused to allow the body of Jabotinsky – who had died in the United States in 1940 – to be reburied in Israel (Aronoff 1989: 21). Even as late as 1963, he argued that if Begin came to power "he will replace the army and police command with his ruffians and rule the way Hitler ruled Germany, using brute force to suppress the labor movement; and will destroy the state" (Aronoff 1989: 24, quoting from Bar-Zohar 1978: 303). Beyond the rhetoric, Ben-Gurion refused to enter into a coalition government with Herut, even though Labor required coalition partners from the very first election and Herut was the second largest party. As a result, Herut did not participate in any of the first fourteen governments of the state of Israel.

Thus, while Herut helped to determine its own fate through the actions and strategies it pursued, Herut's image problems were also the result of a negative framing strategy by Mapai and Ben-Gurion to delegitimize and thereby significantly hamstring its primary opponent. As a consequence of this strategy, even though Herut was the second largest party in Israel, it was not considered a viable alternative to Mapai. "Instead," write Levite and Tarrow, "its image as a party of permanent opposition and that of its leaders as permanent losers was accepted by even its most devout supporters" (Levite and Tarrow 1983: 302). By eliminating Herut as a viable coalition partner, Mapai ensured its centrality to all government formation. It also found it easy to divide and rule the right: Exclude Herut while bringing the Liberal Party into frequent coalition, thereby discouraging the rightist parties from creating a united front (Shalev 1990).[6]

---

[6] Mapai's dominance also stemmed from the relative weakness of the far left, i.e., the Communist Party (Maki). While the sources of weakness on the left were numerous – Shalev (1990) discusses several – a successful deletimization strategy on the part of Mapai played an important role here as well. Shalev notes that the Communist Party had an expanding share of the vote in the early 1950s and drew in both Jews and Arabs. However, "the nationalist sentiment aroused (to some extent deliberately, by Mapai leaders) before and following the 1956 Sinai campaign tarred Maki with a rabidly anti-Zionist appearance in the eyes of the Jewish public and provoked disenchantment among many of the party's Jewish activists" (Shalev 1990: 111). Ben-Gurion facilitated Maki's delegitimation by declaring that he would enter into a coalition

In 1977, Herut's successor, Likud, beat Labor (the Alignment) in a decisive victory and formed a coalition excluding Labor from government for the first time in Israel's history.[7] How did Herut/Likud transform itself from pariah to power? Some of the explanation involved the weakening of Labor from within. For a variety of reasons, reviewed extensively in Shalev (1990), Labor became a less powerful adversary. The party faced significant internal inconsistencies: generational conflict and leadership succession questions; decreasing ideological and organizational coherence due to alliances with other parties; and conflicts between the party's key constituencies. It also became tone deaf to an electorate increasingly frustrated with its "oligarchic" tendencies and put off by a series of corruption scandals. There is evidence that the electorate shifted to the right through generational change (the younger generation lacked their parents' ties to Mapai and tended to be more conservative) and immigration (the Eastern-origin Jews who came to Israel in the later waves of immigration tended to be more traditional, religious, and hawkish on security issues) and Mapai failed to respond. Many of these voters had been "reluctant" supporters of Labor who voted for the party because they depended on it (and the Histadrut) for jobs and services. As the economy grew and diversified, these voters no longer needed Histadrut support and defected to other parties (namely, Likud). Moreover, the growing and diversifying economy created constituencies opposed to Histadrut control and allowed business to grow more powerful, cohesive, and independent, making it difficult for labor to manage the economy for its own ends in the ways it had done in the past. Finally, with the occupation of the Palestinian territories after the Six Day War of 1967, and the difficult and divisive questions this raised for Israel, the Labor Party lost ownership of the nationalism question – which it had so skillfully exploited in the past – to the parties of the right.[8] In sum, Labor's defeat in 1977 was a function in part of a variety of factors – political, economic, and social – that weakened Labor and reduced its attractiveness to the electorate.

At the same time, the weakening of Labor is only part of the story. Had voters lacked a credible alternative to Labor, they might have stuck with the party in spite of their discontent – much as South African voters stick with the ANC or Japanese voters with the LDP. Thus, the second component of the story of Labor's collapse in 1977 was the construction of Likud as a viable alternative. Levite and Tarrow (1983) discuss a variety of strategic moves that Herut made – assisted inadvertently by Labor – that helped it mend its image in the electorate such that, by 1977, when Labor stumbled, it could present

---

with any party except Herut or the Communists. With the far left neutralized, Mapai was free to occupy the political center without fear of major defection on its flank.

[7] Likud took 33% of the vote to Labor's 25%. A new party that split off from Labor – the Democratic Movement for Change, or DMC – took almost 12% of the vote and then subsequently collapsed in the next election, with many of its middle-class voters returning to Labor. Likud formed a coalition with the DMC and the religious parties, excluding Labor from office.

[8] See Shalev (1990) for a thorough discussion of all of these points.

itself as a credible alternative to the long-time ruling party. First, beginning in the mid-1950s, Herut began to moderate some of its policy stances, advocating market liberalism. This did not immediately win the party votes, but it paved the way for later cooperation between Herut and the Liberals. Second, after great internal debate, Herut decided to join the Histadrut, hoping that working within the establishment would allow it to acquire greater legitimacy. Mapai understood the threat posed by Herut's normalization within Histadrut and attempted to block the party from joining. Herut evaded Labor's efforts by forming a joint list with the Liberals for the Histadrut elections of 1965. While the joint list fell far short of a majority, Herut's participation in the Histadrut "proved to be invaluable in reshaping Herut's public image in general and among blue-collar workers in particular" (Levite and Tarrow 1983: 304). Third, Herut and the Liberals also cooperated on the electoral front, forming the coalition Gahal for the 1965 general elections. Gahal, led by Begin, did not do particularly well in the election (its showing in 1965 was less than the combined strength of Herut and the Liberals in the 1961 elections, and 1969 was not much different) but nevertheless marked a critical juncture because it "conferred legitimacy on the party, terminated its political isolation, and moderated its public image." Fourth, and finally, Herut toned down its rhetoric to signal its acceptance of the rules of the democratic game. Gone were the days when Begin would lead stone throwers to march on the Knesset.

In addition to these tactical moves by Herut, Levite and Tarrow suggest that outside events combined with decisions by Labor leaders also helped the party to transform itself. In response to the Six Day War of 1967, Israel's leaders opted to form a National Unity Government that brought together parties from across the political spectrum, including Gahal. For the first time, Begin joined the government. Moreover, once in government, he adopted a cooperative stance, advocated for Ben-Gurion to head the Cabinet, and made very few demands in exchange for joining the coalition. Levite and Tarrow suggest that Gahal's participation in the National Unity Government represented an important turning point in Israeli politics: "Gahal's responsible behavior during this time of national emergency, its participation in the coalition, and its representation in the cabinet won it much needed public respect and provided it almost instantly with the ingredient of legitimacy that it had lacked" (Levite and Tarrow 1983: 304–305). Indeed, it "altered irreversibly the rules of the game" (Levite and Tarrow 1983: 307). Finally, Labor leaders after Ben-Gurion relaxed Labor's stance toward Begin and Herut: Ben-Gurion's successor, Levi Eshkol, approved the reburial of Jabotinsky in 1963; Eshkol also accepted Herut as a partner in the National Unity Government in 1967; and Eshkol and Golda Meir did not seek to terminate the coalition with Gahal after the national emergency ended – indeed, the coalition continued through the 1969 election and into 1970. These proved to be costly political mistakes for Labor because they facilitated Herut's normalization in Israeli politics.

Levite and Tarrow contend that the end result of Herut's efforts was the successful re-engineering of the party's image in the electorate: By 1969, very few Israeli voters polled completely rejected Gahal as a political option and many, including Labor supporters, selected it as a second choice. Positive feelings for Gahal were especially strong in the younger cohort who did not have personal memories of the earlier era. While this shift in the electorate did not translate automatically into increased strength for Gahal, it paved the way for the mass defection from Labor to Gahal almost a decade later, in 1977. Moreover, later efforts by Labor to reverse Herut's (Likud's) legitimation largely failed: Once the genie was out of the bottle, it was very difficult to put back in. The Israeli case thus demonstrates the power of framing for ruling parties, and how framing strategies coexist with and reinforce more materially based techniques like clientelism.

## El Salvador

El Salvador provides a third example of the use of negative framing by a ruling party to delegitimize the opposition. ARENA, the country's predominant party for much of two decades, pursued this strategy to great success, winning four presidential elections (1989, 1994, 1999, and 2004) in part by saturating the electorate with images of the opposing FMLN as un-reconstructed left-wing terrorists. The FMLN, for its part, engaged in self-destructive internal battles that prevented it from presenting a coherent alternative to ARENA's negative portrayal. Moreover, the dominance of the "ortodoxo" faction in the party, with its roots in the wartime leadership and far left of the party, lent substance to ARENA's claims. When the FMLN finally cohered around a nonortodoxo candidate that ARENA had difficulty smearing with the politics of the past, it was able to capitalize on the electorate's fatigue with twenty years of ARENA's policies and capture the presidency in the 2009 elections. The Salvadoran case thus shows how ruling parties can use negative images to delegitimize the opposition and thereby prolong their hold on power, but it also reveals how oppositions sometimes facilitate their own destruction by providing the ruling party with ample material with which to run negative campaigns. I will develop each of these points in greater depth in the following paragraphs.[9]

The Chalpúltepec Peace Accord in January 1992 ended more than a decade of civil war in El Salvador between military-aligned center and right-wing governments and the guerilla organization known as the Farabundo Martí National Liberation Front, or FMLN. Two years later, in 1994, El Salvador conducted its first truly democratic national elections. These elections pitted the left-wing FMLN, now converted into a political party, against the incumbent National Republican Alliance (ARENA), which had held office

---

[9] I am indebted to the input and advice of David Holiday, Carrie Manning, and especially Christine Wade in writing this section. All errors remain my own.

since 1989. ARENA, formed in the early 1980s by Roberto D'Aubuisson, a vice chief of intelligence and death squad organizer for the military governments of the 1970s and 1980s, swept the 1994 elections, winning the presidency by a landslide in the second round of voting, taking a plurality in the legislature, and winning 207 out of 262 municipalities. ARENA dominated the next two presidential elections (in 1999 and 2004), although it lost considerable ground to the FMLN in the legislature (the two parties maintained a rough parity from 1997 on) and in the municipalities (ARENA continued to control a far greater number of municipalities, but the FMLN captured many urban centers, including prominent cities like San Salvador and Santa Tecla).[10]

El Salvador's electoral history raises an interesting question: How did ultra-conservative ARENA, with its links to death squads and the military, manage to win so many elections against the popular and populist FMLN? This question becomes all the more interesting when one considers that ARENA's neoliberal policies like privatization and dollarization, not to mention support for the Iraq war, have not been uniformly popular, nor have all of its presidents (Booth et al. 2006; Holiday 2005).

In the first elections in 1994, fraud and a general climate of fear and violence contributed to ARENA's success. Stahler-Sholk (1994) notes that the FMLN was not represented on the Tribunal Supremo Electoral (TSE) (the body that administered the election). Perhaps as a result, the voter registration process disenfranchised many likely FMLN supporters. He also indicates that fear and distrust formed a constant backdrop to the election, with many FMLN sympathizers afraid to openly support the party. These factors likely diminished in importance over time, however. By 2004, electoral administration was less biased and FMLN supporters no longer felt the need to hide their allegiances (DiNovella 2004).

Perhaps more important than fraud or fear, the incumbent ARENA had a significant edge in terms of campaign finances and media resources. The state distributes campaign funds according to a formula based on the votes won in prior elections – an accounting that gave ARENA significant advantages, especially in the earlier elections. ARENA has also been able to raise far more private money than the FMLN. As a result, ARENA has been able to outspend its opponent by a significant margin (Stahler-Sholk 1994; Holiday 2005). Moreover, as the incumbent party, ARENA also had a distinct advantage with regard to media coverage. Stahler-Sholk (1994) indicates that ARENA had five to fourteen times the number of FMLN advertising spots on television and radio in 1994 and that many government-sponsored ads (ubiquitous prior to the election) used slogans and symbols straight out of ARENA's campaign. Ten years later, the story had not changed significantly (Holiday 2005).

Beyond resources, ARENA successfully presented itself to the electorate as a competent, disciplined, responsible, moderately conservative party,

[10] For a review of election results see Manning (2008).

hiding internal conflict from public view and running attractive candidates who do not have roots in the party's unsavory past (Holiday 2004, 2005; Booth et al. 2006). While in office, it implemented the peace accords, removing the military from government and creating an integrated police force. It delivered economic stability and maintained a privileged relationship with the American government (important in a country where many families depend on remittances). As Lehoucq (1995: 182) writes: ARENA represented the "most viable alternative with which to maintain economic and political stability." In sum, resource asymmetries and successful image control help to explain why ARENA has been successful in spite of unpopular policies and a troubling past.

At the same time, ARENA's success in winning elections resulted not only from its own strengths but also from the weaknesses of its opponent, the FMLN. While the FMLN has successfully competed for lower level offices (municipal and legislative), it has lagged in establishing itself as a credible contender for national office. Wade (2008) reports on a 2004 poll conducted by the Central American University Institute for Public Opinion that showed that 56 percent of respondents believed that the FMLN was "not prepared to govern." The FMLN's credibility problem stemmed in part from its inability to reinvent itself after the war in a way that would make it more compelling to the electorate. According to an analyst of Salvadoran politics cited by Wade: "The Left has not been successful in finding its own identity, and I believe that their participation in the dynamics of power has prevented them from successfully breaking free from a party that came from the war, to transform itself into a peace party."

If image is important to winning elections, why has the FMLN failed to project a more favorable one? Why has it been unable to break free from its past? Some of the FMLN's image problems result from dynamics within the party itself – in particular, bitter internal conflict. As documented in detail by Wade (2008) and Manning (2008), conflict between the "renovadores" or "reformistas" and ortodoxos have wracked the party since shortly after the 1994 elections. The renovadores/reformistas, many of whom have roots in the bread-and-butter politics of the municipalities, urge a more pragmatic approach to politics, including more moderate policies and coalitions with other groups. They also have pushed for greater internal democracy for the FMLN. In contrast, the ortodoxos have fought to keep the party faithful to revolutionary traditions and socialist policies, believing that ideological purity would enhance the FMLN's attractiveness to the electorate. Conflict between the factions flared repeatedly over the decade plus since the 1994 elections, especially when the party had to select presidential candidates, and lead to repeated breakaways of renovadores/reformistas that have gone on to form splinter parties (all of which failed to make an electoral impact).

Internal conflict contributed to FMLN image problems in two ways. First, factional conflict prevented the FMLN from presenting a coherent identity and message to the electorate, and the party has appeared undisciplined and fractious (Manning 2008: 116). It is difficult for a party to present itself as credible and competent when it regularly and publically tears itself apart. Second, until very recently, ortodoxos have won most of the FMLN internal battles. Ortodoxo ascendency within the party has contributed to the FMLN's image of being mired in its revolutionary past. This dynamic is well illustrated by the career of Shafick Handal. Handal, one-time leader of the Communist Party (one of the constituent organizations of the FMLN), became the general coordinator for the FMLN in 1993 and played a central leadership role in the party until his death in January 2006. He won a divisive internal battle against Oscar Ortíz, the popular reformist mayor of Santa Tecla, to take the party's nomination for president in 2003, and he went on to lose the 2004 presidential election to ARENA's Antonio Saca. While Handal was a skillful legislator, he represented a relatively extreme faction within the FMLN. With his roots in the wartime leadership of the Communist Party, his eruptions of anti-American rhetoric, and his statements of support for Castro, he probably had less appeal to the electorate than the moderate FMLN leaders like Ortíz. In selecting this "bearded septuagenarian former leader of the Communist Party," and the "image of guerrilla warfare" he evoked, the FMLN did little to update and moderate its image in the electorate (Holiday 2005: 40).

At the same time, while the FMLN is partially responsible for its problems, ARENA has capitalized very effectively on FMLN weaknesses, eviscerating the party in a series of extremely negative presidential campaigns that portrayed the FMLN as terrorist, communist, and anti-American. Stahler-Sholk (1994: 30) indicates that, in 1994, "ARENA chose to sidestep debate on the issues, preferring to hint darkly that a vote for the FMLN would be a vote for chaos and violence." He notes that, in the months prior to the election, "the television airwaves were saturated with ads that featured gruesome pictures of wartime destruction with ominous voice-overs warning that a vote for the FMLN would mean a return to the past" (Stahler-Sholk 1994: 31). Death squads continued to operate during this time, which further reminded voters of past violence and created an election context that "if not directly fomented by ARENA, worked to [its] advantage" (Stahler-Sholk 1994: 31). One ARENA candidate he interviewed intimated that "citizens are afraid that the FMLN will take up arms again," – an unsurprising sentiment given the negative advertising of the campaign (Stahler-Scholk 1994: fn. 30).[11]

Ten years later, during the 2004 presidential campaign, when the FMLN's Shafick Handal ran against ARENA's Tony Saca, ARENA employed a similar roster of negative campaign tactics. As I noted earlier, Handal made an easy target for ARENA attacks. Seventy-three at the time of the election, he had led the Communist Party during the civil war, supported Castro, and spoke about the "terrorist" and "imperialist" Bush administration (Holiday 2005).

---

[11] Stahler-Sholk (1994: 31) notes that negative advertising was supposedly banned during the election, but ARENA openly flaunted this and the ARENA-dominated Tribunal Supremo Electoral refused to act against the ads.

ARENA took full advantage of the opportunity, predicting "apocalyptic doom" should the FMLN win (Holiday 2005: 80) and portraying Handal as "a terrorist bent on turning El Salvador into another Cuba" (Booth et al. 2006). As part of a "sharp, slick, and expensive campaign," it ran newspaper ads that showed Shafick in full military gear, with a child saluting him and the caption: "Good morning dear teacher! With the FMLN, kindergarten will be free! Is this the education you want for your children?" (Holiday 2004). Saca, a thirty-something, charismatic former sports announcer, compared himself to the gray-bearded Handal, explaining "I have clean hands, I have not engaged in kidnapping" (Holiday 2004). At a Quetzaltepeque rally, he exhorted the crowd: "If we want confrontation, class hatred, unemployment, the loss of credibility, a non-Christian country, street fighting, disorder, if we want this for our country, you know what to do. But if you want a country of brotherhood, a united country, a country with jobs, you know what to do. Tony Saca and ARENA are the answer" (DiNovella, 2004). ARENA also skillfully exploited fears Salvadorans have regarding their dependence on remittances from the United States. The conservative paper *El Diario de Hoy* (widely believed to be a mouthpiece for ARENA) ran an article a few days before the election alleging that the U.S. Congress would cut off remittances to El Salvador if the terrorist FMLN won the election. While the claim was based on skewed information and flawed logic, it struck home for the large number of Salvadoran families dependent on remittances.[12] Moreover, previous representatives of the Bush administration had made clear their dislike of Shafick, lending credibility to the claims (Holiday 2003). In sum, ARENA painted the FMLN as terrorist, communist, and anti-American, intimating that FMLN rule would result in economic disaster for El Salvador and a return of political violence. This strategy paid off nicely for ARENA, which captured 57.7 percent of the vote to the FMLN's 35.6 – even though it had been behind the FMLN in early polls.

Given ARENA's negative campaigns between 1994 and 2004 – and the raw material provided by the FMLN to fuel them – it is not surprising that the FMLN had an image problem. However, by 2009, the FMLN had reversed its fortunes, winning the 2009 presidential election with 51.3 percent of the vote to ARENA's 48.7. Some of the credit for the FMLN's success in 2009 had to do with ARENA's governance failures: general disenchantment with twenty years of ARENA policies, a faltering economy, dependence on remittances, and a stunning homicide rate. However, dissatisfaction with ARENA was nothing new. Some of the change had to do with the FMLN itself, which managed for the first time to gain widespread credibility with the electorate.

---

[12] For a discussion of the remittances issue, see selections from El Salvador political analyst David Holiday's blog from Thursday, March 18, 2004 ("'Unremitting' distortions," and "More twisted news from El Diario de Hoy") and Friday, March 19, 2004 ("Orwellian immigration logic," "LGP gets it right, but ..." and "A slight correction"), http://davidholiday.com/weblog/archive/2004/2004_03_01_archive.html.

How was the party able to do this? In part, the answer lies with the FMLN's continued success in winning lower level elections (especially at the municipalities). Delivering desired goods at the local level helped the party to cultivate an image of competency (see Manning 2008 for a discussion). Also important, however, was the FMLN's choice of presidential candidate – Mauricio Funes – who was harder for ARENA to discredit. ARENA strategies remained the same: Just as in earlier elections, the party pinned its opponent with labels like "terrorist" and "communist," claiming that the FMLN would simply be a puppet of Chavez if it won the election.[13] It ran ads and took out billboards portraying Funes with Castro, Ortega, and Chavez. It focused a great deal of attention on Funes' VP candidate, Salvador Sanchez Ceren, who was a guerrilla commander for a radical faction of the FMLN during the war, arguing that Funes was just a front for Ceren and other ortodoxos. It leaked allegations in *El Diario de Hoy* that the FMLN was conducting military exercises in regions of the country it had formerly controlled, repeating these (unsubstantiated) claims multiple times in the newspaper.[14] However, this time around ARENA's strategies proved much less effective in discrediting the FMLN. Funes, in sharp contrast to Shafick Handal, was young and well known to the electorate as a TV personality. He had not been a combatant during the civil war and had never been a member of the Communist Party. He offered moderate policies and pledged to maintain close ties with the United States. Given his clean past and his familiarity to the electorate, ARENA claims that he was a terrorist or communist lacked credibility. As Salvadoran political analyst Christine Wade put it: "[P]eople felt they had a good idea of who he was – and it wasn't a terrorist."[15] Consequently, ARENA's tactics failed to generate the response they had in previous elections, illustrating the limits of a negative labeling strategy.

As a final note, it is interesting to consider why the FMLN has not followed similar negative strategies vis-à-vis ARENA. Rather than reminding voters of its opponent's role in the civil war and its connection with death squad activities, the FMLN has tended to focus on policies (Holiday 2004; Stahler-Sholk 1994). Why did the party not exploit its opponent's grisly past? First, strategic decisions taken by ARENA may have limited the ability of the FMLN to pursue a negative framing strategy. ARENA has selected candidates that are not tainted with the politics of the past. Even before the end of the war, Roberto D'Aubuisson gave way to the pragmatic, moderate Alfredo Cristiani. In elections since, the party has run men like Tony Saca, who are too young to have participated significantly in the war. ARENA has also presented a united front and a consistent message, hiding internal conflicts from the public eye, which might have allowed it to better control and counter negative attacks.

---

[13] "Left-winger wins El Salvador Poll," BBC News, Monday, March 16, 2009.
[14] For a discussion, see Tim Muth's blog on El Salvador for Thursday, December 18, 2008 ("Armed Groups"), http://luterano.blogspot.com/2008/12/armed-groups.html.
[15] Personal communication, May 5 2009.

And beyond strategy, ARENA's bigger campaign resources and media access have allowed it greater message saturation and control, enhancing its ability to neutralize negative campaign claims. Finally, the FMLN may have been constrained from capitalizing on ARENA's past, especially in early elections, because of the effects this might have had on the peace process. Stahler-Sholk (1994: 32) argues that the FMLN could not be "too aggressive in its attack on the ARENA government because it was, at the same time, trying to convince its supporters to trust the government in its role as interlocutor in the negotiated peace accords."

What important lessons can we pull from the Salvadoran case? First, negative images are big electoral liabilities. Moreover, dominant parties – with their bigger campaign chests and ability to dominate the media – can and do try to manipulate the images of their competitors in ways that make them less credible to the electorate. In El Salvador, as in South Africa, ruling parties saturated the electorate with negative images of opposition parties in attempts – usually successful – to discredit and delegitimize them. In this way, dominant parties manipulate the choice set of voters. If voters do not view an opposition party as credible or legitimate, the dominant party does not need to win its votes through patronage or performance: It gets the votes by default, for voters perceive no alternative. Finally, the Salvadoran case reveals the limits of a negative labeling strategy. Oppositions have difficulty reciprocating in kind because they lack the resources and may face other strategic disadvantages. Moreover, even dominant parties face constraints in manipulating the image of their opponents: When opposition parties send strong credible signals to the electorate – by selecting a presidential candidate, for example, who diverges significantly from the caricature of the opposition being offered by the ruling party – they can counteract some of the effects of negative framing.

From these exercises in comparison, several conclusions about the use of framing strategies by dominant parties emerge. First, these strategies are common across a wide variety of settings: The ANC has used them against "white" and "African" parties in South Africa, against its traditional rivals, and against new parties. Ruling parties in parliamentary Israel and presidential El Salvador have also employed them. Typically ruling parties do not use framing strategies in a vacuum: They employ them alongside other, more materially based strategies like patronage and service delivery. Moreover, the ruling party's command over state resources is part of what makes a framing strategy viable: Significant campaign resources, combined with the ability to saturate the electorate through the media, allow the ruling party to project its message wider and deeper than the opposition. And ruling parties are often assisted in their efforts by the mistakes of their competitors: unfortunate candidate choices, revealing gaffes in rhetoric, and internal divisions that spill out during campaigns. The DA's 1999 campaign, during which it absorbed many conservatives from the NNP and focused on white voters, stands out as perhaps the single greatest regression in the history of its efforts at image transformation – one that continues to haunt it. However, the Israeli and

Salvadoran cases also reveal that ruling parties – with all of their resources – are not perpetually invulnerable. In both cases, opposition parties eventually reversed their delegitimization. In Israel, Herut reigned in its rhetoric, pursued alliances with more moderate parties, and behaved responsibly in the GNU. In El Salvador, the FMLN cultivated a reputation for responsible governance at the municipal level and ran a candidate unconnected to the controversies of the past. Once these opposition parties successfully contested their negative image in the electorate, they were able to exploit ruling party weaknesses and win elections. With these insights as a guide, I return now to South Africa.

## WHERE TO, SOUTH AFRICA?

How and when might we expect an erosion of South Africa's racial census? When might the ANC's grip on the country weaken? On the one hand, slow economic and social change will eventually end the census if nothing else does. As race becomes less predictive of individual circumstance, as South Africans come to believe that what matters to success are individual ability, effort, luck, and connections, and not racial designation, they will come to see the racial credentials of parties as insignificant. Individuals may still identify with their racial group, recognizing it as an important component of their history, culture, and current life, yet if race has little material impact on their life – if it does not shape the education they receive or the job available to them or their treatment at the hands of police officers and judges – then it will matter less whether a party is headed by a white or a black. There are signs that the decoupling of race and destiny has begun. As Seekings and Nattrass (2002) demonstrate, increasing socioeconomic variation marks racial groups in South Africa and a small African middle class has emerged. Should this trend continue, the significance of race in elections will eventually decline.

Alternative paths away from the census involve political change. In this book, I have focused on the white opposition parties – the (New) National Party and the Democratic Party (Alliance) and their struggles to become more competitive by altering their party labels and racial pedigrees. I have focused on these parties because, until the arrival of the Congress of the People (Cope) in 2008, they were the only parties to mount a serious national challenge to the ANC. Nevertheless, the demise of the census and the end of single-party dominance may well come about through the rise of a new party. An entirely new, racially bridging opposition could form, pulling African voters from the ANC and white voters from the DA. Prototypes of such parties exist. The United Democratic Movement (UDM) is one such party and for a brief time glowed brightly. More recently, Patricia de Lille pulled away from the Pan African Congress (PAC) to form the Independent Democrats (ID). The ID had a reasonable showing in 2004 (winning 1.7 percent of the national vote and seven seats in Parliament) and in the 2006 local elections (winning 16 wards out of nearly 4,000) but collapsed below 1 percent of the vote in 2009. Another new party, built on a similar multiracial chassis, could eventually have more success. And even if a new multiracial party does not succeed in breaking down the census, the arrival of a radical African party with social and economic policies to the left of the ANC and a sound organizational basis could force the ANC to court white votes, eroding the census from a different direction. Prototypes of such parties also exist – the Pan African Congress (PAC) and Azanian Peoples Organization (Azapo) being two – but have never been able to solve organizational problems or raise sufficient resources to pose any serious threat to the ANC. Finally, the ANC itself could split – to the left, if Cosatu or the SACP leave (long anticipated by observers of South African politics) – or to the right, as has recently happened when moderate ANC leaders left to form Cope. In either event, competition between the ANC and its splinter could increase the value of white votes, pulling support away from the DA (which would presumably become irrelevant under this scenario).

While analysts of South African politics have tended to focus on the prospects for new parties, especially those that form as splinters from the ANC, relegating the DA and its ilk to the footnotes of South Africa's political history, we might pause before dismissing the party so quickly. It has many advantages over any new party: organizational skills, branch structures, experience running campaigns and working in Parliament, international connections, and, not insignificantly, considerable financial resources. Unlike many opposition parties in Africa and elsewhere in the developing world, it has a wealthy constituency from which to raise funds and connections to the business world. As the recent experience of Cope shows, the challenges of starting from scratch are real and formidable, even for an ANC splinter party. It is not clear that overcoming these challenges is easier than changing a party label. Moreover, nonwhite opposition parties have faced many of the same image issues as the NNP and the DA. The ANC has used negative labeling strategies across the board, not just on white parties. Finally, the ANC's monopoly hold on African talent affects all opposition parties.

If the DA does hold the key to political change in South Africa, how might this come about? The previous section on Israel and El Salvador offers clues. Like the FMLN in El Salvador, the DA might focus on winning municipal elections, cultivating a reputation for success at the local level, and developing a cadre of home-grown talent that might eventually fill the party ranks at the national level. Indeed, the DA's competent administration of Cape Town has already given it a measure of credibility with some new voters and almost certainly contributed to its success in the 2009 election (when its support grew to 16 percent of the national vote and it captured the Western Cape). If the party can gain control over additional municipalities, especially those with sizeable African populations, it might continue to contest its image through delivery and performance.[16] The DA also might change its image through the selection

---

[16] The DA reportedly hopes to take not only Cape Town but also the Nelson Mandela metropolitan council in the Eastern Cape. See Carol Paton. "The nation has spoken." *Financial Mail*, May 1, 2009.

## Conclusion: South Africa in Comparative Perspective 241

of its top leadership, as the FMLN did to win the 2009 presidential election. In 2007, the party replaced Tony Leon with Helen Zille, who is widely regarded as having a more conciliatory style than Leon. This replacement might soften the edges of the DA's image, a step in the right direction, but the selection of a credible nonwhite politician would go even further. Finally, the DA might follow the path of Herut in Israel, reigning in reactionaries, practicing strict message control, and pursuing an alliance with a party with legitimate African credentials.[17] Campaigning with such a party at the national level or governing in coalition with it at the local level could help the DA contest some of its negative image amongst Africans. Finally, although not a factor in El Salvador or Israel, any event or process that loosens the ANC's monopoly over African talent could benefit the DA and other opposition parties.

Significantly, the arrival of Cope to the South African electoral scene expands, rather than restricts, the options available to the DA. Because Cope is a split to the right of the ruling party, it opens up opportunities for alliances. If correctly implemented, an alliance between the DA and Cope could grant the DA greater legitimacy, while boosting Cope's access to financial and organizational resources.[18] Indeed, already during the 2009 election campaigns there was much discussion of this possibility. Even without a formal alliance between opposition parties, the advent of Cope loosens up the South African political space. For the first time, there is a sizeable nationally representative opposition party led by Africans.[19] If Cope actively participates as an opposition party (rather than allowing itself to be coopted), it could remove the racial dimension to opposition. In the past, criticism by the opposition could be dismissed in racial terms, whether race was relevant or not to the issue.[20] With active Cope participation, it will be harder for the ruling party to use this tactic, perhaps diminishing its ability to use racial framing to discredit the DA. Moreover, Cope could eventually have an even bigger impact in the realm of local politics. If Cope replicates its 2009 performance in the next set of local elections, the ANC may lose its majority status in a number of municipalities, creating the possibility of coalition governments and granting various opposition parties, including the DA, the chance to rule in coalition. Hence, the ultimate impact of Cope may not lie in the number of votes it pulls

---

[17] The DA formed an alliance with the IFP in 2004, but this did little to change its reputation as a white party. Quite possibly the IFP was too discredited itself at that time to have much of a positive effect on the DA.

[18] This is far from guaranteed, however. It is instructive here to recall the Israeli case of Herut. Herut aligned with the Liberal Party, which already had considerable legitimacy with the electorate. Had the Liberal Party not already had this legitimacy, it seems unlikely that the alliance would have helped Herut change its image. In South Africa, the legitimacy of Cope is less established, so the ability of the DA to "borrow" from it through an alliance is uncertain.

[19] The IFP was regional. Moreover, for most of the Mandela/Mbeki period, it participated in government.

[20] Patricia de Lille and Bantu Holomisa and their parties have certainly been active and visible members of the opposition, but their numbers have simply been too small to make much of an impact on the racialization of opposition.

away from the ANC, but rather in how it reconfigures the South African political space.

Yet much remains to be seen. The ruling party has proved itself to be a strategic, well-resourced party many times in the past. It will fight to neutralize the effects of Cope. If it cannot lure or shame Cope leaders back to the fold, it will attempt to discredit them, as it did with Bantu Holomisa. If a Cope/DA alliance were to form, the ANC would brand it in elitist and racial terms, hoping to stunt its credibility with the electorate. And if it can no longer use framing strategies to maintain power, it might increasingly turn to clientelistic methods.

Decisions by the opposition will also shape the trajectory of South African politics. Will the DA continue to move in the direction of racial diversification in its candidate lists? Will it marginalize members opposed to transformation, putting substance behind its claims to multiracialism? If it wins control over municipalities, will it use its power to win over black voters or will it narrowly favor its white base? More broadly, can opposition parties overcome their differences and work in unison? Or will they allow petty rivalries to divide them? Certainly, opposition coordination in single-party dominant countries is no easy task, as Magaloni (2006), Scheiner (2006), and others have shown. Hence, while Cope raises new possibilities for the opposition and new challenges for the ruling party, the ultimate effect of these remain unknown. For the time being, the racial census and single-party dominance persist as the defining factors of the South African political system.

# References

Abrajano, Marisa, Jonathan Nagler, and R. Michael Alvarez. 2004. "A Natural Experiment of Race-Based and Issue-Voting: the 2001 City of Los Angeles Elections." Paper draft October 13, 2004.

Adams, Sheena. "Disbelieving Rugby Residents Jostle to Get 'Kisses for Free' from Mbeki. *Cape Times*, March 15, 2004.

Aitchison, John J. W. 1993. *Numbering the Dead: The Course and Pattern of Political Violence in the Natal Midlands: 1987–1989*. Pietermaritzburg: University of Natal.

    2003. "KwaZulu-Natal: The Pre-Election Wars of the 1990s." In *The Role of Political Violence in South Africa's Democratization*, edited by Dr. Ran Greenstein. Johannesburg: Community Agency for Social Enquiry.

Aldrich, John. 1995. *Why Parties? The Origin and Transformation of Political Parties in America*. Chicago: University of Chicago Press.

Alesina, Alberto F., Reza Baqir, and William Easterly. 1998. "Redistributive Public Employment." NBER Working Paper No. W6746.

Ames, Barry. 2001. *The Deadlock of Democracy in Brazil*. Ann Arbor: University of Michigan Press.

Andrew, Miranda. 2009. "Cosatu Vows to Spread Anti-Cope Booklet." *Mail & Guardian Online*. January 28, 2009.

Aranes, Joe, Blackman Ngoro, and Clive Sawyer. 1999. "Blows for Nats as Three Black Members Defect," *Star*, March 26.

Aronoff, Myron J. 1989. *Israeli Visions and Divisions: Cultural Change and Political Conflict*. New Brunswick, NJ: Transaction Publishers.

    1990. "Israel under Labor and the Likud: The Role of Dominance Considered." In *Uncommon Democracies: The One-Party Dominant Regimes*, edited by T. J. Pempel. Ithaca: Cornell University Press.

Arriola, Leonardo. 2008. "A Theory of Opposition Coordination." Book chapters presented at the WGAPE Meetings, UCLA, May 2008.

Atkinson, Doreen. 2007. "Taking to the Streets: Has Developmental Local Government Failed in South Africa." In *State of the Nation South Africa 2007*, edited by Sakhela Buhlungu, John Daniel, Roger Southall, and Jessica Lutchman. Cape Town: Human Science Research Council Press.

Bannon, Alicia, Edward Miguel, and Daniel Posner. 2005. "Sources of Ethnic Identification in Africa." *Afrobarometer* Working Paper Number 44.

Bar-Zohar, Michael. 1978. *Ben-Gurion: A Biography*. Translated by Peretz Kidron. Jerusalem: Steimatzky.

Barchiesi, Franco. 1999. "The Public Sector Strikes in South Africa." *Monthly Review* 51(5), October 1999.

Barrell, Howard. 1999a. "Liberal Invasion of the Platteland." *Mail & Guardian*, April 23.

1999b. "Leon Campaigns with His Heart and Cell." *Mail & Guardian*, April 30.

Barrell, Howard, and Sipho Seepe. 2001. "Leon and Hungry." *Daily Mail & Guardian*, July 11.

Bates, Robert. 1974. "Ethnic Competition and Modernization in Contemporary Africa." *Comparative Political Studies* 6(4): 457–483.

BBC News. 2009. "Left-Winter Wins El Salvador Poll." Monday, March 16, 2009.

Behrens, Gerd. 1989. "The Other Two Houses: The First Five Years of the Houses of Representatives and Delegates," unpublished Ph.D. dissertation, University of Cape Town.

Beilin, Yossi. 1993. *Israel: A Concise Political History*. New York: St. Martin's Press.

Beinart, William. 2001. *Twentieth-Century South Africa*. Oxford: Oxford University Press.

Bell, Paul. 1997. "White Rule's Last Post," *Leadership*: 66–67.

Berelson, Bernard, Paul Lazarsfeld, and William McPhee. 1954. *Voting: A Study of Opinion Formation in a Presidential Campaign*. Chicago: University of Chicago Press.

Blaine, Sue. "Mbeki Vows to Beat the New Enemy." *The Star*, March 12, 2004.

Booth, John, Christine Wade, and Thomas Walker. 2006. *Understanding Central America: Global Forces, Rebellion, and Change, Fourth Edition*. Boulder, CO: Westview Press.

Booysen, Susan. 2005. "The Democratic Alliance: Progress and Pitfalls." In *Electoral Politics in South Africa: Assessing the First Democratic Decade*, edited by Jessica Piombo and Lia Nijzink. New York: Palgrave.

2009. "The ANC and COPE: Fleeting phenomenon or substantive opposition?" EISA South Africa Election Update #2, March 2009.

Bothma, Stephane, and Stephen Laufer. 1998. "Opposition to Take Bar-Code Ruling to Court." *Business Day*, December.

Bratton, Michael and Robert Mattes. 2003. "Support for Economic Reform? Popular Attitudes in Southern Africa," *World Development* 31 (2): 303–323.

Breytenbach, Willie. 1999. "The New National Party." In *Election '99 South Africa: From Mandela to Mbeki*, edited by Andrew Reynolds. New York: St. Martin's Press.

Bullock, Charles S. III. 1984. "Racial Crossover Voting and the Election of Black Officials." *The Journal of Politics* 46(1): 238–51.

Business Day. 2004. "FF+ Will Hold Mbeki to His 'Poor-Whites' Vow." March 23, 2004.

Buthelezi, Mangosuthu. "But Life Was Worse in the Desert." Letter to the editor, *This Day*, March 3, 2004.

Butler, Anthony. 2007. "The State of the African National Congress." In *State of the Nation South Africa 2007*, edited by Sakhela Buhlungu, John Daniel, Roger Southall, and Jessica Lutchman. Cape Town: Human Science Research Council Press.

Caliguire, Daria. 1996. "Voices from the Community." In *Now That We Are Free: Coloured Communities in a Democratic South Africa*, edited by Wilmot James, Daria Caliguire, and Kerry Cullinan. Cape Town: Idasa.
Calland, Richard. 2008. "Creating a Case to Bend the Law." *Mail & Guardian Online*, September 12 2008.
   2009. "The High Price of Political Solutions." *Mail & Guardian Online*, April 27 2009.
Calland, Richard, and Sean Jacobs. 1999. "Western Cape." In EISA *Election Update* 99, 8, March 12.
Calvo, Ernesto, and Maria Victoria Murillo. 2004. "Who Delivers? Partisan Clients in the Argentine Electoral Market." *American Journal of Political Science* 48(4): 742–757.
Cape Times. 2004. "HIV/Aids 'Used to Scavenge Votes.'" March 16, 2004.
Carey, John M. and Matthew Soberg Shugart. 1995. "Incentives to Cultivate a Personal Vote: A Rank Ordering of Electoral Formulas." *Electoral Studies* 14, 4 (December, 1995): 417–39.
Carrim, Yunus. 1996. "Minorities Together and Apart." In *Now That We Are Free: Coloured Communities in a Democratic South Africa*, edited by Wilmot James, Daria Caliguire, and Kerry Cullinan. Cape Town: Idasa.
Carter, Chiara. "'Back the ANC Despite Its Negatives.'" *This Day*, March 18, 2004.
Chalmers, Robyn. 2004. "Remedies Aplenty to Kickstart SA Economy." *Business Day*, March 18, 2004.
Chandra, Kanchan. 2004. *Why Ethnic Parties Succeed: Patronage and Ethnic Headcounts in India*, Cambridge: Cambridge University Press, 2004.
Cherry, Janet. 2004. "Elections 2004: The Party Lists and Issues of Identity." *Election Synopsis* 1(3), 2004: 8.
Chetty, Sharon. 1999. "Mandela Allays Minority Fears," *Sowetan*, April 20.
Cho, Wonbin. 2002. "Attitudes to Democracy and Markets in South Africa, July–August 2000." *Afrobarometer Data Codebook*. Michigan State University.
*Citizen*. 1998. "Cape Court to Hear NP Objections." December 10.
*Citizen*. 1999. "FW Urges Whites: Don't Withdraw from Politics." February 4.
*City Press*. 2004. "The People Have Faith in Tomorrow." Interview with Thabo Mbeki, April 11.
Classen, Tom. 2004a. "Endorsing the DA Is Wasteful." Letter to the editor, *The Star*, February 24.
   2004b. "Stirring Up Hatred Will Not Gain Votes," letter to the editor, *Sowetan*, March 4.
Coovadia, Hoosen. "When Voting Is as Risky as Unprotected Sex." *Mail & Guardian*, March 19, 2004.
Cox, Gary. 1997. *Making Votes Count: Strategic Coordination in the World's Electoral Systems*. New York: Cambridge University Press.
   1999. "Electoral Rules and the Calculus of Mobilization." *Legislative Studies Quarterly*, XXIV: 387–419.
Cox, Gary, and Mathew McCubbins. 2001. "The Institutional Determinants of Economic Policy Outcomes." In *Presidents, Parliaments, and Policy*, edited by Stephan Haggard and Mathew McCubbins, Cambridge: Cambridge University Press.
Cresswell, Ryan, Rapule Tabane, and Cecilia Russell. 1999. "Parties Employ Same Old Tricks." *Star*, January 28.

Cullinan, Kerry. 1995. "'Subtle Racism' Blamed for Split." *Democracy in Action* Volume 9(1): 21.
Curtis, Gerald L. 1988. *The Japanese Way of Politics.* New York: Columbia University Press.
*Daily Mail & Guardian.* 1997. "Apla Blamed for Farm Murders," October 23.
Davis, Gavin. 2004. "Proportional Representation and Racial Campaigning in South Africa." *Nationalism and Ethnic Politics* 10: 297–324.
   2005. "Media Coverage in Election 2004." In *Electoral Politics in South Africa: Assessing the First Democratic Decade,* edited by Jessica Piombo and Lia Nijzink. New York: Palgrave.
Dawes, Nic. 2008. "Court's Giant Blow to Zuma." *Mail & Guardian Online,* August 1 2008.
   2009a. "Reform the X." *Mail & Guardian Online,* January 18.
   2009b. "Saving Cope – the Breech Baby." *Mail & Guardian Online,* March 7.
Dawson, Michael. 1994. *Behind the Mule: Race and Class in African-American Politics.* Princeton, NJ: Princeton University Press.
Desai, Ashwin, and Brij Maharaj. 1996. "Minorities in the Rainbow Nation: The Indian Vote in 1994." *South African Journal of Sociology,* 27(4): 118–125.
Dhlamini, Dan. 2004a. "AWB, FF Members Flocking to the ANC." *City Press,* February 22.
   2004b. "Members of the Volk Find Home in the ANC." *City Press,* February 29.
Diaz-Cayeros, Alberto, Beatriz Magaloni, and Barry Weingast. 2004. "Democratization and the Economy in Mexico: Equilibrium (PRI) Hegemony and Its Demise." Unpublished manuscript, Stanford University.
Dickson, Eric, and Kenneth Scheve. 2006. "Social Identity, Political Speech, and Electoral Competition," *Journal of Theoretical Politics* 18(1):5–39.
Dickson, Peter. 1998. "Eastern Cape Chiefs Block Voter Registration." *Mail &Guardian,* December 11.
Dixit, Avinash, and John Londregan. 1996. "The Determinants of Success of Special Interests in Redistributive Politics." *Journal of Politics* 58(November): 1132–55.
Dixon, Norm. 2007. "South Africa: Strike Ends, COSATU Declares Victory." *Green Left Weekly,* Issue 716, 4 July 2007.
DiNovella, Elizabeth. 2004. "Salvador: From the Bullet to the Ballot." *The Progressive.* http://www.progressive.org/node/871.
Dominguez, Jorge I., and James A. McCann. 1995. "Shaping Mexico's Electoral Arena: Construction of Partisan Cleavages in the 1988 and 1991 National Elections." *American Political Science Review* 89: 34–48.
Downs, Anthony. 1957. *An Economic Theory of Democracy.* New York: Harper.
Dreyer, Nazma. 2004a. "DA Dares ANC/NNP Alliance to Name Their Candidates for Premier." *Cape Times,* February 25.
   2004b. "Van Schalkwyk Confident He'll Stay On as Premier after 'Rightwinger' DA Candidate's 'Racist' Remarks." *Cape Times,* March 2.
Eifert, Benn, Edward Miguel, and Daniel Posner. 2007. "Political Competition and Ethnic Identification in Africa," *Afrobarometer* Working Paper No. 89.
Eldridge, Matthew, and Jeremy Seekings. 1996. "Mandela's Lost Province: The African National Congress and the Western Cape Electorate in the 1994 South African Elections." *Journal of Southern African Studies,* 22(4), December.
Electoral Institute of South Africa (EISA). 1998a. *Election Update* 99, 1, November 13.

1998b. *Election Update 99*, 2, November 27.
1998c. *Election Update 99*, 3, December 11.
1999a. *Election Update 99*, 4, January 15.
1999b. *Election Update 99*, 5, January 29.
Electoral Institute of South Africa (EISA). 1999c. *Election Update 99*, 6, February.
Electoral Institute of South Africa (EISA). 1999d. *Election Update 99*, 7, February 26.
1999e. *Election Update 99*, 8, March 12.
Evans, Jenni, and Riaan Wolmarans. 2006. "Timeline of the Jacob Zuma Rape Trial." *Mail & Guardian*, March 21, 2006.
Fearon, James. 1999. "Why Ethnic Politics and 'Pork' Tend to Go Together." Presented at an SSRC–MacArthur sponsored conference on "Ethnic Politics and Democratic Stability," University of Chicago, May 21–23, 1999.
Ferejohn, John. 1986. "Incumbent Performance and Electoral Control." *Public Choice* 30: 5–25.
Ferreira, Emsie. "Cope Launches Battle to Gain Votes." *Mail & Guardian Online*, December 11, 2008.
*Financial Mail*. 1999. "The Fight for a Free and Fair Ballot." February 5.
Fiorina, Morris. 1981. *Retrospective Voting in American National Elections*. New Haven, CT: Yale University Press.
Forrest, Drew. 2004. *Mail & Guardian*, January 30.
Freund, Bill. 1995. *Insiders and Outsiders: The Indian Working Class of Durban 1910–1990*. Portsmouth, NH: Heinemann.
Friedman, Steven. 2004. "Why We Vote: The Issue of Identity." *Electionsynopsis* 1(2): 2–4.
   2005. "A Vote for Some: South Africa's Ten Years of Democracy." In *Electoral Politics in South Africa*, edited by Jessica Piombo and Lia Nijzink. New York: Palgrave, pp. 3–22.
Georgy, Michael. "Cope: Affirmative Action Misdirected." *Mail & Guardian Online*, March 13 2009.
Gibson, Clark C., and Barak D. Hoffman. 2007. "Can Foreign Aid Help Produce Democracy? A Political Concessions Model of African Democracy." Unpublished manuscript, UCSD.
Gibson, Douglas. "DA Offers Hope of a Better SA," Letter to the editor, *Business Day*, March 3, 2004.
Gigaba, Malusi, and Brij Maharaj. 1996. "Land Invasions during Political Transition: The Wiggins Saga in Cato Manor." *Development South Africa*, 13(2), April: 217–235.
Giliomee, Herman. 1994. "The National Party's Campaign for a Liberation Election." In *Election '94 South Africa*, edited by Andrew Reynolds. New York: St. Martin's Press.
   1996. "A Politically Incorrect View of Non-Racialism and Majority Rule." In *Now That We Are Free: Coloured Communities in a Democratic South Africa*, edited by Wilmot James, Daria Caliguire, and Kerry Cullinan. Cape Town: Idasa.
Giliomee, Hermann, and Charles Simkins, eds. 1999. *The Awkward Embrace: One Party-Domination and Democracy*. Cape Town: Tafelberg Press.
Gimpelson, Valdimir, and Daniel Treisman. 2002. "Fiscal Games and Public Employment: Theory with Evidence from Russia." *World Politics* 54(2): 145–183).

Gordon, Diana. 2006. *Transformation & Trouble: Crime, Justice, and Participation in Democratic South Africa*. Ann Arbor: University of Michigan Press.

Gouws, Amanda. 1999. "The Gender Dimension." In *Election '99 South Africa: From Mandela to Mbeki*, edited by Andrew Reynolds. New York: St. Martin's Press.

Gouws, Piet, and PH " Tienie " Groenwald. 1998. "A Second Look," *Weekly Mail & Guardian*, August 21.

Green, Donald Philip, and Jonathan S. Krasno. 1988. "Salvation for the Spendthrift Incumbent: Reestimating the Effects of Campaign Spending in House Elections." *American Journal of Political Science* 32: 884–907.

Greenberg, Stanley. 2009. *Dispatches from the War Room: In the Trenches with Five Extraordinary Leaders*. New York: Thomas Dunne Books, St. Martin's Press.

Greene, Kenneth F. 2007. *Why Dominant Parties Lose: Mexico's Democratization in Comparative Perspective*. Cambridge: Cambridge University Press.

Greybe, David. 1999. "IEC Rejects Yet Another Round of Registration." *Business Day*, March 3.

Groenewald, Yolandi. 2006. "Who Else Can We Vote for?" *Mail & Guardian*, 27 January 2006.

Gumede, William. 2009. "The Power of the Poor." *Mail & Guardian Online*. April 25, 2009.

Gumede, William Mervin. 2005. *Thabo Mbeki and the Battle for the Soul of the ANC*. Cape Town: Zebra Press.

Haffajee, Ferial. 2003. "ANC Top Dogs to Rejig Lists." *Mail & Guardian*, 28 November 2003.

Haffajee, Ferial, and Marianne Merton. 2003. 'Floor-Crossers or Double Crossers." *Mail & Guardian*, 9 April 2003.

Hamilton, Georgina, and Gerhard Mare. 1994. "The Inkatha Freedom Party." In *Election '94 South Africa*, edited by Andrew Reynolds. New York: St. Martin's Press.

Hamlyn, Michael. 2008a. "Zuma Takes Charm Offensive to the JSE." *Mail & Guardian Online*, January 31.

2008b. "The ANC Is Not Divided." *Mail & Guardian Online*, January 11.

2008. "Manuel Not Concerned over Future Fiscal Policy." *Mail & Guardian Online*, January 10, 2008.

Harper, Paddy. "DA Spin Machine Sells Slick Self-Confidence." *The Star*, February 22, 2004.

Harris, Mari, Anneke Greyling, Robert Mattes, Cherrel Africa, and Helen Taylor. 1999. "The Leaders (IV)." *Opinion '99*, press release, May 24.

Hartley, Wyndham. 2004a. "NNP Steps Up Bid for Cape Coloured Vote." *Business Day*, March 31.

2004b. "ANC Not Planning a Third Term – Mbeki." *Business Day*, March 8.

Heard, Janet, and Carol Paton. 1999. "'Brown Afrikaners' Ready to Stand Fast in Cape of Storms," *Sunday Times*, May 16: 18.

Hechter, Michael. 1975. *Internal Colonialism: The Celtic Fringe in British National Development*. New Brunswick, NJ: Transaction Publishers.

Hlope, Dumisane. "A Real Communist Has My Vote." *City Press*, February 22, 2004.

Hogan, Heather, Nawaal Deane, Marianne Merten, Connie Selebogo, and Paul Kirk. 2000. "Interacial Conflict Still Impedes Tertiary Education," *Weekly Mail & Guardian*, March 17.

Hogarth, "Election Marred by Foot in Mouth." *Sunday Times*, March 14, 2004.
Holiday, David. 2003. *Noticen.* 8(43), November 20, 2003. Latin America Data Base.
    2004. "Polarization or Politicization in the Campaign?" Commentary in blog, Sunday, March 14, 2004. http://davidholiday.com/weblog/archive/2004/2004_03_01_archive.html.
    2005. "El Slavador's 'Model' Democracy." *Current History*, February 2005: 77–82.
Horowitz, Donald L. 1985. *Ethnic Groups in Conflict*. Berkeley: University of California Press.
    1991. *A Democratic South Africa? Constitutional Engineering in a Divided Society*. Berkeley: University of California Press.
Huntington, Samuel. 1968. *Political Order in Changing Societies*. New Haven, CT: Yale University Press.
Idasa. 1994. "National Election Study 1994, Codebook." Cape Town: Idasa.
    1998a. "Voter Participation in the 1999 Elections." Opinion '99, press release, November 10.
    1998b. "Party Support and Voting Intention." *Opinion '99*, press release, November 11.
    1998c. "The Opposition." *Opinion '99*, press release, November 13.
    1999a. "The Provinces: Eastern Cape." *Opinion '99*, press release, February 24.
    1999b. "The Provinces: Gauteng." *Opinion '99*, press release, February 24.
    1999c. "*Opinion '99*: Technical Background." At http://www.idasa.org.za/pos/op99/op99_tech.htm.
    1999d. "The Public Agenda," *Opinion '99* press release, November 13 1999.
    2003. *Regulation of Private Funding to Political Parties*. Cape Town: IDASA.
Independent Electoral Council (IEC) . "2002 Floor Crossing Results – Graphs." Data found at http://www.elections.org.za/library1.asp?KSId=13&iKid=3, accessed 13 July 2006.
Independent Electoral Council (IEC). "2004 Floor Crossing – Summary Reports." Data found at http://www.elections.org.za/library1.asp?KSId=13&iKid=3, accessed 13 July 2006.
Jacobs, Sean, and Richard Calland. 1999. "Western Cape." In EISA *Election Update* '99, 7, February 26.
Jacobson, Celean. 1999. "Mbeki Turns on the Charm as ANC Goes All Out to Keep Gauteng." *Sunday Times*, January 8.
Jacobson, Gary. 1990. "The Effects of Campaign Spending in House Elections: New Evidence for Old Arguments." *American Journal of Political Science* 34: 334–362.
Jacobson, Gary, and Samuel Kernell. 1983. *Strategy and Choice in Congressional Elections, Second Edition*. New Haven: Yale University Press.
Jaffer, Zubeida. 1999. "'Chimo' Chant and Songs Greet NNP Leader," *Star*, May 27.
James, Wilmot , Daria Caliguire, and Kerry Cullinan, eds. 1996. *Now That We Are Free: Coloured Communities in a Democratic South Africa*. Cape Town: Idasa.
Johnson, Angella. 1997. "Fight for the Right to Be Coloured," *Mail & Guardian*, February 14: 9.
Johnson, Anthony. 2004. "Looking Backwards and Forwards in the Run-Up to Elections." *Cape Times*, March 15.
Johnson, R. W. 1996. "The 1994 Election: Outcome and Analysis." In *Launching Democracy in South Africa: The First Open Election, April 1994*, edited by R.W. Johnson and Lawrence Schlemmer. New Haven, CT: Yale University Press.

1997. "The South African Electorate at Mid-Term." *Focus Letter*, Issue 6, February.
Johnson, R. W., and Lawrence Schlemmer, eds. 1996. *Launching Democracy in South Africa: The First Open Election, April 1994*. New Haven, CT: Yale University Press.
Johnson, R. W., and Paulus Zulu. 1996. "Public Opinion in KwaZulu-Natal." In *Launching Democracy in South Africa: The First Open Election, April 1994*, edited by R. W. Johnson and Lawrence Schlemmer. New Haven, CT: Yale University Press.
Ka' Nkosi, Sechaba. 1999. "Louis Luyt's leading lady," *Mail and Guardian*, February.
Kane-Berman, John. 2004. "Political Mudslinging as Vicious as It Ever Was." *Business Day*, March 9, 2004.
Keefer, Philip. 2007. "Clientelism, credibility and the policy choices of young democracies." *American Journal of Political Science* 51:4, 804–821 (October).
Keefer, Philip, and Razvan Vlaicu. 2008. "Democracy, Credibility, and Clientelism." *Journal of Law and Economics*, September 2008.
Kgosana, Caiphus. "Grumbles about Empty Promises at DA Meeting." *The Star*, February 25, 2004.
Kilian, Juli. "Opposition Irrelevant." Letter to the editor, *The Star*, March 17, 2004.
Kinder, Donald R., and Lynn Sanders. 1996. *Divided by Color: Racial Politics and Democratic Ideals*. Chicago: University of Chicago Press.
Kinder, Donald R., and David O. Sears. 1981. "Prejudice and Politics: Symbolic Racism Versus Racial Threats to the Good Life." *Journal of Personality and Social Psychology* 40 (3): 414–31.
Kindra, Jaspreet. 1999. "Reforms 'Not Just for Africans,'" *Natal Witness*, March 15. 2003. "'Too May Pahads on the ANC List.'" *Mail & Guardian*, 21 November 2003.
King, Gary, Michael Tomz, and Jason Wittenberg. 2000. "Making the Most of Statistical Analysis: Improving Interpretation and Presentation." *American Journal of Political Science* 44(2): 347–61.
Kitschelt, Herbert. 2007. "The Demise of Clientelism in Affluent Capitalist Democracies." In *Patrons, Clients, and Politics: Patterns of Democratic Accountability and Political Competition*, edited by Herbert Kitschelt and Steven I. Wilkinson. New York: Cambridge University Press.
Kitschelt, Herbert, and Steven I. Wilkinson. 2007. "Citizen-Politican Linkages: An Introduction." In *Patrons, Clients, and Politics: Patterns of Democratic Accountability and Political Competition*, edited by Herbert Kitschelt and Steven I. Wilkinson. New York: Cambridge University Press.
Kohno, Masaru. 1997. "Electoral Origins of Japanese Socialists' Stagnation." *Comparative Political Studies* 30(1), February: 55–77.
Koorts, Hermene. "DA Revives Hope Lost Because of ANC." Letter to the editor, *The Star*, February 27, 2004.
Kotlolo, McKeed. "Mbeki Visit Has Tshwane Abuzz." *Sowetan*, March 8, 2004.
Kotz, Dirk. 2004. "The Nomination Processes of Candidates on Party Lists." In EISA *Election Update 2004*, No. 7.
Kramer, Gerald. 1966. "A Decision-Theoretic Analysis of a Problem in Political Campaigning." In *Mathematical Applications in Political Science II*, edited by Joseph L. Bernd. Dallas: Southern Methodist University Press.

1970. "The Effects of Precinct-Level Canvassing on Voting Behavior." *Public Opinion Quarterly*, 34(4): 560–572.
Krasno, Jonathan S., and Donald Philip Green. 1988. "Preempting Quality Challengers in House Elections." *Journal of Politics* 50: 920–936.
Lakoff, George. 2004. *Don't Think of an Elephant: Know Your Values and Frame the Debate*. White River Junction, VT: Chelsea Green Publishing.
Laurence, Patrick. 1999a. "Is SA Liberal Legacy Alive?" *Financial Mail*, April 16:38–40.
Lehoucq, Fabrice Edouard. 1995. "The Election of 1994 in El Salvador." *Electoral Studies* 14(2): 179–240.
Leibbrandt, Murray, Laura Poswell, Pranushka Naidoo, Matthew Welch, and Ingrid Woolard. 2004. "Measuring Recent Changes in South African Inequality and Poverty using 1996 and 2001 Census Data." CSSR Working Paper No. 84. Cape Town: University of Cape Town, Centre for Social Science Research.
Lekota, Ido. 2004a. "'De Klerk Never Cared for Blacks.'" *Sowetan*, March 29.
2004b. "ANC Attack on Shenge Continues." *Sowetan*, April 2.
Le Roux, Mariette. 2008. "Zuma Backers Put SA Judges on Trial." *Mail & Guardian Online*, January 12, 2008.
Letsoalo, Matuma. 2009. "Last Chance Saloon for Mbeki-ites." *Mail & Guardian Online*, January 30, 2009.
Letsoalo, Matuma, Mandy Rossouw, and Sello S Alcock. 2008. "ANC Boss Accuses Judges of Conspiracy against Zuma." *Mail & Guardian Online*, July 4 2008.
*Mail & Guardian Online* Levite, Ariel, and Sidney Tarrow. 1983. "The Legitimation of Excluded Parties in Dominant Party Systems: A Comparison of Israel and Italy." *Comparative Politics*, 15(3): April 1983, 295–327.
Lijphart, Arend. 1977. *Democracy in Plural Societies: A Comparative Exploration*. New Haven, CT: Yale University Press.
1999. *Patterns of Democracy*. New Haven, CT: Yale University Press.
Lodge, Tom. 1983. *Black Politics Since 1945*. New York: Longman.
1994. "The African National Congress and its Allies." In *Election '94 South Africa*, edited by Andrew Reynolds. New York: St. Martin's Press.
1999a. *Consolidating Democracy: South Africa's Second Popular Election*. Johannesburg, South Africa: Witwatersrand Unibersity Press.
1999b. *South African Politics Since 1994*. Cape Town: David Phillip Publishers.
Lodge, Tom. 2003. "DA Raises Its Profile in Black Townships." *Focus* 32. Johannesburg: Helen Suzman Foundation.
"Parties not People: An Opinion Piece." EISA *Election Update* 2004 3, 1 March 2004.
2005. "The African National Congress: There Is No Party Like It; Ayikho Efana Nayo." In *Electoral Politics in South Africa: Assessing the First Democratic Decade*, edited by Jessica Piombo and Lia Nijzink. New York: Palgrave.
Lodge, Tom, and Bill Nasson. 1991. *All Here and Now: Black Politics in South Africa in the 1980s*. London: C. Hurst and Company.
Lombard, Edwin, and S ' Thembiso Msomi, "Leon 'the Ultimate Prima Donna,' says Van Schalkwyk." *Sunday Times*, February 22, 2004.
Loock, Steve. 1999. "Opposition Parties Slam Registration." *Citizen*, February 1.
Lupia, Arthur, and Mathew McCubbins. 1998. *The Democratic Dilemma: Can Citizens Learn What They Need to Know?* Cambridge: Cambridge University Press.

Lyne, Mona M. 2007. "Rethinking Economics and Institutions: The Voter's Dilemma and Democratic Accountability." In *Patrons, Clients, and Politics: Patterns of Democratic Accountability and Political Competition*, edited by Herbert Kitschelt and Steven I. Wilkinson. New York: Cambridge University Press.
Mabanga, Thebe. 2009. "Party Poopers." *Financial Mail*, February 20, 2009.
Magaloni, Beatriz. 2006. *Voting for Autocracy: Hegemonic Party Survival and Its Demise in Mexico*. Cambridge: Cambridge University Press.
Magaloni, Beatriz, Alberto Diaz-Cayeros, and Federico Estévez. 2007. "Clientelism and Portfolio Diversification: A Model of Electoral Investment with Application to Mexico." In *Patrons, Clients, and Politics: Patterns of Democratic Accountability and Political Competition*, edited by Herbert Kitschelt and Steven I. Wilkinson. New York: Cambridge University Press.
*Mail & Guardian Online*. 2007a. "Report card: Cabinet Ministers from A to G." 21 December.
*Mail & Guardian Online*. 2007b. "Rebellion at Polokwane." 17 December.
*Mail & Guardian Online*. 2007c. "Zuma vs Mbeki: Battle Lines Drawn." 23 December.
*Mail & Guardian Online*. 2007d. "COSATU Condemns Zuma indictment." 29 December.
*Mail & Guardian Online*. 2008a. "Ngonyama Resigns from the ANC over 'disrespect.'" November 13.
*Mail & Guardian Online*. 2008b. "'ANC Must Go Back to the masses.'" 12 February.
*Mail & Guardian Online*. 2008c. "Let the Courts Decide on Zuma, Say Top Legal Minds." January 5.
*Mail & Guardian Online*. 2008d. "ANC Stands by Zuma Despite Charges." January 8.
*Mail & Guardian Online*. 2008e. "Court Decides in Hlophe's Favour." September 26.
*Mail & Guardian Online*. 2008f. "Cops to Beef Up Security for Zuma's Court Appearance." September 10.
*Mail & Guardian Online*. 2008. "Cope: Public Service Should Be Depoliticized." December 11.
*Mail & Guardian Online*. 2008g. "Round One to Zuma." September 12.
*Mail & Guardian Online*. 2008h. "Deal? No Deal!" August 22.
*Mail & Guardian Online*. 2008i. "Meet the COP: Dissidents Finally Settle on Party Name." November 7.
*Mail & Guardian Online*. 2008j. "Cope Clarifies Position on Affirmative Action." December 18.
*Mail & Guardian Online*. 2008k. "Battle Lines Drawn for 2009 Poll. December 16.
*Mail & Guardian Online*. 2008l. "Black Lawyers Say Lekota a 'Threat' to Empowerment." December 17.
*Mail & Guardian Online*. 2009a. "An Election Year Budget." February 13.
*Mail & Guardian Online*. 2009b. "ANC Spends R200-Million on Election Campaign." April 17.
*Mail & Guardian Online*. 2009c. "Lekota Says Cope Won't Tolerate Cronyism." February 24.
*Mail & Guardian Online*. 2009d. "'Cope Is Like the ANC by Father Joined." January 24.
*Mail & Guardian Online*. 2009e. "Cope's New Leader in Stark Contrast to Zuma." February 24.
*Mail & Guardian Online*. 2009f. "Mpshe: Zuma Decision Not an Acquittal." April 6.
*Mail & Guardian Online*. 2009g. "NPA Drops Corruption Charges against Zuma." *Mail & Guardian Online*

*Mail & Guardian Online.* 2009h. "NPA Confirms Correspondence from Zuma's Lawyers." January 13.
*Mail & Guardian Online.* 2009i. "Malema: NPA Must Drop Zuma Charges." January 15.
*Mail & Guardian Online.* 2009j. "Trengove: Zuma Decision 'Tipping Point.'" April 16.
*Mail & Guardian Online.* 2009k. "Cope: South Africans Must Elect Their President." January 30.
*Mail & Guardian Online.* 2009l. "Dandala Tours Soweto." April 9.
*Mail & Guardian Online.* 2009m. "Cope Struggles to Win Support." April 16.
*Mail & Guardian Online.* 2009n. "Cope Unveils Election Posters." March 13.
*Mail & Guardian Online.* 2009o. "Cope Faltering, ANC Going Strong." March 14.
*Mail & Guardian Online.* 2009p. "'Parties Failed to Push the Zuma Factor.'" April 21.
*Mail & Guardian* Mataboge, Mmanaledi. 2009. "Who's Hot, Who's Not." *Mail & Guardian Online*, February 22, 2009.
Makgotho, Selby. 2004. "Crowds Besiege Mbeki in Limpopo." *Sowetan*, March 29.
Makhado, Khangale. 2004. "Shilowa Says Critics Have Short Memories." *Sowetan*, March 8.
Makhanya, Mondii. 2009. "ANC's Election Campaign a Triumph of Getting Down and Funking It Up." *The Sunday Times*, April 4, 2009.
Makhura, David. 2004. "Ready to Market, Not Ready to Govern." *This Day*, March 17.
Malala, Justice. 1999. "Mbeki Close to Tears," *Sunday Times*, May 16.
Malefane, Pule. "DA Doesn't Support Workers." *City Press*, March 7, 2004
Maloka, Eddy. 2004. "More Subtle, but Racist All the Same." *Sowetan*, March 8.
Mandela, Nelson. 1995. *Long Walk to Freedom*. Boston: Little, Brown and Company.
Mandela, Nelson. 1996. "Citizens of a Single Rainbow Nation." In *Now That We are Free: Coloured Communities in a Democratic South Africa*, edited by Wilmot James, Daria Caliguire and Kerry Cullinan, Cape Town: Idasa.
Manning, Carrie. 2008. *The Making of Democrats: Elections and Party Development in Postwar Bosnia, El Salvador, and Mozambique*. New York: Palgrave Macmillan.
Manson, A., N. Roos, and J. Self. 1999a. "North West Province." EISA *Election Update* 99, No. 6, February.
1999b. "North West Province." EISA *Election Update* 99, No. 8, March 12.
Manuel, Trevor. 1998. "National Budget Speech." Delivered to Parliament, 11 March 1998.
Marais, Peter. 1996. "Too Long in the Twilight." In *Now That We Are Free: Coloured Communities in a Democratic South Africa*, edited by Wilmot James, Daria Caliguire, and Kerry Cullinan. Cape Town: Idasa.
Mare, Gerhard. 1999. "The Inkatha Freedom Party." In *Election '99 South Africa: From Mandela to Mbeki*, edited by Andrew Reynolds. New York: St. Martin's Press.
Marx, Anthony. 1992. *Lessons of Struggle: South African Internal Opposition, 1960–1990*. New York: Oxford University Press.
Mataboge, Mmanaledi. 2009. "On the Train with Mvume Dandala." *Mail & Guardian Online*, April 1, 2009.
Mataboge, Mmanaledi, Mandy Rossouw, and Matuma Letsoalo, 2009. "What the ANC's Victory Means." *Mail & Guardian Onlie*, April 17.
Mattes, Robert. 1995. *The Election Book: Judgement and Choice in South Africa's 1994 Election*. Cape Town: Idasa.

2005. "Voter Information, Government Evaluations, and Party Images in the First Democratic Decade." In *Electoral Politics in South Africa: Assessing the First Democratic Decade*, edited by Jessica Piombo and Lia Nijzink. New York: Palgrave.

Mattes, Robert, and Cherrel Africa. 1999. "The Opposition (II)." *Opinion '99*, press release, May 24.

Mattes, Robert and Jessica Piombo. 2001. "Opposition Parties and the Voters in South Africa's General Election of 1999," *Democratization* 8, 3, Autumn: 101–128.

Mattes, Robert, Hermann Giliomee, and Wilmot James. 1996. "The Election in the Western Cape." In *Launching Democracy in South Africa: The First Open Election, April 1994*, edited by R. W. Johnson and Lawrence Schlemmer. New Haven, CT: Yale University Press.

Mattes, Robert, Helen Taylor, and Cherrel Africa. 1999. "Public Opinion & Voter Preferences: 1994–1999. In *Election '99 South Africa: From Mandela to Mbeki*, edited by Andrew Reynolds. New York: St. Martin's Press.

Mbaya, Kennedy. 2004. "The Use of State Resources during Elections in South Africa." In *The politics of State Resources: Party Funding in South Africa*, edited by Khabele Matlosa. Johannesburg: Konrad-Adenauer-Stiftung Occasional Papers.

Mboyane, Sphiwe. "Mbeki Puts on Caring, Human Face for Voters." *Business Day*, April 6, 2004.

McGreal, Chris. 2008. "Mbeki Fights for Survival after Zuma's Showdown." *Mail & Guardian Online*, September 15 2008.

Mdhlela, Joe. 1999. "ANC in R2.1m Poll Drive." *Sowetan*, 28 January.

Medina, Luis Fernando and Susan C. Stokes. 2007. "Monopoly and Monitoring: An Approach to Political Clientelism." In *Patrons, Clients, and Politics: Patterns of Democratic Accountability and Political Competition*, edited by Herbert Kitschelt and Steven I. Wilkinson. New York: Cambridge University Press.

Mendelberg, Tali. 2001. *The Race Card: Campaign Strategy, Implicit Messages, and the Norm of Equality*. Princeton, NJ: Princeton University Press.

Merten, Marianne. 2004. "DA to 'Take on the ANC in Its Own Backyard'." *Mail and Guardian*, January 9, 2004.

Metz, David Haywood, and Katherine Tate. 1995. "The Color of Urban Campaigns." In *Classifying by Race*, edited by Paul E. Peterson. Princeton, NJ: Princeton University Press.

Misbach, Waghled. "NNP Only Rainbow Party in SA." *Sowetan*, February 23, 2004.

Mkhabela, Mpumelelo. 2004a. "Mbeki on Harsh Soil in Election Walkabout." *City Press*, March 7.

2004b. "Poor Won't Rebel – Mbeki." *City Press*, February 22.

2004c. "Mbeki Faces Critics on Campaign Trail," *City Press*, March 14.

Mohau, Nkululeko Kaizer. "The APF Misleads the People." *City Press*, February 22, 2004.

Molinar Horcasitas, Juan. 1996. "Changing the Balance of Power in a Hegemonic Party System: the Case of Mexico." In Arendt Lijphart and Carlos Waisman (eds.), *Institutional Design in New Democracies: Eastern Europe and Latin America*. Boulder, Colorado: Westview Press.

Monare, Moshoeshoe. "Whites Using 'Swaart Gevaar' Tactics, Says Mbeki." *Sunday Independent*, March 7, 2004.

Moodley, Nashen. 1999. "Parties Appeal to Indian Fears." *Mail and Guardian*, May 28:6.
Motsepe, Cecil. "Tony Leon's Soweto Boo-Boo." *The Sowetan*, March 23, 2004.
Msomi, S ' Thembiso. "The DA Bops to Afropop." *Sunday Times*, March 14, 2004.
Msomi, S' Thembiso, Sabelo Ndlangisa and Bongani Mththwa, "Mbeki, Buthelezi Savage Each Other in Poll War." *Sunday Times*, March 28, 2004.
Müller, J. J., Fanie Cloete, William Fox, Kobus Müller, Erwin Schwella, Frederik Uys, and Andries van Rooyen. 1997. "Civil Service Systems in Comparative Perspective. South Africa: a Country Study." Paper presented at *Civil Service Systems in Comparative Perspective*, a conference held at the School of Public and Environmental Affairs, Indiana University, Bloomington, Indiana, April 5–8, 1997.
Müller, Wolfgang C,. and Kaare Strøm, eds. 1999. *Policy, Office, or Votes: How Political Parties in Western Europe Make Hard Decisions*. Cambridge: Cambridge University Press.
Muth, Tim. 2008. "Armed Groups." Commentary in blog for Thursday, December 18, 2008. http://luterano.blogspot.com/2008/12/armed-groups.html.
Myburgh, James. 2003. "Floor Crossing Adds New Muscle to ANC." *Focus* 30 2003.
*Natal Witness*. 1999. "DP and New NP lash out at Mandela's 'racist' speech," March 10.
Ndlangisa, Sabelo. 2004. "Mpumalanga List Surprise." *Sunday Times*, February 29, 2004.
Ndletyana, Mcebisi. 2007. "Municipal Elections 2006: Protests, Independent Candidates, and Cross-Border Municipalities." In *State of the Nation South Africa 2007*, edited by Sakhela Buhlungu, John Daniel, Roger Southall, and Jessica Lutchman. Cape Town: Human Science Research Council Press.
Norris, Pippa. 1996. "The Impact of Electoral Reform on Women's Representation." *Acta Politica*. 41(2), July 1996: 197–213.
  2004. *Electoral Engineering: Voting Rule and Political Behavior*. Cambridge: Cambridge University Press.
Nqayi, Zolile. 1999. "ANC Benefits from Defections," *City Press*, April 11.
Nzimande, Blade. 2006. "Red Alert: ANC National General Council: An Important Turning Point." *Umsebenzi Online*, South African Communist Party website. Accessed July 31, 2009. http://www.sacp.org.za/main.php?include=pubs/umsebenzi/2005/no38.html
O'Grady, Kevin, Rob Rose, and Sphiwe Mboyane. 2004. "Vindication or the Scrapheap for Opposition DA." *Business Day*, April 13.
Padayachee, Marlan. 1999. "Mbeki Engages in Battle of Words to Secure Indian Vote," *The Sunday Independent*, May 30: 8.
Paton, Carol. 1999a. "Fighting the Losing Battle." *Sunday Times*, February 14.
  1999b. "Dissenting Adults in Unlikely Love Match Etched in Venom," *Sunday Times*, May 2.
  2009. "The Nation Has Spoken." *Financial Mail*, May 1, 2009.
Paton, Carol, and Henry Ludski. 1998. "Shock Figures in Voting Debacle." *Sunday Times*, November 29.
Patterson, Samuel C., and Gregory A. Caldeira. 1983. "Getting Out the Vote: Participation in Gubernatorial Elections." *American Political Science Review*. 77(3): 675–689.
Pempel, T. J. 1990. "Introduction." In *Uncommon Democracies: the One-Party Dominant Regimes*, edited by T. J. Pempel. Ithaca: Cornell University Press.

Perry, Alex. "South Africa Looks for a Leader." *Time* April 27, 2009.
Perry, Dan. 2008. "Zuma's Charm Offensive in Davos." *Mail & Guardian Online*, January 27, 2008.
Phanlane, Charles. 1999. "More Defections from NNP to Ruling Party," *Star*, April 20.
   2004a. "Postman Thabo's Delivery a Hit in Pretoria." *The Star*, March 9, 2004.
   2004b. "IFP-ANC Debate Over Who Is Provoking Pre-Poll Violence." *The Star*, March 2, 2004.
Pillay, Devan. "Mirror, Mirror on the Wall, Is the ANC Tony Leon in Disguise?" *Sunday Times*, February 29, 2004.
Piombo, Jessica. 1999. "The UCDP, Minority Front, ACDP and Federal Alliance." In *Election '99 South Africa: From Mandela to Mbeki*, edited by Andrew Reynolds. New York: St. Martin's Press.
Piombo, Jessica, and Lia Nijzink, eds. 2005. *Electoral Politics in South Africa: Assessing the First Democratic Decade*. New York: Palgrave.
Piper, Laurence. 2002. "Nationalism without a Nation: The Rise and Fall of Zulu Nationalism in South Africa's Transition to Democracy, 1975–1999." *Nations and Nationalism*, 8(1): 73–94.
   2005. "The Inkatha Freedom Party: Between the Impossible and the Ineffective." In *Electoral Politics in South Africa: Assessing the First Democratic Decade*, edited by Jessica Piomobo and Lia Nijzink. London: Palgrave.
Pityana, Sipho M. 2008. "A 'Political Deal': Let's Consider the Options." *Mail & Guardian Online*, September 12 2008.
Popkin, Samuel. 1991. *The Reasoning Voter: Communication and Persuasion in Presidential Campaigns*. Chicago: University of Chicago Press.
Posner, Daniel. 2005. *Institutions and Identities: Regime Change and Ethnic Cleavages in Africa*. Cambridge: Cambridge University Press.
Powers, Cathy, and Rapule Tabane. 1999. "Freedom Day a Convenient Election Platform." *Star*, April 27.
Rabushka, Alvin, and Kenneth Shepsle. 1972. *Politics in Plural Societies: A Theory of Democratic Instability*. Columbus, OH: Charles E. Merrill.
Radebe, Hopewell. "ANC Women Beat Quotas on Poll Lists." *Business Day*, March 15, 2004.
Rakosa, Paseka. "DA Must Approach Issues Differently," letter to the editor, *Soweten*, March 11, 2004.
Ramseyer, J. Mark, and Rosenbluth, Frances M. 1993. *Japan's Political Marketplace*. Cambridge, MA: Harvard University Press.
Randall, Duncan. 1998. "The 1996 Municipal Election in KwaZulu-Natal: An Eyewitness Account." *Politikon*, 25(1): 103–128.
Randall, Estelle. 1999. "Manuel's Manual Electioneering Brings Home the Bacon," *The Sunday Independent*, May 30: 4.
Ray, Malcolm. 1999. "Here's the Final Countdown." *Sowetan*, 28 May.
Reilly, Ben. 2001. *Democracy in Divided Societies: Electoral Engineering for Conflict Management*. Cambridge: Cambridge University Press.
Reilly, Ben, and Andrew Reynolds. 1999. *Electoral Systems and Conflict in Divided Societies*. Washington, DC: National Academy Press.
Republic of South Africa. 2000. "The State of Representativeness in the Public Service." Pretoria: Public Service Commission.
   2005. "Provincial Budgets and Expenditure Review: 2001/02–2007/08. Pretoria: National Treasury, September 2005.

2006. "State of the Public Service Report 2006: Assessing the Capacity of the State to Deliver." Pretoria: Public Service Commission.
2007. "Provincial Budgets and Expenditure Review: 2003/04–2009/10. Pretoria: National Treasury, September 2007.
ed. 1994. *Election '94 South Africa: The Campaigns, Results, and Future Prospects.* New York: St. Martin's Press.
ed. 1999a. *Election '99 South Africa: From Mandela to Mbeki.* New York: St. Martin's Press.
1999b. *Electoral Systems and Democratization in Southern Africa.* Oxford: Oxford University Press.
ed. 2002. *The Architecture of Democracy: Constitutional Design, Conflict Management, and Democracy.* Oxford: Oxford University Press.
Robins, Steve. 1999a. "The Northern Cape: Coloured Support of the ANC in Namaqualand." In EISA *Election Update 99*, 5, January 29.
1999b. "Northern Cape." In EISA *Election Update '99*, 7, February 26.
Robinson, James A. and Thierry Verdier. 2002. "The Political Economy of Clientelism." February 2002. CEPR Discussion Paper No. 3205.
Robinson, Vicki. 2007. "ANC Chiefs Meet on Mbeki Third Term." *Mail and Guardian*, May 4, 2007.
2004. "Weary of Warfare." *Mail and Guardian*, February 27, 2004.
Robinson, Vicki and Stefaans Brümmer, 2006. "SA Democracy Incorporated: Corporate fronts and political party funding." Institute for Security Studies Paper 129, November 2006.
Rose, Richard, and Ian McAllister. 1991, *The Loyalties of Voters.* London: Sage.
Rossouw, Mandy. 2008a. "Rolling Action for Zuma." 2008. *Mail & Guardian Online*, July 28.
2008b. "ANC Dumps Mbeki, Moves to Heal 'Rift.' *Mail & Guardian Online*, September 20.
2008c. "Lekota Serves 'Divorce Papers' on ANC." *Mail & Guardian Online*, October 8.
2009. "MPs Sweat over Jobs." *Mail & Guardian Online*, February 22.
Rossouw, Mandy, and Mmanaldi Mataboge. 2009a. "How Terror Lost Cope." *Mail & Guardian Online*, February 27, 2009.
2009b. "No Campaign, No Votes." *Mail & Guardian Online*, March.
Rossouw, Mandy, and Rapule Tabane. 2008. "Business Wants a Political Solution." *Mail & Guardian Online*, August 22.
Rostron, Bryan. "But for the Accident of Pigment." *This Day*, March 8, 2004.
Rule, Stephen. 2004. "Motivations Behind Voting Behaviour in South Africa." *Electionsynopsis* 1(2): 7–9.
Sartori, Giovanni. 1976. *Parties and Party Systems: A Framework for Analysis.* Cambridge: Cambridge University Press.
Scheiner, Ethan. 2006. *Democracy without Competition in Japan: Opposition Failure in a One-Party Dominant State.* Cambridge: Cambridge University Press.
Schoonakker, Bonny. "Battle Looms as Parties View for 'Cape Soweto.'" *Sunday Times*, March 7, 2004.
Seekings, Jeremy. 1996. "From Independence to Identification." In *Now That We Are Free: Coloured Communities in a Democratic South Africa*, edited by Wilmot James, Daria Caliguire, and Kerry Cullinan. Cape Town: Idasa.
Seekings, Jeremy, and Nicoli Nattrass. 2002. "Class, Distribution and Redistribution in Post-Apartheid South Africa." *Transformation* 50.

Seepe, Sipho. "Mbeki no Match for Leon." *Sowetan Times*, March 4, 2004.
Sepotokele, Themba. 1999. "Political Parties Do Battle in Soweto." *Star*, April 6.
Seremane, Joe. 2004. "Nobody Cares What Azapo Says – It Has Nothing to Offer." Letter to the Editor, *The Star*, February 24.
Shalev, Michael. 1990. "The Political Economy of Labor-Party Dominance and Decline in Israel." In *Uncommon Democracies: the One-Party Dominant Regimes*, edited by T.J. Pempel. Ithaca: Cornell University Press.
Shefter, Martin. 1977. "Party and Patronage: Germany, England, and Italy," *Politics and Society* 7: 403–51.
    1994. *Political Parties and the State: the American Historical Experience*. Princeton: Princeton University Press.
Shugart, Matthew. 1999. "Presidentlialism, Parliamentarism, and the Provisions of Collective Goods in Less-Developed Countries." *Constitutional Political Economy* 10: 53–88.
Siegfried, Kristy. "Leaders Laud Woman with Loads of Love." *The Star*, March 26, 2004.
Sigelman, Carol K., Lee Sigelman, Barbara J. Walkosz, and Michael Nitz. 1995. "Black Candidates, White Voters: Understanding Racial Bias in Political Perceptions." *American Journal of Political Science* 39(1): 243–265.
Simao, Paul. 2008. "Cope Unlikely to Alter Economic Agenda." *Mail & Guardian Online*, December 7 2008.
Sisk, Timothy D., and Andrew Reynolds. 1998. *Elections and Conflict Management in Africa*. Washington, DC: United States Institute of Peace Press.
Sitas, Ari. 1986. "Inanda, August 1985: 'Where Wealth and Power and Blood Reign Worshipped Gods.'" *Southern African Labour Bulletin* 11(4): 85–21.
Smith, David. 2009. "Jacob Zuma the Chameleon Brings South Africans Joy and Fear." *Mail & Guardian Online*. April 20 2009.
Smith, Giles. 2008. "Sit-Ins and Picketing in KZN." *Mail & Guardian Online*, September 2 2008.
Sniderman, Paul M., and Edward G. Carmines. 1997. *Reaching Beyond Race*. Cambridge MA: Harvard University Press.
Snyder, Jack. 2000. *From Voting to Violence: Democratization and Nationalist Conflict*. New York: W.W. Norton and Company.
Snyder, James, and Michael Ting. 2002. "An Informational Rationale for Political Parties." *American Journal of Political Science* 46(1):90–110.
Sole, Sam, and Adriaan Basson. 2008. "Zuma's Lawyers Open New Front." *Mail & Guardian Online*, June 27 2008.
Southall, Roger. 1999a. "Eastern Cape." In EISA *Election Update* 99, No. 4, January 15.
    1999b. "Eastern Cape." In EISA *Election Update* 99, No. 7, February 26.
    1999c. "Eastern Cape." In EISA *Election Update* 99, No. 8, March 12.
    2007. "The ANC State, More Dysfunctional Than Developmental?" In *State of the Nation South Africa 2007*, edited by Sakhela Buhlungu, John Daniel, Roger Southall, and Jessica Lutchman. Cape Town: Human Science Research Council Press.
*Sowetan*. 2004. "'Remember the Suffering.'" March 23, 2004.
Squires, J. Judgment for "The State versus Schabir Shaik and 11 Others," Case Number CC27/04, 31 May 2005, The High Court of South Africa, Durban and Coast Local Division Durban.

Stahler-Sholk, Richard. 1994. "El Salvador's Negotiated Transition: From Low-Intensity Conflict to Low-Intensity Democracy." *Journal of Interamerican Studies and World Affairs* 36(4), Winter 1994: 1–59.
Star. 1999a. "Racial-Quota Policy Smacks of Discrimination, Says Leon," April 8.
   1999b. "ANC, DP and Their War of Posters," May 6.
   1999c. "Mandela Lambasts Opposition Parties," May 19.
   1999d. "Mandela Thanks Fismer for Support," May 20.
   1999e. "Mandela Tells Coloured Community to Be Proud," May 27: 7.
   2004. "Leon Sets Sights on Labour Laws." March 11, 2004.
   2004 "Buthelezi Berates ANC over Its HIV/Aids Policy." March 9, 2004.
Statistics South Africa. 2006. "Mid-year Population Estimates, South Africa." Statistical Release P0302. Pretoria: Statistics South Africa.
Steytler, Nico. 2004. "The Legislative Framework Governing Party Funding in South Africa." In *The politics of state resources: Party funding in South Africa*, edited by Khabele Matlosa. Johannesburg: Konrad-Adenauer-Stiftung Occasional Papers.
Stokes, Susan, ed. 2001. *Public Support for Market Reforms in New Democracies*. New York: Cambridge University Press.
Stokes, Susan. 2005. "Perverse Accountability: A Formal Model of Machine Politics with Evidence from Argentina." *American Political Science Review* 99(3): 315–326.
Stolley, Giordano. 2008a. "Zuma Charges: NPA Denies Political Interference." *Mail & Guardian Online*, January 2.
   2008b. "Hlophe Accused Of Zuma Interference." *Mail & Guardian Online*, May 30.
Strøm, Kaare, Wolfgang C. Müller, and Torbjörn Bergman, eds. 2003. *Delegation and Accountability in Parliamentary Democracies*. Oxford: Oxford University Press.
*Sunday Times*. 1999. "Election Watch: Shilowa lashes out at DP," May 2.
*Sunday Times*. 2004. The Good, the Bad, and the Redeployed." March 21 2004.
Suzman, Helen. 1993. *In No Uncertain Terms: A South African Memoir*. New York: Knopf.
Tabane, Rapule. 1999a. "Mbeki Turns on the Charm as ANC Goes All Out to Keep Gauteng." *Star*, January 8.
   1999b. "Mbeki Sets the Tone in Build-Up to Registration." *Star*, January 9.
   2004a. "'There Is No Secret to Our Success.'" *Mail and Guardian*, April 2–7.
   2004b. "ANC Targets Mlungu Vote," *Mail and Guardian*, January 23.
   2004c. "Squeeze + Spin = 30%." *Mail and Guardian*, April 7.
   2004d. "DA Wracked by Racial Tensions." *Mail and Guardian*, March 12, 2004.
   2009. "How Cope Lost It." *Mail & Guardian Online*, April 24, 2009.
Tabane, Rapule, and Hopewell Radebe. 1999. "Dismal Turnout of Teen Voters Spurs Youth Groups into Action." *Star*, January 7.
Tabane, Rapule, and Frank Wegner. 1999. "Parties Far Apart on Creating Jobs." *Star*, April 9.
Taylor, Helen, and Robert Mattes. 1999. "The Public Agenda (IV)," press release from *Opinion99*, 24 May 1999
Taylor, Helen, Robert Mattes, and Cherrel Africa. 1999. "Party Support and Voting Intention (IV)." *Opinion99*, press release, May 24.
ter Horst, Peter. 1999. "A Constituency Changes Its Colours," *Star*, June 1:17.
Terkildsen, Nayda. 1993. "When White Voters Evaluate Black Candidates: the Processing Implications of Candidate Skin Color, Prejudice, and Self-Monitoring." *American Journal of Political Science* 37(4): 1032–1053.

Terreblanche, Christelle. 2004. "Tony Leon Accuses ANC of Corruption." *The Star*, March 19.
*This Day*. 2004a. "Digging for Gauteng's Pot of Gold." March 31.
*This Day*. 2004b. "Leon Uses Army-Style Campaign Tactics, Says ANC." March 24.
Thom, Anso, and Clive Sawyer. 1998. "IEC Struggling." *Star*, November 23.
Thompson, Leonard. 1990. *A History of South Africa*. New Haven, CT: Yale University Press.
Tleane, Console. 2004. "DA Reveals Its Racist Attitude." *City Press*, March 7.
Tolsi, Niren. 2008. "JZ's Backers Are Like Bad Songs ..." *Mail & Guardian Online*, August 10.
 2009a. "Mantashe: Zuma's Prosecution Is an Attack on ANC." *Mail & Guardian Online*, February 4.
 2009b. "The Cult of Zuma." *Mail & Guardian Online*, March 6.
Tomz, Michael. 1998. CLARIFY: Software for Presenting and Interpreting Statistical Results. Version 1.0. Cambridge MA: Harvard University, August. http://gking.harvard.edu/.
Turkington, Tara. 1999. "ANC, NNP ready to lead N Cape," *Mail and Guardian*, May 28.
van de Walle, Nicolas. 2007. "Meet the New Boss, Same As The Old Boss? The Evolution Of Political Clientelism in Africa." In *Patrons, Clients, and Politics: Patterns of Democratic Accountability and Political Competition*, edited by Herbert Kitschelt and Steven I. Wilkinson. Cambridge: Cambridge University Press.
van der Vliet, Virginia. 2003. "Has Upcoming Poll Yielded Full Roll-Out?" *Focus* 32. Johannesburg: Helen Suzman Foundation.
van Niekerk, Phillip, and Barbara Ludman. 1999. *A-Z of South African Politics 1999: The Essential Handbook*. London: Penguin Books.
van Rooyen, Johann. 1994. "The White Right." In *Election '94 South Africa*, edited by Andrew Reynolds. New York: St. Martin's Press.
Vapi, Xolisa. "ANC Chases Afrikaner Voters in Brixton with Koeksister Politics." *This Day*, February 23, 2004.
Vavi, Zwelinzima. 2004a . "DA Does Not Care for Workers or Poor," *Sowetan*, March 9.
 2004b. "Vote in the Name of Struggle Heroes." *The Sowetan*, March 23.
wa Sepotokele, Themba, 2004. "ANC Slams Intimidation by IFP Followers in Gauteng." *Cape Times* March 16 2004.
Wade, Christine. 2008. "El Salvador: The Success of the FMLN." In *From Soldiers to Politicians: Transforming Rebel Movement After Civil War*, edited by Jeroen de Zeeuw. Boulder: Lynne Rienner Publishers.
Waldner, Mariechen. 2004a. "How to Catch a Boer for the ANC." *City Press*, April 11.
 2004b. "NNP Still Alive, Says Korbroek." *City Press*, March 7.
Walshe, Peter. 1987. *The Rise of African Nationalism in South Africa: The African National Congress, 1912–52*. London: AD. Donker.
*Weekly Mail & Guardian*. 1996. February 2.
*Weekly Mail & Guardian*. 1999a. "At the End of the Rainbow," March 12.
*Weekly Mail & Guardian*. 1999b. "Abuse Deeply Rooted in Land," July 30.
*Weekly Mail & Guardian*. 2000. "'Racisim Didn't Die in 1994: It Is a Growing Problem,'" December 22.

Welsh, David. 1994. "The Democratic Party." In *Election '94 South Africa*, edited by Andrew Reynolds. New York: St. Martin's Press.

   1999. "The Democratic Party." In *Election '99 South Africa: From Mandela to Mbeki*, edited by Andrew Reynolds. New York: St. Martin's Press.

Werth, Carl. 2004. "Be Careful What You Wish For." Letter to the Editor, *Mail and Guardian*, January 9.

Western, John. 1996. *Outcast Cape Town*. Berkeley: University of California Press.

Williams, Brian. 1996. "The Power of Propaganda." In *Now That We Are Free: Coloured Communities in a Democratic South Africa*, edited by Wilmot James, Daria Caliguire, and Kerry Cullinan. Cape Town: Idasa.

Wilson, Francis. 1971. *Labour in South African Gold Mines*. Cambridge: Cambridge University Press.

Wolfinger, Raymond E.. 1965. "The Development and Persistence of Ethnic Voting." *American Political Science Review* 59: 896–906.

Xayiya, Sobantu. 1994. "Cape of Great Gloom." *Democracy in Action* Volume 8(3).

# Index

NOTE: page numbers followed by n or t indicate notes or tables, respectively.

Abrajano, Marisa, 35, 39
affirmative action. *See also* policy issues
  ANC's Reconstruction and Development Plan on, 71
  Black Lawyer's Association on Lekota's views on, 217n
  Cope on ANC's policies regarding, 213
  divergence of white and black opinions on, 35
  DP on ANC policies' of, 94, 100
  as re-racializing South Africa, DP on ANC's policies of, 99–100
Africa, Cherrel, 36, 38–39
African candidates/politicians. *See also* African opposition parties; African voters; Africanization; Africans, in South Africa
  ANC monopoly on talent among, 23, 192
  ANC's monopoly on, opposition parties and, 240
  defections from NP by, 189
  list rankings of ANC, NP, and DP for 1999 and 2004 elections, 175
  loosening ANC's monopoly on, 241
  party-specific effects on retention of, 178, 179t
  retention patterns across South African parties, 175–176, 176t
  switching parties, 182–183
African Christian Democratic Party (ACDP), 4
African National Congress (ANC). *See also* Mandela, Nelson; Mbeki, Thabo; Zuma, Jacob
  African social mobilization prior to enfranchisement and, 11–12n
  African voter allegiances and, 5n, 9–10
  African voters, uncertain or cross-over voting and support for, 53–61, 55t, 62t
  African voters' uncertainty about, 1, 10
  as African vs. multiracial organization, 48
  Africans as captured constituency for, 9
  campaign against UDM by, 202–203
  campaign fundraising and spending by, 134–136
  campaign missteps in 1994 Western Cape by, 77–78
  campaign of 1994
    late strategies of, 78–79
    lessons learned by, 80
    national strategies in, 70–71
    party image after, 66
    party image in Western Cape for, 74–75
    persuasion in, 67–69
  campaign of 1999
    DP and NNP on performance record of, 101, 102
    DP's on racial campaigning by, 104–105
    for African voters by, 84–89
    for coloured voters by, 89–90
    for Indian voters by, 90
    NNP's negative campaigning against, 96
    performance record as issue in, 100–101
    persuasion by, 84–86
    racial campaigning in and performance record of, 105
    racial focus by, 102–104

263

African National Congress (ANC) (cont.)
  campaign of 2004
    attacks DA's image in, 126–129
    DA's rhetoric and competition with, 116–118
    events of, 113–116, 115t
    performance record as issue for, 123–126, 124–125n, 134t
    policies named by other parties and, 122t
    race and party images in, 122t, 126–133, 132t, 133t, 134t
    rhetoric on issues and policies by, 118–122, 120t
    rhetorical sparring partners for, 116t, 116–118
    types of rhetoric in, 133t
  campaign of 2009, campaign resources and events in, 218
  campaign resources available to IFP vs., 201
  on candidate characteristics' important to, 148–149
  candidate lists
    Indian views on Africanization and exclusivity of, 158–159, 159t
    racial balancing in, 151–152, 152t, 184
    racial scorecarding by, 145–146
    white and coloured views on Africanization and exclusivity of, 157–158, 158t
  candidate rank and retention by, 175–176, 176t, 178–179, 180t, 180–181
  candidate recruitment of Africans, 154t, 154–155
  candidate recruitment of coloureds and Indians, 166–167
  candidate retention by, racial effect of, 178, 179t
  candidates
    advancement on national list of, 184
    advancement on provincial lists of, 184–185
    of NP and DA poached by, 182–183
    poaching success by, 181t, 181–182
    presidential, Zuma vs. Mbeki as, 218
  on candidates for NP, Africans as, 187–188
  civil war with IFP and UDF in KwaZulu Natal, 195, 195n, 196n
  clientelism and macroeconomic policies of, 12–13, 13–14n
  Cope as splinter from, 23–24, 217n, 217–218
  Cope on potential defections from, 216, 216n
  core constituency size and loyalty and mobilization or persuasion by, 97–98
  on credibility of coloured or Indian participants in Tricameral Parliament, 165–166, 166n
  dominance without clientelism by, 26n, 28–29
  election of 1994
    party image change difficulties during, 80–81
    results for, 65–66
  election of 1999
    goals and results for, 82–83, 106
    goals for, 83–84
    manifesto of, 99, 100
    mobilization efforts by, 83, 86–89, 88n, 89n
  election of 2004
    NNP alliance with, 111
    results for, 107
  election of 2009
    framing of, 219–220
    manifesto of Cope vs., 213–214
  elections of 1994, 1999, and 2000, coding race of candidates for, 160–162
  elections of 1999 and 2004, list rankings of new, returning, and poached candidates for, 173t, 173–175, 174t, 191
  Holomisa's expulsion from, 202
  IFP as challenger to, 4
  IFP defections to, 199
  IFP's early alliance with, 194–195
  internal party dynamics and leaders leaving, 23–24
  leadership change at 2007 National Conference for, 207–208
  leadership succession from Mandela to Mbeki, 203–204
  legislative seat control by, 171–172, 172t
  local volunteers and branch structures for, 164–165
  media coverage of, 136–137, 137t
  monopoly on African political talent of, 23, 192
  Motlanthe on Mbeki's loss and revitalization of, 208
  National General Council on Zuma as Deputy President of, 206
  negative framing of IFP by, 199–201
  neutralizing Cope, methods available for, 242
  NP's image due to legalizing of, 20
  NP's leadership defections to, 188n, 188–189

# Index

opposition
 African, negative framing by, 194, 220–221
 negative framing by, 2, 19–20, 21, 222
 opposition parties' credibility and trustworthiness vs., 58–61
 opposition parties, micro African and, 193
 opposition party labels/images and, 17
 opposition party leadership recruitment and, 22
 parliamentary system and dominance by, 3–4
 partisan voters over time for, 42, 43t
 party image for voters of, 17–18
 party image, framing to appeal to IFP constituency by, 201–202
 party image, origins of, 47–49
 patronage and, 1–2
 political history and lack of clientelistic linkages to voters of, 11
 on political solution to Zuma's problems, 210–211
 positive achievements by, 7
 redistributive social spending by, 14, 14n
 responses to NP's negative Western Cape campaign by, 77
 splinter parties from, racial censuses and, 240
 strategies for dominance by, 3, 24
 unity governments and, 4n
African opposition parties. *See also* Cope; Inkatha Freedom Party; United Democratic Movement
 ANC's negative framing of, 220–221
 erosion of racial censuses and, 240
 importance of Cope's participation as, 241–242
 micro-, ANC response to, 193
African voters. *See also* African candidates/politicians; Africans, in South Africa
 as ANC captured constituency, 5n, 9
 ANC's 1999 campaign for, 84–89
 on ANC's policies and performance, 36
 campaign rhetoric by ANC vs. DA in 2004 to, 116–118
 Cope's alienation of, 217n, 217n
 DA's 2004 campaign events for, 112–113
 DA's 2004 targeting of, 108, 111
 diverse political identities among, 1, 10
 DP's 1999 campaign alienating, 92, 94
 DP's 1999 campaign belief as out of reach of, 92
 in Gauteng, ANC perception by, 91
 on government policies, 43–45, 44t
 ideological differentiation in South Africa by, 37n
 ideological links of parties to, 11–12n
 NNP's 1999 campaign for multiracialism and, 94–97
 NP courting during 1994 campaign of, 69–70, 72–73
 as NP supporters during 1994 election, 67–69
 NP's campaign appeals to, 20
 opposition parties' credibility/trustworthiness for, 58–59n, 58–61, 60t
 opposition parties' images among, 19
 opposition votes by, effect on ANC of, 3n
 parties voted for, 5
 party labels and choices by, 33
 performance evaluations and party images for, 53–61, 55t, 62t
 performance voting by, 45–46, 46t
Africanism, ANC's Freedom Charter on multiracialism vs., 47
Africanization
 of ANC candidate lists (1994–2004), 151–152
 of DP/DA candidate lists by 2004, 154, 157
 of NP candidate lists (1994–2004), 153
 by recruiting new candidates for ANC, NP, and DP, 154–155, 155t
Africans, in South Africa. *See also* African voters
 analyzing names for coding race of, 160–162
 ANC on criticism of ANC's performance as criticism of, 125
 as candidates, struggle credentials of, 165–166
 clashes in Western Cape with coloureds and Indians, 75–76
 DA's 2004 positioning its image to appeal to, 127n, 127–129
 definition of, 5n
 discontent with ANC's performance in Eastern Cape and, 84, 84n
 election of 1999 and, 82–83
 legacy of apartheid for, 38
 NP's multiracial message in 1994 and, 76–77
 in public service jobs, 13–14n
 views of political parties by, 51–53, 52t
Afrikaners. *See also* white South Africans; white voters
 as DP's target constituency in 1999 campaign, 92, 95–96
 National Party and, 49–50
 terms describing, 93n

*Afrobarometer* survey (2000). *See also* Idasa surveys
  characteristics of, 41n
  cross-over voting and uncertainty studies using, 54n
  on hypothetical policy differences, 43–45
  logit models of African vote choice, 63t
  on South African voter choices, 40–41
age
  African cross-over voting and uncertainty and (*Opinion99*), 54–55, 55t, 62t
  credibility and trustworthiness of South African opposition parties and, 58–61
  cross-over voting and, 56
  performance evaluations, voting decisions and, 58, 59t
age of candidates
  list rankings of ANC, NP, and DP for 1999 and 2004 elections, 175
  logit analysis of candidate retention patterns across South African parties and, 176–178, 177t, 179–180
  of new, returned, and poached candidates for 1999 and 2004 elections, 172–173, 173n
Ahdut Avoda (Israeli party), 225–226n. *See also* Labor Party
*Alatalena* affair, Israel (1940s), 227–228
Alvarez, R. Michael, 35, 39
Anti-Defection Clause, of South African Constitution, 182
apartheid. *See also* racial inequality
  ANC's 2004 rhetoric on its performance record and, 124–125n, 124–126
  ANC's roots in movement against, 47–48
  credibility of candidates associated with, 165–166, 166n
  IFP's 1994 image of association with, 196–197
  NNP as ruling party during, 17–18
  NP's distancing during campaigns from, 20
  NP's party image and association with, 49–50
  Progressive Party's opposition to, 50
  racial classifications due to, 37n, 37–38
  racial heuristics and legacy of, 38
Arab parties, Israel, 225–226n
ARENA (El Salvador's ruling party)
  electoral success from 1989 to 2004, 233
  FMLN's lack of credibility and, 29–30
  image presentation and control by, 233–234
  limiting FMLN's use of negative framing, 237–238
  negative framing of FMLN by, 223–224, 232
Aronoff, Myron J., 228–229
Arriola, Leonardo, 27
Asmal, Kadar, 85n, 90–91
Azanian Peoples Organization (Azapo), South Africa, 240

Barrell, Howard, 149–150
Bates, Robert, 35
Begin, Menachim, 227–228, 231
Ben-Gurion, David
  *Alatalena* affair and, 227–228
  Begin's resistance to German reparations and, 228
  as charismatic leader, 226
  Communist Party delegitimation by, 229–230n
  cooperation with Begin in National Unity Government, 231
  framing Herut's image by, 228
  as Labor leader, 227
  as prime minister, 225
"A Better Life for All" (ANC motto in 1994 election), 70–71
Bizos, George, 209n
Black Consciousness movement, African voting during 1970s and, 9
Black Economic Empowerment (BEE) companies, 135, 203–204, 213, 217
Black Lawyer's Association, South Africa, 217n
Boers, Joggie, 148–149
Boesak, Allan, 77–79
bonding events or rhetoric. *See also* rhetoric, campaign
  by ANC vs. DA in 2004, 116–118
  coding rules for, 109
  election of 2004 analysis of, 115t, 115–116
Booysen, Susan, 217n, 220
Borain, Nic, 147
Bosnia, census elections in, 25–26
Botha, Theuns, 127n, 127–129, 128n, 150–151, 168
Bratton, Michael, 36, 43–45
Breytenbach, Willie, 96–97, 100
bridging events or rhetoric. *See also* rhetoric, campaign
  by ANC vs. DA in 2004, 116–118
  coding rules for, 109
  election of 2004 analysis of, 115t, 115–116

# Index

Bruce, Nigel, 93
Brümmer, Stefaans, 135
Bullock, Charles III, 39
Bush administration, on Handal as El Salvador presidential candidate, 236
*Business Day* (newspaper), 108–109, 139
Buthelezi, Mangosuthu
   ANC's 2004 racial rhetoric and, 124–125, 125n
   on ANC's performance record and 2004 campaign, 124, 124n
   campaigning for 2004 African vote, 112–113
   early goals for IFP of, 194–195
   efforts to change IFP's image by, 194, 198
   Mandela's appointments to government positions for, 196
   Mbeki's racial rhetoric in 2004 against, 130–131
   Zwelithini and, 195
Butler, Anthony, 206n, 208

Calland, Richard, 90n, 146–147, 188
campaign activities. *See also* bonding events or rhetoric; bridging events or rhetoric
   electoral campaign analysis using, 109
campaign rhetoric. *See* rhetoric, campaign
campaign spending, 134–136, 135n.
   *See also* funding for campaigns
campaigns, electoral. *See also specific elections*
   ANC funding for, 3
   images of opposition parties during, 19
   negative framing of opposition by ANC during, 2
   as opportunities to change party labels, 80
   polarizing style with census-style elections, 7
   Popkin on party image during, 20
   themes in party label change efforts over time, 66
candidate demographics
   ANC on importance of racial and/or gender balance in, 148–149, 184, 185, 186
   ANC's racial scorecarding, 145–146
   coding party lists for 1994, 1999, and 2000 elections using, 151, 160–162
   DA's image change through changes in, 240–241
   of opposition parties during 1994 campaign, 149
   of opposition parties during 1999 campaign, 149–150
   of opposition parties during 2004 campaign, 150–151
   overview of South African party label change and, 144–145
   popular views of party labels and, 155–160
   preference effect and signaling effect of, 141
   racial balance of South African party lists and, 151–155, 152t, 153t, 154t, 155t, 160
   racial composition of DP lists, 147
   racial composition of NP/NNP lists, 146–147
   small parties, candidate quality and, 190–192
   South African discussions on racial balance of, 147–148
   undeveloped ideological labels, party labels and, 142n, 142–144
candidate pools. *See also* elite incorporation; new candidate recruits; poached candidates; political talent; returning candidates
   local and municipal councilors in South Africa and, 172
   NNP implosion after aggressive diversification of, 23
   racial diversification by opposition parties of, 2, 21–22
   for small opposition parties, 23
candidate quality. *See also* political talent
   elite incorporation problem and, 167n, 167–168
   elite incorporation theories and, 164
   internal and external dimensions of, 164–167
   of new recruits vs. poached or returning candidates, 171
   NP's diversification of candidate lists and, 187–188
   small political parties and, 168n, 168–170, 169–172n, 190–192
   struggle credentials, credibility of candidates and, 165–166, 166n
candidates. *See specific aspects of*, e.g. retention of candidates
*Cape Times*, 108–109, 139
Carmines, Edward G., 35
Cele, Bheki, 200
census elections. *See* racial censuses
Central American University Institute for Public Opinion, 234

Centre for Social Science Research, University of Cape Town, 38
Ceren, Salvador Sanchez, 236–237
Chalmers, Robyn, 147
Chandra, Kanchan
  on elite incorporation as intractable problem, 163
  on ethnic favoritism in "patronage democracies," 142–143
  on ethnic politics and clientelism, 11
  on ethnicity as informational shortcut for voters, 36, 36n
  on internal party structure and elite incorporation, 170, 186
  on parties with competitive vs. centralized rules for candidate advancement, 183–184
Chapúltepec Peace Accord (1992), 232
Charterist tradition, characteristics of, 47
Chaskalson, Arthur, 209n
Cherry, Janet, 147, 165
chiefs. See traditional leaders
Chikane, Frank, 87
Christians, Ferlon, 103
church leaders, ANC's 1999 voter registration campaigns and, 87
City Press, 108–109, 139
civil conflict. See also apartheid
  in Gauteng, South Africa, 195–196
  in Israel and El Salvador, 223–224
  in KwaZulu Natal, 195, 195n, 196n
Classen, Tom, 125–126
Clelland-Stokes, Nick, 20, 111, 113, 150–151
clientelism. See also patronage
  ANC dominance without use of, 28–29
  corruption vs., 16n
  as explanation for racial censuses, 10–16
  as explanation for single-party dominance, 26–27
  fraud and violence as supplemental to, 27–28
  image control and negative framing as alternatives to, 222
  mediation in Japan and Italy of, 11n
  public sector size as symptom of, 13n
  South Africa's economy and, 12
  South Africa's political institutions and political history and, 11, 11n
coding rules for content analysis, 109–111
Coetzee, Ryan, 130–131
coloured candidates/politicians.
  See also coloured South Africans; coloured voters

defections from NP by, 188–189
party-specific effects on retention of, 178, 179t
retention patterns across South African parties for, 175–176, 176t
switching parties by, 182–183
in Western and Northern Capes for NP, 187
coloured South Africans. See also coloured candidates/politicians
  African South African clashes with, 75–76
  analyzing names for coding race of, 160–162
  ANC at close of apartheid and, 47–48, 48n
  ANC's image for, 48
  apartheid legacy for, 37–38n, 38
  definition of, 5n
  on exclusivity of the ANC and Africanization of ANC's candidate lists, 157–158, 158t
  as middlemen minorities, 38
  as NP candidates in 1999, 149–150
  Tricameral Parliament participation and credentials as ANC or UDF candidates of, 165–166, 166n
  views of political parties by, 51–53, 52t
coloured voters. See also coloured candidates/politicians
  ANC polling for 1994 election on attitudes of, 68–69
  ANC's 1994 campaigning for, 78–79
  ANC's 1999 campaigning for, 89–90
  as DA supporters in South Africa, 5n
  DP's 1999 campaigning for, 92, 94
  on government policies, 43–45, 44t
  ideological differentiation in South Africa by, 37n
  Marais–Morkel conflict during NNP's 1999 campaign and, 96–97
  NP local branches and, 164–165
  NP's 1994 campaigning for, 69n, 69–70
  NP's campaign appeals to, 20
  NP's multiracial message in 1994 and, 76–77
  parties voted for, 5
  performance voting by, 45–46, 46t
comic book, in 1994 campaign by NP, 75
Communist Party, El Salvador. See Handal, Shafick
Communist Party (Maki), Israel, 225–226n, 229–230n
Communist Party, South Africa. See South African Communist Party

Index 269

Comparative National Elections Project (CNEP), South Africa, 5n, 40–41, 41n
competence. *See* performance
Congress of South African Trade Unions. *See* COSATU
Congress of the People (1955), 47. *See also* African National Congress
Congress of the People (party). *See* Cope
Constitutional Court, South Africa, 210, 210n
constitutional engineering. *See* electoral systems
content, electoral campaign. *See also* politics-as-usual issues
　ANC's performance record in 1999 campaign, 100–102
　campaign rhetoric and activities in 2004 as evidence of, 109
　of election of 1999, 98–99
　party images in 1999 campaign, 102–105
　policy issues in 1999 campaign, 99–100
content analysis. *See* newspaper content analysis of 2004 election
CONTRALESA (Congress of Traditional Leaders of South Africa), 85n
Cope (Congress of the People)
　ANC dominance over, 3
　ANC's negative framing of, 194, 220
　as ANC-splinter party, 23–24, 217n, 217–218
　campaign of 2009, as official opposition in Eastern Cape, 203
　campaign of 2009, slow roll-out by, 216–217
　challenges for success of, 24, 240
　Dandala as presidential candidate for, 214
　election manifesto of ANC vs., 213–214
　election of 2009 and, 215, 220
　electoral openness in South Africa and, 241–242
　formation by leaders who left the ANC, 23–24, 203
　internal tensions over Dandala's selection, 214–215
　as multiracial party, 2
　as opposition party, 4
　significance as ANC competitor, 193–194
　strategic campaign blunders by, 217
　structural challenges for, 215–216, 217n
　Western Cape by-elections and, 213, 213n
　Zuma-Mbeki leadership crisis and formation of, 212
corporate campaign contributors, 134–135

corruption. *See also* fraud
　under ANC rule in South Africa, 16n
COSATU (Congress of South African Trade Unions)
　ANC's 1999 persuasion campaign for African voters and, 85
　ANC's 1999 voter registration campaigns and, 87
　ANC's anti-apartheid movement and, 47–48
　ANC's labor market policies and alliance with, 121–122
　anti-apartheid ads for ANC's 1994 campaign and, 78–79
　on Cope as the "Black DA," 220
　DA's 2004 threats of legal action against, 127–129
　discontent with Mbeki's fiscal policies by, 205
　end of apartheid and, 9
　on NPA's indictment of Zuma, 209n, 209–210
　potential split from ANC by, 240
　Shilowa and, 212n
　support for Zuma by, 205–208, 206n
credibility, Ben-Gurion's, Begin's attempt to undermine, 228
credibility of candidates, struggle credentials, candidate quality and, 165–166, 166n
credibility of opposition parties
　ANC's racial campaigning in 1999 against, 102–104
　ANC's racist party labeling in 1999 campaign and, 105
　DP's response to racism in ANC's party labeling and, 104–105
　FMLN as contender for national office and, 234
　FMLN's presidential election win in 2009 and, 236–237
　locked-out, party image change and, 29n, 29–30
　in Mexico, 29n
　racial images of parties during 1994 election and, 66
　racialized party images, South African voting and, 33
　in South Africa, African voters' beliefs about, 58–59n, 58–61, 60t
crime policy in South Africa, racial differences in preferences about, 43–45, 45t
Cristiani, Alfredo, 237

cross-over voters
  as bell-wethers of change, 33
  performance evaluations and party images for, 53–61, 55t, 62t
  in South Africa, characteristics of, 40n
  survey sources for tests of, 40–41
  tests of racial heuristics in choices by, 40

Dandala, Mvume, 214, 217
D'Aubuisson, Roberto, 233, 237.
  *See also* ARENA
Davis, Gavin, 98n, 136n, 136–137
Dawson, Michael, 17, 36, 36n, 38–39, 239
de Beer, Sam, 148–149
de Klerk, F. W., 69–70, 73–74, 76–77, 130–131
de Lille, Patricia, 107, 239, 241n.
  *See also* Independent Democrats
de Wet, Boetie, 189
Delft, South Africa, housing take-overs (1993) in
  ANC response to, 78
  NP response to, 75–76
Delport, Tertius, 93, 189
democracy. *See also* single-party-dominance states
  consensual, Lijphart on identity voting and, 8
  fixed majorities and, 5
  opposition parties in South Africa and, 7
  predominant party or uncommon types of, 26n
  prospects in ethnically-divided countries for, 25–26
Democratic Alliance (DA).
  *See also* Democratic Party; Democratic Party/Democratic Alliance; Leon, Tony
  advantages over any new party of, 240
  as ANC alternative, 24
  ANC voters and, goals for converting to, 7
  on ANC's performance record, racial rhetoric in, 124–125
  campaign fundraising and spending by, 134–135
  campaign of 2004
    ANC's rhetoric and competition with, 116–118, 130–131
    events in, 112n, 112–113, 113n, 115t, 115–116
    IFP's coalition with, 111, 198, 241n
    on ANC's performance record, 124
    policies named by other parties and, 122t
    rhetorical sparring partners for, 116t
  campaign of 2009, ANC's linking Cope to, 219
  campaign rhetoric of 2004
    bridging, 117–118n
    on issues and policies, 120t
    racial, 129–133, 133t, 134t
    types about, 133t
  candidate list racial balancing for 2004 election, 150–151
  on candidate quality and elite incorporation problem, 168
  candidate switching with ANC, 182–183
  Cope alliance with, potential in, 241
  demographics of supporters for, 5n
  election of 2004, voting results, 107
  election of 2009 and, 215
  formation of, 4n
  legislative seats controlled by, 171–172, 172t
  local volunteers and branch structures for, 164–165
  media coverage of, 136–137, 137t
  public opinion on image over time of, 199n
Democratic Movement for Change (DMC), Israel, 230n
Democratic Party (DP). *See also* Democratic Alliance; Democratic Party/Democratic Alliance; Leon, Tony
  ANC and post-apartheid party labels/images of, 17
  ANC's leaders' mocking references to, 90–91
  campaign of 1994
    in Western Cape by, 79–80
    lessons learned by, 80
    national campaign themes and, 72
    persuasion campaign by, 70
  campaign of 1999
    Afrikaners as target constituency for, 92–94
    ANC's persuasion campaign for coloured voters in Western and Northern Capes, 89–90
    ANC's racial campaigning against, 102–104
    coloured and Indian voters as target for, 92, 94
    mobilization efforts by, 83
    on ANC's performance record in, 101, 102
    policy manifesto of, 99–100
    response to ANC's racial campaigning by, 104–105
    van Schalkwyk on campaign targeting of whites by, 95–96
  candidate advancement, effect of centralized rules for, 185–186

# Index

candidate defections from NNP to, 189
candidate lists, racial scorecarding of, 147
candidate poaching success by, 181t, 181–182
candidate rank and retention by, 175–176, 176t, 180–181
candidate retention by, racial effects of, 178, 179t
candidate retention in Western Cape, 178–179
candidate switching effects on, 183n
candidates for 1999 and 2004 elections, list rankings of, 173t, 173–175, 174t, 191
core constituency size and loyalty and mobilization or persuasion by, 97–98
DA formation and, 4n
election of 1994 results for, 65–66
election of 1999 goals and results for, 82–83, 106
election of 1999 party image regression for, 238
image change efforts through campaigns by, 20–21
political image, origins of, 50
white image of, apartheid and, 18–19, 19t
Democratic Party/Democratic Alliance (DP/DA). *See also* Democratic Alliance; Democratic Party
African views on exclusivity of and African candidates for, 156t, 157
candidate lists, racial balancing in, 154, 154t
candidate race, coding for 1994, 1999, and 2000 elections, 160–162
candidate recruits, African, 154t, 154–155
Indian views on Africanization of candidate lists and exclusivity of, 158–159, 159t
as opposition party, 4, 239
party image for voters of, 17–18
party image framed by ANC, 2, 19–20, 21
*El Diario de Hoy*, 236–237
Dipico, Manne, 146
Dlamini-Zuma, Nkosazana, 207
dominant parties. *See also* African National Congress; ruling parties; single-party-dominance states
democracy and, 26n
electoral system revision and manipulation by, 28
framing strategies of, 238–239
image control and negative framing by, 222
in Israel and El Salvador, 3
opposition parties and negative framing by, 223–224

Salvadoran lessons on limits to negative framing by, 238
Dominguez, Jorge I., 29n
Downs, Anthony, 36
Dugmore, Cameron, 103

Eastern Cape, South Africa
African discontent with ANC's performance in, 84, 84n
ANC's 1999 persuasion campaign for African voters in, 84–86, 85n
ANC's cultivation of traditional leaders in, 202
Chiefs' control of African vote in, ANC's 1999 campaign and, 85–86
election of 1999 results in, 82–83
electoral results for UDM in, 203
economy. *See also* social spending programs
African voters on changes in, 1
ANC electoral campaigns and, 10
ANC's policies and, 7, 9
clientelism in South Africa and, 12
end of racial censuses in South Africa and changes in, 239
education
African cross-over voting and uncertainty and (*Opinion 99*), 54–55, 55t, 62t
credibility and trustworthiness of South African opposition parties and, 58–61
cross-over voting and, 56
effects, electoral campaign. *See specific elections*
Eifert, Benn, 41n
El Salvador. *See also* ARENA; FMLN
dominant parties in, 3
election of 1994 in, 235
election of 2004 in, 235–236
election of 2009 in, 236–237
negative framing of opposition by ruling party of, 24–25
party image change and credibility in, 29–30
Eldridge, Matthew
on ANC's late strategies in 1994 Western Cape campaign, 78–79
on ANC's persuasion strategy for 1994 campaign, 68–69, 71
on ANC's response to NP's negative Western Cape campaigning, 77
on nonracialism vs. multiracialism focus for ANC, 74
on NP's 1994 negative campaigning in Western Cape, 74–75

election of 1994 South Africa
  ANC's negative framing of IFP during, 199
  ANC's racial balancing of candidate list
    for, 148
  candidate demographics of opposition
    parties during, 149
  goals of campaigns during, 66
  IFP's results in, 195–196
  lessons from, 66–67
  national, party images and persuasion in,
    70–74
  party images of NP and ANC after, 66
  percent votes by race in, 6t
  racial images of parties in, 66
  views of exclusivity of political parties
    for, 52t
  voting results for, 65n, 65–66
  Western Cape, party images and
    persuasion in, 74–80
election of 1999 South Africa.
    See also mobilization; persuasion
  ANC's negative framing of IFP during, 199
  ANC's racial balancing of candidate list
    for, 148
  campaign content, 98–99
  candidate demographics of opposition
    parties during, 149–150
  party labels in, 102–105, 106
  percent votes by race in, 6t
  performance issues, 100–102
  policy issues, 99–100
  views of exclusivity of political parties
    for, 52t
  voting results and campaign themes
    for, 82–83
election of 2004 South Africa
  ANC's negative framing of IFP during,
    199–201
  ANC's performance record and, 123–126
  campaign content for, 118
  campaign events for, 111–116, 115t
  campaign spending for, 134–136
  candidate demographics of opposition
    parties during, 150–151
  dataset for content analysis of, 108–111,
    138–140
  image change as challenge during, 138
  issues and policies of, 118–122, 119t,
    120t, 122t
  media coverage of, 136–137, 137t
  percent votes by race in, 6t
  persuasion and mobilization during, 111
  race and party images during, 126–133,
    132t, 133t, 134t

rhetoric, 116t, 116–118
views of exclusivity of political parties
  for, 52t
voting results for, 107
election of 2009 South Africa. See also Cope
  Cope's performance in, 220
  results of all parties in, 215
  shift in ANC's support base during, 215n
elections, South Africa
  fairness of, 15, 15n
  post-apartheid South African, generalizing
    explanations for, 24–25
  as racial censuses, 1, 5
  voting statistics in, 5n
Electoral Act (1998), South Africa, 86–87
Electoral Institute of South Africa (EISA),
  145–146
electoral systems
  Cope on reform of, 213, 217
  in ethnically divided countries, expressive
    voting and, 34–35
  opposition party opportunities or
    incentives and, 28n
  proportional, in Israel, 225–226n
  revision and manipulation by dominant
    parties of, 27–28
elite incorporation. See also candidate pools;
    new party elites; old party elites
  candidate quality and, 167n, 167–168
  candidate quality issues for small political
    parties and, 168–170
  Chandra on internal party competition
    and, 170
  methodology for candidate career path
    evaluation, 172–173, 173n
  party size and, 163–164
  testable implications regarding, 171
employment policies, racial differences in
  preferences about, 43–45, 44t
Eshkol, Levi, 231
*Ethnic Groups in Conflict* (Horowitz), 34
ethnic politics. See also ruling parties
  clientelism and, 11
ethnically divided countries. See also racial
    censuses
  political scientists' views of elections in,
    25–26
ethnicity
  ANC's efforts at list balancing by, 201–202
  apartheid state and cognitive cues from,
    38–39n
  candidate characteristics and group
    identity with, 142n, 142–143
  survey questions on identity and, 41n

# Index

Etzel (right-wing Israeli militia), 227–228
exclusivity of political parties
   African candidates on ANC's lists
      and white or coloured views of,
      157–158, 158t
   African candidates on DP/DA's lists and
      African views of, 156t, 157
   African candidates on NP's list and
      African views of, 156, 156t
   Indian candidates on party lists and Indian
      views of, 158–159, 159t
   performance evaluations, voting decisions
      and, 57t, 57–58, 59t
   summary of popular views of, 159–160
   views of, for 1994, 1999, and 2004,
      51–53, 52t
expressive voting. *See also* identity voting
   definition of, 32
   differentiating race-as-information voting
      from, 39
   Horowitz on, 34
   racial censuses in South Africa and, 34–35
external candidate quality. *See also* candidate
   quality
   NP's diversification of candidate lists and,
      187–188
   in South Africa, local communities and,
      164–167

Fearon, James, 11
Federal Alliance, South Africa, 4n, 189, 190n
Ferejohn, John, 36
Fick, Lampie, 188
*The Financial Mail*, 108–109, 139
Fiorina, Morris, 36
fiscal centralization, single-party dominance
   and, 27–28
floor crossing periods. *See* party switching,
   South Africa
FMLN (Farabundo Martí National
   Liberation Front)
   ARENA's success in 1994 elections and,
      233, 235
   avoidance of negative campaigning by,
      237–238
   contests negative image of, 223
   credibility as contender for national office,
      234
   Handal's image and 2004 presidential
      campaign by, 235–236
   internal conflict and image problems of,
      234–235
   internal conflict by renovadores/reformistas
      vs. ortodoxos in, 234

   ortodoxos and negative framing by
      ARENA of, 232
   party image change and credibility of, 29–30
   presidential campaign win in 2009 by,
      236–237
   reverses delegitimation of, 238–239
Ford, Gerald, 20
fractionalization, of opposition parties,
   resource asymmetry and, 27
framing political discourse. *See also* party
   labels/images
   ANC power due to, 28–29
   by dominant parties, 223–224, 238–239
   by Herut (Likud) in Israel, 232
   negative, Salvadoran lessons on limits
      to, 238
fraud. *See also* corruption
   ARENA's electoral success in El Salvador
      and, 233
   and clientelism in semi-democracies by
      ruling party, 27–28
   perceived, in KwaZulu Natal's 1994
      elections, 15n, 195–196, 196n
Free State, South Africa, ANC social
   spending in, 15n
Freedom Charter, ANC's, 47, 148–149
Freedom Front (FF), South Africa, 4
Friedman, Steven, 9, 35
funding for campaigns
   ANC's resources for, 3, 135
   by ARENA vs. FMLN in El Salvador, 233
   IEC allocations for, 134–135, 135n
   restraints on Cope, 216, 217n
Funes, Mauricio, 236–237

Gahal (Israeli coalition), 225–226n, 231, 232
Gauteng, South Africa
   ANC's 1999 persuasion campaign for
      African voters in, 85n
   ANC's 1999 voter registration campaigns
      in, 87
   ANC's ignoring of potential white
      supporters in, 91n, 91
   ANC's social spending in, 15n
   civil war in, 195–196
   DA's 2004 campaign events in, 112n,
      112–113
   DP's 1999 campaign targeting Indian
      voters in, 94
   DP's 1999 campaign targeting whites in,
      93–94
   UDM presence in shantytowns (1999)
      of, 85n
   voting results for 1994 election, 65n

GEAR (Growth, Employment, Redistribution), South Africa, 12–13, 13n, 90–91
gender
  African cross-over voting and uncertainty and (*Opinion 99*), 54–55, 55t, 62t
  ANC's candidate list requirements on, 184, 185, 186
  credibility and trustworthiness of South African opposition parties and, 58–61
  cross-over voting and, 56
  list rankings of ANC, NP, and DP for 1999 and 2004 elections and, 175
  logit analysis of candidate retention patterns across South African parties and, 176–178, 177t, 179–180
  of new, returned, and poached candidates for 1999 and 2004 elections, 172–173, 173n
  performance evaluations, voting decisions and, 58, 59t
General Zionist party, Israel, 225–226n
George, Mluleki, 23–24, 85n, 212–213
Gerber, Jean-Pierre, 188, 189
Gibson, Douglas, 113n, 126–129
Giliomee, Hermann
  on ANC's persuasion strategy for 1994 campaign, 73–74
  on ANC's response to NP's negative Western Cape campaigning, 77
  on NP's 1994 national campaign, 71–73
  on NP's 1994 negative campaigning in Western Cape, 74–75
  on NP's choices of African candidates, 187–188
  on NP's image change efforts through campaigns, 20
  on racial demographics of NNP's candidate lists, 146–147
  on unopposed parties, 5–7
Government of National Unity, Israel, 224–225
Government of National Unity, South Africa, 4n
grassroots memberships, candidates in South Africa and, 164–165
Greenberg, Stanley
  on ANC's attacks on NP during 1994 national campaign, 73–74
  ANC's campaign themes in 1994 and, 70–71
  ANC's disagreements on 1994 strategy with, 73–74
  on ANC's focus during campaigns, 21
  on ANC's performance record in 1999 campaign, 101
  on ANC's persuasion strategy for 1994 campaign, 71
  as polling expert for ANC in 1994, 67–69, 68n
Greene, Kenneth F., 27, 224
Greer, Frank, 67–69, 68n, 73–74
grow-your-own candidates
  Chandra on internal party competition and, 170
  effectiveness as large- vs. small-party strategy, 169, 171
Gumede, William, 219
Gwala, Blessed, 200

Haffajee, Ferial, 139
Haganah (Israeli military organization), 227–228
Handal, Shafick, 235–236
Hanekom, Derek, 148–149
Hani, Chris, 77–78
Harms, Louis, 211
Hechter, Michael, 35
hegemonic party autocracies, 26n.
  *See also* dominant parties; single-party-dominance states
Hertzog, James, 49
Herut (Israeli party). *See also* Begin, Menachim; Likud
  Ben-Gurion's refusal to include in coalition government of, 228–229
  contests negative image of, 223
  lessons for South Africa's DA from, 241
  Liberal Party legitimacy and alliance with, 241n
  Mapai's strength vs. weakness of, 227
  National Unity Government and legitimation of, 231
  negative public image of, 227
  as opposition party in Israel, 225–226
  party image change and credibility of, 29–30
  reverses delegitimation of, 238–239
  rightest coalition and, 225–226n
he said/she said situations, South Africa's electoral campaigns as, 21, 108, 118
Histadrut (Israeli labor union), 226, 226n, 228–229, 230, 231
HIV/AIDS, in South Africa
  racial rhetoric of 2004 campaign and, 124–125n
  rhetoric in 2004 campaign on, 134t
Hlope, Dumisane, 121n

# Index

Hlope, John, 210n
Holomisa, Bantu
  ANC's efforts to discredit, 203
  ANC's negative framing of, 194
  expulsion from the ANC, 202
  formation of UDM by Meyer and, 84, 96–97, 189, 202
  impact on racialization of opposition and, 241n
  as political talent who left the ANC, 23
Holomisa, Chief Phathekile, 85n
Horowitz, Donald L.
  on criteria for racial censuses, 5n
  on ethnic census characteristics, 4–5, 7, 82–83
  on ethnicity and party persuasion vs. mobilization, 67
  on expressive voting, 34
  on identity voting and racial censuses, 8
  on international frequency of census elections, 25–26
  on mobilization campaigns in divided countries, 97–98, 106
  on voter identity and partisanship, 42
Huntington, Samuel, 7
hyper-incumbency advantages, ruling parties and, 26–27

Idasa surveys. *See also* Afrobarometer survey; *Opinion99*
  African vote choice in 1994, 55t, 56, 62t
  characteristics of, 41n
  coloured perceptions of ANC in 1994, 78–79
  cross-over voting and uncertainty studies using, 54n
  on identity voting, 41–42
  on perceptions about IFP, 196–197
  on South African voter choices, 40–41
identity voting. *See also* expressive voting; racial identities
  African voters' concerns about party labels and, 33
  cross-over voting in South Africa and, 61
  as explanation for racial censuses, 8–10
  Horowitz on census-style elections and, 8
  partisanship and, 42, 43t
  prevalence of racial identities in South Africa, 41–42, 42t
  survey questions on, 41n
ideology
  convergence of 2004 party rhetoric and, 120–121, 121n

differentiation of South African political parties and, 36–37
grow-your-own candidate strategy driven by, 169–172n
opposition party extremism, party image and, 27
racial signaling using, 109–110
South African political party links to African voters and, 11–12n
undeveloped, candidate characteristics as alternative for, 142n, 142–144
in the United States, white voters' links to, 35
image politics. *See also* identity voting; party labels/images
  in Israel and El Salvador, 223–224
Independent Democrats (ID), South Africa
  campaign of 2004
    policies named by other parties and, 122t
    rhetoric on issues and policies by, 118–122, 120t
    rhetorical sparring partners for, 116t
    types of rhetoric about, 133t
  election of 2004, voting results for, 107
  election of 2009 and, 215
  media coverage of, 137t
  as opposition party, 4, 239
  racialization of opposition and small size of, 241n
Independent Electoral Commission (IEC), South Africa
  ANC's 1999 voter registration campaigns in rural areas and, 87–89, 88n
  campaign funding allocations (1998–2004) by, 134–135, 135n
  election administration and, 26n
  party switching data and, 182
  voter education and, 86–87
independent voters
  importance of party images for partisans vs., 56–57
  in South Africa, 42, 43t
Indian candidates/politicians, defections from NP to Minority Front by, 188
Indian South Africans. *See also* Indian voters
  African South African clashes with, 75–76
  analyzing names for coding race of, 160–162
  ANC at close of apartheid and, 47–48, 48n
  ANC's image for, 48
  definition of, 5n
  in KwaZulu Natal, 1999 registration for voting of, 89n

Indian South Africans (*cont.*)
  legacy of apartheid for, 37–38n, 38
  as middlemen minorities, 38
  on NP candidate lists (1999 and 2004), 153
  on party exclusivity, 52t
  and Africanization of candidate lists, 158–159, 159t
  on political parties, 51–53
  represented in South African government, Mandela on, 148
  Tricameral Parliament participation and credentials as ANC or UDF candidates of, 165–166, 166n
Indian voters. *See also* Indian South Africans
  ANC's 1999 campaign for, 90
  campaign of 1994, ANC polling on attitudes of, 68–69
  as DA supporters in South Africa, 5n
  DP's 1999 campaign targeting, 92, 94
  on government policies, 43–45, 44t
  ideological differentiation in South Africa by, 37n
  NP courting during 1994 campaign of, 69–70
  NP's campaign appeals to, 20
  NP's multiracial message in 1994 and, 76–77
  parties voted for, 5
  performance voting by, 45–46, 46t
information for voting. *See* racial heuristics
Inkatha Freedom Party (IFP)
  as African challenger to ANC, 4
  ANC defections to, 199
  ANC dominance over, 3
  ANC's 1999 campaign, KwaZulu Natal chiefs' support for, 85–86
  ANC's 1999 persuasion campaign for Indian voters and, 90
  ANC's 2004 rhetoric and, 116–118
  ANC's appeals to core constituency of, 201–202
  ANC's blame for performance record due to apartheid and, 124–125
  ANC's negative framing of, 199–201, 202
  Buthelezi and early goals for, 194–195
  campaign of 1994
    benefits/liabilities of image of, 197–198
    later decline in support for, 196
  campaign of 1999, as ANC threat, 84–86
  campaign of 2004
    ANC/NNP rhetoric on, 131–132
    DA alliance with, 111, 241n
    Mbeki's racial rhetoric against, 130–131
  on ANC's performance record, 124, 124n
  policies named by other parties and, 122t
  rhetoric on issues and policies by, 118–122, 120t
  rhetorical sparring partners for, 116t
  types of rhetoric about, 133t
  campaign resources available to ANC vs., 201
  civil war with UDF and ANC in KwaZulu Natal, 195, 195n, 196n
  election of 1994 results for, 65n, 195–196
  election of 1999 results for, 82–83
  election of 1999, voter registration in KwaZulu Natal and, 89n
  election of 2004 results for, 107
  election of 2009 and, 215
  Government of National Unity and, 4n
  image change efforts and ANC's negative framing of, 194
  internal culture and image change efforts for, 199
  media coverage of, 136–137, 137t
  as opposition party, 4, 239
  origins of, 194n
  Piper on image and campaign-style changes by, 198
  post-apartheid image of, 196–197
  public opinion on image over time of, 198–199
  as regional party and government participant, 241n
  significance as ANC competitor, 193–194
Inkatha yeSizwe. *See* Inkatha Freedom Party
instrumental voting, as explanation for racial or ethnic voting, 34n
internal candidate quality, 164–167
Iraq, census elections in, 25–26
Irgun Zvai Leumi (IZL) Israeli militia, 227. *See also* Etzel
Ismail, Anwar, 75–76
Israel. *See also* Herut; Labor Party; Likud
  dominant parties in, 3
  Labor governments without Herut in coalition for, 228–229
  Labor's dominance in, 223–224
  National Unity Government, 231
  negative framing of opposition by ruling party of, 24–25
  party image change and credibility in, 29–30
Israel Defense Forces (IDF), 227–228

# Index

Israeli Labor Party, 225n. *See also* Labor Party
issue priorities. *See also* policy issues
   about different parties in 2004, 133t
   categorizing, in campaign of 2004, 118–122, 119n, 119t
Italy
   mechanisms mediating clientelism in, 11n
   single-party dominance in, 26
IZL (Irgun Zvai Leumi) Israeli militia, 227. *See also* Etzel

Jabotinsky, Vladimer Zeev, 227, 228–229, 231
Jacobs, Sean, 90n, 146–147, 188
James, Wilmot, 73–74, 77, 146–147
Japan
   clientelism mediated by businesses in, 11n
   clientelistic strategy by LDP for, 16
   LDP dominance in, 3
   opposition parties' problems finding leadership for, 23
   single-party dominance in, 26
Johannesburg High Court, South Africa, 210n
Johnson, R. W., 5–7, 9, 35
Jordan, Pallo, 129, 200
Judicial Services Commission (JSC), South Africa, 210n

Kilian, Johan, 95
Kilian, Juli, 130
Kinder, Donald R., 35
Kitschelt, Herbert, 11n, 16
Koornhof, Gerhard, 148–149
Koorts, Hermene, 112–113
Kotz, Dirk, 185–186
Kramer, Gerald, 67
Kriel, Hernus, 76–77, 78–79, 96–97, 187
KwaZulu Natal, South Africa
   African–Indian conflict in, 38
   ANC social spending in, 14–15, 15n
   ANC's 1994 negative framing of IFP in, 199
   ANC's 1999 campaign for Indian voters in, 90
   ANC's 1999 candidate list for, racial demographics of, 145–146
   ANC's 1999 persuasion campaign for African voters in, 84–86
   ANC's 1999 politician recruitment in, 166–167
   ANC's 2004 campaign events for whites in, 113–115
   ANC's cultivation of traditional leaders in, 202
   chiefs' control of African vote in, ANC's 1999 campaign and, 85–86, 86n
   civil war in, 195, 195n
   election of 1994 results in, 65n, 65–66
   election of 1999 results in, 82–83
   election of 2004 results in, 107
   fraud in 1994 elections in, 15n
   IFP control in, 193–194
   IFP's decline in, 196
   IFP's roots in, 194–195
   IFP's strength during 1994 election in, 67–69
   IFP's support in, 4
   voter registration for 1999 election in, 88–89, 89n
   Zuma's appeal as 2009 candidate in, 218

Labor Alignment, Israel, 225–226n. *See also* Labor Party
labor market policies, South Africa, differences in 2004 party rhetoric on, 121n, 121–122, 134t
Labor Party (Israel). *See also* Ben-Gurion, David
   cooperation with Gahal in National Unity Government, 231
   failure to reverse Herut's (Likud's) legitimation by, 232
   formation and dominance of, 225
   framing Herut's image by, 228
   history of rivalry with Revisionists/Herut, 227
   Likud as credible alternative to, 224–225
   loses 1977 election to Likud, 230, 230n
   negative framing of opposition by, 223–224, 227
   sources of dominance by, 226
Lakoff, George, 28–29, 201n
large political parties
   candidate quality, candidate retention, and poaching by, 171
   candidate retention in South Africa and, 175–176, 176t
   logit analysis of candidate retention patterns across South African parties and, 176–178, 177t
   poaching candidates by small parties vs., 181, 181t
LDP. *See* Japan

leadership demographics. *See also* candidate demographics; elite incorporation
    diversification to change party image, 21–22
    of opposition parties, party image and, 19
Lechi (Stern Gang), Israel, *Alatalena* affair and, 227–228
leftist bloc, Israel, composition of, 225–226n
Lehoucq, Fabrice Edouard, 233–234
Lekota, Mosiuoa "Terror"
    Cope formation after leaving the ANC by, 23–24, 212–213
    on Cope's affirmative action and BEE policies, 213
    Dandala's selection as Cope presidential candidate and, 214–215
    heckled in 2007 ANC National Conference, 207–208
    struggle credentials of, 212n
Leon, Tony. *See also* Democratic Party
    ANC leaders' racial attacks on, 102–103
    ANC's portrayal of apartheid role of, 129
    Asmal's mocking references to, 90–91
    campaign of 1999
        African rating of, 94
        approval ratings decline among Africans for, 105
        as street fighter for DP, 92
        on goal for DP's persuasion campaign, 92
    campaign of 2004
        on labor market policies in, 121–122
        racial rhetoric by, 127–129
    campaigning for 1999 African vote, 94n
    campaigning for 1999 Afrikaner vote, 92–94, 95–96
    campaigning for 1999 coloured and Indian vote, 94
    campaigning for 2004 African vote, 112n, 112–113
    on candidate quality and elite incorporation problem, 168
    on candidate ranking by the DP, 186
    on DA's candidate lists reflecting South Africa, 150–151
    DA's portrayal of apartheid role of, 126–129
    DP's campaigns to change party image and, 20–21
    Zille as replacement for, 240–241
Levite, Ariel, 227, 228–229, 231, 232
Liberal Party, Israel
    Herut cooperation with, 231
    Mapai's exclusion of Herut and coalition with, 229
    Mapai's strength vs. weakness of, 227
    rightest coalition and, 225–226n
Lijphart, Arend, 5, 8, 34
Likud (Israeli party)
    as credible alternative to Labor, 224–225
    development as viable alternative to Labor, 230–231
    political antecedents of, 225–226n
    wins 1977 election over Labor, 230, 230n
local communities. *See also* municipalities
    candidate connection in South Africa to, 164–165
Lodge, Tom
    on 1999 policy manifestos, 100
    on ANC ignoring potential white supporters in Gauteng, 91
    on ANC missteps in 1994 Western Cape campaign, 77–78
    on ANC's 1994 negative framing of IFP, 199
    on ANC's 1999 persuasion strategy for Africans, 85, 85n
    on ANC's 1999 persuasion strategy for coloureds and Indians, 89–90
    on ANC's 1999 policy manifesto, 99
    on ANC's 1999 voter registration campaign in rural areas, 87–88
    on ANC's campaign contributors, 135
    on ANC's campaign spending, 135–136
    on ANC's centralized rules for candidate advancement, 184
    on ANC's national interference with provincial candidate lists, 184–185
    on ANC's performance record in 1999 campaign, 101
    on ANC's persuasion strategy for 1994 campaign, 67–69, 71
    on ANC's racial scorecarding in, 145–146
    on ANC's Reconstruction and Development Plan, 71
    on apartheid as ANC theme in 1944 national campaign, 73
    on DP's 1999 campaign targeting coloured and Indian voters, 94
    on DP's 1999 campaign to capture whites from NP, 92, 93–94
    on DP's and NNP's 1999 policy manifestos, 99–100
    on NNP's 1999 efforts at targeting Africans, 96
    on NP's image change efforts through campaigns, 20
Ludman, Barbara, 50
Luzipho, Zet, 209n

Mackenzie, Patrick, 166–167, 188, 188n
Madikizela-Mandela, Winnie
  on ANC militancy in 1994, 77–78
  ANC's 1999 persuasion campaign for African voters and, 85, 85n
  on ANC's performance record in 1999 campaign, 101
  DP's 1999 campaign criticisms of, 92
  racial campaigning in 1999 by, 103
Magaloni, Beatriz, 14–15, 26n, 29n, 224, 242
*Mail & Guardian*, 108–109, 139
Makhanya, Mondli, 139
Makhura, David, 131–132, 200
Malan, D. F., 49
malapportionment, single-party dominance and, 27–28
Malatsi, David, 95, 146–147, 187
Malema, Julius, 210, 211n
Mandela, Nelson. *See also* African National Congress
  as ANC leader, 47
  ANC's 1994 campaign attacks on apartheid and, 73–74
  ANC's 1994 election, on coloured and Indian voters during, 68–69, 77–78
  ANC's 1999 persuasion campaign for African voters and, 85n, 85
  ANC's 1999 persuasion campaign for coloured and Indian voters and, 89–90
  ANC's 2009 campaign and, 218
  conservative coloured South Africans and, 48
  on DP and NNP as "Mickey Mouse" parties, 90–91
  on fiscal mess ANC inherited, 13n
  government appointments for Buthelezi by, 196
  homage to traditional leaders by, 86n, 201
  on IFP and election of 1994, 195–196
  Mbeki's succession to presidency after, 203–204
  on NP's claim of ending apartheid, 21
  NP's image due to release of, 20
  on racial balancing of regional candidate lists, 148
  racial campaigning in 1999 by, 102–104
Mandela, Winnie. *See* Madikizela-Mandela, Winnie
manifestos, South African party
  for election of 1999, 99–100
  for election of 2004, 119, 119n
  for election of 2004, DA's launch used as courting of Africans with, 127–129
  for election of 2009 of ANC vs. Cope, 213–214
Manning, Carrie, 234
Mantashe, Gwede, 211n
Manuel, Trevor, 208–209
Mapai. *See* Labor Party
Mapam (Israeli party), 225–226n
Marais, Peter, 95, 96–97, 166–167
Masher, Mario, 166–167, 188
Mattes, Robert
  on ANC's persuasion strategy for 1994 campaign, 73–74
  on ANC's response to NP's negative Western Cape campaigning, 77
  on Dawson's racial heuristic theories, 17
  Idasa identity data analysis in 1994 by, 41–42
  on NP's 1994 negative campaigning in Western Cape, 74–75
  on opposition image among disillusioned ANC voters, 55
  on racial demographics of NNP's candidate lists, 146–147
  on racial differences in policy preferences, 43–45
  on racial heuristics in South Africa, 38–39
  on voter satisfaction with ANC's policies and performance, 36
  on white vs. African views of ANC performance, 60, 60n
Mbalula, Fikile, 210
Mbeki, Thabo. *See also* African National Congress
  ANC's 1999 persuasion campaign for African voters and, 85n, 85
  ANC's 1999 persuasion campaign for coloured and Indian voters and, 89–90, 90n
  ANC's 2004 campaign on performance record of, 123n, 123–124
  ANC's prospects for revitalization after loss by, 208
  on apartheid's effect on ANC's 2004 performance record, 124–125n
  campaigning in 2004 for white votes by, 113–116
  Cope's leaders association with, 217–218
  DA's 2004 attacks on, 112–113, 125–126, 126n
  expels B. Holomisa from the ANC, 202
  failure to court potential white supporters in Gauteng by, 91, 91n

Mbeki, Thabo (*cont.*)
  homage to traditional leaders by, 86n
  racial rhetoric in 2004 campaigning by, 127–129, 130–131
  resignation of, 211
  second term voter discontent with presidency of, 205–206
  Zuma as candidate vs., 218
  Zuma defeats as ANC president, 207–208
  Zuma released from Deputy President duties by, 205
  Zuma replacement considerations for, 207
  Zuma's 2009 campaign linking ANC's failures to, 219
McCann, James A., 29n
McCarthy, Leonard, 212
Meir, Golda, 231
Mendelberg, Tali, 35, 109–110
Merten, Marianne, 147
Metcalfe, Mary, 148–149
Mexico
  clientelistic strategy by PRI for, 14–15, 16
  credibility of opposition parties in, 29n
  PRI dominance in, 3
  single-party dominance in, 26
  social spending programs (PRONOSAL) in, 13
Meyer, Roelf, 84, 96–97, 189, 202
Miguel, Edward, 41n
Minority Front (MF), South Africa, 94, 188, 190n
mixed-member systems, single-party dominance and, 27–28
MK Military Veterans' Association (MKMVA), South Africa, 210
Mlambo-Ngcuka, Phumzile, 207
mobilization
  as ANC focus in 1999 election, 82–83, 86–89, 88n, 89n
  ANC's 2004 persuasion efforts and, 111
  in DP's 1999 campaign, 92–94
  Horowitz on ethnicity and party persuasion vs., 67
  Kramer on party strategies of persuasion and, 67
  in NNP's 1999 campaign, 94–97
  as party strategy, 67–70
  persuasion as campaign goal vs., 66
  persuasion in election of 1999 vs., 83, 97–98, 98n
Modise, Jan, 188–189
Modise, Ken, 71
Mohau, Nkululeko Kaizer, 129, 129n
Mokaba, Peter, 77–78

Mokonyane, Nomvula, 113–115, 148–149, 165
Moorcroft, Errol, 104
Morkel, Gerald, 96–97, 103, 187
Motlanthe, Kgalema, 208, 211
Mpshe, Mokothedi, 211–212, 212n
Mthimkhulu, Mtholephi, 124–125n
Mugabe, Robert, 125–126, 126n
multiracialism
  ANC and DA claims in 2004 of inclusivity and, 111
  ANC at close of apartheid and, 47–48
  Freedom Charter on, 47
  indicators of ANC's lack of commitment to, 48
  nonracialism as ANC theme vs., 74
  NP's 1994 Western Cape campaign as party of, 76–77
  political parties in South Africa and, 239–240
municipalities. *See also* local communities
  ANC domination of elections in, 172
  ARENA vs. FMLN electoral domination of, 233, 234
  elections in, as focus for DA's image cultivation, 240, 240n
  FMLN's electoral success in, 236–237, 238–239
  FMLN's renovadores/reformistas on politics of, 234
  social spending programs for, 14–15
  South African, party switching in 2004 in, 182

Nagler, Jonathan, 35, 39
Naidoo, Mann, 188
National Director of Public Prosecutions (NDPP), South Africa, 210, 211
National Executive Committee (NEC), ANC's, 207–208, 210, 211
National Federation of Labor (NFL), Israel, 227
National List Committee, ANC's, 184–185
National Party (NP), South Africa. *See also* National Party/New National Party; New National Party
  African recruits as candidates for, 154t, 154–155
  on African seizures of coloured and Indian property, 76
  African views on exclusivity of and African candidates for, 156, 156t
  African voters during 1994 election for, 67–69

# Index

ANC and post-apartheid party labels/
  images of, 17
ANC voters, and goals for converting to, 7
on ANC's plans for coloureds and Indians,
  75–76
campaign of 1994
  difficulties in changing party image
    during, 80–81
  IEC bans campaign comic book of, 75
  lessons learned by, 80
  multiracial message in, 76–77
  negative campaigning in Western Cape
    by, 74–75
  party image after, 66
  racial images as subtext in, 72–73
  using persuasion, 69–70
candidate list diversification by, 187
candidate lists, racial balancing in,
  153, 153t
candidate lists, racial scorecarding of,
  146–147
candidate poaching by, 181t, 181–182
candidate quality and list diversification
  by, 187–188
candidate rank and retention by, 180–181
candidate retention from 1994 to 2004
  elections by, 175–176, 176t
candidate retention in Western Cape by,
  178–179, 180t
candidate retention, racial effect of, 178,
  179t
candidates for 1994, 1999, and 2000
  elections, coding race of candidates
  for, 160–162
candidates for 1999 and 2004 elections,
  list rankings of new, returning, and
  poached, 173t, 173–175, 174t, 191
candidates lost to the DP or the ANC by,
  182–183
case study on collapse of, 187–190,
  191–192
competition and centralized rules for
  candidate advancement in, 185–186
defections, effects on party of, 188–189
election of 1994, national campaign themes
  for, 71–72
election of 1994, voting results for, 65–66
election of 1999, non-white candidates for,
  149–150
electoral machinery erosion from
  defections from, 189–190
Government of National Unity and, 4n
image change efforts through campaigns
  by, 20

Indian views on Africanization of
  candidate lists and exclusivity of,
  158–159, 159t
legalizes the ANC, 47
local branch structures for, 164–165
name change and image of, 16n
name change by, 4n
as opposition party, 4
political image, origins of, 49–50
white image of, apartheid and, 18–19, 19t
National Party (NP), Zambia, 144
National Party/New National Party (NP/
  NNP). See also National Party, South
  Africa; New National Party
image framed by ANC, 2, 19–20
National Prosecuting Authority (NPA)
  case against Zuma by, 206–207
  charges Zuma with corruption, 204–205
  drops charges against Zuma, 211–212
  Nicholson on Mbeki's encouragement of
    Zuma case by, 211
  pressure to drop charges against
    Zuma, 211n
  SCA reverses Nicholson's decision in favor
    of, 211
  Zuma indictment after ANC power shift at
    Polokwane, 209–210
National Religious Party (NRP), Israel,
  225–226n
National Republican Alliance. See ARENA
National Unity Government, Israel, 231
Nattrass, Nicoli, 239
Ndlangisa, Sabelo, 147
Ndoni, Andiswa, 217n
Nel, Lucas, 189
Netshitenzhe, Joel, 76–77
new candidate recruits
  list rankings of ANC, NP, and DP for 1999
    and 2004 elections, 173t, 173–175,
    174t
  rank of, in large vs. small parties, 171, 191
  testing candidate quality and list rankings
    of, 172–173
New National Party (NNP).
  See also National Party, South Africa;
  National Party/New National Party
African voters' uncertainty and support
  for, 54, 55t, 62t
ANC's leaders' mocking references to,
  90–91
on ANC's performance record, racial
  rhetoric in, 124–125
campaign image as framed by ANC, 21
campaign of 1999

New National Party (NNP) (*cont.*)
    ANC's persuasion campaign against,
        85, 85n
    ANC's persuasion campaign for coloured
        voters and, 89–90
    ANC's racial campaigning against,
        102–104
    DP's effort to capture coloured and
        Indian voters from, 94
    DP's effort to capture white voters from,
        92, 93–94
    multiracial goals for, 94–97
    on ANC's performance record in,
        101, 102
    policy manifesto of, 99–100
    campaign of 2004
        ANC's rhetoric and, 116–118
        attacks DA's image in, 126–129
        policies named by other parties
            and, 122t
        racial rhetoric in, 127–129, 130,
            131–132, 132t
        rhetoric on issues and policies by,
            118–122, 120t
        rhetorical sparring partners for, 116t
        types of rhetoric about, 133t
    and coloured community, Mackenzie's role
        in, 166–167
    core constituency size and loyalty and
        mobilization or persuasion by, 97–98
    DA formation and, 4n
    education, age, gender, political interest
        and support for, 56
    election of 1999 goals and results for,
        82–83
    election of 1999, persuasion efforts in, 83
    election of 2004, ANC alliance with, 111
    election of 2004, voting results for, 107
    image for voters of, 17–18
    implosion after diversifying candidate lists
        of, 23
    legislative seats controlled by,
        171–172, 172t
    media coverage of, 137t
    as opposition party, 4, 239
    public opinion on image over time of, 199n
    van Schalkwyk on racial balance of
        candidate list for, 150
new party elites. *See also* elite incorporation;
    new candidate recruits
    quality of, electoral success and, 164
New Zionist Organization (NZO), 227
news media
    ARENA's 1994 campaign ads using, 235
    ARENA's campaign coverage by, 233

campaign coverage in South Africa by,
    136–137, 137t
on identity voting, 9
newspaper content analysis of 2004 election
    coding rules for, 109–111
    dailies and weeklies in study, 108–109,
        138–140
    media coverage analysis using, 136, 137t
    using campaign rhetoric and
        activities, 109
Ngcuka, Bulelani, 204–205, 207, 212
Ngonyama, Smuts, 129
Nicholson, Chris, 210, 211
Niemann, J. J., 188–189
Nitz, Michael, 35
Nonkonyana, Chief Mwelo, 85n
Nonracial identity rhetoric, categorizing, in
    campaign of 2004, 118–122, 119n, 119t
nonracialism, multiracialism as ANC theme
    vs., 74
Norris, Pippa, on internal party structure
    and elite incorporation, 170–171, 186
North West Province, South Africa
    ANC's 1999 voter registration campaigns
        in, 87–88
    ethnic demographics of ANC's candidate
        pool for, 146
Northern Cape, South Africa
    ANC's 1999 campaign for coloured voters
        in, 89–90
    ethnic demographics of ANC's candidate
        pool for, 146
    IEC and ANC collaboration on voter
        registration in, 87–88
    NNP's 1999 campaign on multiracialism
        in, 95–96
    NP's diversification of candidate lists
        for, 187
    NP's leadership defections in, 188–189
Northern Province, South Africa, ANC's
    1999 voter registration campaigns in,
    87–88
"Now is the Time" (ANC motto in 1994
    election), 70–71
Nujoma, Sam, 77–78

old party elites. *See also* candidate pools;
    elite incorporation
    Chandra on net negative with loss of, 163
*Opinion99* (survey)
    characteristics of, 41n
    control variables in uncertainty and cross-
        over voting studies, 54–55, 55t, 62t
    cross-over voting and uncertainty studies
        using, 54

importance of party images for partisans vs. nonpartisans, 64t
on policy preferences, 43–45
opposition parties. *See also* small political parties
African. *See* African opposition parties
African images of, 19, 19t
ANC dominance over, 3
ANC's racial campaigning in 1999 against, 102–104
candidate demographics' awareness over time by, 149–151
candidate switching effects on, 182–183, 183n
challenge of recruiting high-quality African candidates for, 22
challenges for success of, 24
control over legislative seats by, 171–172, 172t
credibility and trustworthiness for African voters of, 58–59n, 58–61, 60t
on election fairness in South Africa, 15n
electoral systems and opportunities or incentives for, 28n
Greene on resource asymmetry for, 27
image changing strategies for, 2–3
image framed by ANC, 2, 240
inclusive/exclusive views of, good/bad performance and, 57–58
locked-out, credibility and image of, 29n, 29–30
logit analysis of candidate retention patterns across South African parties and, 178
negative framing by dominant parties and, 224
party label change as challenge for, 2, 18, 21, 224, 240
racial diversification of candidate lists by, 21–22
trajectory of South African politics and decisions by, 242
voting behavior and images of, 18
Ortíz, Oscar, 235
ortodoxos, FMLN (El Salvador), 232, 234, 235
Our Plan campaign (ANC, 1994), 78–79

Padyachee, Roy, 48
Palestine Worker's Party (Mapai). *See* Labor Party
Palestinian territories, occupation after Six Day War by Israel, 230
Pan African Congress (PAC), South Africa, 4, 9, 240

parliamentary system
ANC electoral dominance and, 3–4
as clientelism mitigation mechanism in South Africa, 11
partisans and partisanship
African cross-over voting and uncertainty and (*Opinion 99*), 54–55, 55t, 62t
identity voting in South Africa and, 42, 43t, 61
importance of party images for independent voters vs., 56–57, 64t
party image and performance evaluations by Africans and, 55t, 56
party labels/images
African cross-over voting and uncertainty and (*Opinion 99*), 55t, 56, 62t
of ANC, origins of, 47–49
ANC control as ruling party over, 220–221
ANC's negative framing of opposition and, 2, 21
changing, as challenge for opposition parties, 18
changing, as lesson learned from election of 1994 on, 80–81
changing, in Israel and El Salvador, 224
of Cope on its launch as a party, 214
of Dandala as Cope presidential candidate, 214
DP's campaigns to change, 20–21
election of 1999 and, 106
election of 2004 and, 108, 138
identity voting in South Africa and, 61
ideological differentiation issues in South Africa and, 36–37, 37n
for IFP, ANC neutralization of changes to, 194
of IFP during post-apartheid period, 196–197, 197n
inclusive/exclusive views of opposition, good/bad performance and, 57t, 57–58, 59t
lessons learned from election of 1994 on, 80
NP's campaigns to change, 16n, 20
of opposition parties during campaigns, 19
origins of ANC's, 47–49
origins of DP's, 50
origins of NP's, 49–50
Popkin on campaigns and, 20
preference effect and, 143
race in 2004 campaigns and, 126–133
racial, in South Africa, 17
racial campaigning in 1999 and, 102–105
racial diversification of candidate lists and, 2, 21–22

party labels/images (*cont.*)
    racial heuristics operationalization based on, 33
    racialized, South African voting and, 61
    rhetoric in 2004 campaign on, 133t
    as subtle measure of racial identification, 53n
    tracking through survey data over time, 51–53, 52t
    undeveloped ideological labels, candidate characteristics and, 142n, 142–144
    use of term, 16–17
    voting decisions and, 58
party loyalists, signaling effect of displacing, 143–144
party switching, South Africa. *See also* poached candidates; poaching candidates
    due to NP's candidate diversification plan, 188–189
    effects for NP's leadership of, 190
    legal basis for, 182
    as white/coloured phenomenon, 181t, 181–182
patronage. *See also* clientelism
    ANC and, 1–2, 13n, 13–14n
    Chandra and Posner on ethnic favoritism in democracies based on, 142–143
    as explanation for single-party dominance, 26–27
    in Israel, decline in importance of, 230
    in Israel, Histadrut's link with Mapai and, 226
    opposition parties' lack of control over, 19
Pempel, T. J., 26, 26n, 28
performance. *See also* politics-as-usual issues
    African cross-over voting and uncertainty and (*Opinion 99*), 55t, 56, 62t
    *Afrobarometer* survey (2000) on, 43–45
    categorizing, in campaign of 2004, 118–122, 119n, 119t
    claims of, content coding rules for, 109–111
    content analysis of 2004 election and, 109–111
    credibility and trustworthiness of opposition parties and, 58–61
    good/bad, inclusive/exclusive views of opposition and, 57t, 57–58
    identity voting in South Africa and, 61
    as issue in 1999 campaign, 100–102
    racial differences in concerns about, 45–46, 46t
    racial or ethnic voting model and, 35–36
    rhetoric in 2004 campaign on, 123–126, 133t, 134t
    voting decisions and, 58, 59t
persuasion. *See also* rhetoric, campaign
    by ANC and DA in 2004 campaign, 111
    by ANC for African voters in 1999, 84–86, 85n
    by ANC for coloured and Indian voters in 1999, 89–90
    by ANC for white voters from the NP in 1999, 92
    as ANC strategy during 1994 election, 67–69
    campaign rhetoric in 2004 as, 109
    in DP's 1999 campaign, 92–94
    mobilization as campaign goal vs., 66
    mobilization in election of 1999 vs., 83, 97–98, 98n
    in NNP's 1999 campaign, 94–97
    as NP strategy in 1994 campaign, 69–70
    party images and, 70
    party images as key during 1994 election to, 80
    as party strategy, 67–70
Peru, social spending programs (FONCODES) in, 13
Peterson, Hector, 112, 112n
Pietermaritzburg High Court, mass gathering of Zuma supporters around, 210
Piombo, Jessica, 36, 38–39, 55, 60, 60n
Piper, Laurence, 197n, 198, 199, 200
poached candidates
    legal permission for party switching and, 182
    list rankings of ANC, NP, and DP for 1999 and 2004 elections for, 173t, 173–175
    rank of, in large vs. small parties, 171
    testing candidate quality and list rankings of, 172–173
    as white/coloured phenomenon, 181t, 181–182
poaching candidates
    Cope's expectations for, 216, 216n
    effectiveness as large- vs. small-party strategy, 169
    success of large vs. small parties in, 171, 181, 181t
polarization of the electorate, symbolic manipulation by dominant parties for, 28
policy issues. *See also* politics-as-usual issues
    *Afrobarometer* survey (2000) on voting and, 43–45, 44t

categorizing, in campaign of 2004,
  118–122, 119n, 119t, 122t
characteristics of voting on, 35–36
comparative ethnic politics theorists on
  racial voting and voting on, 35
content analysis of 2004 election and,
  109–111
of election of 1999, 99–100
grow-your-own candidate strategy driven
  by, 169–172n
racial attachments in 1994 election and, 9
policy rhetoric. *See also* rhetoric, campaign
  in campaign of 2004, 121n, 133t
  categorizing, in campaign of 2004,
    118–122, 119n, 119t
political identity. *See also* identity voting;
  racial identities
of African voters, 1, 2
Idasa 1999 post-election survey on voter
  identity and, 41n
political institutions, in South Africa,
  clientelism and, 11, 11n
political interest
African cross-over voting and uncertainty
  and (*Opinion 99*), 54–55, 55t, 62t
credibility and trustworthiness of
  South African opposition parties
  and, 58–61
cross-over voting and, 56
performance evaluations, voting decisions
  and, 58, 59t
political parties. *See also* candidate pools;
  exclusivity of political parties; large
  political parties; manifestos, South
  African party; opposition parties; party
  labels/images; single-party-dominance
  states; small political parties
Chandra on competitive vs. centralized
  rules for candidate advancement in,
  183–184
Chandra on elite incorporation and
  internal competition in, 170
core constituency size and loyalty and
  tactics by, 97–98
elite incorporation and size of, 163–164
racial balance of South African candidate
  lists, 151–155, 152t, 153t, 154t, 155t
unopposed, risks associated with, 5–7
political talent. *See also* candidate pools;
  candidate quality
African, loosening ANC's monopoly on,
  241
ANC's monopoly on, 23, 192
high-quality, challenge of recruiting, 22

high-quality Japanese, challenge of
  recruiting, 23
low-quality, NNP implosion and, 23
politics-as-usual issues. *See also* performance;
  policy issues
African voters' concerns about party labels
  and, 33
as hypothesis for voting, 32
racial censuses in South Africa and, 35–36
voters' criteria for decisions on, 34n
polls
on DA's image and NNP's image over
  time, 199n
on IFP's image over time, 198–199
pre-1994 election, citizen distrust of, 196n
Polokwane, South Africa
perspectives on Zuma's ANC election at,
  208–210
as power shifting among ANC elites, 208n
Zuma elected ANC president at 2007
  National Conference in, 207–208
Polokwane losers
ANC's image of Cope as black elitists and,
  24, 215, 217–218
press's use of term, 218n
Popkin, Samuel, 20, 36, 80–81
popular press. *See* news media
Posner, Daniel, 11, 36, 41n, 142–143, 144
poverty
African frustration with, 1
clientelism in South Africa and, 12, 12n
predominant party democracies, 26n.
  *See also* dominant parties; single-party-
  dominance states
preference effect, candidate demographics,
  party image and, 141, 143
prevalence of racial identities in South Africa,
  41–42, 42t
PRI. *See* Mexico
Progressive Party, Israel, 225–226n
Progressive Party, South Africa, 50.
  *See also* Democratic Party
Prohibition of Political Interference Act,
  South Africa, 50
proportional representation
centralized party systems and candidate
  diversification in, 170–171
closed list, to mitigate clientelism, 11
Cope on electoral form and, 213
single-party dominance and, 27–28
as South African model, 7
public appearances, for ANC's 1999
  persuasion campaign for African voters,
  85, 85n

Public Funding of Represented Political
    Parties Act 103 (1998), South Africa,
    134–136
public opinion. *See* polls
public policies
  opposition parties' lack of control over, 19
  racial attachments vs. preferences of
    parties on, 9
public-sector employees
  number of, as potential for clientelism, 13n
  in South Africa, clientelism and, 12–13
punishment regimes
  ANC's social spending patterns as evidence
    against, 14–15, 15n
  in Mexico vs. South Africa, 14–15
  single-party-dominance states as, 26–27
Purified National Party. *See* National Party

Rabushka, Alvin, 35
race of candidates
  group identity with, 142n, 142–143
  list rankings of ANC, NP, and DP for 1999
    and 2004 elections and, 175
  models of retention patterns across South
    African parties and, 176–178, 177t
  of new, returned, and poached candidates
    for 1999 and 2004 elections, 172–173
  party-specific effects on candidate
    retention and, 178, 179t
racial censuses
  ANC dominance and, 3
  clientelism in South Africa as explanation
    for, 10–16
  criteria for, 5n
  elections as, 1, 5, 25–26
  identity voting in South Africa as
    explanation for, 8–10
  overview of political origins of, 16–17
  political basis of South African elections
    vs., 26
  political roots of, 3
  political vs. identity change and, 2
  rise of a new party and end to, 239–240
  in South Africa, potential erosion of, 239
racial framing, Mendelberg on subtleties of,
  109–110
racial heuristics. *See also* party labels/images
  African partisanship over time and, 42, 43t
  in ANC's 1994 national campaign, 73–74
  classifications due to apartheid, 37n, 37–38
  criteria for, 34n
  Dawson on, 17
  described, 32
  election of 1999 and, 82–83
  innovations in, 33
  legacy of apartheid and, 38
  in NP's 1994 campaign, 72–73
  overview of, 36–40
  performance evaluations as indicator of,
    45–46, 46t
  policy preferences as indicator of, 43–45,
    44t, 45t
  prevalence of racial identities in South
    Africa and, 41–42, 42t
  racialized party images, South African
    voting and, 61
  South African ethnic heuristics compared
    to, 38–39n
  South African voting behavior and, 46
  survey sources for tests of, 40–41
  tests of, 40
  value in keeping separate different strands
    of, 39–40
racial identities. *See also* identity voting
  African images of, 53n
  cross-over voting in South Africa and, 61
  identity voting and, 9
  party labels as subtle measure of, 53n
  prevalence in South Africa, 41–42, 42t
racial inequality. *See also* apartheid
  within as well as across South African
    racial groups, 38n
racial or ethnic voting. *See also* racial
    censuses
  theories on, 34, 34n
racial priming, content analysis of 2004
  election and issues of, 109–111
racial rhetoric
  the ANC/NNP and, 132t
  on ANC's performance record and 2004
    campaign, 123–126, 124–125n,
    126n
  categorizing, in campaign of 2004,
    118–122, 119n, 119t, 132–133
  the DA in 2004 and, 133t
  DA's portrayal of its image and use of,
    127n, 127–129
radio coverage of 2004 campaign, 136–137
Rajbansi, Armichand, 166–167
Ramaphosa, Cyril, 203–204n, 203–204
rank of candidates
  of ANC, NP, and DP for 1999
    election, 173t
  of ANC, NP, and DP for 2004
    election, 174t
  elite incorporation theories on, 171
  logit analysis of candidate retention
    patterns across South African parties
    and, 176–178, 177t, 180–181
  retention patterns and, 171

testing quality of new, returned, or
poached candidates and, 172–173
Rasool, Ebrahim
on ANC image and balancing candidate
lists, 148
on ANC's 2004 targeting of whites, 113–115
on ANC's recruitment of coloured and
Indian politicians, 166–167
ANC's Western Cape canvassing and,
89–90, 90n
complains to IEC of racism by Botha,
150–151
rational choice, as explanation for racial or
ethnic voting, 34n
Reconstruction and Development Plan/
Program, ANC's, 14, 71
religious bloc, Israel, composition of,
225–226n
remittances from U.S. to El Salvador, 236
renovadores/reformistas, of FMLN, 234
repression, and clientelism in semi-
democracies by ruling party, 27–28
resource asymmetry. *See also* funding for
campaigns
dominant parties in Israel and El Salvador
and, 224
in El Salvador, 233
as tool in single-party dominance states,
26–27
retention of candidates
across South African parties from 1994 to
2004, 175–176, 176t
NP's list diversification and, 188–189
party-specific effects vs. racial effects on,
178, 179t
race, age, and gender across South African
parties and, 176–178, 177t
rank of, in large vs. small parties, 171
returning candidates
list rankings of ANC, NP, and DP for
1999 and 2004 elections for, 173t,
173–175, 174t
rank of, in large vs. small parties, 171
testing candidate quality and list rankings
of, 172–173
Revisionists, Israel. *See also* Herut
history of rivalry with Labor (Mapai), 227
negative public image of, 227
rhetoric, campaign. *See also* candidate
demographics; news media; persuasion;
racial rhetoric
by ANC on IFP during 2004 campaign,
199–201
competition patterns of 2004 reflected in,
116t, 116–118

content analysis for 2004 election using,
109–111
electoral campaign analysis using, 109,
115t, 115–116
issues emphasized by different parties, 120t
most frequent topics in 2004, 134t
policies named in 2004 by different
parties, 122t
types of, about different parties, 133t
types of, by different parties, 119t
rhetoric, political, Likud's moderation of, 231
rightest bloc, Israel, composition of,
225–226n
"Rise and Fall of Bantu Holomisa, The"
(ANC Department of Information and
Publicity), 203
road shows, for ANC's 1999 persuasion
campaign for African voters, 85
Robins, Steve, 146–147
Robinson, Vicki, 135
ruling parties. *See also* African National
Congress; ARENA; Labor Party
government role of IFP as part of, 241n
negative framing of opposition by, 238
policies and strategies for remaining in
office, 26–27
vulnerabilities in Israel and El Salvador of,
238–239
rural areas
African voters' allegiances to traditional
leaders in, 9–10
ANC's 1999 voter registration campaigns
in, 87–88

Saaiman, Pieter Willem, 95, 149–150
Saca, Antonio, 235–236, 237–238
SACP. *See* South African Communist Party
Scheiner, Ethan, 23, 224, 242
Schlemmer, Lawrence, 5–7, 9, 35
Scorpions. *See also* McCarthy, Leonard
Cope on reinstatement of, 213
Sears, David O., 35
Seekings, Jeremy
on ANC's late strategies in 1994 Western
Cape campaign, 78–79
on ANC's persuasion strategy for 1994
campaign, 68–69, 71
on ANC's response to NP's negative
Western Cape campaigning, 77
on increasing socioeconomic variation in
South Africa, 239
on nonracialism vs. multiracialism focus
for ANC, 74
on NP's 1994 negative campaigning in
Western Cape, 74–75

Serfontein, Jan, 146
Sexwale, Tokyo, 203–204n, 203–204
Shaik, Schabir, 204–205
Shalev, Michael, 226n, 227, 229–230n
Shepsle, Kenneth, 35
Shilowa, Mbhazima
  ANC nomination as Gauteng province premier of, 91
  Cope formation after leaving the ANC and, 23–24, 212–213
  Dandala's selection as Cope presidential candidate and, 214–215
  on inclusiveness of ANC, 131–132
  racial campaigning in 1999 by, 104
  on racial rhetoric over ANC's performance record, 125n
  struggle credentials of, 212n
Sigcau, King Mpondobini, 86n
Sigcau, Stella, 86n, 202
Sigelman, Carol K., 35
Sigelman, Lee, 35
signaling effect, candidate demographics, party image and, 141, 143–144
Simkins, Charles, 5–7
Single-member districts, candidate quality issues for elite incorporation and, 168n
single-nontransferable votes, single-party dominance and, 27–28
single-party-dominance states.
  *See also* dominant parties
  characteristics of, 26n
  commonalities between South Africa and, 26
  explanations for, 26–27
  factors contributing to, 27–28
  negative framing and resource-based strategies in, 224
  opposition coordination in, 242
Sisulu, Walter, 47
Sithole, Antoinette, 112n
Six Day War (1967), 230
Slovo, Joe, 48n
small political parties. *See also* African opposition parties; opposition parties
  candidate quality and, 168–170, 190–192
  candidate quality and list rankings of, 171
  elite incorporation and internal structure of, 170–171
  elite incorporation as intractable problem for, 164
  list rankings of new, returning, and poached candidates for 1999 and 2004 elections, 173t, 173–175, 174t, 191

logit analysis of candidate retention patterns across South African parties and, 176–178, 177t
poaching candidates by large parties vs., 181, 181t
testing candidate quality and list rankings of, 172–173
Smith, Ian, 95, 130
Sniderman, Paul M., 35
Snyder, Jack, 7
social spending programs
  ANC's, clientelism and, 12–13, 13–14n
  in Mexico, 13, 14–15
  in Peru, 13
  transparency, clientelism and, 14–15
Sonn, Franklin, 77–78
Sono, Themba, 183n
South Africa. *See also specific South African political parties*
  political origins of census elections in, 25–26
  racial terminology in, 5n
South African Broadcasting Corporation (SABC), 104, 137
South African Communist Party (SACP)
  ANC's alignment with, 47–48
  DA's 2004 threats of legal action against, 127–129
  discontent with Mbeki's fiscal policies by, 205
  potential split from ANC by, 240
  support for Zuma by, 205–208, 206n
Southall, Roger, 208
*Sowetan* (newspaper), 108–109, 139
spatial voting model, Downs's, 36
Squires, Hilary, 205
Stahler-Sholk, Richard, 233, 235, 235n, 238
*The Star*, 108–109, 139
"struggle credentials," as sign of South African candidate quality, 165–166, 166n, 212n
*The Sunday Independent*, 108–109, 139
*Sunday Times*, 108–109, 139
Supreme Court of Appeal (SCA), South Africa, 206–207, 211, 211n
Suzman, Helen, 50, 94n, 126–129
Sweden, single-party dominance in, 26
symbolic manipulation, by dominant parties, 28
symbolic racism, racially-polarized voting in the U.S. and, 35

Tabane, Rapule, 147
Tajfel, Henri, 8, 34

# Index

Tambo, Oliver, 47
Tarrow, Sidney, 227, 228–229, 231
Taylor, Helen, 36, 38–39
television coverage of 2004 campaign, South Africa, 136–137
Terklidsen, Nayda, 35
Theron, Moza Mayman, 95
*This Day* (newspaper), 108–109, 139
traditional leaders
    ANC's 1999 persuasion campaign for African voters and, 85n, 85–86, 86n
    ANC's homage to fight against colonialism by, 201
    IFP support by, 196
    as IFP supporters, ANC's cultivation of, 202
    rural African voters' allegiances to, 9–10
    as UDM supporters, ANC's cultivation of, 203
Transkei (Bantustan), (B.) Holomisa as head of state in, 202
Transkei, South Africa
    ANC's 1999 persuasion campaign for African voters in, 85n, 85
    chiefs' control of African vote in, ANC's 1999 campaign and, 86n
    voter registration for 1999 election in, 88n, 88–89
transparency on social spending, clientelism and, 14–15
Tribunal Supremo Electoral (TSE), El Salvador, 233, 235n
Tricameral Parliament, South Africa, 69–70, 76–77, 165–166, 166n
trustworthiness of the opposition
    African voters' beliefs about, 58–61, 60t
    racialized party images, South African voting and, 33
Truth and Reconciliation Commission, South Africa, 196–197, 202
Tsedu, Mathatha, 139
Tshwete, Steve, 85n

Umkhonto we Sizwe (Spear of the Nation), 47, 48n
uncertain responses, about opposition parties, 51–53
uncertain voters
    Africans with negative evaluations of the ANC and, 56
    as bell-wethers of change, 33
    inclusive/exclusive views of opposition, good/bad performance and, 57–58
    informational shortcuts for, 36–40
    performance evaluations and party images for, 53–61, 55t, 62t
    racial heuristic theories on, 34n
    survey sources for tests of, 40–41
    tests of racial heuristics in choices by, 40
United Democratic Front (UDF)
    ANC's anti-apartheid movement and, 47–48
    civil war with IFP and ANC in KwaZulu Natal, 195, 195n, 196n
    end of apartheid and, 9
    Lekota and, 212n
United Democratic Movement (UDM)
    as ANC threat in 1999, 84–86
    ANC's 1999 persuasion campaign against, 85, 85n, 202–203
    ANC's 1999 persuasion campaign for Eastern Cape chief's support vs., 85–86
    ANC's negative framing of, 194
    burnout of, 203
    challenge to ANC in Transkei, 1999 voter registration and, 88–89
    election of 1999 results for, 82–83
    election of 2009 and, 215
    Meyer's and Holomisa's goals for, 202
    mission of, 189
    NP's leadership defections to, 190n
    as opposition party, 4, 239
    racialization of opposition and small size of, 241n
    significance as ANC competitor, 193–194
    voting results for 2004 election, 107
United National Independence Party (UNIP), Zambia, 144
United Party (UP), South Africa, 49, 49n
United States, explanations for racially-polarized voting in, 35
urban areas, ANC's 1999 voter registration campaigns in, 87

van Niekerk, Phillip, 50
van Schalkwyk, Marthinus
    joins the ANC (2004), 187
    Mandela's racial attacks on, 102–103
    on modernization of NNP, 95
    NP's 1994 Western Cape campaign and, 75–76
    NP's 1999 multiracial campaign and, 95–96
    on racial balance of NP's 2004 candidate list, 150
    racial rhetoric in 2004 campaigning by, 130, 132n

Vavi, Zwelinzima, 129, 129n
Verwoerd, Hendrik Frensch, 49
violence
    ANC 2004 association of IFP with, 200
    and clientelism in semi-democracies by
        ruling party, 27–28
    election-induced, Horowitz on census-style
        elections and, 7
    IFP's 1994 image of association with,
        196–197
    image control and negative framing as
        alternatives to, 222
Vos, Suzanne, 198
Votani Mawethu (voter registration 1999)
    campaign, ANC's, 87–88
vote buying/monitoring, lack of in South
    Africa, 15
voter registration campaigns, as ANC
    mobilization campaigns in 1999, 86–89
voters. See also uncertain voters
voters, South African. See also African
    voters; coloured voters; Indian voters;
    party labels/images; white voters
    evidence of party label racialization, 33
    explaining choices by, 53–61
    expressive or identity voting by, 34–35
    hypotheses about behavior of, 32
    identity voting in South Africa (1994 and
        2000), 41–42, 42t
    income and responses to clientelism by, 12n
    innovations in theories about choices by, 33
    lack of understanding of Electoral Act
        requirements for, 86–87
    material inducements by ANC for, 28–29
    partisanship issues and, 42, 43t
    performance voting by, 35–36
    policy voting by, 35–36, 43–45, 44t
    questions about choices by, 32
    use of party images to guide voting
        decisions by, 17–18

Wade, Christine, 234, 237
Walkosz, Barbara J., 35
Welsh, David
    on ANC's racial campaigning in 1999,
        102, 104
    on DP's national campaign for 1994
        election, 72
    on DP's persuasion strategy for 1994
        campaign, 70
    on DP's response to racism in ANC's party
        labeling, 104–105
    on DP's Western Cape campaign for 1994
        election, 79–80

on goal for 1999 DP's persuasion
    campaign, 92
Western Cape, South Africa
    ANC social spending in, 14–15, 15n
    ANC's 1999 campaign for coloured voters
        in, 89–90
    ANC's racial campaigning in 1999 against
        opposition parties in, 103
    attention to party image in, 70
    campaign of 1994, NP's in, 69–70
    campaign of 1999, NNP's, Marais–Morkel
        conflict and, 96–97
    candidate retention patterns across
        political parties in, 176–177, 180–181
    debate over race in 1994 campaign in,
        74–80
    DP's 1999 campaign targeting coloured
        voters in, 94
    DP's use of Afrikaans-speaking candidates
        in, 149–150
    election of 1994, voting results for, 65–66
    election of 1999, voting results for, 82–83
    election of 2004, voting results for, 107
    election of 2009, Cope successes in,
        213, 213n
    logit analysis of candidate retention
        patterns across political parties in,
        178–179, 180t
    Mandela on racial balancing of 1994
        candidate lists in, 148
    NNP tensions over list diversification
        in, 188
    NP's diversification of candidate lists
        for, 187
    NP's leadership defections in, 188
    racial demographics of ANC's candidate
        lists for, 145–146
    racial tensions in, 38
white candidates/politicians
    party-specific effects on retention of, 178,
        179t
    retention patterns across South African
        parties, 175–176, 176t
    switching parties, 182–183
white opposition parties. See Democratic
    Party; National Party, South Africa
white South Africans. See also Afrikaners;
    National Party, South Africa
    ANC at close of apartheid and,
        47–48, 48n
    ANC courting by white candidates of,
        148–149
    conservative, on DP's 1999 party list, 93
    definition of, 5n

*Index*

DP's 1999 campaign techniques to attract, 93–94
on exclusivity of the ANC and Africanization of ANC's candidate lists, 157–158, 158t
legacy of apartheid for, 38
in public service jobs, 13–14n
views of exclusivity of political parties by, 52t
views of political parties by, 51–53
white voters. *See also* Afrikaners; National Party, South Africa
ANC on opposition parties composed of, 2
campaign of 1994, NP and, 69–70
campaign of 1999
DP's to capture, 92
ignored by ANC in, 90–91, 91n
NNP's, Marais–Morkel conflict during, 96–97
campaign of 2004
ANC's events courting, 113–115
ANC's targeting of DA party label and, 108, 111
rhetoric by ANC vs. DA to, 116–118
election of 1994, for IFP in KwaZulu Natal, 197n
election of 1999 and, 82–83
on government policies, 43–45, 44t
ideological differentiation in South Africa by, 37n
parties voted for, 5
performance voting by, 45–46, 46t
racial censuses and, 1
Wiggins, South Africa, housing take-overs (1993) in
ANC response to, 78
NP response to, 75–76
Wilkinson, Steven I., 16
Women's League, ANC's, 208
World Zionist Organization (WZO), 227, 228–229

Xhosa politicians, dominance in Mbeki's cabinet, 205

Youth League, ANC's, 205–207, 208, 210

Zambia
Posner on ethnic favoritism in, 142–143
Posner on party labels and party leader ethnicity in, 144
Zille, Helen, 240–241
Zionist movement
early rivalries for control of, 227
Mapai's role in, 226
Zondi, Musa, 200, 201
Zulu, Paulus, 50
Zulu credentials, ANC's cultivation of, 201–202
Zuma, Jacob. *See also* African National Congress
ANC seeks political solution to problems of, 210–211
ANC's National General Council support for, 206
as appealing candidate in 2009 election, 218
as champion of the poor and dispossessed, 205–206
charges against dropped, 211–212
chosen as Deputy President under Mbeki, 204
corruption allegations and charges against, 204–205, 208
corruption in South Africa under, 16n
Dandala as stark contrast to, 214
elected ANC president over Mbeki, 207–208
as first non-Xhosa African president in South Africa, 201–202
IFP's 2004 confrontation with, 200
lawyers appeal cases against, 210
Nicholson sets aside charges against, 211
sexual practices and image of, 206n
shadow campaign for the presidency by, 206
Zwelithini, Zulu King Goodwill, 86n, 195

**Other Books in the Series** *(continued from page iii)*

Michael Bratton, Robert Mattes, and E. Gyimah-Boadi, *Public Opinion, Democracy, and Market Reform in Africa*
Michael Bratton and Nicolas van de Walle, *Democratic Experiments in Africa: Regime Transitions in Comparative Perspective*
Valerie Bunce, *Leaving Socialism and Leaving the State: The End of Yugoslavia, the Soviet Union, and Czechoslovakia*
Daniele Caramani, *The Nationalization of Politics: The Formation of National Electorates and Party Systems in Europe*
John M. Carey, *Legislative Voting and Accountability*
Kanchan Chandra, *Why Ethnic Parties Succeed: Patronage and Ethnic Headcounts in India*
José Antonio Cheibub, *Presidentialism, Parliamentarism, and Democracy*
Ruth Berins Collier, *Paths toward Democracy: The Working Class and Elites in Western Europe and South America*
Christian Davenport, *State Repression and the Domestic Democratic Peace*
Donatella della Porta, *Social Movements, Political Violence, and the State*
Alberto Diaz-Cayeros, *Federalism, Fiscal Authority, and Centralization in Latin America*
Thad Dunning, *Crude Democracy: Natural Resource Wealth and Political Regimes*
Gerald Easter, *Reconstructing the State: Personal Networks and Elite Identity*
Margarita Estevez-Abe, *Welfare and Capitalism in Postwar Japan: Party, Bureaucracy, and Business*
Henry Farrell, *The Political Economy of Trust: Institutions, Interests, and Inter-Firm Cooperation in Italy and Germany*
M. Steven Fish, *Democracy Derailed in Russia: The Failure of Open Politics*
Robert F. Franzese, *Macroeconomic Policies of Developed Democracies*
Roberto Franzosi, *The Puzzle of Strikes: Class and State Strategies in Postwar Italy*
Geoffrey Garrett, *Partisan Politics in the Global Economy*
Scott Gehlbach, *Representation through Taxation: Revenue, Politics, and Development in Postcommunist States*
Miriam Golden, *Heroic Defeats: The Politics of Job Loss*
Jeff Goodwin, *No Other Way Out: States and Revolutionary Movements*
Merilee Serrill Grindle, *Changing the State*
Anna Grzymala-Busse, *Rebuilding Leviathan: Party Competition and State Exploitation in Post-Communist Democracies*

Anna Grzymala-Busse, *Redeeming the Communist Past: The Regeneration of Communist Parties in East Central Europe*
Frances Hagopian, *Traditional Politics and Regime Change in Brazil*
Mark Hallerberg, Rolf Ranier Strauch, and Jürgen von Hagen, *Fiscal Governance in Europe*
Henry E. Hale, *The Foundations of Ethnic Politics: Separatism of States and Nations in Eurasia and the World*
Gretchen Helmke, *Courts Under Constraints: Judges, Generals, and Presidents in Argentina*
Yoshiko Herrera, *Imagined Economies: The Sources of Russian Regionalism*
J. Rogers Hollingsworth and Robert Boyer, eds., *Contemporary Capitalism: The Embeddedness of Institutions*
John D. Huber and Charles R. Shipan, *Deliberate Discretion? The Institutional Foundations of Bureaucratic Autonomy*
Ellen Immergut, *Health Politics: Interests and Institutions in Western Europe*
Torben Iversen, *Capitalism, Democracy, and Welfare*
Torben Iversen, *Contested Economic Institutions*
Torben Iversen, Jonas Pontussen, and David Soskice, eds., *Unions, Employers, and Central Banks: Macroeconomic Coordination and Institutional Change in Social Market Economies*
Thomas Janoski and Alexander M. Hicks, eds., *The Comparative Political Economy of the Welfare State*
Joseph Jupille, *Procedural Politics: Issues, Influence, and Institutional Choice in the European Union*
Stathis Kalyvas, *The Logic of Violence in Civil War*
David C. Kang, *Crony Capitalism: Corruption and Capitalism in South Korea and the Philippines*
Junko Kato, *Regressive Taxation and the Welfare State*
Orit Kedar, *Voting for Policy, Not Parties: How Voters Compensate for Power Sharing*
Robert O. Keohane and Helen B. Milner, eds., *Internationalization and Domestic Politics*
Herbert Kitschelt, *The Transformation of European Social Democracy*
Herbert Kitschelt, Peter Lange, Gary Marks, and John D. Stephens, eds., *Continuity and Change in Contemporary Capitalism*
Herbert Kitschelt, Zdenka Mansfeldova, Radek Markowski, and Gabor Toka, *Post-Communist Party Systems*
David Knoke, Franz Urban Pappi, Jeffrey Broadbent, and Yutaka Tsujinaka, eds., *Comparing Policy Networks*
Allan Kornberg and Harold D. Clarke, *Citizens and Community: Political Support in a Representative Democracy*

Amie Kreppel, *The European Parliament and the Supranational Party System*
David D. Laitin, *Language Repertoires and State Construction in Africa*
Fabrice E. Lehoucq and Ivan Molina, *Stuffing the Ballot Box: Fraud, Electoral Reform, and Democratization in Costa Rica*
Mark Irving Lichbach and Alan S. Zuckerman, eds., *Comparative Politics: Rationality, Culture, and Structure, second edition*
Evan Lieberman, *Race and Regionalism in the Politics of Taxation in Brazil and South Africa*
Pauline Jones Luong, *Institutional Change and Political Continuity in Post-Soviet Central Asia*
Julia Lynch, *Age in the Welfare State: The Origins of Social Spending on Pensioners, Workers, and Children*
Doug McAdam, John McCarthy, and Mayer Zald, eds., *Comparative Perspectives on Social Movements*
Beatriz Magaloni, *Voting for Autocracy: Hegemonic Party Survival and Its Demise in Mexico*
James Mahoney and Dietrich Rueschemeyer, eds., *Historical Analysis and the Social Sciences*
Scott Mainwaring and Matthew Soberg Shugart, eds., *Presidentialism and Democracy in Latin America*
Isabela Mares, *The Politics of Social Risk: Business and Welfare State Development*
Isabela Mares, *Taxation, Wage Bargaining, and Unemployment*
Anthony W. Marx, *Making Race, Making Nations: A Comparison of South Africa, the United States, and Brazil*
Bonnie Meguid, *Competition between Unequals: Strategies and Electoral Fortunes in Western Europe*
Joel S. Migdal, *State in Society: Studying How States and Societies Constitute One Another*
Joel S. Migdal, Atul Kohli, and Vivienne Shue, eds., *State Power and Social Forces: Domination and Transformation in the Third World*
Scott Morgenstern and Benito Nacif, eds., *Legislative Politics in Latin America*
Layna Mosley, *Global Capital and National Governments*
Wolfgang C. Müller and Kaare Strøm, *Policy, Office, or Votes?*
Maria Victoria Murillo, *Labor Unions, Partisan Coalitions, and Market Reforms in Latin America*
Maria Victoria Murillo, *Political Competition, Partisanship, and Policy Making in Latin American Public Utilities*
Monika Nalepa, *Skeletons in the Closet: Transitional Justice in Post-Communist Europe*

Ton Notermans, *Money, Markets, and the State: Social Democratic Economic Policies since 1918*
Aníbal Pérez-Liñán, *Presidential Impeachment and the New Political Instability in Latin America*
Roger Petersen, *Understanding Ethnic Violence: Fear, Hatred, and Resentment in Twentieth-Century Eastern Europe*
Simona Piattoni, ed., *Clientelism, Interests, and Democratic Representation*
Paul Pierson, *Dismantling the Welfare State? Reagan, Thatcher, and the Politics of Retrenchment*
Marino Regini, *Uncertain Boundaries: The Social and Political Construction of European Economies*
Marc Howard Ross, *Cultural Contestation in Ethnic Conflict*
Lyle Scruggs, *Sustaining Abundance: Environmental Performance in Industrial Democracies*
Jefferey M. Sellers, *Governing from Below: Urban Regions and the Global Economy*
Yossi Shain and Juan Linz, eds., *Interim Governments and Democratic Transitions*
Beverly Silver, *Forces of Labor: Workers' Movements and Globalization since 1870*
Theda Skocpol, *Social Revolutions in the Modern World*
Regina Smyth, *Candidate Strategies and Electoral Competition in the Russian Federation: Democracy Without Foundation*
Richard Snyder, *Politics after Neoliberalism: Reregulation in Mexico*
David Stark and László Bruszt, *Postsocialist Pathways: Transforming Politics and Property in East Central Europe*
Sven Steinmo, Kathleen Thelen, and Frank Longstreth, eds., *Structuring Politics: Historical Institutionalism in Comparative Analysis*
Susan C. Stokes, *Mandates and Democracy: Neoliberalism by Surprise in Latin America*
Susan C. Stokes, ed., *Public Support for Market Reforms in New Democracies*
Duane Swank, *Global Capital, Political Institutions, and Policy Change in Developed Welfare States*
Sidney Tarrow, *Power in Movement: Social Movements and Contentious Politics*
Kathleen Thelen, *How Institutions Evolve: The Political Economy of Skills in Germany, Britain, the United States, and Japan*
Charles Tilly, *Trust and Rule*
Daniel Treisman, *The Architecture of Government: Rethinking Political Decentralization*
Lily Lee Tsai, *Accountability without Democracy: How Solidary Groups Provide Public Goods in Rural China*

Joshua Tucker, *Regional Economic Voting: Russia, Poland, Hungary, Slovakia, and the Czech Republic, 1990–1999*
Ashutosh Varshney, *Democracy, Development, and the Countryside*
Jeremy M. Weinstein, *Inside Rebellion: The Politics of Insurgent Violence*
Stephen I. Wilkinson, *Votes and Violence: Electoral Competition and Ethnic Riots in India*
Jason Wittenberg, *Crucibles of Political Loyalty: Church Institutions and Electoral Continuity in Hungary*
Elisabeth J. Wood, *Forging Democracy from Below: Insurgent Transitions in South Africa and El Salvador*
Elisabeth J. Wood, *Insurgent Collective Action and Civil War in El Salvador*